Guidance
and Counseling Services
An Introduction

Guidance and Counseling Services
An Introduction

Lester N. Downing, Ed.D.

*Professor of Educational Psychology
and Coordinator of Counselor Education
Brigham Young University*

McGraw-Hill Book Company

*New York / St. Louis / San Francisco
Toronto / London / Sydney*

Guidance and Counseling Services
An Introduction

Preface

The tremendous scientific and technological advancements of the past decade have resulted in some overwhelming challenges to education. The anticipated advancements of the immediate future make the task of providing appropriate educational experiences for all children and youth even more formidable, but also exciting. A well-organized guidance program is an important element in this educational program of the present and the future.

The purposes of this text may be summarized as follows: (1) to clarify the relationship of the guidance service to instruction and to show how the teacher, the counselor, and the administrator contribute to the total education of a child in a reciprocal relationship; (2) to identify the major functions of the counselor, teacher, and administrator as co-contributors in the educational process; and (3) to provide a framework of principles and procedures from which a well-organized guidance service can be developed for the elementary and secondary schools.

The book attempts to synthesize the intangibles of philosophy and attitudes with the tangibles of techniques and tools into a meaningful, understandable pattern for conducting the guidance service in its contribution to the development of each student. Knowledge from the past, current thinking, research data, and experience are utilized in describing the guidance service and its relation to the educational process.

This book is designed as an introduction to the guidance field. It may be used as a text in appropriate courses at the upper-division and graduate levels, to help prospective elementary and secondary school teachers, counselors, and administrators come to a better understanding of guidance, its role in education, and its basic elements. It was written also to assist the professionals in their work by outlining procedures to follow in organizing and conducting the guidance service.

Appreciation is expressed to everyone who by design or accident aided in the completion of the book. Dr. Percy E. Burrup and Dr. Sterling Callahan were generous with their wisdom, and they provided the encouragment for dedicated effort by virtue of their literary successes. The suggestions made by Dr. Howard T. Reid for making the material appealing to students were helpful. The editorial suggestions of Joanne Thomas and Richard Cracroft resulted in improvements, and the author is indebted to the guidance professionals who read the manuscript with patience and responded with kind and favorable reactions. Dr. Walter Johnson, as consulting editor, deserves considerable credit for the strengths in the text but is responsible for none of its weaknesses. Ruth Downing and all the young Downings deserve credit for their enduring faith in seeing a demanding task ultimately realized.

Lester N. Downing

Contents /

PART 1/

An introduction to guidance

ONE

/GUIDANCE SERVICES IN MODERN EDUCATION

A modern educational system requires organized programs of guidance services. To conduct their activities such services must have active support in materials, facilities, and personnel with an attitude of concern for the welfare of youngsters and dedication to effort in their behalf. The belief that the maximum development of children is basic to the whole educational structure and to society has strong support. Confidence in the guidance service, a faith in its outcome, and a commitment to its philosophy are essential elements for its success. As the guidance service helps to fulfill many social needs, it presents an opportunity for strengthening the framework of society. The theme of this chapter is that the guidance service provides the opportunities for assisting children and youth in their development. A justification is also made for the guidance program in terms of the needs of growing children and of society itself.

The Guidance Program: An Opportunity

The guidance program provides many opportunities for service to young people, for aiding them educationally and personally. Flexibility is possible within the structure of the program, and it permits variations in the services among schools as adjustments are made to local conditions. A statement by Frank H. Bowles reflects quite accurately the thinking of many people concerning their responsibility to youth.[1] "We all believe in guidance—that is, in the idea that the older generation has a responsibility to counsel and assist the rising generation—but it is only the idea on which we agree. We differ widely in our belief as to the nature of guidance."

This responsibility is an opportunity from which both the giving and the receiving generations may profit. The concern for the younger generation may be prompted in part by a sense of obligation, but a genuine spirit of altruism and love also plays a major motivating role. The desire felt by many adults to be of service to others is the generating force behind many of the activities designed to aid young people. The guidance service is an important contributor to these activities. It shares in the responsibilities and takes pride in the outcomes.

Progress of the Guidance Movement

From the early twentieth century of Frank Parsons in Boston to the present, the guidance movement has experienced both historical discouragements and advancements.[2] Perhaps greater progress should have been made; however, any worthy endeavor takes time and the dedication of many people. Optimism is justified in terms of startling accomplishments of the past and exciting promises for the future. A succinct and profound statement from James Cribbin summarizes well what has taken place in the guidance movement: [3]

> In the short space of approximately half a century, guidance has developed from a hesitant, groping, unstructured effort in behalf of students to become one of the most potent forces for good in our educational

[1] Frank H. Bowles, "Nature of Guidance," *Personnel and Guidance Journal*, vol. 38, p. 112, October, 1959.

[2] For a brief history see Merle M. Ohlsen, *Guidance Services in the Modern School*, Harcourt, Brace & World, Inc., New York, 1964, pp. 7–12.

[3] James J. Cribbin, "Essentials and Incidentals in Guidance," *The Catholic Education Review*, vol. 59, no. 9, p. 608, December, 1961.

system. It has been publicized, popularized, and propagandized. Books on the subject abound. Authorities range the country explaining its alpha and omega. Counselors flock to universities to learn more about the matter. Teachers are constantly urged to be "guidance minded." Institutes are conducted under governmental sponsorship and special funds are made available to the states for guidance purposes. . . . To say that guidance has arrived is surely to bark one's shins against the obvious. In fact some schools would as soon admit that they lacked an enriched curriculum as own up to the fact that they lacked a guidance program.

Guidance has indeed arrived, and rare is the school administrator who unabashedly admits that no provision has been made for a guidance program within his school. The intent to provide these services prevails, but intentions have not, in all cases, resulted in tangible practices. However, foundations have been established and structures are being developed from which creditable programs are emerging.

A major problem and deterrent to progress has been the diversity of ideas as to the nature and purposes of guidance. Although agreement is relatively high among guidance specialists, the same degree of agreement is not reached among nonspecialists, or between the latter and the specialist. Views also differ as to whether these special services being provided for children and youth should be called "pupil personnel services" or "guidance services." A brief look at this problem may be helpful in avoiding possible confusion in later discussions.

"Pupil Personnel Services" or "Guidance Services"?

Whether the term "pupil personnel services" or "guidance services" is used in describing the program of pupil services in a school depends upon the nature, number, and breadth of services included. Both terms are valid and have a place in the description and delineation of activities taking place within various schools. The personal preference of the personnel worker also plays a part in title selection. This prerogative is to be exercised as long as agreement prevails as to the nature and extent of the services to be included and as long as there are competent, qualified people to perform the necessary services.

Since the two terms are not mutually exclusive, nothing is to be gained by regarding them as separate and distinct areas of service, nor is there any justification for creating a controversy. A simple and appropriate guide is to use the term "guidance" in describing a program of services which include the usual basic elements of the guidance service as outlined in this chapter. "Pupil personnel service" is more appropriate as a title of services which are broader and more inclusive than the guidance program. It includes not only the guidance service but also the health services, attendance services, socio-psychological services, and all other personal services apart from instruction and administration designed to provide the student with individual and personal attention and aid.[4] Some attention is, of course, given to these areas by the typical guidance service. However, it is the function of the counselor to refer pupils to other specialists and to cooperate with them in providing these pupils with needed services. It is not the prerogative of the counselor to attempt treatment or perform services outside his realm of competence.

One well-known text uses the term "pupil personnel" in the title.[5] Another popular author uses "personnel" in the title of her book.[6] Still another excellent text uses both the terms "guidance" and the term "pupil personnel" in the title,[4] and Jones uses "guidance" in the title of his equally excellent book.[7] Both terms are appropriately used and consistent with the topics covered. Froehlich makes this statement: [8] " 'Personnel' is a term that appears to have been borrowed by education from industry. In an industrial setting, the term has long been used to cover the administrative activities which relate to the management of workers." He also states: [9] "It was a logical transition for the educators to use the term 'pupil personnel' to identify the activities of school administration that dealt with the management of pupils." There are appropriate uses for both terms; in this text "guidance" is preferred, since many activities of the pupil personnel services are not included in the discussion.

[4] For an excellent discussion see Walter F. Johnson, Buford Stefflre, and Roy A. Edelfelt, *Pupil Personnel and Guidance Services*, McGraw-Hill Book Company, New York, 1961, pp. 14–15.

[5] Dugald S. Arbuckle, *Pupil Personnel Services in American Schools*, Allyn and Bacon, Inc., Boston, 1962.

[6] Jane Warters, *High School Personnel Work Today*, 2d ed., McGraw-Hill Book Company, New York, 1956.

[7] Arthur J. Jones, *Principles of Guidance*, 5th ed., McGraw-Hill Book Company, New York, 1962, and Johnson, *op. cit.*

[8] Clifford P. Froehlich, *Guidance Services in Schools*, 2d ed., McGraw-Hill Book Company, New York, 1958, p. 5.

[9] *Ibid.*, p. 6.

Guidance Defined

A common problem in defining guidance is one of keeping the definition short but sufficiently broad to be informative. The criteria of brevity and breadth are difficult to attain but may be observed with clarity in the following two-part definition:

1 Guidance is an organized set of specialized services established as an integral part of the school environment designed to promote the development of students and assist them toward a realization of sound, wholesome adjustment and maximum accomplishments commensurate with their potentialities.
2 Guidance is a point of view that includes a positive attitude toward children and a realization that it is to supplement, strengthen, and make more meaningful all other phases of a youngster's education.

An analysis of this definition reveals the following elements:

1 The program is organized; it has structure, system, and personnel.
2 The program includes specialized services of testing, counseling, educational and vocational information, placement, and follow-up.
3 The guidance service, along with its conceptual and technical aspects, is an integral part of the school environment.
4 The promotion of student development is a major aim of guidance.
5 The realization of adjustment as a developmental process is promoted, and as children develop under superior tutelage, they gain in their ability to deal with problems.
6 The guidance program provides for the identification and development of talents and potentialities.
7 The intangible elements are recognized as a point of view or as an attitude.

There are many definitions and explanations of guidance.[10] No single definition is likely to satisfy everyone completely. Each guidance worker may profit from the experience of writing his own definition.

[10] Some representative definitions are to be found in Froehlich, *op. cit.*, p. 8; Edward C. Glanz, *Foundations and Principles of Guidance*, Allyn and Bacon, Inc., Boston, 1964, pp. 5–6; George E. Hill, *Management and Improvement of Guidance*, Appleton-Century-Crofts, Inc., New York, 1965, p. 9; Herman J. Peters and Gail F. Farwell, *Guidance: A Developmental Approach*, Rand McNally & Company, Chicago, 1959, p. 20.

Basic Elements in the Program

The following services constitute the usual pattern of activities within a guidance program and are called "basic elements":

1   Pupil inventory service—records
2   Pupil appraisal—tests and inventories
3   Counseling
4   Information service
5   Placement
6   Follow-up

Items 1 and 2 may be combined and classified as "pupil appraisal."

The Relationship to Education

The guidance service is an integral part of the educational program and as such is one of several elements within that program. Although the teaching-learning situation constitutes the heart of education, it is made to be more meaningful through the aid and influence of the guidance service. There is guidance within the classroom as the teacher exemplifies an interest in, and a genuine concern for, the educational and personal welfare of each student. There are also specialized services which constitute a second dimension of the guidance program and are designated as the basic elements. While guidance is a part of education, at the same time it provides specialized services that would otherwise be neglected.

The Need for Guidance Programs

The need for guidance programs within all schools became increasingly evident in the recent past and is currently regarded as a foregone conclusion. Not all schools have a guidance program, but very few deny its need. A number of studies dealing with the problem of dropouts include recommendations for more and better guidance and counseling programs in the schools.[11] Much of the current research concludes that potential dropouts can be identified early and that many can be kept in school through broader programs of

[11] Three representative reports include the following: Monica Bayley, "A Renewed Effort to Solve the Problem of Dropouts," *School Life*, vol. 46, pp. 11–16, December, 1963; "Results of the 1963 Dropout Campaign," *The Education Digest*, vol. 30, pp. 27–29, September, 1964; Robert R. Ritchie, "The High School Dropout: An Educational Dilemma," *Bulletin of the National Association of Secondary-school Principals*, vol. 46, pp. 45–47, November, 1962.

services and activities. Preponderant evidence supports the position that there is a great need for guidance services and that this need will become increasingly persistent in the future. A greater utilization of the capabilities of all people must be realized if the demands of the times are to be met even minimally. L. G. Derthick stresses a similar point in this statement: [12]

> The United States has been a world leader in many respects with only about seven percent of the world's population. We consume about half of the goods produced in the entire world. . . . Yet these very same statistics clearly bring home a point upon which our future prosperity and security may well depend. It is this: Possessing only a small fraction of the world's population, we must in the days and years immediately ahead exert an unprecedented effort to make the utmost utilization of all our native skills and talents—we must develop to the maximum the brainpower of all our citizens.

Thus there is a greater need for guidance services now than ever before. Rapid technological advances, an increasingly complex society, new concepts of government and its role in the lives of people, the need for outstanding leadership talents, a shift in standards of morality and integrity, and a condition of unusual demands upon the young people all contribute to the need for the philosophy espoused by the services provided under the guidance program.

Conditions Which Contribute to the Need for the Guidance Service

Specific conditions within the educational setting contribute to the need for the guidance service. These conditions are in addition to, but related to, the factors of change and advancement within the total society. The following are some of these conditions:

1 The teacher's major responsibility is instruction; this leaves little time or energy for assisting youngsters with problems unrelated to instructional activities. Problems of social adjustments and personality reorientation require the services of a competent counselor and the availability of appropriate facilities and time.

2 The concept of individual differences is critical in education. A careful consideration of the needs of children on an individual

[12] L. G. Derthick, "Guidance and the Nation's Needs," *Personnel and Guidance Journal,* vol. 37, p. 107, October, 1958.

basis is essential. This concept is emphasized in the philosophy and the specialized services provided in the guidance service. Individual attention and direction are essential for quality productivity.

3 The psychological aspects of pupil development are receiving more attention. A better understanding of children is being realized as a more intensive and comprehensive study of all aspects of development is made.

4 The emotional needs of children must also be met, and efforts must be made to satisfy them. The needs for affection, recognition, status, and acceptance are all in this category. Symptoms of aggressiveness—bullying, timidity, or other kinds of undesirable behavior—can be expected when emotional needs are left unsatisfied.

5 Problems occur as concomitants to growth and development. The need for providing assistance with these problems, if good adjustment is to be realized, is apparent. Physical growth takes place at a rapid rate, and new insights are needed for a valid understanding of these physical changes. Wholesome attitudes toward the whole process of development are needed as learning occurs and understandings increase through instruction and guidance activities. Mental development is taking place at a rapid rate during childhood. The implications become apparent: there is the need to provide an educational environment conducive to maximum development with appropriate challenges and some assurance of successful accomplishments.

6 The increased industrialization of the United States with its technological advancements has served to multiply and complicate the problems of youth. Instead of choosing from a relatively few vocational pursuits, as was once the case, modern youth have a great variety of vocations from which to choose and must therefore be more selective. The systematic utilization of time and energies in intelligent vocational preparation and selection is most essential. Man's personal and emotional life has also experienced new demands as technology has advanced. Continuous adjustment to these complexities is a daily challenge to many people.

7 New and formidable challenges in serving a great variety of youngsters have resulted in a broadening of the school's responsibilities. An expansion in services and improved quality in all educational functions have been brought about as schools have attempted to meet these challenges. Schools are now providing instruction and activities once regarded as the prerogatives of the home. The home is doing no less for youngsters but has also had demands of a different variety thrust upon it and has attempted to make the necessary adjustments.

8   Changing conditions and a highly complex society have made necessary an increase in the functions of the home. Technologically, the typical home is prepared to perform many of its daily functions, but in the psychological and sociological realms preparation and improved competence have required attention. A concomitant to the acceptance of new responsibilities by the home has been the gradual relinquishing of some of its activities to the school. The school is better prepared than the home to provide certain kinds of information and experiences needed by children at various times in their lives. The home, on the other hand, is the logical place for other activities equally essential to a child's development.

9   Problems of misconduct and delinquency require attention and emphasize the need for agencies and services to avoid circumstances which contribute to misbehavior. Guidance programs have the potential for the prevention of problem behavior and for providing therapeutic assistance as needed. Youngsters may also be aided toward rehabilitation and fruitful productivity following mistakes in conduct.

Accomplishments through Guidance Services

Certain accomplishments are realized as the activities of a guidance program are carried on. Youngsters are aided in their educational pursuits, and outcomes of greater educational and personal progress are achieved. The conditions which contribute to the need for guidance may now be utilized as efforts are made to help youngsters accomplish more in life and make satisfactory adjustments to the environment.

Goals become attainable as students are given needed assistance and direction. Better adjustments to the realities of life are made. These adjustments are better realized during the early years of life when a person is more flexible and teachable than during the adult years. Unsolved problems may become more serious with time, particularly since additional difficulties encountered also require attention. A condition of accumulated unsolved problems is a serious deterrent to satisfactory emotional well-being. This is a basic principle underlying the guidance service, and its corollary is prevention. Aid is given as needed, and preventive measures are taken, all in the interest of maximum development for each child. Students do not realize the same degree of accomplishment if they flounder in an atmosphere of neglect and fail to proceed satisfactorily by themselves.

Positive attitudes toward people and the circumstances of life have their beginning during the early years. A person learns to be friendly, cooperative, and agreeable, and his understandings increase as appropriate experiences are gained during the formative years when he is amenable to change, and it is in this period of maximum influence that the bases for his attitudes are developed and the thoughts and attitude patterns established that have their outcome in adult behavior.

The home and the school are influential in attitude formation. The former provides the first and most critical environment from which many character and personality traits emerge. Conversely, unfavorable home conditions contribute to maladjustment, including unhealthy attitudes. The school may also contribute to these maladjustments. Both also provide for wholesome attitude formation.

Opportunities for a cooperative relationship with the home are increased and strengthened through the guidance program. Services become more effective as contacts are maintained and as the home-school relationship is improved. Effective guidance requires parental and school understanding of pupil needs and the resources for satisfying these needs. A realistic appraisal of student development becomes possible as data are accumulated and used intelligently. An ultimate goal of the guidance program is better pupil self-understanding from which greater self-fulfillment is realized. The following benefits may then accrue:

1 Satisfaction with school is achieved, leading to successful accomplishments in academic pursuits.
2 Plans for the future are made with care, confidence, and logic.
3 Personal satisfactions are enhanced as achievements increase and improve.
4 Emotional adjustments are more readily attained and maintained.
5 Vocational possibilities are explored intelligently, and wise decisions are made.

A systematic exploration of educational and training opportunities is provided within the classroom and through guidance activities. The teacher contributes to these activities by providing information about schools in which further academic or vocational training may be received and by identifying the occupational possibilities associated with his particular subject fields. For example, the English teacher knows and calls to the attention of youngsters some of the possible vocations open to people with interests and competence in the field of English. The same is true with teachers in the other academic areas. This can be done without neglecting the fundamental aims of teaching.

Successes in academic endeavors bring increasing self-confidence. A bolstered self-esteem and improved self-concept result as students meet and satisfactorily handle school and social problems. An improved and strengthened personality serves as a means by which creative endeavors are attempted, resourcefulness is enhanced, leadership qualities are improved, and greater total progress is realized.

Needed aid and comfort are provided as crises occur in the lives of young people. In some cases these crises may be avoided as alert adults anticipate problems. Emotional reactions may occur as a result of family problems such as parental conflicts, separation, death, or law violations. Sympathetic, interested school people can lessen the frustration at these times and provide aid for a satisfactory adjustment.

The development of interests is aided through guidance activities. This can be done by giving the student personal attention and by providing him with the opportunities to participate in stimulating and challenging activities. Many potentially strong interests remain dormant for lack of attention and opportunities for development.

Guiding Principles

The nature of the activities of the guidance program should be in harmony with the established objectives. Once agreement has been reached on objectives, appropriate plans can be made for accomplishing them. The activities provided are structured with these objectives in mind, resulting in a close relationship between the goals and the activities by which they are accomplished. Principles serve as guides in conducting these activities. Their observance contributes to the efficiency with which activities are conducted and to their effectiveness in serving students.

1   Guidance activities must be related to the total development of students. As the needs of children are determined, appropriate activities and services are provided to meet these needs.
2   Guidance services are for everyone. A common fallacy has been that only children with serious problems are to receive aid. The variety and quality of experiences provided have the potential for being helpful and stimulating to everyone irrespective of status.

3 Increasing independence and maturity are encouraged. All guidance activities serve as means to ends. Goals of independence and maturity constitute these ends.

4 Guidance services and instructional activities are interdependent and reciprocal. Instruction becomes more meaningful as children profit from the attention accorded them in counseling and other guidance activities. Learning is enhanced as potentialities are identified and developed. The classroom provides the setting for learning, adjustment, and the suitable application of new understandings and insights. The counselor depends upon the teacher to provide opportunities for the implementation of the plans made.

5 Adequate time is needed for guidance activities. Certain functions require planning and time within the school day. Failure to provide the necessary time for such activities as testing and counseling inevitably is followed by disappointing results.

6 Proper tools and adequate facilities are essential. No craftsman is capable of quality production without good tools and satisfactory facilities. Conditions must be favorable and conducive to effort. Since the essentials for guidance work are quite modest, this requirement is attainable.

7 Broad participation and interest, with strong leadership and active participation by the various staff members, are essential. Benefits to students may be anticipated as efforts are coordinated and energies properly utilized.

8 Responsibilities within the total program should be shared. Major obligations are assumed by guidance personnel. All teachers should, however, have a part in planning and in carrying out certain activities. This participation need not be burdensome or time-consuming and should be satisfying to the participants.

9 Standards of ethics should be observed in counseling and in using personal information. The welfare of the children should be the paramount consideration in all cases. Youngsters should be protected against unkind remarks and maliciousness of any sort.

10 The guidance program is continuous. Planning should be long-range and should anticipate activities of the future in addition to a concentration upon the present. The guidance service moves as an integral part of the total educational program throughout the school life of the student.

11 Objective data should be gained and properly utilized. The cumulative record provides for the recording and use of data synthesized from various sources. The scientific attitude is essential in all aspects of data collection and use.

12 Guidance and counseling functions require certain compe-

tences. Adequate training, appropriate experiences, and proper personal characteristics are all basic requirements of the personnel worker.

13   There is a distinction between guidance work and administrative functions. Tasks of a supervisory, administrative, or clerical nature, where unrelated to guidance activities, should be performed by the proper personnel and not by the counselor.

The Guidance Service as a Response to National and World Needs

The rapidity with which technological and scientific advancements are taking place in the United States and throughout the world is beyond the comprehension of the typical person. Sociological advancements are far less spectacular, but the time may come when the discoveries and innovations of the social sciences will equal those of the natural sciences. And perhaps there should be no division between areas of scientific endeavor. The objective is the same—a better, richer, freer life for all mankind—for all the sciences irrespective of title or classification. Guidance and student personnel services are responding to the needs of the nation and of the world. This is done through the specialized services they provide and through the philosophy espoused by guidance workers. The fullest development possible of each individual within the various societies of the world is the ultimate objective of the guidance service. This is, indeed, a lofty aim with its ultimate achievement little more than a dream. However, the sincere dedication of guidance personnel to the concept of a better life for everyone is bound to bring results.

SUMMARY/

Schools of modern society benefit from the philosophy and services of organized guidance programs. The needs of children and youth are met more efficiently and satisfactorily through the activities of these programs. Providing these services constitutes an opportunity for the adult generation to be of service to the younger generation and help to fulfill the obligation adults have toward youth.

The educational program includes guidance services as one of several areas of activity and regards it as an integral part of the total program. Guidance is defined both as an organized set of special services and as a concept.

Guidance services are needed as evidenced by conditions within the society. The maximum development of pupils and the intelligent utilization of all human resources are worthy aims of society. The need for guidance activities becomes evident as efforts are made to attain these aims. Accomplishments beyond those realized in the conventional classroom can be attained through these services.

Principles have been developed by which schools can be guided in providing essential aids and services for the youngsters. An observance of these principles will result in a broad, comprehensive program designed to aid and stimulate youth.

The guidance service has a responsibility beyond providing for the individual and personal needs of its students. Its ultimate aim is to help society achieve greater heights of accomplishment and a more fruitful, satisfying life for its citizens.

PROBLEMS/

1 Justify and defend the statement that a modern educational system should have an organized system of guidance services.

2 What major objective underlies all educational offerings of the school? That is, why do these services exist?

3 An educational program should contribute to the society and should also benefit from the contributions of that society. Explain how the guidance service contributes to society. In what ways does the guidance service depend upon society?

4 Why does the author speak of the guidance program as an opportunity? Is providing a guidance program also a responsibility of the school? Explain.

5 Explain briefly some of the historical highlights of the guidance movement.

6 Justify optimism for the guidance movement. Note some important events and conditions which have contributed to this optimism.

7 Note the criteria you may use in determining whether a school might use the term "guidance" or "personnel services" in describing its noninstructional services to students. Under what circumstances might both terms be used?

8 Take a critical look at the author's definition of guidance. What are some merits and weaknesses in the definition?

9 Explain in one or two brief statements the relationship of the guidance service to the total educational program.

10 Some conditions which contribute to the need for guidance are given. Show how the guidance service might help to meet these conditions. What does the guidance service hope to accomplish?

11 What are the possible benefits to be gained from the establishment and utilization of guiding principles in conducting the guidance service?

12 How could this chapter have been of more help to you as a functioning or prospective guidance worker? How can you best make use of the information given here?

13 Do you feel that this chapter may be equally beneficial for both the elementary and the secondary school guidance worker? Defend your answer.

14 How realistic is the claim that the guidance service can contribute to a better life for the citizens of all societies?

Selected References

Textbooks

ARBUCKLE, DUGALD S.: *Pupil Personnel Services in American Schools,* Allyn and Bacon, Inc., Boston, 1962, chap. 1.

BARR, JOHN A.: *The Elementary Teacher and Guidance,* Holt, Rinehart and Winston, Inc., New York, 1957, chap. 1.

COTTINGHAM, HAROLD F.: *Guidance in Elementary Schools,* McKnight & McKnight Publishing Company, Bloomington, Ill., 1956, chap. 1.

FARWELL, GAIL F., and HERMAN J. PETERS: *Guidance Readings for Counselors,* Rand McNally & Company, Chicago, 1960, chap. 2.

FROEHLICH, CLIFFORD P.: *Guidance Services in Schools,* 2d ed., McGraw-Hill Book Company, New York, 1958, chaps. 1 and 2.

GLANZ, EDWARD C.: *Foundations and Principles of Guidance,* Allyn and Bacon, Inc., Boston, 1964, chap. 1.

HILL, GEORGE E.: *Management and Improvement of Guidance,* Appleton-Century-Crofts, Inc., New York, 1965, chap. 1.

HUMPHREYS, J. ANTHONY, ARTHUR E. TRAXLER, and ROBERT D. NORTH: *Guidance Services,* Science Research Associates, Inc., Chicago, 1960, chap. 1.

HUTSON, PERCIVAL W.: *The Guidance Function in Education,* Appleton-Century-Crofts, Inc., New York, 1958, chap. 1.

JONES, ARTHUR J.: *Principles of Guidance and Pupil Personnel Work,* McGraw-Hill Book Company, New York, 1951, chap. 1.

JOHNSON, WALTER F., BUFORD STEFFLRE, and ROY A. EDELFELT: *Pupil Personnel and Guidance Services*, McGraw-Hill Book Company, New York, 1961, chap. 1.

JOHNSTON, EDGAR G., MILDRED PETERS, and WILLIAM EVRAIFF: *The Role of the Teacher in Guidance*, Prentice-Hall, Inc., Englewood Cliffs, N.J., 1959.

KOWITZ, GERALD T., and NORMA G. KOWITZ: *Guidance in the Elementary Classroom*, McGraw-Hill Book Company, New York, 1959, chap. 1.

MC DANIEL, HENRY B.: *Guidance in the Modern School*, The Dryden Press, Inc., New York, 1956, chap. 1.

MARTINSON, RUTH A., and HARRY SMALLENBURG: *Guidance in Elementary Schools*, Prentice-Hall, Inc., Englewood Cliffs, N.J., 1958, chap. 1.

MATHEWSON, ROBERT HENDRY: *Guidance Policy and Practice*, Harper & Row, Publishers, Incorporated, New York, 1955, chaps. 1 and 2.

MILLER, CARROLL: *Foundations of Guidance*, Harper & Row, Publishers, Incorporated, New York, 1961, chap. 1.

MILLER, FRANK W.: *Guidance Principles and Services*, Charles E. Merrill Books, Inc., Englewood Cliffs, N.J., 1961, chap. 1.

MORTENSEN, DONALD G., and ALLEN M. SCHMULLER: *Guidance in Today's Schools*, John Wiley & Sons, Inc., New York, 1959, chap. 1.

OHLSEN, MERLE M.: *Guidance Services in the Modern School*, Harcourt, Brace & World, Inc., New York, 1964, chap. 1.

PETERS, HERMAN J., and GAIL F. FARWELL: *Guidance: A Developmental Approach*, Rand McNally & Company, Chicago, 1959, chap. 1.

ROTHNEY, JOHN W. M.: *Guidance Practices and Results*, Harper & Row, Publishers, Incorporated, New York, 1958, chap. 1.

SHERTZER, BRUCE, and HERMAN J. PETERS: *Guidance: Techniques for Individual Appraisal and Development*, The Macmillan Company, New York, 1965, chap. 1.

SMITH, GLENN E.: *Principles and Practices of the Guidance Program*, The Macmillan Company, New York, 1951, chap. 1.

WARTERS, JANE: *High School Personnel Work Today*, 2d ed., McGraw-Hill Book Company, 1956, chap. 2.

WILLEY, ROY DE VERL, and DEAN C. ANDREW: *Modern Methods and Techniques in Guidance*, Harper & Row, Publishers, Incorporated, New York, 1955, chap. 1.

WRENN, C. GILBERT: *The Counselor in a Changing World*, American Personnel and Guidance Association, Washington, D.C., 1962, chap. 1.

Journals

DUNSMOOR, C. C.: "Yes, More Than Vigilantes," *Personnel and Guidance Journal*, vol. 41, p. 651, March, 1963.

EDERLE, HELEN: "Guidance Services in the Public Schools," *Teachers College Journal*, vol. 29, pp. 72–74, March, 1958.

GUNNEN, R. E.: "Guidance is the Concern of All," *Montana Education*, vol. 41, p. 16, April, 1965.

HITCHCOCK, ARTHUR A., and others: "Milestones in the Development of the Personnel Services in Education," *Personnel Services in Education*, Fifty-eighth Yearbook of the National Society for the Study of Education, 1959, part II, pp. 283–298.

JOSEPH, E. A.: "Unphilosophical Tendencies in the Philosophy of Guidance," *Peabody Journal of Education*, vol. 41, pp. 332–337, May, 1964.

KAVRUCK, SAMUEL: "Guidance Draws on Many Fields," *School Life*, vol. 44, p. 28, March, 1962.

RAYBURN, J. D.: "Guidance Is an All-Time Thing," *Ohio School*, vol. 42, p. 24, February, 1964.

ROGERS, J. H.: "Broader Concept of Guidance Is Needed," *Agriculture Education Magazine*, vol. 36, p. 233, April, 1964.

SAUM, JAMES A.: "Current Events and Materials in Guidance," *California Journal of Secondary Education*, vol. 33, pp. 217–223, April, 1958.

SAIPETTE, K. F.: "School Board Member Looks at Guidance," *California Education*, vol. 2, pp. 9–10, November, 1964.

SMITH, HYRUM M.: "Preventing Difficulties through Guidance," *Education*, vol. 83, pp. 266–269, January, 1963.

STREET, PAUL: "Guidance: The Century's Educational Necessity," *Personnel and Guidance Journal*, vol. 35, pp. 460–462, March, 1957.

WILKINS, W. D., and B. J. PERLMUTTER: "Philosophical Foundations of Guidance and Personnel Work," *Review of Educational Research*, vol. 30, pp. 97–104, April, 1960.

TWO

/THE ROLE OF GUIDANCE SERVICES

The guidance program includes specialized services, but guidance is also a concept. Some of the influences of guidance on other phases of education are thus subtle and sometimes obscure. Professional people within the schools are aware of the benefits being realized as these influences manifest themselves in more mature behavior by students. Student achievement improves, time and energy are more efficiently utilized, creative potentialities are given greater expression, and other accomplishments are noted. The guidance function has the potentiality for marked influences in the lives of young people.

A study conducted by Austin H. Turney and Charles G. Morehead reports findings typical of similar studies. Two schools in Kansas with enrollments of about 150 students, in the seventh through twelfth grades, were used. In the experimental school a trained counselor spent fifteen hours a week in counseling activities with students. There was no formal counseling in the second school. The study reports four major findings from the experimental school. It claims that the average student was (1) superior in personality adjustment, (2) superior in academic achievement, (3) higher in his achievement in accordance with abilities, and (4) more intelligent in vocational choices. The researchers concluded that the experiment clearly showed the constructive value of counseling.[1]

A well-trained, highly competent counselor is essential to the guidance service. There is no place for serious errors in judgment, inefficiency, or incompetence in the counselor's office. The guidance program also has a definite relationship with the instructional phases of education. The nature of this relationship is considered in this chapter as the role and functions of the guidance service are reviewed.

Functions of the Guidance Service

If a guidance program is to justify its existence within the scheme of the educational program, it must accomplish tasks and perform functions not otherwise accomplished. It must provide services not normally made available in the conventional school program, and it must constitute a source of inspiration and direction for both students and teachers. The total educational program becomes meaningful as the guidance philosophy is accepted and promoted by the staff and as guidance functions are performed. These major functions include a philosophy and provide activities by which all phases of the educational program are supplemented and strengthened. This improvement in the educational program is noted as pupils improve in their own self-understanding and as various aspects of the educational endeavor are closely coordinated and properly utilized. Counseling and its related activities are other functions of the guidance service. These activities too are closely integrated with, but do not duplicate, the instructional and administrative phases of the school's organization. In-service training constitutes another function of the guidance program, one through which all school personnel are aided and encouraged toward a higher level of competence in their professional work. These three functions do not cover all the specifics of the guidance program. However, they do provide the framework upon which all phases of the guidance service are built. The more detailed functions of the guidance program are covered in separate chapters which deal with each basic element individually.

[1] Barbara Kirk (ed.), "Higher Achievement in School with Trained Counselor," *Personnel and Guidance Journal,* vol. 35, p. 455, March, 1957.

The Guidance Service as an Agency
Augmenting Instruction

The guidance service supplements, strengthens, and adds meaning to the regular educational experiences. The classroom is of necessity devoted to activities designed to serve youth in the development of the fundamental skills of learning. The importance of a close working relationship between the teacher and the counselor must be emphasized. Within this concept rests the key to the success of the program. The next few paragraphs point out how guidance programs can make instruction more meaningful to students. The teacher-learning function becomes more interesting, fruitful, and satisfying to teacher and learner as the aims of the guidance service are realized. The goals of the guidance service are enumerated in the following discussion.

To improve pupil self-understanding. Test results, counseling, and proper utilization of records are some of the means by which students arrive at a more objective, realistic, and enlightened attitude about themselves. This improved understanding should minimize frustrations experienced by students lacking the necessary comprehension to account for the discrepancy between their accomplishments and the school's expectations. The same principle applies as well to the brighter students, many of whom never become aware of their unusual potentialities or aptitudes. Services fostered by an organized program provide helpful information for identifying the more capable children.

To increase pupil understanding of self in relation to others. The guidance program encourages pupil participation and social interaction. Achieving a satisfactory working relationship with others is essential because of society's expectations and because of the desire of each child to be liked and accepted.

To emphasize relationships between academic pursuits and personal development. Because of the importance of self-knowledge and satisfactory social relationships, all learning experiences, in order to be meaningful and to result in new skills and understanding, should have a relationship to other activities within the lives of individuals. These activities are more intimate than the typical activities of the classroom, and they may occur in the home or in relationships with other children and adults. To confine learning only to the classroom and thus ignore other facets of living and additional influences denotes a failure to capitalize on other equally important and dynamic factors.

To promote better pupil understanding of the teacher.   To achieve such an important role in relating learning to life, the student should have understanding of his teacher. A more wholesome, positive, fruitful attitude exists if students have an appreciation for the teacher as a person and if they can be aware of the motives which prompt teacher actions. Personal development is a major aim of guidance. It is fostered through a personal interest shown in each child and by means of the technical services provided. A concomitant of self-understanding is a better understanding of other people. This condition too is fostered by the attitudes and services found within the guidance program.

To contribute to feelings of security.   An increase in self-understanding, which includes a realistic appraisal and awareness of limitations and abilities, should contribute to a student's feelings of adequacy. Good counseling contributes to his self-adjustment and to his ability to accept his limitations and capitalize on his strengths. It is anticipated that feelings of adequacy and security are strengthened as a student becomes familiar with objective data about himself, particularly if competent assistance is provided in making this information meaningful and understandable.

To supplement teachers' efforts in assisting children with problems. The majority of the students in a typical classroom can, with some attention, patience, and direction on the part of the teacher, make a satisfactory adjustment to school. They occasionally experience minor problems which can be resolved satisfactorily through the teacher's assistance. Typically, each classroom has a few youngsters with more serious problems which require more time and attention than the schedules of most teachers permit. The concerned teacher welcomes assistance with such problems. There are, however, several steps which the teacher can take in such cases. He can:

1   Maintain an attitude of sympathy.
2   Make an effort to understand these children and convey a feeling of genuine understanding.
3   Provide counseling in appropriate cases.
4   Make referrals to the counselor.
5   Maintain contact with the home.

6 Provide for the needs of individual pupils within the instructional setting.
7 Provide personal attention incident to classroom and other activities.

To provide for the establishment and attainment of long-range goals.
All students, with or without problems, are looking to the future. Here again, guidance activities help them to give more serious attention to goals. Immediate goals also receive consideration, and with their accomplishment comes increased confidence. More challenging achievements are realized as poise and determination increase. Successful achievement of immediate goals provide the impetus for attaining higher goals.

To provide encouragement and stimulation for new and varied classroom activities. As noted, the purposes of guidance programs include stimulating and contributing to the learning process. Therefore, teacher-counselor conferences are held for purposes of considering procedures to be used by the teacher in accommodating children according to their needs within the classroom. From this conference and through the utilization of information at hand the teacher may learn the possible courses to follow in providing classroom activities that will be helpful to the youngsters.

To accumulate and interpret important information. The welfare of each student is somewhat dependent upon the systematic accumulation and appropriate interpretation of important data. One new emphasis in education is that of being more objective in gaining and utilizing scientific data through research and through the use of dependable instruments. Personal judgment still has its place in education but generally as a supplement to objective data. Information and data relevant to the development and progress of students are accumulated systematically and routinely as a guidance service. The data are available to professional people with a personal interest in these children.

These guidance services include the proper recording of test data and other information in the cumulative records. Guidance personnel provide teachers with aid in proper recording methods. Standardization of procedures and recording contribute to the effectiveness of the records and the efficiency with which they are used.

The systematic and efficient accumulation of data is just one phase of this service and should include the interpretation of data to teachers, pupils, and parents. Teachers are then prepared to interpret test data to students and may need only occasional help or direction from the counselor. A periodic meeting might be held with teachers in which current information is reviewed and decisions are made on how this information might be most appropriately used.

It is unnecessary to review with children all the various data obtained. However, students seeking this information should be given the benefit of a proper interpretation of significant data. This may be done by either the teacher or the counselor, depending on the nature of the information and the time available to each for this function. If information is worth gathering, it deserves careful and considerate use with students concerned.

To provide information and stimulation essential to the development of the curriculum. Another important area in which guidance can make a tangible contribution to the effectiveness of the educational program is in making available accumulated information essential to the development of a sound curriculum and in providing the stimulation for making progressive changes. Sound educational practices call for modifications in the curriculum in order to accommodate students more intelligently. The intent is to make the needed changes for purposes of improving the educational offering. The curriculum must be subject to constant observation, scrutiny, and evaluation. The central core of evaluation is under administrative authority and responsibility, but this core must have a definite and strong relationship with the several units of activity within the school, including guidance.

The Guidance Service as a Provider of Counseling and Other Specialized Services

Guidance services are designed to supplement and strengthen the efforts of the classroom but never to supplant these efforts. Some of the functions of the guidance service are not the sole prerogatives of the guidance worker but are performed by the classroom teacher. However, if these services are to be made available to the degree necessary and at a high level of quality, they must be provided under an organized, systematic approach, designed to function with the highest possible efficiency and effectiveness.

*The Guidance Service as an Agency for In-service
Training Activities*

To help in strengthening the efforts of the teacher, guidance personnel are often called upon to provide in-service training for the teaching staff. The school administration is responsible for the establishment of an in-service training program. These activities provide teacher and counselor with learning experiences and training which will contribute to their effectiveness in their various positions.

Factors Related to the Role and Functions of Guidance in the Educational Program

The guidance service, as part of the educational program, must be considered in its true perspective. An educational activity is a part of the guidance service to the degree to which the activity capitalizes on guidance as a sound concept or the extent to which it utilizes the instruments, tools, and techniques of the guidance service. Considerable guidance-type activity of an incidental or informal nature takes place in education. These activities are essential to the educational process. Personal contacts between teachers and pupils, wherein genuine concern and interest are exemplified, have real value for pupil development. It is important that every child experience a warm feeling for his teacher. The services and activities of an organized guidance program are also essential to his development. The guidance worker plays his role as a member of the educational team by performing the tasks his position provides. The teacher does likewise. Their combined efforts provide experiences for, and promote the development of, youngsters to a higher and more effective degree than either could do alone.

A sharp delineation of functions and an arbitrary separation of responsibilities between teacher and guidance worker would be unwise at this time in the typical school. This is not to suggest that there is no place for various personnel specialists who may function somewhat apart from the classroom in a clinical setting. These clinicians do, indeed, have an important place in the personnel services of a modern school district. However, these people are not replacing the school counselor any more than the teacher is replacing the counselor.

The school district that is prepared both financially and philosophically to provide a team of highly trained specialists is the exception rather than the rule at the time when this statement is written. However, most districts are prepared to sponsor a guidance service which includes at least a minimum number of counselors to work directly with the students, teachers, and administrators in a close, warm professional relationship from which all may profit. Nor can certification requirements for guidance workers within states be ignored. Where teachers certification is required for certification as a counselor, conformity is desirable. Appropriate changes may certainly be made within the states through legislative action, as such changes are deemed desirable and as they gain enough support to bring them about.

Three important concepts should prevail: (1) each professional person should devote himself to the services he is trained to perform; (2) a total pupil personnel services program should be broad and inclusive, thus requiring a variety of qualified people to carry out the functions in a number of specialties; (3) an atmosphere of cooperation in both spirit and performances should prevail among all school personnel as each person does his job and as each lends his support to everyone else on the educational team.

Hoyt [2] makes a strong case for guidance as an integral part of education and for continuing to use the term "guidance." The plan he opposes would make the counselor a member of a team of pupil personnel specialists including the counselor, school psychologist, school social worker, health officer, and attendance officer. He says that although this staff would work with educators, there would be no need for them to regard themselves as educators.[3] There is a continuing need for a guidance service which is closely allied with all other phases of the educational program. Too much haste and zeal for any plan which would broaden the gap between the counselor and the teacher should be resisted. However, support should be given to any sound plan which will provide additional specialists required to meet the needs of students within any school.

The factors considered in the following paragraphs are important to the educational endeavor and relevant to all phases of the educational program.

[2] Kenneth B. Hoyt, "Guidance: A Constellation of Services," *Personnel and Guidance Journal*, vol. 40, pp. 690–697, April, 1962.

[3] *Ibid.*, p. 691. He also discusses four reasons for opposing a plan which would change the concept of guidance from its current position as a closely related part of the educational program to a more specialized role with a resulting gap between the counselor and the teacher.

Formal Counseling

An organized counseling program is essential to the success of the guidance service. A report on a Wisconsin study emphasizes this point. Three hundred Wisconsin high school students were included in a study in which one group was counseled by a teacher-counselor. The experimental group received counseling from the teacher-counselor and from a guidance specialist. The study, conducted over a period of three years, reported the following:

1   The differences in the number of graduates employed one year after graduation was insignificant.
2   A greater number of the experimental group were continuing their education beyond high school.
3   A greater percentage of the experimental group (*a*) had made specific vocational choices and (*b*) had designated the last three years of high school as the period when they had chosen their future occupations.
4   The experimental group planned their school programs more carefully.
5   The interpretation of guidance tests was a more profitable experience for the experimental group.
6   The experimental group also received more help in employment following high school.
7   More help in planning post-high school training was received by the experimental group.
8   Personal problems received greater attention, and more help was gained by the second group.

Considerably more help was received from the counselor than from the teacher-counselor. The research concluded that the counseling of students by a full-time counselor produced more favorable results.[4]

Obviously, this study does not tell the whole story, and there are many factors to be considered. The important point is that to be most effective, counseling should be done by competent well-trained, experienced people who have the time and the resources to do the best job possible.

Fulfillment of Needs

The nature of children's needs must be known in order to help them appropriately and adequately. Whereas each child has his own needs

[4] Santo J. Caravello, "Effectiveness of High School Guidance Services," *Personnel and Guidance Journal,* vol. 36, p. 325, January, 1958.

peculiar to his particular situation, he has certain basic needs common to all children. The following discussion includes some of the most basic and essential needs of children.

Essentials of food and clothing.   The importance of supplying subsistence needs is obvious, and the demand for these essentials transcends anything of an educational nature. Other agencies are responsible for the fulfillment of these needs. The educational environment merely capitalizes on the achievement of others who help the child to satisfy these basic needs. Children who are properly and adequately fed and clothed make better participants in the classroom and profit more from guidance activities than neglected children. They are also more receptive and amenable to encouragement.

Adequate activity and rest.   Although food and clothing cannot be provided by the school, the school can do much to provide the child with adequate activity and proper rest. Growing youngsters have an abundance of energy, drive, and natural exuberance. As energies are dissipated, drives are satisfied and exuberance lessens. A satisfactory balance between activity and rest, in accordance with the individual needs of the children, becomes an aim of the school.

An assurance of acceptance.   There is probably no influence in the lives of children more devastating than a realization that they are unwanted by, and unacceptable to, others. A feeling of being wanted and accepted is basic to a healthy personality. Feelings to the contrary contribute markedly to emotional and personality breakdown. Wholesome, adequate personality development depends upon the assurance that one is acceptable to, and liked by, other people.

Guidance can help in developing an awareness of the fact that social acceptance is important to young people. This concept is inherent in the guidance point of view. The awareness is made manifest in the teachers' relationship with youngsters. Teachers can structure the classroom situation in such a way as to contribute to the children's awareness of their acceptability. Counseling also provides the potential and possibility for understandings and the insights essential to good adjustment and adequate development. These benefits are provided by both the teacher and the counselor, and they should prove particularly beneficial to children who may be deprived of proper love and attention at home.

A close association with friends.   Basic to the personality of every normal human being is the fundamental desire for friends. This group of friends should provide at least one person with whom each child can form a strong bond of close friendship. Making and losing friends is a dynamic experience for most children, resulting in an occasional change of the best friend. Despite these changes, however, the need for a close friend is realized by children, and essential satisfactions are gained from these associations.

A wholesome atmosphere of permissiveness and controls. A logical and sensible balance between freedom of children and controls by adults is essential. Children need to feel good in their relationships with parents and teachers. A permissive atmosphere provides an environment in which the communication between children and adults is positive, understandable, and agreeable to both. Children are permitted a degree of freedom to share in the making of decisions. This freedom contributes to the utilization and promotion of their sense of initiative to assume responsibility for behavior and the completion of tasks. Permissiveness of this sort is essential to proper development and to a realization of independence and development.

Understanding regulated controls and knowing how to use freedom sensibly and profitably are not intuitive in children but must be learned. This learning occurs as a result of the controls which are strategically and wisely imposed. The controls provide direction and help children keep within acceptable bounds of good judgment and propriety in their activities. These restrictions are acceptable to them and welcomed by them. A free rein with few or no restrictions on conduct constitutes a frightening and threatening situation for most children.

A realization of successful achievement. Another important basic need in every child—and every human being—is to excel in something and perform with greater proficiency than his associates. The nature of the proficiency is not important, but the prestige, attention, and satisfaction gained from a creditable performance are.

High academic achievement is not always of major importance to many students. Superior athletic performance may be the ultimate in the minds of some youngsters and may actually take precedence over academic achievement. Music, dramatics, art, homemaking, workmanship, mechanics, and other activities receive their share of emphasis, demonstration of skills, and participation in which some students are able to excel. However, high academic accomplishments occupy the foremost position among possible achievements for the following reasons: (1) these activities occupy the major part of a youngster's day; (2) much of their intellectual energies are devoted to schoolwork; and (3) society stresses academic competence and achievement.

Opportunities to gain independence. As children develop and find satisfaction in various activities and are successful in meeting the demands of society, they are also gaining in independence. They become stronger, more proficient, and more mature as self-confidence increases. To be delayed in, restricted in, or denied the opportunities for gaining independence results in frustration and unhappiness in the same way that any thwarting of wishes or limiting of opportunities will result in frustration.

Purposes and Aims of Guidance Programs

The aims of the guidance service are similar to the aims of education itself—to help the student fulfill as many as possible of the above-mentioned needs. The aims of guidance lend emphasis and strength to the educational program and make it more dynamic. The guidance program purports to define an objective and scientific attitude in education. It also provides some stimulation in the establishment of educational aims and contributes to their attainment and fulfillment. A closer look at some of the purposes and aims of the guidance program will illustrate this thesis.

To provide services which contribute to a realization of potentialities. Each teacher should possess a full awareness of the desires and potentialities of youngsters. Efforts may then be directed toward assisting children in the realization of these desires and in the development of their potentialities. A significant function of education is to help children identify and develop their talents and abilities. The emphasis on pure academic achievement for its own sake has, however, resulted in the exclusion of other worthy activities and left little time and energy for their fulfillment.

Most children are aware of their desires but are unable, without assistance, to understand them or see them to their fulfillment. A strong program of educational services staffed by competent, sympathetic, professional people can thus make its impact felt in providing teacher and child with this needed assistance. The need of children is great for sympathetic, understanding, skillful adults to help them discover talents and identify promising potentialities.

Children left to their own resources will fail to realize the maximum fulfillment of their capabilities.

To provide teachers with encouragement and stimulation toward better teaching. Another principal purpose of the guidance activity is to provide incentive, encouragement, and stimulation to the teacher and to help the student benefit from more effective instruction. The responsibility for instruction rests with the teachers; however, the guidance program contributes to the educational processes through the encouragement provided teachers toward a stronger, more effective relationship with students. The guidance program provides encouragement and stimulation toward better teaching in the following ways:

1 By taking a personal interest in each teacher
2 By recognizing commendable work and worthy efforts of teachers
3 By discussing with teachers problems incident to their teaching
4 By providing teachers with information about children which may prove helpful and contribute to their understanding of children
5 By making suggestions on how to assist children who may be experiencing problems
6 By giving teachers the benefit of a guidance point of view and by demonstrating how this philosophy might make teaching a happier, more satisfying experience

Encouragement and stimulation often occur as a result of incidental contacts and from experiences which provide additional incentives for better teaching. The teacher often becomes the forgotten person and the one who receives the least attention and praise.

To provide teachers with technical assistance. The conventional training program for teachers includes very little experience with the more technical aspects of guidance work. A need thus exists for assistance with guidance functions essential to the educational program. The guidance worker is trained to provide for the more technical and complex aspects of guidance services. He is thus qualified to assist the teacher in the following ways:

1 Selecting, administering, and interpreting tests
2 Selecting and using cumulative, anecdotal, and other kinds of records and forms
3 Providing help and suggestions relative to counseling techniques

which may be employed by teachers in their counseling with pupils

4 Providing leadership in the development of a philosophy which emphasizes the importance of each pupil
5 Providing vocational information and suggesting appropriate vocational exploratory experiences
6 Providing leadership in promoting and conducting in-service training

To contribute to the mutual adjustment of children and the school. A reciprocal relationship must exist between children and the school wherein each is concerned about the other. Rights are accepted and responsibilities assumed in an atmosphere of respect. The school's obligations include modifications in its activities and offerings in order to provide essential educational experiences. An awareness as to the individual and collective needs of students is essential. Guidance has a responsibility for this cooperative relationship. Teachers and counselors must be alert in order to identify and ascertain student needs. Pupils must also make adjustments and adaptations to the school. They also have the obligation to contribute something to the school. Thus, a major contribution of students is that of making intelligent use of the school's resources and working toward greater accomplishments.

The mutual adjustment of child and school is facilitated by the guidance program and its services in the following ways:

1 By providing some stimulus and direction for the faculty in the development of a guidance philosophy
2 By gaining and making available information obtained through special guidance activities
3 By providing suggestions for program improvements
4 By conducting research and providing data needed for educational improvements

Guidance services are also helpful in assisting pupils toward better school adjustment by observing the following suggestions:

1 By making known to pupils why certain procedures within the educational framework are essential
2 By contributing to pupil adjustment through counseling
3 By providing pupils with information about the school by which they can become more knowledgeable
4 By utilizing guidance activities to minimize children's anxieties and tensions
5 By fostering and promoting wholesome attitudes toward the school and the home

To identify children with developing problems. The guidance service provides for the prevention of school-related problems and aids in providing remedial assistance. Prevention should receive major attention, since most children are within the range of normality and can thus be helped. Remedial assistance suggests the presence of problems which the typical teacher may be unable to handle. Where therapy or remediation is indicated, the counselor may provide the needed assistance or obtain clinical treatment for the child through the appropriate agency.

The identification of children with developing problems may be accomplished in several ways:

1　By taking a personal interest in each child and noting any unusual behavior or deviation
2　By conducting periodic interviews with each pupil
3　By noting the quality of work performed by each child and being alert for any abrupt deviation from the usual pattern
4　By utilizing objective data and coordinating it with other important information
5　By conducting case studies and making use of all information gained in improving the school situation for all children

Relationship Between Guidance Services and the Curriculum

A school may provide an adequate program of instructional activities and yet have no organized guidance service. A program of broad, inclusive educational activities should, however, provide for guidance services. Although instruction and the guidance program each has its unique functions, there is an overlap of responsibilities which requires cooperative effort from both areas. The relationship is thus positive and reciprocal, with each making its best contribution to the educational process and each supplementing the efforts of the other in achieving the same goals.

Twofold function of the teacher. A teacher may have a sound philosophy about guidance but be unable to carry out the activities of the service because of time and training limitations. The teacher is still the key person in the promotion of a strong educational program and in providing activities essential for the development of children. A positive view toward the guidance program and a degree of technical skill constitute a combination of proficiencies that should produce excellent results.

Points of emphasis in guidance activities and instruction. The aims of the guidance service and the aims of instruction are essentially the same. These aims include the maximum development of children. The guidance function emphasizes personal development, while instruction emphasizes educational achievement and progress. However, both services are concerned with the personal and educational development of children: neither leaves the aims or the tasks for accomplishing them entirely to the other. Both areas of service give maximum consideration to the following points:

1 Each makes an effort to accommodate students according to their needs.
2 Each utilizes community resources in furthering the educational offering and in stimulating people to participation.
3 Each assists in the learning process and provides meaningful learning experiences.
4 Each provides encouragement and direction for high pupil motivation.
5 Each promotes and stimulates children's interests.
6 Each contributes to knowledge through experimentation and research.
7 Each provides a variety of services to teachers and pupils.

Guidance programs and instruction. The following list provides suggestions on how the guidance program aids instruction:

1 By contributing to an understanding of human development for teachers and students
2 By providing objective data on students to be used in curriculum improvement
3 By counseling students toward realistic subject choices
4 By providing activities designed to contribute to adjustment and achievement

Instruction and the guidance service. Instruction, on the other hand, also contributes to the effectiveness of the guidance service. The teacher can aid in the guidance function by observing certain guides and principles. The following items may serve as aids in improving the guidance service and in making it possible for children to benefit from the activities provided.

1 Accommodating children in accordance to their academic needs, thus minimizing the occurrence of problems
2 Providing library and literary aids and materials

3 Providing for vocational exploration activities
4 Having socializing experiences in conjunction with classroom activities
5 Scheduling time for guidance activities to take place

Utilization of All School Personnel

The effectiveness of a guidance program is determined largely by the amount and quality of participation by all staff members. Everyone with educational responsibilities shares in the guidance of young people. Although this participation may be limited in specific functions, the influence and stimulus exerted through a positive philosophy is of great value. The position of each school official is unique and offers special opportunities for service to children. The educational program and the quality of the experiences are improved as a result of the interests and participation of these people.

Administrators.   Administrative officers occupy strategic positions for promoting the guidance program. Maximum utilization should be made of their positions and capabilities. The following suggestions on the functions of the administrator may be helpful in accomplishing this goal:

1 Providing dynamic, stimulating leadership
2 Encouraging broad participation
3 Providing for expenditures in the budget
4 Arranging for guidance activities in the daily schedules
5 Identifying children in need of assistance
6 Establishing the procedures for pupil referrals to counselors
7 Being informed on community referral agencies and encouraging their use
8 Recommending competent people for employment on the staff
9 Commending the effective teachers and counselors and encouraging them in their efforts

Teachers.   Teachers must be well-informed about programs and activities and take an active part in their establishment and conduct. They contribute to the guidance function in many ways:

1 By creating a warm, friendly atmosphere in the classroom
2 By being alert and noting behavior symptomatic of developing problems
3 By referring children to counselors for additional help
4 By providing for released time for counseling purposes

5   By providing opportunities for self-expression and activities essential to good mental health
6   By accepting youngsters and encouraging them to discuss their concerns
7   By lending cooperative effort to improve the educational program
8   By encouraging parental interest and participation in school activities
9   By talking periodically during the year with each child on a personal and confidential basis
10 By making each child feel that he is liked and appreciated
11 By serving on committees where needed for program improvement
12 By assisting with the activities of the guidance program

Counselors.   School counselors have leadership responsibilities in addition to counseling. The head counselor or director of the guidance program gives some time to leadership activities. The typical counselor engages in the following functions:

1   Assumes responsibilities for guidance functions delegated by the principal
2   Accepts referrals for counseling and personal assistance
3   Initiates procedures for making pupil contacts and for making counseling available
4   Observes students in the classroom and works with the teacher in improving classroom conditions
5   Conducts case studies and advises teachers in an effort to promote the optimum adjustment and welfare of each child
6   Provides leadership in the development of all phases of the guidance program
7   Assists in planning and conducting in-service training activities
8   Provides for the selection and use of guidance materials
9   Gives lectures and leads discussions for community groups and stimulates interest and participation in school activities

Nonteaching personnel.   Custodians, lunchroom supervisors, and bus drivers are all people with influence on the lives of youngsters. The participation of these people strengthens the pupil services, especially if they:

1   Note any unusual behavior and report it to the proper person.
2   Encourage children in proper conduct.
3   Provide assistance in settling misunderstandings or differences.
4   Protect youngsters against bullying or mistreatment.

5   Suggest and structure recreational activities.
6   Demonstrate a genuine interest in, and concern for, youngsters.

Community groups.   The various organizations within the community make fruitful contributions to the educational effort. They augment the school program by providing funds and leadership for additional activities. These community groups include service organizations, churches, labor and professional organizations, and business and employment agencies. Several activities come under their sponsorship possibilities. They can:

1   Provide financial aid for worthy youngsters.
2   Sponsor summer camps and other educational-recreational activities.
3   Develop and supervise playground and youth centers.
4   Provide medical, psychological, and sociological services for children in special need of these services.
5   Sponsor field trips and career days for vocational exploratory experiences.
6   Provide work experiences and earning opportunities.

Special professional personnel.   Psychologists, psychiatrists, and social workers are essential as resource people. A district may provide a clinic in which such resource people are available. This clinic may also serve more than one district in the interest of economy. Pupils receive many benefits as specific services are given. Such personnel may:

1   Provide for diagnostic services.
2   Administer and interpret clinical tests.
3   Provide the school with information gained in the clinic.
4   Provide special counseling or therapy.
5   Assist in case conferences and in-service training programs.

Reciprocal Relationship of Teachers and Counselors

The counselor may devote full time to counseling activities, or he may have teaching responsibilities as well. In either case there is a major allegiance to counseling or teaching, and the activity of his main commitment receives the major share of his attention. The school program should be so structured as to include adequate numbers of both teachers and counselors. These two groups then combine their efforts in a cooperative endeavor to serve students.

This shared responsibility is more fruitful if the activities of teachers and counselors augment and supplement each other by:

1 Sharing information which may be mutually beneficial.
2 Joining efforts in finding solutions to pupil problems.
3 Encouraging pupils to utilize appropriate services within the school.
4 Consulting and assisting in program modifications.
5 Sharing resources and knowledge in conducting case studies.
6 Making referrals to the proper unit or person.
7 Promoting a sound professional relationship based on established ethics.
8 Sharing responsibilities and functions and minimizing a clear-cut distinction between functions.
9 Observing flexibility in attitudes, duties, and responsibilities.

Guidance, then, is a concept, a belief, a commitment, a philosophy, and an attitude. It is upon this framework of intangibles that teachers, counselors, administrators, and other specialists can build a better program of educational experiences for each student. The subjectivity inherent in each of the above terms makes it no less influential and no less critical in the shaping of young lives. Guidance also has its tangibles in tests, cumulative records, diagnostic data, and some aspects of the counseling it provides. The tangibles and the intangibles of guidance are thus combined under the framework of the total educational endeavor in an alliance of commitment and dedication to the children and youth of the society.

Allport says: [5] "Guidance is not a matter of gimmicks, nor of rules of thumb. A guide, like a philosopher and friend, is a person who loves wisdom and loves his fellow men." The terms "commitment" and "dedication" used in this text both imply and assume that a genuine love for, interest in, and concern for children and youth prevail in the heart and mind of the guidance worker. In posing a question as to the personal attitudes of guidance specialists and teachers, Allport asks: [6] "Should we not cultivate the same twin virtues that we recommend to client and student: tentativeness and commitment? . . . Tentativeness and commitment are twin ideals for both counselor and client. To my mind they lie at the heart and center of guidance, of teaching, and of living." The reciprocal relationship between instruction and the guidance service, as it is herein emphasized, would presumably receive support from Allport's

[5] Gordon W. Allport, "Psychological Models for Guidance," *Harvard Educational Review,* vol. 32, p. 380, Fall, 1962.
[6] *Ibid.,* p. 381.

statement. Commitment is certainly an essential element of the guidance service, and tentativeness is likewise an ideal, as it suggests the need for continuous development, expansion, and improvement in the educational fare of each child.

SUMMARY/

The guidance program includes a philosophy as well as specialized services. The latter include the basic elements of the program, while the former is primarily an attitude. Guidance is also a concept. The guidance service is a part of the educational program. It supplements and strengthens the total educational program by making activities more meaningful and profitable to students, but at no time does it supplant any existing service or activity.

Counseling and other guidance services assist in providing for the needs of young people and in aiding them toward a realization of their potentialities. Instructional opportunities improve and teachers and pupils profit from the specialized services provided through the guidance program. As children make a better adjustment to school and their peers, their schoolwork usually improves.

Cooperative effort is essential to a successful program. School personnel combine resources and abilities and solicit the participation of community agencies in a combined effort to better the educational experiences and the recreational activities within the school and the community.

PROBLEMS/

1 Guidance is regarded as a concept as well as a set of organized services. Explain the meaning of this statement. Give some examples to illustrate the point.

2 The behavior of students might improve and their academic achievements become more pronounced with no immediate, observable explanation. Explain how this might be possible, and identify the possible influences in this case.

3 Explain how it is possible for students to demonstrate more mature behavior and realize greater achievement as a result of counseling. What are some major limitations of this kind of a study?

4 Some studies conclude that counseling is beneficial in contributing to the development of students, while other studies find no significant improvements following counseling. How do you explain this?

5 If the guidance service is not to replace another service or activity in the school, what is its value? What are its major contributions?

6 Note the merits and weaknesses of the goals of guid-ance as stated in the chapter. What additions would you make?

7 What justification is there for having an organized guidance service rather than leaving these activities to the class-room teacher?

8 What are the principal benefits to come from an in-service training program? What school officer is responsible for this program? How might the various staff members assist?

9 Note the differences between incidental guidance and the guidance provided under an organized program. Of what value is the former?

10 Why do you think a number of guidance people con-tinue to emphasize the importance of a close working relationship between the teacher and counselor? What results would likely occur if there were to be a sharp division between the two?

11 Children have certain basic needs for which the guid-ance service is not directly responsible. How can the guidance serv-ice help in meeting these needs?

12 How do the aims of education and the aims of guid-ance compare?

13 If the aims and purposes of the guidance service are quite well fulfilled, how will the life of each child be affected?

14 How can there be some overlap of functions between instruction and guidance without its resulting in duplications and inefficiency?

15 Give some examples in which you show how instruc-tion can aid the guidance service, and then give some examples to show how the guidance service aids instruction.

16 Support the concept that all staff members have a part in the guidance service. What are some possible dangers of this attitude?

17   What does the statement that there is a reciprocal relationship between the teacher and the counselor mean? How might this relationship be strengthened and improved?

Selected References

Textbooks

ARBUCKLE, DUGALD S.: *Pupil Personnel Services in American Schools*, Allyn and Bacon, Inc., Boston, 1962, chap. 3.

BERNARD, HAROLD W., C. EVAN JAMES, and FRANKLIN R. ZERAN: *Guidance Services in Elementary Schools*, Chartwell House, New York, 1954, chap. 1.

FARWELL, GAIL F., and HERMAN J. PETERS: *Guidance Readings for Counselors*, Rand McNally & Company, Chicago, 1960, chap. 3.

FROEHLICH, CLIFFORD P.: *Guidance Services in Schools*, 2d ed., McGraw-Hill Book Company, New York, 1958, chap. 3.

GLANZ, EDWARD C.: *Foundations and Principles of Guidance*, Allyn and Bacon, Inc., Boston, 1964, chap. 4.

HILL, GEORGE E.: *Management and Improvement of Guidance*, Appleton-Century-Crofts, Inc., New York, 1965, chap. 2.

HUMPHREYS, J. ANTHONY, ARTHUR E. TRAXLER, and ROBERT D. NORTH: *Guidance Services*, Science Research Associates, Inc., Chicago, 1960, chap. 2.

HUTSON, PERCIVAL W.: *The Guidance Function in Education*, Appleton-Century-Crofts, Inc., New York, 1958, chaps. 3 and 4.

JONES, ARTHUR J.: *Principles of Guidance and Pupil Personnel Work*, McGraw-Hill Book Company, New York, 1951, chap. 3.

KELLEY, JANET A.: *Guidance and Curriculum*, Prentice-Hall, Inc., Englewood Cliffs, N.J., 1955, chap. 1.

KOWITZ, GERALD T., and NORMA G. KOWITZ: *Guidance in the Elementary Classroom*, McGraw-Hill Book Company, New York, 1959, chap. 2.

MC DANIEL, HENRY B.: *Guidance in the Modern School*, The Dryden Press, Inc., New York, 1956, chaps. 2–4.

———, JOHN E. LALLAS, JAMES A. SAUM, and JAMES L. GILMORE: *Readings in Guidance*, Holt, Rinehart and Winston, Inc., New York, 1959, chaps. 2 and 3.

MATHEWSON, ROBERT HENDRY: *Guidance Policy and Practice*, Harper & Row, Publishers, Incorporated, New York, 1955, chap. 3.

MILLER, CARROLL: *Foundations of Guidance*, Harper & Row, Publishers, Incorporated, New York, 1961, chap. 2.

MORTENSEN, DONALD G., and ALLEN M. SCHMULLER: *Guidance in Today's Schools*, John Wiley & Sons, Inc., New York, 1959, chap. 2.

OHLSEN, MERLE M., *Guidance Services in the Modern School*, Harcourt, Brace & World, Inc., New York, 1964, chap. 2.

SMITH, GLENN E.: *Principles and Practices of the Guidance Program*, The Macmillan Company, New York, 1951, chaps. 2–4.

STOOPS, EMERY, and GUNNAR L. WAHLQUIST, *Principles and Practices in Guidance*, McGraw-Hill Book Company, New York, 1958, chap. 1.

WARTERS, JANE: *High School Personnel Work Today*, 2nd ed., McGraw-Hill Book Company, New York, 1956, chap. 1.

WILLEY, ROY DE VERL: *Guidance in Elementary Education,* Harper & Row, Publishers, Incorporated, New York, 1960, chaps. 1 and 2.

WRENN, C. GILBERT: *The Counselor in a Changing World,* American Personnel and Guidance Association, Washington, D.C., 1962, chap. 2.

Journals

BERSTON, H. M.: "School Dropout Problem," *Clearing House,* vol. 35, pp. 207–210, December, 1960.

BURNETT, COLLINS W.: "Strategy in the Guidance Program," *Clearing House,* vol. 35, pp. 305–307, January, 1961.

CARLSON, RUTH K.: "Emergence of Creative Personality," *Childhood Education,* vol. 36, pp. 402–404, May, 1960.

CASSEL, RUSSELL N.: "Basic Program of the Guidance Counselor," *Education,* vol. 82, pp. 323–326, February, 1962.

CODY, JOHN J.: "Rethinking the Purposes of Guidance," *Bulletin of the National Association of Secondary-school Principals,* vol. 48, pp. 10–20, April, 1964.

COMBS, ARTHUR W.: "Adjustment through Guidance and Special Services," *Educational Leadership,* vol. 16, pp. 89–92, November, 1958.

DANSKIN, DAVID G., C. E. KENNEDY, JR., and WALTER S. FRIESEN: "Guidance: The Ecology of Student," *Personnel and Guidance Journal,* vol. 44, pp. 130–135, October, 1965.

DERTHICK, LAWRENCE G.: "Guidance and the Educational Challenge," *American Association of University Women Journal,* vol. 52, pp. 137–140, March, 1959.

DIFFENBAUGH, DONALD J., and DOUGLAS J. BOWMAN: "Guidance Services at the Intermediate Level," *Personnel and Guidance Journal,* vol. 41, pp. 25–28, September, 1962.

FELDSCHUH, S. G.: "Guidance and the Law of Diminishing Returns," *High Points,* vol. 46, pp. 36–40, May, 1964.

FOX, M.: "Counseling the College Bound," *National Education Association Journal,* vol. 50, pp. 16–18, January, 1961.

HOPPOCK, ROBERT: "Place of Guidance in the Instructional Program," *Virginia Journal of Education,* vol. 55, pp. 11–15, November, 1961.

JENSEN, GRANT, and A. DUNSTAN: "Individualizing Guidance Services: Help for Johnny and Mary," *California Journal of Secondary Education,* vol. 34, pp. 79–82, February, 1959.

KATZ, MARTIN: "Role of the Guidance Counselor," *Bulletin of the National Association of Secondary-school Principals,* vol. 47, pp. 1–9, September, 1963.

KETRON, SARAH R.: "Guidance, Junior High School Style," *Teachers College Journal,* vol. 34, pp. 59–61, November, 1962.

MICHAEL, JACK, and LEE MEYERSON: "Behavioral Approach to Counseling and Guidance," *Harvard Education Review,* vol. 32, pp. 382–402, Fall, 1962.

PETERS, HERMAN J.: "Fostering the Developmental Approach in Guidance," *Education Forum,* vol. 28, pp. 87–93, November, 1963.

———: "Interferences to Guidance Program Development," *Personnel and Guidance Journal,* vol. 42, pp. 119–124, October, 1963.

PLA, J. E.: "Personality and Guidance Practices," *Teacher's College Record,* vol. 66, pp. 266–269, December, 1964.

REAVES, GAYLE C., and LEONARD REAVES III: "The Counselor and Preventive

Psychiatry," *Personnel and Guidance Journal*, vol. 43, pp. 661–664, March, 1965.

SAMLER, JOSEPH: "Higher Achievement in School with Trained Counselor," *Personnel and Guidance Journal*, vol. 35, p. 455, March, 1957.

SHERTZER, BRUCE, and SHELLEY C. STONE: "Administrative Deterrents to Effective Guidance Programs," *Education Digest*, vol. 29, pp. 40–43, October, 1963.

———, and ———: "The School Counselor and His Publics: A Problem in Role Definition," *Personnel and Guidance Journal*, vol. 41, pp. 687–692, April, 1963.

SMITH, HYRUM M.: "Pupil Personnel Services: What and How," *School Life*, vol. 43, pp. 16–18, June, 1961.

STEEL, CAROLYN: "Emerging Programs of Counseling and Guidance," *Bulletin of the National Association of Secondary-school Principals*, vol. 47, no. 284, pp. 10–18, September, 1963.

WILDMAN, J.: "More Quality Through Guidance," *Ohio School*, vol. 40, pp. 22–23, January, 1962.

WRENN, C. GILBERT: "Philosophical and Psychological Bases of Personnel Services in Education," *Personnel Services in Education*, Fifty-eighth Yearbook of the National Society for the Study of Education, 1959, part II, pp. 41–80.

THREE

/THE TEACHER IN THE GUIDANCE PROGRAM

Responsibilities for carrying out the functions of the guidance service rest with both the teacher and the counselor. The teacher's major commitment is to instructional activities, but he is also an active participant in functions designed to promote the personal welfare of students. The counselor's major commitment is to the personal development of individuals, with emphasis upon services of a specialized nature. The aims of both workers include fulfillment, self-actualization, and maximum development of all youngsters under their charge. However, the procedures used by the teacher and by the counselor in trying to realize these aims are not necessarily the same. The teacher is skilled in the techniques of instruction, and the counselor is adept in the use of the tools, materials, and techniques of the guidance worker. Together they are able to provide the stimulation and the enrichment experience by which each child is helped toward goals of realistic achievement and appropriate personal development.

Since the teacher's role is critical in the

educational lives of youngsters, the major aspects of this role and its importance in influencing the thinking and attitudes of each student are emphasized in this chapter. Some activities of the teacher within the classroom setting with implications for stimulating and assisting youngsters are enumerated and discussed briefly. The teacher's role in working closely with each child, noting possible problems, demonstrating a personal interest, and making certain that needed aid is provided is also reviewed. It is noted that the teacher is a guidance worker as he demonstrates a belief in, and a love for, each student in his class and as he provides for activities and enrichment experiences for youngsters beyond those normally provided in the typical classroom. He also aids and supports the guidance workers by rendering service in keeping with his qualifications and in harmony with time and energy limits imposed by his teaching.

Importance of the Teacher's Role

The teacher is the most important single individual in the educational life of each student. The teacher-pupil relationship should be characterized by warmth, acceptance, and friendliness. The quality of this relationship is a determining factor in the character and efficiency of learning experiences and in the emotional and mental state of the student.

The teacher is the person in the child's school day most conveniently accessible for assistance and understanding. Although schoolmates and friends fulfill needs for companionship, other essential needs must be provided for by an interested adult. The teacher fulfills this role as he remains close, accessible, and sympathetic and as he provides the necessary structure for classroom activities.

Influence on Thinking and Attitudes

The influence of the teacher is far-reaching. The extent of this influence and the implications it has in the lives of young people are not entirely known. Characters are developed and strengthened and personalities improved through the forceful influence of the teacher. Youngsters are stimulated toward higher achievement, energies are utilized, and potentialities are developed as the subtle but genuine impact of the teacher's personality and behavior is felt by each child.

Appropriate structuring makes learning experiences more

fruitful and pleasant. Thought processes are enhanced and greater depths achieved in the pursuit of knowledge as intelligent guidance is given and as opportunities for self-direction and personal fulfillment are provided. Satisfactory answers to problems and stimulating, enriching experiences gained in the educational setting during the early years of life provide positive influences on thinking and attitudes with permanent results. Patterns of thinking and behavior generally persist indefinitely once they have become well-established and reinforced; logic and the intellect may do very little to change them.

Imitation and emulation characterize the behavior of every child. Thoughts, expressions, speech, attitudes, and behavior pervade and influence the child. The teacher is often the model and should therefore set the best example possible. The child's behavior reflects his attitudes toward the teacher, and it also becomes a reflection of teacher behavior.

Influence through Encouragement and Stimulation

A desirable objective of education is to provide an environment from which may come the maximal realization and fulfillment of the child's potentialities and possibilities. The anticipation of accomplishments for each child must, of course, be realistic. The adult with unrealistic expectations is destined to disappointment and frustration. The child likewise experiences frustration as he finds himself the victim of an ambitious, misguided adult. However, failure by the school to identify potentialities and develop capabilities is also a serious affront to the child's integrity and dignity. Unrealistically high expectations and neglect are serious deterrents to a child's progress and development.

The teacher is a dynamic source of encouragement from which admirable accomplishments are attained. He provides imaginative, challenging activities which stimulate a child to give tasks his full attention and energies. The culmination of desires and aspirations is realized as a pupil is aided in identifying and testing his proficiencies. The opportunities of the teacher for influencing a pupil toward high achievement and appropriate self-realization are perhaps without limits.

The teacher fosters and promotes feelings of security and self-confidence. The nature of the classroom environment determines to a high degree the quality of each child's adjustment and his feelings toward school and toward himself. Self-confidence, attitudes of personal worth, and level of self-esteem are influenced by the school atmosphere. The prevention of problems and maladjustments is also accomplished by the alert teacher who notes symptoms of potential difficulties and takes appropriate action to avert them.

The attitude of the teacher toward the guidance service and his participation in these activities have a definite influence upon each child. His attitudes and behavior are often reflections of the teacher's attitude. The teacher can encourage participation and encourage positive attitudes of acceptance, or he can minimize the importance of the guidance service and thus depreciate it.

Activities of the Teacher

The teacher has many opportunities for active participation in various guidance activities. Some opportunities are associated with the instructional function, while others are available within the more specific activities of the guidance service. Permeating all these activities are a positive attitude of helpfulness and a genuine interest in young people. These elements are more important than the specific nature of the service being provided.

Providing for group activities. Active participation within small groups provides opportunities to share ideas and to profit from these intimate associations. Social skills are developed, self-understandings enhanced, verbal abilities improved, and insights gained through organized group activities. Innumerable possibilities are available to the resourceful teacher. For example, instead of the conventional approaches wherein each student does his own work, groups might be organized. Considerable interaction, mutual stimulation, and cooperative efforts are thus made possible. Individual groups may also share their findings and conclusions with those of other groups and of the class as a whole.

Providing for meaningful projects and activities. The whole learning process is made far more meaningful and valuable as opportunities for a variety of experiences are provided. The teacher's contribution to education is most significant as he capitalizes on opportunities for teaching through active pupil participation in projects. Reactions of enthusiasm, interest, and dedication are often demonstrated by a student, and a wholesome respect for all learning develops as he becomes actively involved in a variety of appealing activities.

Instead of the traditional teacher-dominated approach, students may be permitted and encouraged to take the initiative in planning procedures to be used. Assignments may also be made to individuals and to committees from which suggestions may come for more interesting ways to deal with materials and ideas.

Encouraging individual performance and activity.   Self-confidence improves and self-esteem is bolstered as a child profits from his experiences. Many of these experiences include contact with other people from whom he learns and gains stimulation. Individual performances in which he depends upon his own resources and capabilities are also essential to his development. These activities might include oral reports, written expressions, directing other pupils in an activity, artwork, manual skills, or decorating the classroom. Each student should learn to function effectively in an atmosphere of self-dependence, which requires resourcefulness, imagination, and a plumbing of the creative potential. These are the kinds of experiences which contribute to maximum development.

The teacher is thus making the learning of the basic skills and the accumulation of essential information realities in the lives of students. He is also contributing to each student's personal welfare and progress and is to this extent a member of the guidance team. The teacher controls the structuring of classroom experiences in which learning takes place and in which attitudes are formed. He also helps to create the atmosphere which is conducive to learning and appropriate for the mental and emotional well-being of students.

Making referrals to others.   An important function of the teacher is to identify a child with developing problems. Suitable measures may then be taken to deal with these problems through environmental manipulation and treatment. The teacher is sometimes able to deal satisfactorily with the youngster, while in other cases assistance is required. The welfare of the child should be the major criterion upon which decisions for action are based. The enlistment of assistance through referral is often the logical procedure. The student in need of help thus profits from the interest and concern of his teacher, and he also receives benefits from treatment or aid provided by other competent people.

Problems of an emotional, psychological, or sociological nature should receive assistance beyond that provided by the typical classroom. Problems directly associated with the classroom which are nonpathological might be handled satisfactorily by the teacher.

However, referral may still be warranted with relatively minor problems, since the counselor's efforts may supplement those of the teacher.

Assisting in making case studies. The case study involves a concentration of efforts by the teacher and the counselor in an analysis and synthesis of pertinent data on a child. The benefits to come from this cooperative effort and data utilization include a better understanding of the child. The teacher observes a child under varying conditions in the classroom. A general conclusion may thus be made as to the apparent adjustment being realized by the student and appropriate efforts made to improve conditions for his benefit. The ultimate worth of case studies is determined to a significant degree by the participation of the teacher, who has many opportunities for observing the child in a variety of activities.

Conclusions and decisions reached from any one case study are useful in dealing with another child. The case-study process contributes to a better understanding of all children, although their problems differ. The teacher is also the logical person to carry out the decisions of the study group and to apply them. Recommendations may be made by any member of the case-study group, but it is the teacher who must ultimately put these suggestions into operation. The recommendations of the group might, for example, suggest that the teacher provide materials at a lower level of difficulty for a particular child. The youngster may thus make a better adjustment to school as his frustrations are reduced. The teacher may also apply the same principles in assisting other youngsters experiencing similar problems.

Maintaining contact with the home. Pertinent information gained from the home also improves the teacher's understanding of a youngster. An occasional request for data or parent reactions to certain matters might be made. Discretion should be used and a respect maintained for the family and its right to privacy. Short questionnaires, checklists, or requests for statements are means by which information may be gained. Telephone calls and home visits help to keep the channels of communication open.

Teacher-parent conferences serve as a device for improving relationships between the school and the home. Their use at the elementary level is quite common. High schools often encourage parents to visit the schools and provide special evenings for this purpose.

Providing appropriate stimulating experiences. A pupil is unable to assess accurately the quality of his potentialities or capabilities. Nor can the teacher know all these facts. He can, however, provide varied, stimulating, interesting experiences which present new opportunities for the development of potentialities. Such experiences will, for example, assist the bright child who may be frustrated by the mediocrity of the educational fare provided and who may be confused by his inability to reconcile his high intellectual capabilities with the relatively low expectations of the school. All pupils need the guidance and intelligent leadership of a competent teacher and the challenges provided by a variety of educational experiences. Motivation increases as pupils respond to the guidance of a perceptive teacher and as they experience the thrill of successful accomplishments.

A child may demonstrate very little interest in creative endeavors and take no initiative in promoting his own development when limited to his own resources. Interests are developed and initiative stimulated when the teacher shows a personal concern for a child and aids him in discovering new interests and in furthering their actuality. The alert teacher will notice each child and will provide experiences which will stimulate him to greater activity. The particular nature of the activity is not important, but involvement in worthwhile activities is.

Providing for role-playing and dramatic experiences. Role-playing opportunities may be provided as events make their use profitable. Conflicts among children, misunderstandings with family members, or historical events are examples of role-playing situations. These experiences contribute to verbal skills, stimulate thinking, provide information about human relationships, and add to knowledge. Many aspects of the basic school subjects can be made more meaningful through dramatizations. Characters in history and literature may be played by youngsters. Geography, government, and science also take on new life as students participate in dramatizations, structured to emphasize learning. These activities constitute enrichment experiences through which interests can be stimulated and learning enhanced.

The Teacher's Role in Personal Assistance

A favorable, positive relationship between teacher and pupil includes personal assistance, for the teacher is concerned with all aspects of a child's experiences. He should be helpful in many problem areas, even though his major commitment is to teaching. Opportunities for closer personal contact with individual students other than those afforded in the typical classroom setting are made possible through personal and academic advisement, working with parents, and individualizing instruction. There are specific means by which the teacher can accomplish these important functions. These means are discussed later in this section.

Although the teacher is an important member of the guidance function and has unique contributions to make to it, the inadvisability of classifying the teacher as *a* or *the* counselor is quite evident. The teacher is a specialist in the processes of instruction. These instructional experiences are made more meaningful and profitable to students as the teacher also applies his knowledge of child development and as he demonstrates his concern for the personal welfare of each youngster.

One textbook notes that there are differences in method and timing between teaching and guidance work.[1] These writers state that the school teaches facts and rules and that the immediate purpose of teaching is to create an awareness in the children that there is order and pattern in the world, and then to get them to conform.[2] The function of guidance, on the other hand, is one of developing individuality rather than conformity.[3] Children should understand that there is order in the educational process and that they will profit from being systematic in the pursuit of knowledge. Individuality also has a place in the educational scheme, particularly if it fosters the creative spirit.

A somewhat more liberal view may be taken than that expressed by Arbuckle when he says: "The teacher cannot participate as a counselor, but he can be a member of the personnel services team." [4] This statement correctly emphasizes that there is a division between the work of the teacher and of the counselor but that there are also areas of shared efforts and cooperation. The work of the teacher, however, in a setting of privacy with individual students may constitute a form of counseling, although it is generally more

[1] These differences between teaching and guidance are discussed in some detail in Gerald T. Kowitz and Norma G. Kowitz, *Guidance in the Elementary Classroom*, McGraw-Hill Book Company, 1959, chap. 4.

[2] *Ibid.*, p. 56.

[3] *Ibid.*, p. 58.

[4] Dugald S. Arbuckle, *Pupil Personnel Services in American Schools*, Allyn and Bacon, Inc., Boston, 1962, pp. 101–102.

informal than the counseling provided by the counselor and it may also have different aims.[5]

The controversy as to whether or not the teacher should be the counselor has little relevance if the role of the teacher is correctly perceived.[6] He is not a counselor in the same sense that the counselor is and, therefore, is not attempting to fulfill two incongruent or incompatible roles. He is, however, a warm, approachable person who gives time to personal interviews with students.

In examining a statement the nature and purposes of the work of the researcher or writer must be considered. For example, in a recent book devoted entirely to the role of the teacher in the guidance service,[7] the point of view expressed is that "Notwithstanding the controversies regarding meaning and function, an effective teacher cannot avoid being a counselor." [8] Perhaps what the teacher does, as described by these writers, is more closely allied to teaching, interviewing, advisement, or conducting a conference with a child than it is to counseling. They note that if the objective of assisting the child is reached, there is little profit in quibbling over terms.[9] However, both teacher and counselor should be cognizant of their major responsibilities and limitations and function accordingly. Also, there will be less confusion if the service being provided is given the most appropriate term available. The arbitrary mislabeling of services is misleading and confusing to students and parents, and it detracts from the dignity and integrity of the educational system.

The teacher, then, contributes to the guidance function through effective teaching and through his involvement in specific activities which constitute a formal part of the organized guidance service. This point of view is assumed in the discussion that follows, in which consideration is given to the specific functions of the teacher as a member of the guidance team. It is also assumed that the better the qualifications of the teacher in guidance, the more valuable his services will be to students. Additional academic preparation beyond that required for teaching certification should be

[5] Arbuckle notes and discusses some difficulties faced by the teacher who attempts to function as a counselor (*ibid.,* pp. 108–121).

[6] See Edward V. Daubner, "Teacher as a Counselor," *Catholic Educational Review,* vol. 62, pp. 91–99, January, 1964.

[7] Roy DeVerl Willey and Melvin Dunn, *The Role of the Teacher in the Guidance Program,* McKnight & McKnight Publishing Company, Bloomington, Ill., 1964.

[8] *Ibid.,* p. 14.

[9] *Ibid.*

obtained by every person with a serious interest in giving help to youngsters beyond that provided in the conventional classroom. Additional preparation also can add to the teacher's understanding of behavior, enabling him to identify children showing symptoms of deviant behavior. As he better understands the human personality and the significance of a child's behavior, the teacher is also better prepared to provide for the child's needs within the classroom. Prevention is the keynote of guidance in the schools, and the teacher is the person in the best position to note and seek assistance for the child in need of help before the problem gets out of hand. He is also the one with the responsibility for providing a wholesome classroom environment which minimizes frustrations and anxieties and maximizes unrestricted development. Not only can the teacher thus reduce suffering on the part of victims of emotional disturbances, but also he has an effect on society as a whole and the price it pays for indifference to these problems.

Supporting the Counseling Function

The teacher furthers the counseling function by calling this service to the attention of students and by making appropriate referrals. Students react to the attitudes and behavior of the teacher, who can be a power in promoting counseling activities—or in deterring their effectiveness. His willingness to serve and his attitude of cooperation likewise influence other teachers to assume a healthy attitude of cooperation with the guidance personnel.

Another area of teacher activity is participation in in-service training functions. Benefits are reciprocal as the teacher contributes to the in-service training program and is in turn benefited personally and professionally by his participation. A constant increase in skills and in improved self-understanding depend upon continuous study and research and an organized plan for the exchange of ideas and information. Active participation by the total staff in these training functions can result in professional progress and improvements in the counseling service. The teacher's knowledge of test data and his ability to administer tests and interpret the results to students also strengthen the program.

Local conditions, availability of counselors, teacher competency as a counselor, and the amount of time available to the teacher are the major criteria for deciding when the teacher should refer a child to the counselor and when he should attempt to provide the personal assistance himself. A general guide is for the teacher to counsel on problems associated directly with the classroom situation. This activity may be more appropriately designated as "academic advisement" or "interviewing." Emotional, personality, family, or social problems are appropriately handled by the counselor.

Aiding in Personal Adjustment

Although many of the teacher's activities involve all students within a classroom, there are opportunities for personal contacts and a demonstration of interest in individuals. These manifestations of concern are most influential in bringing about improvements in the attitudes and behavior of youngsters. The realization that his teacher cares, is concerned, and wants to be helpful is a source of stimulation for self-improvement for most students.

Exactly what constitutes improved adjustment may be difficult to describe. Certainty as to just which activities may result in better pupil adjustment may be equally elusive. However, the following principles to be observed in teaching and serving youth may be used as guides in determining the nature of activities to be provided:

1 The ultimate welfare of the child is the major consideration.
2 All activities are means to ends and are not to be regarded as ends themselves.
3 Resourcefulness, imagination, and enthusiasm are essential in devising activities which will be profitable for boys and girls.
4 Parents, other teachers, and community agencies have abilities that can be utilized by soliciting their assistance.
5 All procedures should be planned carefully.
6 Appropriateness of activities for each student is essential for his development and for satisfying results.
7 Existing conditions within the school determine to a great extent the activities to be provided. Practicability and logic are essential factors.
8 Personal services and activities should be consistent with the philosophy and aims of the school.

Promoting a Wholesome Classroom Atmosphere

The happiness, satisfaction, and achievements of youngsters are influenced to a high degree by the climate of the classroom. An atmosphere of meaningful activity with a minimum of tension is conducive to learning and accomplishments. There is no single means, or combination of means, by which a desirable classroom climate is achieved. The teacher is probably the determining factor through his skill, personality, and character. Suggestions on procedures, however, may be used in conjunction with superior teaching. The teacher should:

1 Recognize and praise a child for commendable achievement and proper behavior.
2 Encourage each student to dedicate himself and devote his best efforts to each task at hand.
3 Provide enrichment experiences to accommodate learners at all levels of ability.
4 Use humor in handling minor incidents and avoid unnecessary tensions and anxieties.
5 Plan work well ahead and have several alternatives ready when a change in plans is necessary.
6 Provide incentives and recognition for bolstering the self-confidence of students.
7 Provide a variety of experiences in order to stimulate and accommodate everyone.
8 Note persisting symptoms of developing difficulties and take necessary remedial and preventive measures.
9 Take a personal interest in each student and demonstrate concern through greetings, gestures, and words of encouragement.
10 Deal firmly but kindly with a child when his behavior indicates a need for adult supervision and direction.

Providing Opportunities for Participation and Leadership

Satisfaction is felt, new skills develop, and understandings increase as youngsters win the attention and approbation of others through their achievements. Individual initiative by the student, or even an awareness as to how to proceed, is unlikely without close teacher direction and encouragement. Teacher personality and competence are again the controlling factors. However, teachers at all levels of competence may profit from suggestions such as those given below on how to provide for broad participation and for the development of leadership. The teacher may:

1 Arrange for pupil participation in the planning of classroom activities.
2 Encourage thinking and permit expressions on needed decisions on classroom procedures and subject-matter study.

3 Organize groups for panel discussions, demonstrations, and dramatizations for presenting academic material.
4 Structure activities to permit the more capable students to assist others in need of personal help.
5 Withdraw from active participation periodically and permit maximum student participation and decision making.
6 Refer controversial topics or questions to selected students for decisions or recommendations.

Working with Parents

Basic to the personal welfare of every child is the quality and stability of his home. An affiliate of this condition is the quality of the relationship between the home and the school. His status, security, and personal welfare depend upon the cooperative efforts of his parents and teachers. The initiation of these personal contacts is the major responsibility of the school. Parents may then respond to the actions of the school and lend their support in carrying out these activities. The capabilities of parents and favorable home conditions are thus utilized to the benefit of the children. Imaginative, resourceful teachers will find the means for exploiting the more favorable circumstances and conditions to achieve a stronger, more intimate relationship with these youngsters.

Study groups composed of teachers and parents are excellent for improving understandings and for arriving at decisions on important issues concerning children. They may be held in the evening during times when parents are able to participate. The sessions should be kept lively and interesting and should be directed at problems of current concern. Other contacts might be made with parents through telephone calls, informal meetings, and notes sent to the home. As teacher and parents reach a better understanding of each other, improve in their knowledge of child development, and share in the responsibilities and decisions on mutual problems, all children are directly benefited.

Providing for a Variety of Activities

The teacher, then, provides or assists in providing a variety of activities for students. These activities may be of an instructional or a guidance nature, or they may be both. A favorable environment for learning and the emotional well-being of the learner are concerns of the teacher, since he realizes their importance in the learning process. He therefore does not limit himself to the routine procedures of teaching, but he also assumes the responsibility for improving the learning environment and for aiding each child toward the full realization of his capabilities. Stimulating each child toward an attitude of receptiveness and enthusiasm for learning, aiding him in his personal development, assessing his level of readiness, and structuring appropriate learning experiences for him constitute the real challenges for the teacher.

Each student should seek the counsel of his teachers and by so doing continue to profit from the stimulation and the insights gained from this relationship. The student in the modern school is thus more fortunate than his parents and grandparents, as he has the advantages of both highly competent teachers and well-qualified counselors.

SUMMARY/

Both the teacher and the counselor are essential to the educational program. The teacher is essentially an instructional technician and as such gives teaching his first allegiance. This responsibility provides opportunities for him to give personal attention to his class members. He is not a counselor in the same sense that the guidance counselor is, but he does provide needed personal assistance to members of his class.

The vital nature of the teacher's influence is made manifest as he shapes, often unwittingly, the thinking and the attitudes of his students. The teacher also organizes activities within the classroom which provide encouragement and stimulation for youngsters. These activities should normally be offered with or without benefit of a guidance service.

The teacher also has a role in giving students personal assistance which is closely allied with the guidance service. Herein is found a reciprocal relationship between instruction and the guidance function where teacher and counselor augment the efforts of each other but do not duplicate or supplant.

The teacher provides for a variety of activities of both an instructional and a guidance nature. No hard, fast line of distinction between all instructional and all guidance functions is necessary. If the teacher is fulfilling his major responsibilities creditably and the counselor is doing likewise, the overlapping functions will be handled adequately with no need for conflict.

PROBLEMS/

1 Outline the major functions and responsibilities of the teacher.

2 Outline the major responsibilities of the counselor.

3 Note how the above two lists differ. That is, indicate what characterizes the work of the teacher and of the counselor.

4 What elements have you found to be somewhat common to both teaching and counseling?

5 The point is made in the chapter that the teacher is a highly influential person in the life of each child. Identify some of the major aspects of this influence.

6 What are some of the specific activities a teacher can provide which will have beneficial results in the lives of youngsters? Do all teachers use these procedures? Why?

7 Some controversy has persisted on the problem of whether or not the teacher is a guidance worker. Settle this argument once and for all to the satisfaction of everyone.

8 Someone asks you the question "Should the teacher also counsel?" Answer this question.

9 A teacher may have a genuine interest in becoming an effective counselor. What should this teacher do?

10 A teacher enjoys teaching, and he also wants to be of all the help possible to his students, but he is not interested in preparing for, or engaging in, formal counseling work. How can he be of most help to his students?

11 A condition of warmth between teacher and pupil probably enhances the learning process. Why?

12 Most of a teacher's activities are those which take place as a part of instruction. Other activities may be closely allied with the guidance service. Point out the differences in these two kinds of activities.

Selected References

Textbooks

ARBUCKLE, DUGALD S.: *Pupil Personnel Services in American Schools,* Allyn and Bacon, Inc., Boston, 1962, chap. 4.

FROEHLICH, CLIFFORD P.: *Guidance Services in Schools,* McGraw-Hill Book Company, New York, 1958, chap. 3.

HILL, GEORGE E.: *Management and Improvement of Guidance*, Appleton-Century-Crofts, Inc., New York, 1965, pp. 143–150.

JOHNSON, WALTER F., BUFORD STEFFLRE, and ROY A. EDELFELT: *Pupil Personnel and Guidance Services*, McGraw-Hill Book Company, New York, 1961, chap. 7.

JOHNSTON, EDGAR G., MILDRED PETERS, and WILLIAM EVRAIFF: *The Role of the Teacher in Guidance*, Prentice-Hall, Inc., Englewood Cliffs, N.J., 1959.

KOWITZ, GERALD T., and NORMA G. KOWITZ: *Guidance in the Elementary Classroom*, McGraw-Hill Book Company, New York, 1959, chap. 4.

LEE, JAMES M., and NATHANIEL J. PALLONE, *Guidance and Counseling in Schools*, McGraw-Hill Book Company, New York, 1966, chap. 5.

MILLER, FRANK W.: *Guidance Principles and Services*, Charles E. Merrill, Columbus, Ohio, 1961, chap. 4.

OHLSEN, MERLE M., *Guidance Services in the Modern School*, Harcourt, Brace & World, Inc., New York, 1964, chap. 15.

PETERS, HERMAN J., and GAIL F. FARWELL: *Guidance: A Developmental Approach*, Rand McNally & Company, Chicago, 1959, chap. 2.

TRAXLER, ARTHUR E.: *Techniques of Guidance*, Harper & Row, Publishers, Incorporated, New York, 1966, chap. 16.

WILLEY, ROY DE VERL, and MELVIN DUNN: *The Role of the Teacher in the Guidance Program*, McKnight & McKnight Publishing Company, Bloomington, Ill., 1964, chaps. 1, 11, 12, 14, and 15.

Journals

BENTLEY, JOSEPH C.: "Teacher's Role in Mental Health," *Education Forum*, vol. 29, pp. 199–205, January, 1965.

COTTINGHAM, HAROLD F.: "Guidance and Instruction," *Grade Teacher*, vol. 77, p. 50, October, 1959.

DAY, G. R.: "Imitation Counselors," *Clearing House*, vol. 39, pp. 76–79, October, 1964.

FREER, JAMES J.: "Teacher as Counselor," *Education*, vol. 82, pp. 336–338, February, 1962.

GARDNER, P. L.: "Teacher's Role in Guidance," *Ohio School*, vol. 38, p. 30, March, 1960.

GRANT, CLAUDE W.: "The Teacher-Student Relationship Is Not Counseling," *Journal of Counseling Psychology*, vol. 7, no. 2, pp. 148–149, 1960.

MALCOLM, DAVID D.: "Every Teacher a Counselor, But . . . ," *Education*, vol. 81, pp. 195–197, December, 1960.

MATHIS, G. K.: "Guidance Needs the Classroom Teacher," *Elementary Education*, vol. 50, pp. 398–399, May, 1962.

MC CABE, GEORGE E.: "Guidance in the Classroom: A Series of Hypotheses," *Educational Administration and Supervision*, vol. 44, pp. 213–218, July, 1958.

PULLEN, MILTON J.: "Classroom Guidance," *Instructor*, vol. 74, pp. 38–39, September, 1964; pp. 36–37, October, 1964; pp. 28–29, November, 1964.

RESNICK, JOSEPH: "Teacher-Counselor's Role," *Education*, vol. 80, pp. 206–209, December, 1959.

RICH, JEANNE and JACK I. BARDON: "Teacher and the School Psychologist," *Elementary School Journal*, vol. 64, pp. 318–323, March, 1964.

STEWART, J. A.: "Factors influencing Teacher Attitudes toward and Participation in Guidance Services," *Personnel and Guidance Journal,* vol. 39, pp. 729–734, May, 1961.

SWINEFORD, E. J.: "Peripatetic Guidance," *Clearing House,* vol. 38, pp. 93–95, October, 1963.

WAGNER, VICTORIA, and LOUIS J. GILBERT: "Team Guidance in a School," *Education,* vol. 81, pp. 359–362, February, 1961.

WALTER, SISTER MARY KNOWLE: "Teaching as Guidance," *Liberal Education,* vol. 47, pp. 345–351, October, 1961.

WATSON, DOROTHY: "A Teacher Looks at Guidance," *National Elementary Principal,* vol. 43, pp. 37–40, April, 1964.

FOUR

/THE INTEGRAL GUIDANCE SERVICE

The guidance service should be organized to reach all educational levels—kindergarten through twelfth grade. The junior college, college, or university should then assume its responsibilities for meeting the personal needs of students through its student personnel services. There is no longer any justification for the position that the guidance service is for the secondary school and that it has no place in the elementary school. There was some justification for this view during the early years of the guidance movement when its main concern was vocational preparation and placement. Guidance in modern education emphasizes personal student development. Obviously, the age or grade level of a student at any one time has no relevance to his receiving or not receiving the aid or having the experiences which will contribute to that development. The differences are in the nature of the experiences, not in the beliefs or commitments of the school.

A few textbooks dealing with elementary school guidance were published in the early

1950s.[1] Additional books gave impetus to the movement for elementary school guidance programs with their appearance in the late 1950s and the early 1960s.

The current attitude which embraces the guidance concept as an integral part of the total educational process minimizes the need for divisions by grade levels. The functions of the elementary school counselor differ somewhat from those of the secondary school counselor; he gives more time to consultations with teachers and parents and less to individual counseling; a counselor may also be more effective at one level than at the other; and the preparation also differs in terms of the functions the counselors are to perform at these educational levels. However, the guidance worker should be well acquainted with all phases of the guidance service at the various educational levels, while his placement nevertheless allows his personal preferences to be accommodated and his best competences properly utilized.

Although there is a place for textbooks written to cover the secondary school guidance program alone and likewise the elementary school guidance service, the point has been reached in the historical development of guidance where it is both possible and desirable to present a basic guidance program for the schools below the college level in one book. There is no longer any need for a sharp division within the guidance service imposed by the artificiality of grade levels. Youngsters require certain types of guidance irrespective of age. There is a continuing need for publications which will provide for the preparation of guidance workers with specialized functions to perform; however, this literature is in addition to the materials covered for purposes of becoming familiar with the basics of the guidance service. As the length and the depth of the preparation program for guidance workers increase, so, too, should the intensity of the training increase and the quality of the materials studied improve.

The present chapter covers the guidance services as a broad, integral part of the educational endeavor. The elements common to both elementary and secondary school guidance are reviewed briefly, and some of the major differences between the two are considered. Basic to this discussion is the assumption that the

[1] Those books that did include Raymond N. Hatch, *Guidance Services in the Elementary School*, William C. Brown, Dubuque, Iowa, 1951, and Roy DeVerl Willey, *Guidance in Elementary Education*, Harper & Row, Publishers, Incorporated, New York, 1952. Others are listed in the Selected References at the end of this and other chapters; a later edition (1960) of Willey's book is also listed in other chapters.

person who plans to engage in guidance work at the elementary school level will receive appropriate training and experience for his work. The secondary school counselor will likewise be prepared for the work he is to do. The development of special skills and techniques takes place as a part of the counselor's preparation. A study of the basic guidance service, as presented in this book, provides the foundation upon which more intensive preparation is built.

The Broad Base of the Guidance Service

The guidance program has a broad base upon which all the specialized services of the program should rest. Testing, counseling, therapy, and all other specialized services operate from this basic structure. It is the framework within which all elements of the guidance service are interrelated and interdependent.

A sound educational program includes an organized guidance service, and the total guidance service is integrated with the whole of the educational enterprise. Many schools of the past have operated without benefit of an organized guidance service, and some such schools still exist. However, the needs of youngsters are not generally being met as well as they could be met with the aid and direction of a guidance program. As Gelatt states,[2] "Guidance services are the focus of the school's effort to see that each individual child has a variety of *appropriate* educational experiences and that he develops and uses his intellectual potential."

Guidance for Meeting Developmental Needs

The developmental process includes growth, change, adaptation, and adjustment.[3] The current concept of the guidance service is that it takes into consideration these developmental phenomena of youth as it provides services and activities which make this development more enriching and rewarding and as it facilitates the various aspects of a child's development. Vocational advisement, job selection, and educational decisions are all essential activities, but they represent oversimplifications of the counselor's work and certainly

[2] H. B. Gelatt, "Early Guidance Essentials," *Education*, vol. 83, p. 263, January, 1963.

[3] See George E. Hill, "The Start of a Continuous Program in Guidance in Elementary Schools," *Clearing House*, vol. 38, pp. 111–116,, October, 1963. He outlines four basic needs of children which constitute the basis for organized guidance services.

of the school's functions. Careful attention and intelligent consideration should be given to all matters involving plans and decisions. However, the guidance view is that this planning is done as a part of the student's total development, as opposed to traditional, arbitrary decision making based only upon immediately available problems and facts. The really important information about a student and facts which may have the greatest relevance for his future are usually not immediately available or observable. The sound concept of guidance as broad and as having a concern for the total development of each student suggests the importance of a well-organized guidance program.

Maturity as a major objective. The continuous development and progress of each student is an immediate objective of the guidance service. As a child's approximate level of growth and attainment is ascertained, it is possible to provide the necessary stimulation, direction, and activity to keep him moving positively toward maximum growth. The principle is the same no matter what the age or maturity level of the child may be. The concern for a youngster's full development is just as pronounced for a high school sophomore as it is for the third-grader. Obviously, the nature of the activities provided by the teacher and the counselor for youngsters at different levels of maturation will vary.

Prevention as a major objective. The prevention of serious problems is the objective of the school—again, at all educational levels. Correction and treatment are also important objectives of the guidance service where it is able to provide the necessary personnel and facilities. Early identification, correction, and treatment are all essential; however, the more successful the program for prevention, the less need there will be for intensive treatment procedure. Prevention is basic to the whole guidance service from early elementary school to high school graduation.

Identification of special needs. There are needs common to all children the fulfillment of which is essential for their physiological and psychological welfare. At the same time each child is unique and has needs peculiar to himself and his situation. The school must provide for both kinds of needs. The needs in the first classification are easier to meet because they involve all children and because a number of children can be accommodated simultaneously. The individual needs of each child, however, require special attention, and the procedures used should be determined by the peculiarities of his unique situation. The broad base of the guidance service provides for a variety of activities and procedures by which this identification of needs can be accomplished and by which the needed treatment facilities can be provided. Meeting the developmental needs of each child is still the objective here.

A variety of activities for meeting developmental needs. Activities within the instructional setting and activities of the guidance service all help to fulfill the developmental needs of students. Many of these are covered in detail elsewhere in this text. Guidance activities within the classroom combine with the activities of the guidance service to provide a broad base of operation from which all children should be helped.

Elements Common to Guidance at All Levels

If great detail were essential in noting the elements of the guidance service which are common to all educational levels, a rather formidable list could be provided. For the purposes of this chapter, a few representative elements have been selected to emphasize that the basics of the guidance service are essentially the same for all educational levels.

The guidance philosophy. A philosophy, or point of view, about guidance and its role in the educational process need not depend upon any particular educational level for its existence or strength. An attitude of concern for the full development of each student is to be fostered by all teachers and counselors at every grade level.

Basic elements of the guidance service. The elements of pupil appraisal, counseling, information services, placement, and follow-up may constitute the base of the total guidance service for elementary and secondary school guidance programs. Modifications in these services should, of course, be made to accommodate the age and maturity level of the students. Other activities will also be introduced to aid youngsters, particularly in the elementary school, but the basic services can remain essentially the same.

Identification of talent. The identification of youngsters with unusual potentialities and capabilities should be taking place at all times and with students of all ages. Early recognition of unusual talents is just as important as early identification of problems. While this statement has implications for the guidance service in the elementary school, there should be no minimum or maximum ages for talented youngsters. They should be identified as early as possible and aided accordingly all the way through school.

An attitude of warmth and acceptance.   An attitude of warmth and acceptance by all staff members toward each child has no grade barriers. Such an attitude is essential to the success of the guidance service, and it has a far-reaching influence in the lives of students. The relationship between teacher and child is closer and of greater duration in the elementary school than in the secondary school. This relationship should be of high quality and a source of inspiration and satisfaction for every student with each of his teachers throughout all his schooling.

Unique Elements at Different Levels

Certain elements of the guidance service are essentially the same at all levels. Other elements in the elementary school or in the secondary school are unique.[4] Some representative elements will be identified in this section. It should be noted, however, that the differences are in degree rather than those that make a clear-cut separation. In this book the unique characteristics of the guidance service in the elementary school are noted with the assumption that the reader knows or can infer the companion condition in the secondary school. For example, it is assumed that the elementary school child needs considerable personal help and direction in the attainment of the basic skills. The secondary school student, on the other hand, may be permitted greater freedom and latitude in the pursuit of his studies. The latter statement represents an assumption that might be made in each case.

Teaching and guidance techniques.   The approaches, techniques, and devices of the teacher and the counselor working with younger

[4] One writer lists some principles which he says describe elementary school guidance work. Although some modifications are in order in light of more recent events, this list of eight principles characterizes the guidance service of the elementary school; see Harold F. Cottingham, "Guidance," *Grade Teacher*, vol. 76, p. 91, January, 1959. Another reference includes a discussion of what the writers call "differential factors in elementary school guidance"; see Gail F. Farwell and Herman J. Peters, "Guidance: A Longitudinal and a Differential View," *Elementary School Journal*, vol. 57, pp. 442–445, May, 1957.

children must be appropriate for their maturity level and in keeping with their capabilities for profiting from the experiences. Greater structure, more detailed instructions, and closer supervision in both instructional and guidance activities are required than for older students. However, as already noted, the differences are a matter of degree.

Learning the basic skills.   Becoming adept in the use of language and the other basic skills is a major objective of the school for the child during his early school years. These skills are improved upon as he is able to deal with more difficult tasks and come to an understanding of more complex concepts. But this development requires time. The activities of the classroom and the guidance service should reflect this major objective of the school—the gaining of the fundamental skills and the acquisition of basic knowledge upon which all future academic progress depends.

Development of the self-concept.   The situation with a young child in the development of the self-concept is characterized by trial, tentative establishment, and fluidity. The adolescent is also in a trial-and-check state, but he is experiencing a rather pronounced emergence of the self-concept with some definite overtones of permanence. The successes, failures, and emotional impressions of the young child all have tremendous influence upon the self-concept, and they have far-reaching implications for his future development and eventual status as an adult.

Tentativeness of choices.   The urgency with which the adolescent may need to respond in making decisions does not normally prevail with the child. The latter has the time to experiment and even to ignore choices, since there is time for thought and preparation. He needs the opportunities for enrichment and exploratory experiences upon which the wisdom of future choices depends. Adjustments in plans may be made and errors corrected as new insights are gained. There is comfort in the fact that the child can be tentative and exploratory in his plans and decisions, since he is not faced with the same urgency as the older student.

A direct approach.   The judgment of the child generally reflects his immaturity, with the indication of need for a direct approach by teacher and counselor in aiding the child. His need for information and for structure in his activities is greater than that of the adolescent. His ability to gain the necessary insights for effective action is limited, thus requiring a close personal relationship with the teacher. His development can be best facilitated by providing direction and by helping him avoid delays and frustrations.

Coordinating role of the teacher. The elementary teacher is the coordinator of many of the guidance activities of his students. The counselor performs such functions for the total guidance service, but the teacher does this for his classroom. At the secondary level coordination of guidance activities is handled primarily by the counselor.

Uninhibited nature of the child. The young child is relatively uninhibited. He is expressive, imaginative, and candid. He has not yet had the time to develop inhibitions or had the experiences from which they result. This condition suggests the importance of a kind, approachable, understanding teacher and counselor who will continue to provide the most fruitful experiences possible for him. These people will continue to foster a stimulating atmosphere in which each child will explore, experience, and create unfettered by the inhibiting influences of the typical adolescent and adult. This free, accepting, naïve attitude of the child makes him a willing subject for learning and a delightful person to observe.

Differing duties of the counselor. The elementary school counselor works closely with the teacher and concerns himself with the learning function of the classroom.[5] He can be of the greatest service by maintaining close contact with the activities of the classroom. He emphasizes prevention and helps in structuring school experiences which foster and promote good mental health. He also identifies youngsters with developing problems and makes certain they receive needed aid or treatment. He also identifies the special talents and capabilities of children and uses his influences in providing appropriate, stimulating experiences for each child. The secondary school counselor gives less direct attention to the classroom activities and more to student counseling and to functions of coordinating the guidance service.

[5] Nine specific counselor duties of the elementary school counselor are listed in George E. Hill, *Management and Improvement of Guidance*, Appleton-Century-Crofts, Inc., New York, 1965, pp. 52–53.

The Reality of a Broad Guidance Service

The concept of guidance as being broad and inclusive but at the same time having some definable limits is quite well accepted. A total, unequivocal acceptance of this concept by all school people depends upon a unity of understanding of both guidance and the total educational process. The problems of low budgets, conservative school boards, ill-informed or uncooperative school personnel, and insufficient numbers of well-qualified counselors will continue to plague the schools. However, many of the more serious deterrents to progress are being reduced or eliminated, and the prospects for the future are encouraging.

Various Specialities within the Guidance Service

The intent here is to emphasize the fact that there are specialties under the framework of the personnel services, for purposes of showing that the concept of guidance as a broad, comprehensive service is logical and realistic. The child guidance consultant in the elementary school, the counselor in the secondary school, the school psychologist, the social worker, and the director of guidance services all have their special functions.

With better counselor preparation programs, including longer and more intensive training, guidance workers will become more proficient, and the quality of services provided for the schools will likewise improve. More teachers too are taking advantage of graduate school offerings, and many are working toward higher degrees with the same promise of higher professional-level service for the students of the schools in both instruction and guidance.

Demands of the Times

The demands of modern life require greater intellectual competence, emotional stability, and social sophistication of its young citizens than ever before. Rapid adjustments and spontaneous adaptations to changing conditions and changing people are first requisites to a young person's well-being, and they are most essential for his personal and professional progress. The fact that today's child is far better informed than his parents should evoke no surprise but should rather be accepted as both inevitable and highly desirable. Indeed, he should be brighter and better prepared to act more quickly, to have greater vision, and to be more productive than the generations that produced him. This presents each child and young person with great challenges and is an even greater challenge to his school to provide him with a variety of educational experiences, each with meaning and with the promise of contributing something to his growth. There is no time for waste, for errors in judgment, for the needless dissipation of energies, or for unstructured experimentation for its sake alone. A related idea is aptly stated: [6] "Events of these times place an added burden on school children to acquire more education in breadth and depth, and on teachers to use new techniques in crowding more knowledge into young heads." Certainly, there is no time or justification for easing the pressure on the schools to do an increasingly better job each day. The demands of the times are great, the anticipations for the future are exciting, and the opportunities for involvement in creative and productive enterprises by everyone with ambition and imagination are tremendous.

Developments and Trends in Guidance

The appearance of some rather definite trends in guidance and some current developments also provide support for the idea of guidance as a broad educational specialty. The details of these developments are covered in Chapter 17. A greater acceptance of the guidance concept by school personnel is taking place, and trends include an even more positive attitude toward the guidance service and a more whole-hearted support for it. Historically, many counselors have been only minimally prepared for their work, and they have often lacked the personal qualities upon which successful guidance work depends. This condition is improving, however, with more stringent admission standards to counselor education programs and with longer, more intensive periods of preparation.

The National Defense Education Act of 1958 (NDEA) currently provides for the preparation of personnel workers for the elementary school, junior college, and technical school as well as for the secondary school. Nineteen NDEA institutes were given during the school year 1966–1967, seven of which were for the elementary school guidance workers. Forty-six institutes were given during the summer of 1966, again with seven designed for the elementary school guidance worker.[7] These and many other developments and

---

[6] Louise O. Eckerson and Hyrum M. Smith, "Guidance in the Elementary School," *School Life*, vol. 44, p. 16, May, 1962.

[7] *The Guidepost*, American Personnel and Guidance Association, Washington, D.C., vol. 8, no. 3, December, 1965.

trends support the reality of guidance as a broad concept with an influence felt throughout the entirety of the educational system from the kindergarten through the university.

SUMMARY/

The guidance service is an integral part of the total educational endeavor. The elementary school is currently receiving consideration for the inclusion of guidance services in its educational program. Colleges and universities are also profiting from the influences of the guidance movement and are making a greater effort to strengthen their personnel services and to meet the needs of all students more adequately.

The broad base of the guidance service provides the structure upon which a variety of activities are made available for purposes of educational enrichment and for the stimulation of youngsters toward worthy achievements. The needs of children occurring as concomitants of the developmental process are recognized within the framework of guidance, and appropriate services are utilized in providing the needed assistance.

The philosophy of guidance is no different at one educational level from that at another. The activities conducted and the amount of emphasis given to a particular procedure or technique may, however, differ. There are elements common to the guidance service at all educational levels, and there are also elements in a particular age group that are unique. The guidance service capitalizes upon this to improve the effectiveness of its activities for all students.

The concept of guidance as broad and inclusive is realistic in terms of the past, emphases of the present, emerging trends, and the anticipations of the future. Events of great significance are providing impetus to the guidance service. Its influence is being felt throughout the educational world.

PROBLEMS/

1 Account for the fact that organized guidance services have been limited largely to the secondary school. Justify the need for some changes in this view.

2 Publishers at one time discouraged the writing of guidance textbooks directed at the elementary school. Was this a defensible position? Is it currently defensible?

3 Why should any school guidance worker be acquainted with the educational process at both the elementary and secondary school levels?

4 Point out some major differences between the work of the elementary school guidance worker and that of the secondary school guidance person.

5 Note the distinct advantages to come from the view that guidance is a broad program and that it influences the whole educational process. What are some weaknesses in this view?

6 How can the guidance service aid in meeting the developmental needs of youngsters? Why are these of some concern to the guidance people?

7 If it is true that there are elements in the guidance service common to all educational levels and some elements at each major educational level that are unique, what are the implications for the guidance service? What influence might this have upon instruction?

8 Identify the elements of the guidance service that are common to both the elementary and the secondary school. Identify the elements that are somewhat limited to one level or the other.

9 With which idea does the typical counselor feel more comfortable: (*a*) guidance as a broad concept in which all areas of education are involved or (*b*) guidance as a set of specific services with only a casual relationship to the rest of the educational program? Describe current thinking or trends on this issue.

Selected References

Textbooks

BARRY, RUTH, and BEVERLY WOLF: *Modern Issues in Guidance Personnel Work*, Bureau of Publications, Teachers College, Columbia University, New York, 1957, chap. 9.

DETJEN, ERVIN WINFRED, and MARY FORD DETJEN: *Elementary School Guidance*, 2d ed. McGraw-Hill Book Company, New York, 1963, chap. 1.

HILL, GEORGE E.: *Management and Improvement of Guidance*, Appleton-Century-Crofts, Inc., New York, 1965, chap. 3.

LEE, JAMES M., and NATHANIEL J. PALLONE: *Guidance and Counseling in*

Schools: Foundations and Process, McGraw-Hill Book Company, New York, 1966, chap. 12.

MARTINSON, RUTH, and HARRY SMALLENBURG: *Guidance in Elementary Schools,* Prentice-Hall, Inc., Englewood Cliffs, N.J., 1958, chaps. 1 and 2.

WRENN, C. GILBERT: *The Counselor in a Changing World,* American Personnel and Guidance Association, Washington, D.C., 1962, chap. 3.

Journals

ANGLIN, ELEANOR M.: "Guidance in the Elementary School," *National Elementary Principal,* vol. 41, pp. 54–58, January, 1962.

BRISON, DAVID W.: "The Role of the Elementary Guidance Counselor," *National Elementary Principal,* vol. 43, pp. 41–44, April, 1964.

FERRIS, R. R., and S. L. LEITER: "Guidance in the Elementary School: Opinions Differ," *National Education Association Journal,* vol. 54, pp. 48–49, September, 1965.

MAHAN, THOMAS W., JR.: "Elementary School Counselor: Disturber of the Peace," *National Elementary Principal,* vol. 44, pp. 72–74, February, 1965.

MEEKS, A. R.: "Guidance in the Elementary School," *National Education Association Journal,* vol. 51, pp. 30–32, March, 1962.

MILLER, D. F.: "Elementary Guidance for All Children," *School and Community,* vol. 47, p. 9, May, 1961.

MOORE, LANIRE H.: "Guidance Project at the Elementary Level," *School and Community,* vol. 49, p. 15, May, 1963.

OLDRIDGE, BUFF: "Two Roles for Elementary School Guidance Personnel," *Personnel and Guidance Journal,* vol. 43, pp. 367–370, December, 1964.

OTTERNESS, JANE, and A. UNTERKER: "Counseling Elementary Children," *Minnesota Journal of Education,* vol. 43, p. 22, December, 1962.

PURKEY, E.: "Elementary School Counseling," *National Education Association Journal,* vol. 51, pp. 18–20, December, 1962.

RAPPORT, A.: "Some Guidance Activities for the Elementary School," *Chicago School Journal,* vol. 45, pp. 32–33, October, 1963.

RICCIO, ANTHONY C.: "Elementary School Guidance: Its Present Status," *Theory into Practice,* vol. 2, pp. 39–43, 1963.

ROYSTER, WILLIAM B.: "Guidance in the Elementary School," *National Elementary Principal,* vol. 43, pp. 6–10, April, 1964.

SMALLENBURG, HARRY: "Studying the Elementary Guidance Program," *National Elementary Principal,* vol. 43, pp. 15–18, April, 1964.

STROWIG, R. WRAY: "Selected References on Guidance in Elementary School," *Elementary School Journal,* vol. 65, pp. 286–289, February, 1965.

WHITE, HELEN, and MARY EDITH BANES: "Practical Guidance Services in the Elementary School," *Teachers College Journal,* vol. 31, pp. 58–62. December, 1959.

PART 2/

*Elements and services
in the guidance program*

FIVE

/THE PUPIL INVENTORY

The pupil inventory is a synthesis of important information gained about each pupil as he progresses through school. Much of this information is utilized in counseling and in planning a pupil's educational and vocational program. Data gained from standardized tests and inventories may also be regarded as part of the pupil inventory. A discussion of testing follows in Chapter 6. The present chapter covers guidance records and related tools and procedures for learning about pupils. Both the guidance records and the accumulated data constitute the pupil inventory.

The most important single record for guidance purposes is the cumulative folder. This folder provides for the recording of salient data and is a depository for profile sheets, health data, samples of work, and other information regarded as pertinent to the welfare of the youngster. The cumulative folder is the core of the pupil inventory. Permanent records are also kept on each child, but these are for administrative purposes and are usually kept in the school's administrative offices. Records and reports of various kinds are maintained by teachers for instructional and administrative purposes. Every school can profit from the availability and proper use of these various records and should have a suitable system for gathering, maintaining, and utilizing significant data.

The pupil inventory is also a system of tools and techniques which contributes to the efficiency of the guidance and the instructional programs, and it is a valuable aid in promoting sound pupil adjustment. In order that the value of the pupil inventory may be fully appreciated, this chapter examines its use as an aid to pupil adjustment, the types of records comprising the pupil inventory, and ways and means of utilizing the accumulated data. Proper use of these records and intelligent interpretation and application of the data are important for the effectiveness of the teacher and the counselor.

The Inventory as an Aid to Adjustment

The data accumulated are used to improve and further the child's personal and educational development, and their use contributes to more satisfactory pupil adjustment to school and to life. The inventory thus serves as a means to an end but never becomes an end itself. Accumulating and recording information are essential activities but only as they serve the purposes of the guidance program.

The search for ideas and procedures which will prove useful in promoting better adjustment is endless. Unfortunately the simple and more obvious possibilities are sometimes overlooked in this search, and the opportunities at hand are not utilized. Thus, three generalizations concerning this probing for new adjustment helps are useful: (1) resourcefulness, imagination, initiative, and ambition by the staff are needed to devise new methods and activities by which pupil development and progress can be enhanced; (2) available resources should be fully utilized for adding variety to a program and for realizing maximum benefits from current conditions and facilities; and (3) cooperative effort and a free exchange of ideas among staff members should be promoted and regarded as essential to the progress and success of the guidance effort.

Many activities within the school contribute directly to the development and adjustment of the pupils. The effectiveness of these activities in fulfilling their purposes is determined to a high degree by the quality of the pupil inventory. Activities and problems which might be carried through to satisfactory conclusions and solutions with an adequate system of records are often left unsolved because of insufficient available data. An appropriate organization for accumulating and recording pertinent information is essential to the instructional functions of a school and to the guidance program. The pupil inventory depends upon, and contributes to, all other phases of the educational program.

Reciprocal Relationship of the Pupil Inventory

The relationship of the pupil inventory to each of the other phases of the guidance service is reciprocal. Each basic element of the guidance program depends upon the availability of information made possible through records, and each element also supplements the pupil inventory and makes it more meaningful. Effective instruction too depends upon the adequacy, availability, and quality of recorded data. The teacher's efforts are more fruitful as essential information is gained and properly utilized in modifying educational offerings and in stimulating youngsters toward greater achievements.

As important data are synthesized, studied, and utilized in an objective, intelligent fashion, the guidance service is improved and the aid given students is made more practical. The significance of various items of information are determined as all data are viewed as a whole and relationships noted. Conclusions are reached, predictions made, and a course of action established only after the information is viewed as an integrated whole and after its meaning and value for the particular child to whom it applies are considered.

Importance of the Pupil Inventory

A sound system of adequate records is essential to any guidance service and to the educational program. It lends system and continuity to many of the educational functions, and it contributes markedly to the efficiency of the total school program.

Effective teaching depends upon the quality and adequacy of the recorded information. The personal as well as the educational welfare of each child is a concern of the teacher. Pertinent personal and educational data are thus helpful in planning programs, in providing for a pupil's individual needs, and in strengthening the teacher-pupil relationship.

The counseling activities are also enhanced and improved

through the proper use of the cumulative record. The counselor works with many youngsters who are experiencing a variety of concerns and problems. An occasional reference to the appropriate information serves as a reminder of information otherwise forgotten and improves the counseling relationship as the counselor's knowledge of the student increases. Better planning results and more logical decisions are reached as both the counselor and the client consider the evidence and data at hand with a calm, objective attitude.

Many other uses are made of records; their importance must be emphasized. Parent-teacher conferences in both elementary and secondary schools depend upon the availability of significant data about each student, for an awareness as to a child's progress and development is essential to both teacher and parents. An objective report is possible through the benefit of the cumulative record. The testing program has only limited value until test results are properly recorded and made available in usable form. Prospective employers seeking certain information about former students are served satisfactorily when requested information is accessible. Letters of recommendation often depend upon records for their authenticity. Requests from colleges for information about a student, including requests for transcripts, are readily met when suitable records are maintained. The pupil inventory is indeed an essential element in the educational program for aiding youngsters toward better adjustment and for providing the community with a record of his activities.

Use of Records in Case Studies

The case study is as much an expression of a philosophy or a belief as it is a technique for learning about and aiding students. If there is a prevailing belief among staff members that they have a responsibility for the adjustment of each child, their activities will reflect this concern. A good record system will provide an accumulation of data needed for aiding the child to adjust. Involvement in the collection of material makes staff members more aware of student limitations and helps them to identify developing problems. The degree of record utilization for any purpose related to better pupil adjustment is a reflection of the school's interest in the student. The case-study method, then, depends upon the adequacy and quality of the records maintained, and the functional utilization of all appropriate information depends upon the philosophy of the school.

Types of Records

Records may be classified into four major types: administrative, instructional, health, and guidance. Although some duplication of recorded information is inevitable, this is generally minimal and considerably less serious than the omission of pertinent information. The important point is that information needed for aiding the student in his schoolwork and in planning his future should be available in usable, meaningful form.

The Permanent Record Card

The permanent record card is the primary administrative record. It includes basic information about each youngster and is kept current in the administrative office of the school. Home and personal data such as the following are recorded: name, birth date, parents' names, address, telephone number, date of school entry, sex, date discontinued or graduated, and occupation of parent. Grades earned in various courses are also recorded here. This record is used in completing transcripts and in fulfilling requests for information about individual students.

The Cumulative Folder

The cumulative folder is the major guidance record and serves as the core of all data accumulated for purposes of providing individual guidance. This folder ordinarily provides four surfaces for the recording of information and also serves as a depository for profile sheets, health records, autobiographies, and samples of a pupil's work.

A school or district might want to develop its own cumulative folder if it is large enough to justify the expenditure. For a small district the selection of a good folder already available for use may be more economical and provide a better record than one developed locally. The use of a form adopted statewide has many advantages. All districts within the state may find it convenient and advantageous to use the same record form.

The Utah Permanent Student Record Form [1] is a good example of the cumulative record and is typical of many used throughout the country. This folder has sections for the following information:

[1] State Department of Public Instruction, Salt Lake City, Utah.

1   Personal data: name, address, and related information
2   Family data
3   Health data
4   Grades earned
5   Learning-aptitude tests
6   Achievement tests
7   Special school activities
8   Special interests, achievements, and talents
9   Significant out-of-school activities and achievements
10   Consecutive addresses and schools attended
11   Withdrawal record
12   Entry record
13   Educational places
14   Educational plans
15   Vocational plans
16   Follow-up record of marriage, education, employment, and transcripts

A folder of this type is initiated for each child upon his entrance into kindergarten or first grade, maintained throughout his school years, and terminated upon his graduation from high school.

Most cumulative records are of the folder type. However, a slightly different format includes the use of four cards of the same size as the typical folder.[2] Each card is a different color and provides space for specific kinds of information. Entries are made on the appropriate card in designated spaces instead of on the folder. The cards are kept in a plain manila folder. Once the forms to be used are selected and a plan for accessibility has been designed, records can be put to proper use.

Filing Plans

Several plans for the filing of the cumulative folders are available. A careful consideration of the most logical plans should result in an appropriate decision for each school. The form to be used and the system of filing to be followed are only incidental to the use of the data. The aim is an improved educational service to students. Records are only instruments by which this aim may be more fully realized. Also, basic to any discussion of the establishment and utilization of guidance records is the realization that this service is one of the major responsibilities of the school counselor. He provides the leadership essential to the success of the service, although the

[2] Form no. 801, Stephenson Supply Company, Lincoln, Nebr.

teacher also has responsibilities in the accumulation of data and in making use of the information gained.

Alphabetical arrangement by grades.   One procedure is to file the folders alphabetically by grades. The records may be located in a central office, under the supervision of the counselor. In elementary schools with no designated counselor, the folders can nevertheless be filed in a central location and kept readily accessible to the teacher. A designated teacher might then have the responsibility for the supervision of their maintenance and use. In junior and senior high schools, particularly where the student population is large, this alphabetical system facilitates the location of any particular folder.

Alphabetical arrangement by school.   The cumulative folders may be filed alphabetically within a school and arranged without regard for grade or classroom. This method is used satisfactorily in schools of all sizes at both the elementary and secondary levels. Care should be taken in keeping the records up-to-date and in making certain that they are readily accessible to the counselor and to the appropriate teachers.

A numerical system.   In a numerical system, each folder is numbered according to a predetermined plan and filed by this number. A guide sheet containing the number and name of each student is necessary; the student's name and number also appear on a tab on the folder. Deletions and additions are made on the guide sheet as children leave or enter the school.

The location of records.   The permanent record card is filed in the central administrative office and is maintained and used by the administration. Since the cumulative folder is a guidance record, it should be located in a central office under the supervision of the counselor, for example, perhaps in a room adjoining the counselor's office.

A system of check-out for records.   A system by which records are accounted for at all times is desirable. Folders should either be filed in their proper places or their location noted by some check-out method. A simple procedure is to make the proper notations on a card and place it in the space occupied by the folder at the time it is withdrawn. The card is removed when the folder is returned.

Filing of confidential information. Data of a confidential nature should be protected by the observance of appropriate filing procedures. A large manila envelope can be used as a depository for confidential information and then placed in the cumulative folder. It is marked "confidential" and is accessible only to authorized personnel. Another procedure is to maintain a separate file drawer for confidential data. Separate folders may be kept for each child, or information on several students may be placed in one folder.

Collecting Information

Collecting information important for pupil guidance is an essential function of the pupil inventory service. The effective and efficient use of information depends upon a systematic procedure for the collection of meaningful data. Criteria are also needed to determine what information should be recorded only temporarily and what should be retained permanently. Data relevant to the child's welfare and development should be retained; other data should be eliminated from the current files. (See Disposing of Irrelevant Material, below.)

There are various procedures and tools to be utilized in the collection of important information. A combination of several of these procedures is reviewed briefly and suggestions are given as to how they might be used.

Teacher observations and anecdotes. A teacher gains considerable knowledge about each student by virtue of his close association with him. Although helpful, this information is not recorded and is therefore limited in its usefulness. Behavior of an unusual nature may be noted and recorded by the teacher as an anecdote. This anecdote is written as a brief objective report in which the child's behavior is described. It becomes a part of the child's record and may be used in coming to a better understanding of all children and in improving their educational experiences.

Information from parents. Information may be gained from parents through interviews, questionnaires, or checklists. A combination of methods and tools is desirable. For example, parents might complete a questionnaire during an interview. This personal contact permits questions and responses and makes the written information more meaningful. Parent responses may also be solicited by sending the instrument by mail or by having it delivered by the child. A cover letter in which explanations are made about the purposes and uses of the information is advisable. Tact and diplomacy should always be used, particularly in soliciting information about which the parents may feel sensitive.

Pupil interviews. Pupils too contribute to the accumulation of data. A fact-finding interview with each student can provide most of the basic information necessary for establishing the cumulative folder. The benefits of the interview method outweigh the disadvantages, one of which is the occasional inaccuracy of the information obtained. Information from small children should be supplemented by that gained from parents. Older children and youth, however, are capable of providing such information. The personal interview provides the opportunity for becoming better acquainted with each child and contributes to his feelings of importance.

Questionnaires, checklists, and other forms. Questionnaires are of value in gaining information to be transferred to the cumulative records, if they have been carefully prepared. The form should require a minimum of writing for the pupil and should be clearly and easily understood. The form used should be patterned after the cumulative record, so that the information gained can be transferred easily and with no loss of information. The teacher, counselor, or clerical assistant assumes the responsibility for actual entries in the cumulative record, but much of the information can be provided by the students, thus expediting the task.

Autobiographies. The autobiography is unique in the manner and kinds of information it yields. It often affords an increased understanding of a student as no other device can, for it is the product of a person's thinking and a report on the significant events of his life. The autobiography is filed in its original form in the cumulative folder. Some structuring by the teacher or counselor as to kinds of events and information to be included in the autobiography is advisable.

Disposing of irrelevant material. Much data gathered during the school years have temporary value only and should be discarded when they lose their usefulness. A periodic examination of all cumulative folders should be made and materials without current or future value removed. These records should be usable, accurate, objective, and meaningful; they should contribute to the personal and educational welfare of each child.

Recording Information

Data should be recorded promptly (in the proper space on the folder) as they become available. Efficiency in the recording and use of records is best attained by designating the persons responsible for the task and by providing for the necessary clerical assistance. The following are guidelines for recording data and the use of the cumulative records:

Planning cooperatively with all members of the staff. A cooperative plan which utilizes the capabilities of teachers and counselors is recommended. Although major responsibilities are assumed by the counselor, others may contribute to the pupil inventory system. Standard procedures for recording data should be agreed upon and observed. Uniformity is essential for ease, accuracy, and speed in both recording and interpreting data.

Following established criteria in selecting information. Criteria to be used in determining which information is to be recorded are usability, recency, objectivity, accuracy, and relevance. Personal judgments are useful if they are combined with established criteria.

Keeping records readily accessible. Accessibility is the key to the utilization of the student inventory. The cumulative folders should be properly filed and conveniently located for easy availability to teachers, counselors, and principals. Clerical and routine functions in using records should be kept to a minimum to permit professional personnel to devote their time and energies to the important tasks for which they were trained.

Following a standard pattern for recording information. Some standardization in the recording of information should be followed. The format of the folder usually provides a guide as to the nature and form of data to be recorded. Test data, for example, should be recorded in the same way by everyone. This can be done by observing the standards and forms agreed upon within the school. A handbook of instructions is provided with some cumulative folders. Such a guide might be provided for use within a school district or within a state. The recording of information according to individual interpretation by teachers and counselors should be discouraged. This practice is uneconomical and limits the efficiency with which recorded data can be used.

Assigning responsibilities for record keeping. The person responsible for maintaining records should be designated. The responsibility may be assigned to one person who directs others in this activity. The director of pupil personnel or the head counselor will in most cases be the logical person to assume this responsibility.

Providing for clerical assistance. The recording of data on forms is primarily a clerical function. Competent help should be made available. Mature students might be employed for recording information of a nonconfidential nature. A secretary may serve the entire school in this function, making the cost relatively low. Efficiency, accuracy, and standardization may be enhanced by this method and professional personnel protected against encroachments upon their time and energies.

Interpretation and Use of Data

Recording pertinent information is only the beginning. Intelligent interpretation and use of all recorded data must be made if the pupil inventory is to fulfill its role as an aid to pupils. Care in the selection of cumulative data to be retained and in the recording of information facilitates and makes more meaningful the interpretations given to data. The usability of material is improved and the application possibilities increased as the quality of the pupil inventory is improved. The effectiveness of the aid given pupils also depends upon the character of the interpretations made of data at hand.

In this section guides are suggested for facilitating data interpretation and for making the records more effective. Principles of record keeping are also enumerated.

An Increasing Interest in Pupil Appraisal

Time was when pupil appraisal and the recording of pertinent information was regarded by the public as prerogatives of the school. Parents did, and still do, expect some kind of reporting by which the status and progress of a child could be ascertained. But the public's interest has been limited largely to a periodic reporting of achievement. Educational innovations and technical advances have, however, contributed to a need for more accurate and meaningful reporting of a child's progress in all areas of development. Parents have become increasingly aware of significant educational develop-ments and have become better informed and more concerned about the educational welfare of their children. Motives underlying ap-praisal and the subsequent recording of information have also been subject to question by the public.[3]

Teachers and counselors are also more aware of the need for careful pupil appraisal as a concomitant of new educational needs and procedures, and they are interested in the tools and techniques for obtaining useful information. Technical advances in recording and duplicating information have made it possible to accumulate more data than was once possible. The minimization of the teacher's role as a clerical worker has increased the need for help and ma-chines by which information can be recorded speedily and accu-rately. Dictating devices, IBM equipment, and more imaginative use of standard machines and equipment have made it possible to obtain more information and to make more intelligent use of all data.[4]

Objective pupil appraisal is most essential in the modern edu-cational system. Effective guidance depends upon the availability of pertinent information upon which future plans may be based and from which logical decisions may be reached.

Guides for Data Interpretation

A variety of procedures for effective interpretation of data will occur to the alert teacher and counselor, and choices will be made in accordance with local conditions. The following suggestions to the counseling and teaching staffs may be modified, or they may serve as a stimulus for the development of other ideas:

1 Meet together and review recorded information. These meetings might be conducted by the head counselor, but ideas and help should be invited from all participants.

2 Arrive at a consensus as to the meaning of various kinds of in-formation and how they are to be utilized. Decisions and agree-ments arrived at by the staff should be used as guides and hon-ored by all teachers.

[3] See W. Wesley Tennyson, "Student Personnel Records: A Vital Tool but a Concern of the Public," *Personnel and Guidance Journal*, vol. 42, pp. 888–893, May, 1964.

[4] Robert Owens and Randy Frank, "How to Stop Wasting Counselor's Time: Direct Dictating Line to Student Records," *School Management*, vol. 8, p. 62, August, 1964; this article reports on a system by which counselors can dictate via telephone to a central secretary.

3 Review the manual of instructions periodically, and utilize other available literature which may contain guides and aids. If a manual has not been provided or does not include information on data interpretation, the counselor or a committee may prepare a bulletin of information and suggestions for use.

4 Utilize profile, or psychograph, sheets in recording and interpreting test data. The counselor should make certain that the tools and techniques used are appropriate for the student being helped and that he understands the interpretations made. The use of profile sheets saves time and simplifies the information for the student.

5 Note the significance of data as they relate to each other. Information used in isolation has only limited value.

6 In interpreting data, point out comparative scores by the use of profile sheets on which percentiles, quartiles, or quintiles have been plotted. The counselor should make certain that the terms used are understood by each student and that he is able to see the personal significance of the information. He should know his relative position with other students on a particular test and should also know how to capitalize on this information for personal development.

7 Study test scores in conjunction with other information gained on students. Any source of data, including tests, provides only a certain amount of information. Accumulated data should be viewed as a whole and their significance for a particular student noted.

Accumulated data are useful only insofar as they are properly interpreted and as the information is intelligently utilized. Recorded data in themselves mean nothing. The application of pupil appraisal in making program adjustments and improvements is the critical test of the value of the information accumulated. The data must be pulled together into a meaningful pattern from which the teacher and the counselor may be better informed as to how best to proceed in order to be of the most help. It is important to distinguish between behavior that has significance and behavior that is irrelevant in both reporting information and in working with a child.[5] The avoidance of labels which have no meaning or which may be misleading is essential.[6] Objectivity in all reporting should be the goal of each teacher and guidance worker.[7]

[5] Raymond T. Steve, "Cumulative Record," *National Educational Association Journal*, vol. 51, p. 48, May, 1962.

[6] *Ibid.*

[7] See Bruce Shertzer and Patricia S. Fessler, "Teachers' Comments about Pupils," *Elementary School Journal*, vol. 62, pp. 371–374, April, 1962.

Principal Uses of the Pupil Inventory

The pupil inventory has many uses within the educational setting. The benefits gained from an efficient system of student appraisal more than justify the expenditures required. A summary of these major uses is presented here:

1 Effective instruction depends to a degree upon the adequacy and availability of significant information about each student.
2 Recorded data and known information about students are utilized in the counseling function. Counselors depend upon such information, and teachers utilize it in their personal as well as their instructional relationships with students.
3 Diagnosis and case studies are possible only as appropriate information is available. Complete, current records simplify and add quality to diagnostic and case-study procedures.
4 Recorded data are helpful in assisting pupils in proper curriculum and course selection. Modification or adjustments in the school program may be made in view of what is known about each child, particularly in respect to his past achievements.
5 Records are useful in planning vocational exploratory activities. Test scores, autobiographies, classroom achievement, plans, interests, and other accumulated information all provide helpful clues for planning with young people for possible future vocational pursuits.
6 Efficient administration depends upon a well-organized and systematic record-keeping system. Records maintained primarily for guidance purposes may be used to supplement those records maintained principally for administrative purposes.
7 Parent conferences can be made more meaningful and profitable as records are used for reviewing pupil progress and adjustment. Parents thus also come to a better understanding of the school's aims and objectives, and they become more familiar with the school's program and activities.
8 Making referrals is a common and necessary practice and one which depends upon the adequacy and availability of objective data. These referrals are made by teachers and administrators to counselors or other teachers and by counselors to teachers or to other personnel either within the school or in the community.
9 Errors of judgment in grouping children for instructional purposes are much less common when significant objective data are available for use in making these judgments.

Increasing parental interests in the accumulated data on youngsters has prompted the school to take a more critical look at its record system, and it has provided some stimulation for the improvement of records. As long as records were unavailable to parents, there was less concern about what information was gathered and how it was recorded. It was just a matter of the school's being satisfied with its particular system. But as parents have shown greater concern for the educational progress of their children, they have also demonstrated greater curiosity about the kinds of records maintained and the meaning these data have. Certain precautions must certainly be taken to protect a child against unwarranted and unauthorized perusal of his records. However, achieving a better utilization of recorded data often entails a more active involvement of parents in the guidance service as accumulated information is properly reviewed and interpreted for them. Some accessibility of records to parents, either through a sense of responsibility by the school or through legal mandate, should result in a more useful set of records from which everyone may profit. The position maintained by a substantial number of schools that all records were confidential and therefore not accessible to anyone outside the school may no longer be defensible.[8]

The Disposition of Records

The proper disposition of the cumulative record should be made when a student moves to another school, terminates his schooling, or graduates. The major consideration in record disposition is the benefit to be derived by the student. A guidance record should accompany the student throughout his school life and should therefore be available to his teachers and counselors in the school he attends. This principle suggests the importance of having a system by which the transfer of records to a student's current school can be quickly expedited.

When a child changes schools. When a child moves to another school, his cumulative record should follow him, since it can no longer serve a useful purpose in his old school but will benefit him in the new one. The permanent record card used for administrative purposes should be retained and a duplicate made and forwarded to the receiving school. Clerical time in effecting the transfer should

[8] Virginia Bailard, "Should Parents See the Cumulative Record? Or Some Answers to Questions Parents Ask Us," *Journal of Secondary Education,* vol. 36, pp. 291–296, May, 1961. This article explains how the Long Beach Unified School District improved its record system after legislation made it possible for parents to see a student's cumulative record.

be kept to a minimum. For example, if the receiving school mails a prepared post card to the former school requesting the child's records, the transfer is made as a routine task, with very little expenditure of time. Another system utilizes a central clearing office, which completes the transfer upon receiving the request from the new school.

When a child finishes elementary school. When the pupil completes elementary school, the cumulative folder is sent to the receiving junior high school. The elementary school needs no record other than the permanent records maintained by the administration. This permanent record card may be duplicated and a copy sent with the cumulative folder. The same procedure may be followed upon the completion of the junior high. The high school to be attended then becomes the receiving school.

When a student terminates or graduates. Although the usefulness of the cumulative record for immediate guidance purposes ends with the termination of formal education, follow-up services and research activities still depend upon accumulated data, thus making it advisable to retain the record for a few years. The availability of filing space is a major consideration in determining how long to keep it. It should be removed from the files of currently enrolled students and kept for about five to seven years, after which it can be destroyed.

Microfilming for storage purposes. Essential pupil records may be microfilmed and stored for an indefinite time in a very small space. This system permits a school to maintain permanent administrative records on all former students at low cost. Time is saved in supplying requests for information about a former student, since the record is immediately accessible and accurate.[9]

Principles of Record Keeping

An observance of, and a reliance upon, certain guiding principles in maintaining records should be helpful to school people and result in a stronger pupil inventory system. Many of these principles have been implied in the discussion thus far. Some major principles

[9] For an interesting account of how this system works, see Paul Abramson, (ed.), "How to Store Permanent Pupil Records and Save Space," *School Management,* vol. 7, pp. 56–58, August, 1963.

may be summarized briefly as follows: (1) the pupil is the focus of concern and the reason for the inventory system; (2) a system is essential for appropriately recording, filing, and utilizing all data; (3) the uses of the inventory system should be broadened to include appropriate staff members and to be of the greatest possible service to students; (4) objectivity, uniformity, and neatness are essential in maintaining records and should be encouraged; (5) uniformity in recording data simplifies their use and eliminates frustration; (6) the relationship between accumulated data and other information gained on a student should be noted and all data intelligently utilized and applied.

Other Tools and Procedures for Learning about Students

The record system has been reviewed as the means by which meaningful data are recorded and utilized, and it is regarded as the core of the pupil inventory. Results of standardized tests constitute a source of objective data which are properly recorded, filed, and made available for pupil guidance. A review of some additional guidance service tools, as well as some suggested procedures for their use, follows.

Instruments for Learning about Pupils

Any instrument or tool of the school used to gain information about a child should be carefully selected and its potential value ascertained before it is used. The device used should provide helpful information which is not otherwise accessible. If the information accumulated will not be of use in improving the environment or aiding the student or if the school fails to follow up with appropriate action, then the device for gaining the information has served no useful purpose.

A number of devices for obtaining information are available; some of the better-known devices, presumably of greater value, are described in the paragraphs that follow.

Sociometric devices. Sociometric devices are used in determining the social groupings within a class. Children are asked to indicate their preferences from among their classmates for partners in a particular activity. The sociogram drawn from these choices shows the pattern of selection and permits the teacher and counselor to identify the less popular and more popular children. This device has definite limitations and should be used with care. The sociogram identifies the isolates and the least popular children, but it provides no information as to why this is true or how the situation may be improved. Answers to these problems must be gained elsewhere.

Careful planning is essential in employing the sociometric device. Instructions must be given to students prior to their making choices. They must be told for what particular purpose they are selecting another person and how their choices are to be reported on the form. For example, the preliminary instructions may point out to the students that the class will permit the students to work in groups of three in which ideas and efforts can be shared. Students are then instructed to write the names of two students each would like most to work with him in this project. Specificity in instructions results in more logical choices by the students. Obviously, not all students will get their choices, since several of them will likely choose the same ones. In anticipation of this situation, instructions could include third and fourth choices. This procedure also increases the possibilities that all students will be chosen by someone.

A completed sociogram shows the location of each student by the use of a symbol or the student's initials. Since the sociogram is for teacher use, nothing is to be gained by making it accessible to the student.

The social-distance scale. The social-distance scale is similar to the sociogram but provides a little more structure in the form used and requires specific responses. Such items as the following are included, and each student responds by writing the appropriate name after each statement:

1 If you were going on a picnic and had your choice of a member of this class to accompany you, who would it be?
2 Name your very best friend.
3 Name a person who makes you feel very good.

The teacher and counselor learn from this scale something about how a youngster feels about other children, and they also get some idea of the degree of popularity each child enjoys with other children.

The "guess who" method. The "guess who" method is another helpful device for improving teacher understanding of pupils. Each child is asked to name someone else in the room who best fits the description given by a class member. This may be done by asking for oral responses or by having class members write their choices on a sheet of paper. This activity calls to the attention of other pupils desirable and commendable behavior worthy of emulation by classmates. It also calls to the attention of the teacher behavior favorably regarded by the pupils. This kind of conduct can then be encouraged by the teacher.

The sentence-completion device. In the sentence-completion activity, an incomplete sentence is submitted to the pupils in written form to be completed. For example, the following sentences might be used:

1 The thing I like best about school is _____.
2 Some time in my life I hope to _____.
3 I like people who _____.
4 My strongest talents are in _____.

Competence in the use of projective techniques is essential if this method is used for diagnostic or clinical purposes. However, clinical diagnosis is not the intent in the classroom setting, but rather the insights that may be gained into the thinking and conduct of the youngsters, relevant to planning educational activities and in providing services to improve the personal welfare of each child.

The interaction-technique device. The interaction-technique device involves having students rate each other on elements of behavior which either bolster or threaten self-esteem. This procedure assumes that a student's actions within a class or small-group setting either contribute to the feelings of self-esteem of other group members or threaten the self-esteem of others. This device may be used at all school levels, since the elements of behavior to appear in the instrument are initiated by the students. The principal procedures to be used include the following:

1   Have the student make a list of actions of other students which contributes to his self-esteem (actions that make him "feel good" when others treat him this way).
2   Make a second list of actions by others which threaten the student's self-esteem and contribute to discomfort. These two lists make up what are known as "interaction techniques."
3   Refine these two lists by eliminating duplications and improving the wording. The refined list is a compilation of the interaction techniques to be used in the instrument.
4   Have each student respond to the various items on the interaction-technique inventory by indicating to what degree each item bolsters or threatens his self-esteem.

5 A computation of student responses is then made by which a relative rating of each it' m on the instrument is made. Thus an identification is made of actions which contribute positively to the self-esteem of oth'.r people and of those which constitute a threat to the self-esteem of others.

A five-point rating scale may be used with this instrument. The directions might include the following:

1 Circle the 2 if this action by another class or group member contributes positively to your self-esteem (makes you feel very good).
2 Circle the 1 if this action contributes to your self-esteem to a small degree.
3 Circle the 0 if this action has no effect upon your self-esteem.
4 Circle the −1 if this action lowers your self-esteem, threatens you, or makes you feel less important.
5 Circle the −2 if this action presents a strong threat to you and has a definite influence in lowering your self-esteem.

As mean rates are computed for each item in the instrument, it is possible to determine what kinds of behavior appear to bolster the self-esteem of individuals and what kinds of behavior threaten self-esteem. Practical applications of this information are possible in structuring school activities.

Procedures for Learning about Pupils

There are several procedures carried out as activities by which an understanding of pupils may be increased without use of a specific tool or instrument. For example, whereas the sentence-completion device requires the use of a prepared form, observing pupils at work needs no such form. Such procedures are presented here as suggestions on how to improve the pupil-school relationship.

Observations. Observing the activities and behavior of pupils under a variety of circumstances is often a rewarding experience for the teacher and the counselor. These observations may be made informally and casually in order to avoid creating an unnatural situation in which children become unduly inhibited or overly stimulated. The observation of a youngster suggests the presence of a real interest in him and a concern for his welfare.

Correspondence. Information and ideas may be exchanged and recommendations made through occasional correspondence with parents, specialists, or other individuals. Any contact which holds the promise of an increased understanding of children and their problems should justify the investment of time.

Home visits. A home visit by the appropriate staff member often proves to be helpful to both the school and the home. Because there are limitations of time for this activity, care should be taken in the selection of homes to be visited. There should be some reasons for these visits, and benefits should be anticipated. The utmost tact and diplomacy should be practiced and the feelings of family members protected.

Pupil interview. The concern shown for the child through periodic personal interviews by the teacher or the counselor—or both— bolsters his self-confidence and improves morale. Troublesome areas or problems may be identified by this means and appropriate action taken to assist the student.

Contact with community members. Personal contacts with community members are often helpful in gaining needed information about youngsters and in assessing community attitudes toward them and toward the school. These individuals may be well informed on family conditions and neighborhood influences. Such shared knowledge can then be utilized by the school.

SUMMARY/

The cumulative folder is the central guidance record for each pupil. Pertinent data are gained throughout each youngster's school life and made available through the cumulative record to teachers and counselors. The furtherance of personal and educational adjustment and development is the major objective of the pupil inventory. It has a reciprocal relationship with all other elements in the guidance program and constitutes an area of service upon which all phases of the educational program depend.

Several kinds of records are included in the pupil inventory and make up the final cumulative record. The cumulative folder serves as the depository for accumulated data, and certain information is recorded upon the folder itself. Various procedures for collecting, recording, and filing data are used. Establishing guidelines for these procedures improves their efficiency and ensures standardization in recording and filing data.

Proper interpretation and intelligent use of data are vital aspects of the pupil inventory. By following guiding principles in the use of information the possibilities of misinterpretations and abuses are minimized.

There are other effective tools and procedures for learning about pupils which have a direct relationship to the pupil inventory. The tools involve the use of prepared instruments, while other procedures are conducted as activities with no need for a specific tool or form.

PROBLEMS/

1 Enumerate the principal functions of a record system. What are these records supposed to do?

2 Why is an adequate record system essential? What are the benefits to be derived from a record system?

3 The permanent record card and the cumulative record folder constitute the principal guidance records. Point out how each is to be used and why each is necessary.

4 Note the principal classifications of information to be included in a cumulative folder.

5 There are several filing plans for use with records. Select any one plan, or combination of plans, and defend its use by noting the advantages.

6 How should confidential information be filed? Where? Accessible to whom?

7 Enumerate the methods to be used in collecting information needed for cumulative records.

8 Make a list of principles, or guidelines, to observe in the recording of information.

9 Some person or group should be responsible for the record system. In your judgment, who should this be? Defend your selection.

10 Make some recommendations with respect to the clerical functions which are essential to maintaining records.

11 Point out how records can be useful in each of the following:

    a Teaching

    b Counseling

    c Diagnosis and case studies
    d Curriculum, or course
        selection
    e Vocational exploratory
        experiences
    f Administration
    g Parent conferences
    h Making referrals
    i Pupil grouping

12   What should the disposition of records be when (*a*) child moves to another school? (*b*) drops school? (*c*) graduates?

13   Make a list of guiding principles to observe in the overall program of keeping guidance records.

14   Note the main uses to be made of sociometric techniques. What precautions should be taken?

15   What are some other appropriate techniques for learning about students? Note their strengths and limitations.

Selected References

Textbooks

ARBUCKLE, DUGALD S.: *Pupil Personnel Services in American Schools,* pp. 252–262, Allyn and Bacon, Inc., Boston, 1962, chap. 7.

BARR, JOHN A.: *The Elementary Teacher and Guidance,* Holt, Rinehart and Winston, Inc., New York, 1957, chaps. 8–10.

BERNARD, HAROLD W., C. EVAN JAMES, and FRANKLIN R. ZERAN: *Guidance Services in Elementary Schools,* Chartwell House, New York, 1954, chap. 9.

COTTINGHAM, HAROLD F.: *Guidance in Elementary Schools,* McKnight & McKnight Publishing Company, Bloomington, Ill., 1956, chap. 2.

FARWELL, GAIL F., and HERMAN J. PETERS: *Guidance Readings for Counselors,* Rand McNally & Company, Chicago, 1960, chap. 5, pp. 247–254.

FROEHLICH, CLIFFORD P.: *Guidance Services in Schools,* 2d ed., McGraw-Hill Book Company, New York, 1958, chap. 9.

GLANZ, EDWARD C.: *Foundations and Principles of Guidance,* Allyn and Bacon, Inc., Boston, 1964, chap. 8, pp. 176–178.

HUMPHREYS, J. ANTHONY, ARTHUR E. TRAXLER, and ROBERT D. NORTH: *Guidance Services,* Science Research Associates, Inc., Chicago, 1960, chap. 7, pp. 150–158.

HUTSON, PERCIVAL W.: *The Guidance Function in Education,* Appleton-Century-Crofts, Inc., New York, 1958, chap. 11.

JONES, ARTHUR J.: *Principles of Guidance and Pupil Personnel Work,* McGraw-Hill Book Company, New York, 1951, chap. 6.

JOHNSTON, EDGAR G., MILDRED PETERS, and WILLIAM EVRAIFF: *The Role of the Teacher in Guidance,* Prentice-Hall, Inc., Englewood Cliffs, N.J., 1959, chap. 6.

KOWITZ, GERALD T., and NORMA G. KOWITZ: *Guidance in the Elementary Classroom*, McGraw-Hill Book Company, New York, 1959, chap. 6.

MARTINSON, RUTH A., and HARRY SMALLENBURG: *Guidance in Elementary Schools*, Prentice-Hall, Inc., Englewood Cliffs, N.J., 1958, chap. 7.

MC DANIEL, HENRY B.: *Guidance in the Modern School*, The Dryden Press, Inc., New York, 1956, chap. 8, pp. 186–197.

——— and others: *Readings in Guidance*, Holt, Rinehart and Winston, Inc., New York, 1959, chap. 17, pp. 112–116.

MORTENSEN, DONALD G., and ALLEN M. SCHMULLER: *Guidance in Today's Schools*, John Wiley & Sons, Inc., New York, 1959, chap. 7, pp. 211–224.

MILLER, FRANK W.: *Guidance Principles and Services*, Charles E. Merrill Books, Inc., Englewood Cliffs, N.J., 1961, chap 5, pp. 111–135.

OHLSEN, MERLE M.: *Guidance*, Harcourt, Brace & World, Inc., New York, 1955, chap. 10, pp. 191–196.

PETERS, HERMAN J., and GAIL F. FARWELL: *Guidance: A Developmental Approach*, Rand McNally & Company, Chicago, 1959, chap. 5, pp. 133–165.

SHERTZER, BRUCE, and HERMAN J. PETERS: *Guidance: Techniques for Individual Appraisal and Development*, The Macmillan Company, New York, 1965, chap. 16.

SMITH, GLENN E.: *Principles and Practices of the Guidance Program*, The Macmillan Company, New York, 1951, chap. 5.

TRAXLER, ARTHUR E., and ROBERT D. NORTH: *Techniques of Guidance*, 3d ed., Harper & Row, Publishers, Incorporated, New York, 1966, chap. 13.

WARTERS, JANE: *High School Personnel Work Today*, 2d ed., McGraw-Hill Book Company, New York, 1956, chap. 7, pp. 146–155.

WILLEY, ROY DE VERL: *Guidance in Elementary Education*, Harper & Row, Publishers, Incorporated, New York, 1960, chap. 3.

——— and DEAN C. ANDREW: *Modern Methods and Techniques in Guidance*, Harper & Row, Publishers, Incorporated, New York, 1955, chap. 21, pp. 584–589.

Journals

ABRAMSON, PAUL (ed.): "Easy Way to Maintain Student Records," *School Management*, vol. 5, pp. 42–43, July, 1961.

ALEXANDER, D. B.: "Parental Misunderstandings," *Education*, vol. 84, pp. 153–155, November, 1963.

ANDERSON, G. E.: "How to File Teacher Comments," *Nations School*, vol. 73, pp. 70–71, June, 1964.

ANGERS, WILLIAM P.: "Dangers of Evaluative Laboring," *Education Digest*, vol. 24, pp. 44–46, January, 1959.

ANGLIN, E. M., and M. L. CARROLL: "They Really Want to Know," *Journal of Teacher Education*, vol. 15, pp. 303–309, September, 1964.

BONNEY, WARREN C., and LOYCE MCGEHEARTY: "Non-test Pupil Data," *Vocational Guidance Quarterly*, vol. 11, pp. 68–72, Autumn, 1962.

BREWSTER, ROYCE E.: "Accumulative Record; Foundation of Guidance Program: A Depository of Objective Information," *School Life*, vol. 42, pp. 16–17, September, 1959.

BRUCE, WILLIAM C. (ed.): "Should Student Records Be Made Available to Parents?" *American School Board Journal*, vol. 143, pp. 14–15, December, 1961.

BURIANCK, E. T., and R. O. FITZSIMMONS: "Confidentiality of Student Records," *National Education Association Journal*, vol. 55, pp. 28–30, January, 1966.

CRIPE, HAROLD W.: "Guiding Principles for a Good School Record System," *Clearing House*, vol. 31, p. 41, September, 1956.

ELLIS, GORDON: "A New Approach to Student Records," *Personnel and Guidance Journal*, vol. 41, pp. 724–726, April, 1963.

FREDENBURG, F. A.: "Interpreting the IQ to Parents," *New York State Education*, vol. 48, pp. 11–13, March, 1961.

GANS, R.: "How Are They Really Doing?" *Grade Teacher*, vol. 83, p. 59, October, 1965.

JAFFA, N. N.: "Disadvantaged Child: Charting the Mobile Child," *Instructor*, vol. 74, p. 37, October, 1964.

MITZEL, M. A.: "Who Keeps Cumulative Records?" *Elementary School Journal*, vol. 66. pp. 195–196, January, 1966.

OHLES, JOHN F., MARGARET SAWKINS, and J. BRIEN MURPHY: "Cumulative Records: A Case Study of a Committee in Operation," *Clearing House*, vol. 36, pp. 531–535, May, 1962.

PAGE, JAMES L.: "Films, Filmstrips, Recordings," *Grade Teacher*, vol. 79, pp. 10–11, June, 1962.

PAUL, H. A.: "Counseling and Student Use of High School Records," *Catholic Education Review*, vol. 59, pp. 376–381, September, 1961.

PUTNAM, J. F.: "Toward Improved Information about Pupils," *School Life*, vol. 44, pp. 23–25, January, 1962.

SAMLER, J.: "School and Self-understanding; Maintaining Self-records," *Harvard Education Review*, vol. 35, pp. 65–67, Winter, 1965.

TAYLOR, DOROTHEA: "How to Obtain Autobiographies," *Personnel and Guidance Journal*, vol. 36, pp. 426–427, February, 1958.

SIX

/PUPIL APPRAISAL THROUGH TESTING

An evaluation of pupil potentiality and progress is made through the utilization of standardized tests. Tests and inventories are tools of appraisal by which plans and decisions may be made more realistically and intelligently. Test results provide valuable information which is utilized in course selection and in vocational planning. A pupil's understanding of himself and of his personal development improves as he gains information about his aptitudes, interests, and personality.

Tests are important tools for the teacher and the counselor in the guidance of young people. Care should therefore be taken in the selection of tests, and the data obtained should be properly interpreted and intelligently utilized in both instructional and guidance activities. Tests are among the most objective and dependable sources of information on pupils. This information is very useful in planning for and providing educational activities for pupils, as it is used in conjunction with other kinds of information. The realization of the school's objectives may be facilitated and brought to fruition as all accumulated data are carefully studied and intelligently applied.

The discussion of the testing service in the present chapter begins by noting that tests and inventories of various kinds are the tools, or instruments, by which certain information may be obtained about pupils. Tests serve certain purposes, but they also have definite limitations of which the users should be aware. Certain precautions are in order. The observation of guiding principles should result in better data utilization. The major activities of the testing service are outlined, and the professional responsibilities of the staff are noted. The six principal areas of tests are given with some typical test titles in each classification. A standard program of testing is outlined with some suggestions on how to interpret test results to pupils.

Tools for Better Pupil Understanding

A noteworthy aim of the guidance service is a better understanding of each pupil in the school. Knowledge about his aptitudes, interests, achievements, and personality characteristics contribute to this understanding. An adequate system of pupil appraisal is essential in gaining needed information.

Incidental appraisal and observations by the teacher and the counselor can be used to supplement objective data. A better understanding of each pupil is thus gained as a variety of information is properly utilized.

Specific Purposes and Aims of Testing

The testing service has specific purposes and aims enumerated in the following discussion, which is concerned only with standardized tests.

To determine pupil achievement level and progress. The approximate achievement capabilities of each pupil in the various subject-matter areas are ascertained with appropriate tests. The degree of progress attained over a period of time is determined. As relatively weak or strong areas are identified, action may be taken to bolster or otherwise aid and accommodate each student. Estimates can be made as to possible attainments to be expected, and enrichment experiences may be provided from which more effective learning may occur.

To gain data for diagnostic purposes. Good teaching involves constant vigilance in noting symptoms of developing difficulties. Early identification of problems and remediation are essential to the satisfactory progress of a pupil. Data gained from testing are utilized for the informal type of diagnosis that is an ongoing occurrence in the school as well as for the formal diagnosis conducted by counselors and clinicians.

To ascertain aptitudes. Appropriate tests provide data on the approximate potentialities of youngsters in various aptitudes. Scholastic aptitude is of great concern to the school, since achievement expectations and predictions are based to a degree upon the measured learning capacity of a child. Environmental factors also contribute to academic excellence and are used along with measured scholastic aptitude to predict success and to provide appropriate educational experiences in order to facilitate high performance levels.

To provide for the identification of interests. Preference tests provide opportunities for the selection of activities which have appeal for the student. Patterns of interests emerge from these tests, improving student self-understanding and helping students to plan for future vocational pursuits. Most of these tests are designed for use at the secondary and college levels, when students are sufficiently mature to profit from their use and when decision making is more critical. Interests of elementary-age youngsters can be assessed through personal observations and by less formal procedures. Exploration is the main activity at this level.

To improve instruction. The constant improvement of instruction is a major aim of education. The strengthening of the teaching-learning relationship serves as a goal toward which considerable effort is directed by all teachers, counselors, and administrators. As testing instruments are refined and as counselors and teachers become better informed on utilization of test data, progress toward superior teaching is realized, and personal relationships between teachers and pupils are bettered.

To determine existing self-concepts and attitudes. A device for determining the exact quality and condition of one's self-concept may not exist. However, how each youngster feels about himself can be determined and an assessment of his approximate level of self-confidence made through observations and specific testing instruments. The knowledge obtained is then helpful in counseling with him, enriching his educational environment, and aiding him toward greater achievements and better personal adjustments.

To ascertain social adjustments. Approximate levels of social adjustment are ascertained through appropriate instruments used in conjunction with observations. Since social development is comparable in importance to other aspects of development, some knowledge of the current status of each child and possible problems each may be experiencing is essential. The accurate and objective assessment of social adjustment is not readily attained with present tools of measurement, but improvements are being realized.

To identify underachievers and overachievers. To ascertain achievement of all pupils is one of the purposes of testing. An important part of the procedure for this is that of identifying pupils who achieve above or below the level of expectation. A scattergram or simple chart may be used for comparing aptitude with achievement. Once test data are available, the scattergram is easily made, and each pupil's relative position is immediately ascertained. Normally, the correlation between academic aptitude and achievement is positive and moderately high. However, factors other than aptitude influence achievement, resulting in an occasional deviation from the usual pattern. A youngster may score high on a scholastic aptitude test but be relatively low in his achievement, or a child may achieve at a relatively high level although his scholastic aptitude score is comparatively low. The scattergram helps to identify and locate these youngsters but provides no explanations as to why this is the case. Once a pupil's academic competence and academic performance are known appropriate action may be initiated by which the most critical needs may be met. Enrichment experiences and exploratory activities may be provided and efforts made to discover and enhance creative capabilities.

Limitations of Testing

Certain limitations are present in virtually all guidance tools. Some limitations are inherent in the instrument, some in its use, or both. Although tests have many of these limitations, the elimination of all testing is hardly justified, but caution and logic are needed in the use of any instrument.

Extreme views are sometimes expressed about test usage. One view holds that tests have no value in the guidance service; the other view maintains that test results are of the greatest importance. A more logical and tenable view is that test data are helpful when used properly with other kinds of information. No one test or combination of tests is infallible or likely to provide more than a fraction of information required for the effective guidance of a student.

Another limitation of testing lies with the student himself. Abilities, attitudes, and interests vary considerably among children. Test performances may reflect only to a limited degree the true quality of the characteristics or traits being assessed. The following are some of the critical limiting factors in test usage:

Low motivation of some pupils. The assumption that all pupils are equally interested in a task or enjoy the same stimulation is erroneous. Relatively low motivation on the part of some pupils during the testing experience is probably inevitable. However, a pupil can be motivated to give the task his best efforts through preliminary activities and the careful structuring of the testing activities. Test scores must represent a pupil's best efforts if they are to be true indications of ability. Indifference, inattention, low commitment, and generally low motivation tend to invalidate test results.

Relative narrowness of the traits measured. A test is designed to measure a certain trait or quality or combination of traits. With even the best of tests the traits being measured constitute a relatively narrow aspect of one's total makeup. Many other factors of perhaps equal significance are not assessed. Other tools and devices must therefore be used if these traits are to be identified and assessed. This statement is made as a precaution, not as a criticism of testing instruments.

Low validity and reliability for some pupils. Scores obtained may be relatively invalid or unreliable for a particular pupil. However, this is not likely to be evident, since computations for validity and reliability are based on large numbers of subjects. Thus, a pupil obtaining scores inappropriate in terms of his true abilities is likely to go unnoticed.

The unavailability of local norms. Local norms are not always computed or made available. Reliance upon the norms in the publisher's test manual for test interpretation is then necessary, although local norms may have greater value for guidance purposes within a particular school. Proper use of both local norms and norms published in the test manual should be made.

Heavy weighting of verbal ability on many tests. High verbal ability is a distinct advantage on many of the current standardized tests. Other characteristics of comparable merit are not assessed to the same degree, nor is the advantage of the student with these other qualities as distinct as the one with high verbal ability. The student with relatively low verbal aptitude is thus penalized on a test in which vocabulary and verbal expression carry a heavy weighting. Conversely, an overestimation of a student's total ability may occur if his verbal aptitude is favorable and he receives a high score on a test. The results may not represent a true picture of his total ability.

Undue influence of environmental conditions upon test results. A test score may reflect more accurately the nature of one's environment than the quality of the traits being measured. The nature of the environment sometimes has a marked influence upon one's test performance. A favorable environment tends to provide more information and more stimulation for better test performance than an unfavorable environment.

Failure to follow directions. A failure by students to follow directions, which provide the standards for a test, can result in an invalidation of the results. This failure may be due to a careless approach by the person giving the test or to the inability of students to comprehend or follow directions. In any case, established procedures must be observed by the test administrator and by the student; otherwise the results are valueless.

Principal Activities of a Testing Program

The five major areas of activity which constitute the total testing service are preparatory activities, administration of tests, scoring and computing results, preparing statistical data, and interpretation and follow-up. A neglect of any of these activities reduces the effectiveness of the testing service. Not all require equal time, but they do require appropriate attention.

Many of the guides suggested for each of the five phases of testing can be appropriately applied in each of the other phases, as well. These suggestions are made in each case for purposes of strengthening the specific activity and for improving the total testing service.

Preparatory Activities

Adequate preparations made by the testing personnel prior to the testing experience make it a more fruitful and enjoyable experience for all concerned and help to ensure that all phases of testing are carried out according to certain essential principles. Explanations by counselors and teachers are useful in preparing students mentally and emotionally for the activity. Since supervision of the testing program is one of the functions of the counselor, he should find the following guides to preparatory activities helpful:

1   Student and school needs should be known before tests are selected. The testing experience and test results should help meet these needs.
2   Tests should be selected by knowledgeable school people who have made an intensive study of test literature and catalogs.
3   Suitable and appropriate test selection depends upon the school's resources and personnel. Staff competence, finances, facilities, school philosophy, and pupil needs and capabilities are all factors to be considered.
4   It is advisable that a standard or minimum program of testing be established. Some basic structure which serves as a guide for the total program is essential. However, flexibility must be possible within the standard program without sacrificing efficiency.
5   The procedures to be observed and the personnel to be used in the test administration should be decided early in the planning stage. Appropriate steps may then be taken to carry out these procedures.
6   Meetings should be held with all school personnel who have assignments in the testing program. The manuals should be reviewed, questions concerning procedures answered, and everyone made familiar with his responsibilities. A practice experience with the test prior to its use with students may be in order if the staff members are not acquainted with the test.
7   Appropriate time scheduling is essential for the administering of the selected tests. Arrangements should be made for the testing well in advance of the time the test is to be administered. It would be a mistake to deny testing its logical claim on time; it would be a waste to provide more time than is necessary.
8   Students too should be apprised of what is taking place. Intro-

ductory and orientation experiences should be provided in which they learn something about the tests to be taken.

Administration of Selected Tests

If adequate preparations have been made, the second phase of the testing—the administering of the selected tests to appropriate student groups—should run smoothly. The student should be able to enjoy the testing experience as a challenge to be met, and he should be interested in the possibilities it holds for gaining useful information. Anxieties or tensions should be at a minimum as students prepare to respond to the tasks and problems presented.

The counselor should make certain that the four conditions listed below prevail. Following these guidelines will result in more efficient utilization of the time available, better performances by each student, and more useful test results. These guides also provide structure and encourage a systematic, objective approach in the testing function.

1   Suitable, adequate facilities must be available. Classrooms are usually satisfactory for testing purposes and provide the advantage of being immediately accessible. Adjustments in seating arrangements may be made as needed. Auditoriums, gymnasiums, or lunchrooms may have the advantage of space but the disadvantage of a mass-production effect in which the true purpose of the testing experience may be lost. Elementary school children, particularly, should be kept in small groups and carefully supervised.

2   Seating should be comfortable and suitable for all students. Desks should be arranged to permit easy access to each student.

3   The mechanics of the test must be thoroughly understood by each student. He should know at what point to start and to stop and the proper place on the booklet or answer sheet to indicate his choices. All questions concerning the mechanics of taking the test should be clarified satisfactorily before it is administered.

4   Appropriate directions clearly given are most essential. The person giving the test should become familiar with the manual directions prior to giving the tests and should observe the directions religiously when the test is administered.

These conditions may appear to be obvious. However, emphasis on them may result in a better testing service through fewer errors and more efficient use of time and resources. Other guides of equal merit and usefulness will occur to the alert teacher and counselor.

Scoring the Tests

Scoring the tests is the third phase of the testing service. The scoring procedures to be used should be decided upon during the preparatory activities, so that appropriate plans may be made. There are three principal alternatives for accomplishing this task:

1. Hand scoring can be accomplished rather quickly in a small school. Large groups can also be handled if some clerical assistance is provided. In most cases answer sheets are available for use with tests which make the scoring a rather simple task. Answers are generally marked directly in the test booklet in the primary grades. This makes the scoring a more time-consuming task.

2. IBM or similar scoring equipment is available locally in some areas. This service is relatively inexpensive and should be utilized when available. Answer sheets are scored quickly, and the results are tabulated for school use.

3. Scoring may be done by a service agency. In this case answer sheets are delivered to the agency. They are scored, statistical data are computed, and the results are returned to the school. The school may then make immediate use of the information.

One general principle to follow is to keep faculty involvement in clerical tasks to a minimum. Testing can become self-defeating if a maze of oppressive chores obscures the real purposes of the testing program. The counselor should make certain that he gives only a logical part of his time to the testing program. The leadership he provides combined with a sharing of responsibilities among the staff should result in a strong program with a minimum of time commitment. In scoring the tests,

1. The best and most appropriate facilities available for scoring should be known by the counselor; intelligent decisions should be made in accordance with this knowledge.

2. Only people with skill and competence should be assigned to scoring tasks. Errors can invalidate the results.

3. The scorers should be knowledgeable on scoring procedures and should observe the directions for properly computing results.

4. The counselor in charge of the scoring should observe and check the work of each assistant to ensure uniformity and correctness.

Preparing Statistical Data

To make maximum use of testing, it is necessary to make some statistical computations of data. Most of these data for ordinary use are relatively simple and easy to compute. The amount and kinds of data to be computed will depend upon the needs and wishes of the school and the uses to be made of the information. A commercial scoring center usually provides all the necessary statistical information at the time tests are scored. However, the essential computations may have to be done by the school.

Following are suggestions for preparing the statistical data:

1   Simplicity is essential in the preparation of data. The data should be in practical, usable form, with an absence of ambiguity and complexity.
2   The amount and form of statistical information to be provided with test results can be determined by the criterion of usefulness to the school and the student. Any information beyond that which fulfills the objectives of the testing service may be superfluous.
3   Simple profile, or psychograph, sheets should be used for reporting results on certain tests and for simplifying the interpretations.

Interpretation of Data and Follow-up Activities

Teachers, counselors, and students should know what the test results mean and how they can be best utilized for student development and improvement. The fifth phase of testing consists of the interpretation of results and follow-up activities in which efforts are made to utilize this new information appropriately in the guidance of young people. These activities are the most easily neglected, particularly if the testing itself has been an onerous task. Everyone may be relieved at its completion, and a general letdown in commitment may follow. Obviously, however, if results are not used and proper applications made, the testing itself is a waste of time.

The following suggestions on how to handle this phase of testing may result in a stronger program:

1   Pupils need to know the quality of their performances and the meaning test results may have for them individually. This information can be provided in small-group discussions or in conferences with individual pupils.
2   Staff members too must be acquainted with test results and know how to use this information in providing for the needs of pupils. Study groups may be formed in which interpretation procedures are explained and a consensus is reached on how to make the best use of the data obtained.
3   Statistical terms and data must be understood by the staff members, and these data must be in usable form. The staff under-

standing can be improved through procedures initiated by the counselor, including private conferences and group instructional activities.

4 Follow-up procedures include the recording of results in the cumulative record and the filing of profile sheets in anticipation of future use.

5 All teachers and counselors must see the pertinence test data may have for the total educational program. Their uses in conjunction with other kinds of information must be known, their limitations recognized, and the data treated accordingly.

Implied in the preceding discussion is the belief that the functions of the testing program are carried out by various members of the staff according to the abilities of each member. The counselor is the director of the program under the administrative authority of the principal, and the teacher works cooperatively with the counselor. The five major phases of testing are thus given appropriate attention and are combined into one major service under the guidance program.

The suitable application of all pertinent knowledge to bettering the teaching-learning process is an aim of the testing service. More effective and profitable learning experiences should result as intelligent use is made of information. Teachers are in the best position to apply this new knowledge, to observe the needs of pupils, and to aid them in their progress. Without such application and benefits the testing service may not be able to justify its existence. The improvement of instruction is an aim of all education, and it becomes a reality as counselors and teachers combine efforts in a worthy cause.

Types of Tests

A great number of tests are available covering a variety of areas. When all tests are viewed as being in one broad classification, confusion often results, and efficiency in test usage is threatened. Traxler has made a simple classification of tests into three areas: (1) aptitude, (2) achievement, and (3) tests of personal qualities, including interests.[1] He lists and describes a great number of tests under each of these three classifications. In the present discussion six classifications are used in an effort to make the value of each area of testing as meaningful as possible. A few test titles are given

---

[1] Arthur E. Traxler, *Techniques of Guidance*, Harper & Row, Publishers, Incorporated, New York, 1966, p. 46.

in each case for purposes of illustration but with no attempt to assess the relative merits of each.

Catalogs, readily provided by test publishers,[2] serve as excellent sources of information about the various tests. These catalogs should be obtained and carefully studied prior to selection. Specimen sets are also obtainable and are most helpful in making appropriate selections.

Scholastic Aptitude Tests

The scholastic aptitude test measures a pupil's potential for learning. Some knowledge as to his learning capabilities is gained from this test. "Aptitude" is a combination of certain characteristics essential to one's success in a particular area of endeavor. "Scholastic aptitude" refers to degree of competence in conventional school subjects. The terms "mental maturity" and "intelligence" are also used in referring to scholastic aptitude tests.

Purposes and uses.   Scholastic aptitude tests are useful in ascertaining the approximate quality of schoolwork a child might be expected to do and predicting possible success in mastering school subjects. They normally yield a mental age, an intelligence quotient, and a percentile rank. These numerical designations denote the approximate performance level of each child as they are compared with established norms. The educational program can be modified accordingly, and other appropriate procedures may be followed by which students can experience both challenges and successes in keeping with their learning aptitudes.

Some typical tests.   Three excellent individual-type tests are the Revised Stanford Binet Scale, published by Houghton Mifflin Company, Boston, and the Wechsler Intelligence Scale for Children (WISC) and Wechsler Adult Intelligence Scale (WAIS), both published by the Psychological Corporation, New York. The Binet and the Wechsler tests have many advantages over the group tests, particularly with youngsters experiencing academic or emotional problems. Since these tests are administered to one child at a time by a qualified examiner, the cost is considerably higher than for a group test. Their use might logically be limited to special cases.

[2] Appendix A provides a list of publishers and addresses; hence the addresses are omitted where publishers' names are given in the discussion in this chapter.

Many group tests are available. Each has its virtues and limitations. The following is a list of some typical tests and the educational levels for which they are intended:

1   American Council on Education Psychological Examination (ACE), Educational Testing Service; secondary and college
2   Army General Classification Test, Civilian Edition, 1947, Science Research Associates, Inc.; secondary and college
3   California Test of Mental Maturity, California Test Bureau; elementary, secondary, and college
4   Henmon-Nelson Tests of Mental Ability, Houghton Mifflin Company; elementary, high school, and college
5   Kuhlman-Anderson Intelligence Tests, The Personnel Press, Inc.; elementary, secondary, and adult
6   Lorge-Thorndike Intelligence Test, Houghton Mifflin Company; elementary, secondary, and college
7   Ohio State Psychological Test, Ohio State University; secondary, and college
8   Otis Quick-scoring Mental Ability Tests, World Book Company; elementary, secondary, and adult
9   Pintner General Ability Test, World Book Company; elementary, secondary, and adult
10 Primary Mental Abilities, Science Research Associates, Inc.; elementary, secondary, and adult
11 School and College Abilities Test (SCAT), Cooperative Test Division, Educational Testing Service; elementary, secondary, and college

Achievement Tests

Achievement tests have been used for many years in elementary and secondary schools and have helped teachers to identify academic strengths and weaknesses. The information is useful, too, in program improvements and in individualizing instruction. "Achievement" refers to a student's level of accomplishment in the various subject-matter areas. The test results are expressed as a profile of numerical designations denoting each student's achievement level.

Purposes and uses. Achievement tests serve several purposes in addition to supplying information on which modifications and adjustments in both curricular content and instructional procedures can be based. The following are some of their specific purposes and uses:

1 They provide a measurement of academic attainment in the various subject areas. This information supplements teacher observations and evaluations of performance in the classroom.
2 They identify certain skills and weaknesses of pupils.
3 They aid in arriving at a diagnosis.
4 They help to determine the readiness of pupils for school tasks and experiences.
5 They serve as guides in the selection and organization of material for enrichment experiences.
6 They reveal the degree of retardation or acceleration experienced by a child in comparison with his age and class group.
7 They provide information for use in ability grouping.

Some typical tests. The tests listed in this section are representative of a substantial number of such tests currently on the market. The reading readiness test is included in this group and is used at the primary grade level. Most of the other tests are available for the various elementary and secondary levels; thus no grade designation is made. Some well-known tests in this area are:

1 Metropolitan Readiness Tests, World Book Company
2 California Achievement Tests, California Test Bureau
3 Iowa Every-pupil Test of Basic Skills, Houghton Mifflin Company
4 Iowa Tests of Basic Skills, Science Research Associates, Inc.
5 Metropolitan Achievement Tests, World Book Company
6 Stanford Achievement Tests, World Book Company
7 Cooperative General Achievement Tests, Educational Testing Service
8 Iowa Tests of Educational Development, Science Research Associates, Inc.
9 Sequential Test of Educational Progress (STEP), Educational Testing Service
10 SRA Achievement Series, Science Research Associates, Inc.

Interest Inventories

Interest inventories provide scores from which patterns of interests are established. These patterns indicate the kinds of vocational activities that have the greatest appeal for an individual. Both low and high interests are shown on the profile sheets. Areas of interests are shown, not specific jobs. Most of the present inventories are designed for use in secondary schools and colleges. The specific assessment of interests at the elementary level would have little value.

Purposes and uses.   As previously noted, there are definite limitations in the use of most test data. The interest tests or inventories are no exception. However, they stimulate youngsters toward giving serious consideration to the matter of vocation selection and making better use of other tools available. The purposes and uses of the interest tests are summarized in the following list:

1   They reveal general broad patterns of interest.
2   They provide some stimulation for a student as a result of which greater effort may be directed toward intelligent vocation selection.
3   They give information both directly and indirectly about the various activities involved in the different vocational fields, thus serving as sources of information for students.
4   Their use contributes to more realistic planning by a student in considering the vocational possibilities open to him.
5   They are used to initiate interviews with a student from which new insights and improved self-understanding may result.
6   Their use may make possible the identification of, and attack upon, other problems and concerns. As test results are reviewed in counseling, the student may feel free to reveal other problems that need attention.

Some popular interest tests.   Several good interest tests have been available for a number of years. The following are some of those that have become popular with users and have provided useful information for making vocational plans:

1   The Kuder Preference Record, Science Research Associates, Inc.; high school and college
2   The Cleeton Interest Inventory, McKnight & McKnight Publishing Company; high school and college
3   Lee and Thorpe Occupational Interest Inventory, California Test Bureau; high school
4   Strong Vocational Interest Blank, The Psychological Corporation; high school and college

Special Aptitude Tests

A special aptitude is one's potential for performance in such areas as art, clerical work, mechanics, and music. Although environment and opportunities have considerable influence upon the development of these aptitudes, they are determined to a degree by characteristics which are apparently innate. The knowledge gained from aptitude tests is helpful to a person in his planning for the future.

Purposes and uses. The information gained from special aptitude tests, may have direct application value, or certain assumptions might be made on the basis of this information. For example, strong musical aptitude may indicate that a person should do well in musical activities. Aptitude is not, however, the only consideration in choosing a vocation. Opportunities for training and for job placement must also be considered. A person may, therefore, select a vocation in an area apart from his highest aptitude. Tests are thus used in conjunction with other information as vocational choices are made. The purposes and uses of the aptitude test may be summarized as follows:

1   The results give some indication as to a person's chances for success in a particular educational endeavor or vocational pursuit.
2   The relationship between scores obtained on an interest test and scores on an aptitude test may need to be determined. A high interest score in a particular area may have little value in vocation selection unless the aptitude in that area is also high.
3   Aptitude tests have use for the counselor in his planning schoolwork and a possible vocation with a student. The counselor views all objective data collectively and is able to counsel with students accordingly.
4   The aptitude test usually appeals to a student's curiosity about himself. He therefore takes some interest in it and is stimulated to plan more carefully and thoughtfully and to exert greater effort toward further self-exploration and eventual vocational selection.
5   The interest that an aptitude test stimulates may carry over into other areas of testing. A student may become more interested in the entire matter of data collection as a result of his experiences with aptitude tests.

Some popular and useful aptitude tests. Five major areas of aptitude are listed here with a few test titles under each. The last area given is an aptitude for occupations and is not a specific aptitude as the other four are:

1   Art aptitude: The Meier Art Tests, State University of Iowa; the Grave Design Judgment Test, The Psychological Corporation; secondary and college.
2   Clerical aptitude: The Minnesota Clerical Test and SRA Clerical Aptitude Test, Science Research Associates, Inc.; the Detroit Clerical Aptitude Examination and the General Clerical Test, The Psychological Corporation; high school and college.

3   Mechanical aptitude: SRA Mechanical Aptitude, Science Research Associates, Inc.; MacQuarrie Test for Mechanical Ability, California Test Bureau; Wrightstone-O'Toole Prognostic Test of Mechanical Abilities, California Test Bureau; Bennett Mechanical Comprehension Test, The Psychological Corporation; high school and college. (The following tests require certain equipment and have value in determining mechanical and dexterity aptitude: Minnesota Rate of Manipulation Test and Minnesota Spatial Relations Test, Educational Test Bureau; Purdue Pegboard, Science Research Associates, Inc.; Small Parts Dexterity Test and Stromberg Dexterity Test, The Psychological Corporation; high school and adult.)

4   Music aptitude: Seashore Measure of Musical Talents, The Psychological Corporation, fifth to fourteenth grades and adult; Musical Aptitude Test by Whistler and Thorpe, California Test Bureau, fourth to tenth grades. The Seashore test requires a record player; the Whistler test requires a piano.

5   Occupation Aptitude Test, California Test Bureau; this test includes these areas: personal-social, computational, clerical, sales, mechanical, and scientific; high school, college and adult.

Adjustment and Personality Inventories

The assessment of adjustment and personality provides considerable challenge to the researcher and developer of measuring instruments. Despite the problems, however, considerable progress has been made in the assessment of personality traits and in the determination of one's adjustment to life situations. Benefits other than numerical designations of measurement, however, are to be gained from the use of these tools.

Purposes and uses.   Several purposes may be realized through the proper utilization of the testing experience and test results. These are outlined as follows:

1   Their use often stimulates the student to giving more serious consideration to his own personality development.

2   The student gains information which is helpful in coming to a better understanding about the human personality and its development.

3   Student contacts with the counselor are encouraged and made easier as opportunities are provided for test-interpretation interviews.

4   Responses to individual items as well as the total scores provide

clues for the counselor and the teacher in identifying areas of difficulty.

5 The results can usefully be coordinated with other data in case studies.

6 The results help to determine the approximate degree of adjustment realized by each student.

Some typical tests and inventories.   Student maturity is an important criterion for the use of the personality test. Very few group personality tests, for example, are currently available for use in the elementary school. The following is a list of some personality tests and adjustment inventories which have been favorably received:

1 Bell Adjustment Inventory, Stanford University Press; secondary, college, and adult

2 Bernreuter Personality Inventory, Stanford University Press; secondary and college

3 California Personality Inventory, Consulting Psychologists Press; secondary and college

4 California Test of Personality, California Test Bureau; elementary, secondary, and college

5 Edwards Personal Preference Schedule, The Psychological Corporation; secondary and college

6 Kuder Preference Record, Form A, Personal, Science Research Associates, Inc.; secondary and college

7 Minnesota Counseling Inventory, The Psychological Corporation; secondary

8 Minnesota Multiphasic Personality Inventory, The Psychological Corporation; secondary, college, and adult

9 Mooney Problem Checklist, The Psychological Corporation; secondary, college, and adult.

10 Personal Audit, Science Research Associates, Inc.; secondary and college

11 SRA Youth Inventory, Science Research Associates, Inc.; secondary

Tests for clinical use.   There are some special tests designed for use by a qualified clinical psychologist. The school psychologist might be qualified to use these tests, but the typical school counselor at the master's degree level of preparation is not likely to be prepared to use them. (The Minnesota Multiphasic Personality Inventory might be classified here rather than with the group tests, since its use requires special training.) Two well-known clinical tests are:

1 The Rorschach Ink Blot Test, The Psychological Corporation; all ages
2 The Thematic Apperception Test, The Psychological Corporation; all ages

Differential Aptitude, or Multifactor, Tests

The differential aptitude test includes a number of specific tests by which several aptitudes are assessed. The results thus yield a profile of scores which indicate a person's aptitude for performance in a variety of activities. The term "multifactor" suggests that a number of factors are measured within a single test battery. The interpretation of these tests is made by a consideration of the combination of scores in the different areas. So, the counselor is interested in both the individual scores in each area and in the pattern of scores for purposes of interpretation.

Some multifactor tests. Multifactor tests have enjoyed a warm reception from some schools, and their usefulness has been demonstrated. Three popular tests in this classification are:

1 Differential Aptitude Test, The Psychological Corporation; secondary and college
2 Flanagan Aptitude Classification Tests (FACT), Science Research Associates, Inc.; secondary
3 General Aptitude Test Battery (GATB), U.S. Employment Service; secondary, college, and adult

A Standard Program of Testing

A standard program of testing is an established pattern by which testing is done throughout a school or district. Certain tests are given at specified grade levels in accordance with this standard program. In addition, however, certain tests should be made available to individuals and to small groups. These tests include special aptitude, personality, and other tests which have only limited value when used for all students.

Advantages of a Standard Program

A standard program of testing has many advantages and is recommended over a system which permits testing on an unplanned basis. It requires systematic planning and the observance of established procedures and justifies this attention through improved efficiency and more fruitful results. Some flexibility is possible and even desirable under a standard program, but the testing is done within a structure. Within the basic structure modifications are made as deemed necessary.

Some of the principal advantages of the standard program over one in which testing is done with little or no planning are that the standard program:

1   Makes for greater efficiency and economy in all phases of the guidance program.
2   Assists the teachers and counselors in planning their work for the year.
3   Provides for better and more effective use of the teacher's time.
4   Makes testing a more integral and closely related part of the educational program.
5   Reduces or eliminates entirely the confusion which often accompanies testing activities.
6   Provides time to prepare pupils for the anticipated testing experience.
7   Reduces or eliminates the anxieties, frustrations, and tensions on the part of both pupils and teachers.
8   Makes possible more efficient planning for the scoring of tests.
9   Permits more time for follow-up and interpretation activities.
10   Encourages and permits better preparation and more willing participation of teachers in the program.
11   Contributes to the total school morale.

Suggested Testing Schedule for All Grades

A testing schedule for all grades provides a guide for all standardized testing to be done within a district. This schedule is prepared or revised well before the testing is done in each school year. The following outline illustrates how this basic schedule may be set up for a school:

Kindergarten: Reading readiness
First grade: Scholastic aptitude (mental maturity)
Second grade: Achievement
Third grade: Scholastic aptitude; achievement
Fourth grade: Achievement
Fifth grade: Scholastic aptitude; achievement
Sixth grade: Achievement
Seventh grade: Scholastic aptitude; reading achievement; problem inventory or personality test

Eighth grade: Achievement

Ninth grade: Achievement; problem inventory or adjustment inventory

Tenth grade: Scholastic aptitude; reading achievement; personality test

Eleventh grade: Vocational interest inventory; General Aptitude Test Battery

Twelfth grade: Adjustment inventory or personality test

Aids in the Interpretation of Test Data

Careful interpretation of test data should result in better use of information gained by the counselor and a clearer understanding by the student as to the significance the information has for him. A sound principle of testing is that counselors, teachers, and students should know and understand the results of the tests. Two extremes should be avoided in test interpretation: (1) revealing exact scores to all students indiscriminately and without interpretation and (2) keeping scores hidden and inaccessible. These two approaches defeat the purposes of testing by failing to provide usable information. A graphic illustration of the results simplifies interpretation and makes the information more meaningful and understandable to both staff members and students. Certain simple statistical designations may also be used for purposes of improving interpretation procedures.

Percentiles, quartiles, and quintiles.   These statistical designations reduce raw scores to a concept which is readily understood by everyone. An exact score from a test is not necessary in order for a pupil to know the significance of his performance. In fact, a raw score has no meaning. Equivalents in educational age, grade placement, mental age, percentile, stanine, standard score, or some other meaningful designation are essential in order for the student to profit from the results.

A *percentile* rank shows a student's relative position in a group of 100 students. The percentile denotes his performance in comparison with other students at his age or grade level. *Quartiles* are points in the distribution, 25, 50, and 75, which divide the scores into sets of four and indicate to a student whether he is in the lowest, second, third, or upper fourth of the total group in his performance. *Quintiles* are points in the distribution, 20, 40, 60, and 80, which divide the distribution into five levels. This too permits the observance of a student's approximate position in the distribution of scores.

Psychograph, or profile, sheets.   The psychograph sheet serves as an aid in simplifying test results and making them meaningful. These sheets may be prepared for duplication by which any number of copies can be made available. The percentile, quartile, or quintile points are plotted across the top of the sheet, and the names of the tests with the appropriate subtests are listed down the left side of the sheet. Grade placements, age equivalents, mental ages, or other meaningful data may be recorded with the percentile designations. The profile sheets should be made to accommodate the particular tests being used.

The advantages of profile-sheet utilization are apparent to most teachers and counselors. It makes possible a frank discussion and intelligent interpretation of test results. Misunderstandings are kept to a minimum, and the whole testing experience is made more meaningful, enjoyable, and profitable.[3]

Z scores and T scores.   If more precise interpretation than that made possible by the use of percentiles is desired, a standard score, or a Z score, might be used. This is a score derived from the raw scores in a distribution. One disadvantage of the Z score is that negative numbers occur in the computations. The T score computation is similar to the Z score, and it has the advantage of dealing with positive numbers.

Stanines.   The use of stanines also simplifies test interpretation and is useful in the assignment of grades in classes, particularly at the college level. Scores in a distribution are divided into nine units. The number 5 stanine is the midpoint, number 9 is at the top, and number 1 is at the bottom of the distribution. In a distribution including one hundred subjects approximately twenty would be included in stanine 5, seventeen in stanines 4 and 6, twelve in stanines 3 and 7, seven in stanines 4 and 8, and four in stanines 1 and 9. Once the necessary computations are made, a student can readily see the quality of his performance in comparison with other individuals in the group.[4]

[3] The type of instrument to be used in test interpretation is illustrated in Appendix C.

[4] Many excellent sources of information on the use of statistical procedures are available. Two representative sources for the person seeking basic information are Herbert J. Klausmeier and William Goodwin, *Learning and Human Abilities*, 2d ed., Harper & Row, Publishers, Incorporated, New York, 1966, chap. 18; and Merle M. Ohlsen, *Guidance Services in the Modern School*, Harcourt, Brace & World, Inc., New York, 1964, appendix A.

SUMMARY/

There are many benefits to be derived from the use of standardized tests if they are carefully selected and properly used. Instruments of evaluation and appraisal are essential in assisting children and youth toward better self-understanding and in making realistic educational and vocational choices. Proper test utilization adds strength to the guidance service and contributes to the effectiveness of the total educational program. The limitations and weaknesses of tests can be minimized if they are used properly and if precautions are taken to protect students against misunderstanding and apprehensions.

There are five major areas of activity in the testing services, each of which is essential to the success of the total program. The preparatory activities and the follow-up procedures should receive attention equal to that given to the actual administration of the tests.

Although the testing program is one of the responsibilities of the counselor, the administrator and the teacher should also be involved in planning and carrying out this program. The interest and participation of everyone are essential to its success.

Standardized tests may be divided into six major classifications. Each of these tests is designed to assess a particular aptitude or trait. Each has value as it is used to gain purposeful and usable information.

A standard program of testing provides for the use of certain designated tests at the various grade levels. The proper interpretation of test data to pupils following a testing experience increases the value of the experience. Interpretation can be simplified through the use of profile, or psychograph, sheets. Statistical data computed from raw scores also make test results more meaningful.

PROBLEMS/

1 What is the meaning of "pupil appraisal"? What other terms might be used?

2 What are the major purposes and aims of a testing program?

3 If a test is an instrument by which pupil self-understanding can be improved, show how this can be accomplished.

4 At what point in educational planning should the decisions be made as to whether or not tests should be given and as to the kinds of tests to be given?

5 Defend the view that any test is merely a means toward an end. What is that end?

6 Explain the nature of the relationship between the realization of aims and the utilization of particular tools. Why use any tool?

7 What are the dangers of a condition in which staff members are unaware of or ignore the limitations of tests?

8 A school states that it has eliminated the use of tests because they do more harm than good. Give your reactions to this statement.

9 How might the limitations of tests be minimized?

10 Review the five principal areas of activity in a testing program. What are the advantages of this type of structure in conducting the testing program?

11 How much information should students be given on test results? What general guides might be used here?

12 What are the major junctions of each of the following people with the testing service: (*a*) counselor, (*b*) teacher, (*c*) principal?

13 Enumerate and explain the principal uses of each of the major classifications of tests.

14 What are the advantages of observing a standard program of testing rather than leaving test selection and administration to chance?

15 List some guides and procedures to be used in making use of the data gained from any test.

Selected References

Textbooks
AHMANN, J. STANLEY, and MARVIN D. GLOCK: *Evaluating Pupil Growth*, Allyn and Bacon, Inc., Boston, 1958.
ARBUCKLE, DUGALD S.: *Pupil Personnel Services in American Schools*, Allyn and Bacon, Inc., Boston, 1962, chap. 7, pp. 252–262.
BARR, JOHN A.: *The Elementary Teacher and Guidance*, Holt, Rinehart and Winston, Inc., New York, 1957, chaps. 6 and 7.

BERNARD, HAROLD W., JAMES C. EVAN, and FRANKLIN R. ZERAN: *Guidance Services in Elementary Schools*, Chartwell House, New York, 1954, chap. 7.

BUROS, OSCAR K.: *Mental Measurements Yearbook*, Rutgers University Press, New Brunswick, N.J., 1959.

COTTINGHAM, HAROLD F.: *Guidance in Elementary Schools*, McKnight & McKnight Publishing Company, Bloomington, Ill., 1956, chap. 7.

FARWELL, GAIL F., and HERMAN J. PETERS: *Guidance Readings for Counselors*, Rand McNally & Company, Chicago, 1960, chap. 5, pp. 247–254.

GLANZ, EDWARD C.: *Foundations and Principles of Guidance*, Allyn and Bacon, Inc., Boston, 1964, chap. 8, pp. 176–178.

GOLDMAN, LEO: *Using Tests in Counseling*, Appleton-Century-Crofts, Inc., New York, 1961.

HUTSON, PERCIVAL W.: *The Guidance Function in Education*, Appleton-Century-Crofts, Inc., New York, 1958, chap. 12, pp. 376–399.

JONES, ARTHUR J.: *Principles of Guidance and Pupil Personnel Work*, McGraw-Hill Book Company, New York, 1951, chap. 8.

KOWITZ, GERALD T., and NORMA G. KOWITZ: *Guidance in the Elementary Classroom*, McGraw-Hill Book Company, New York, 1959, chap. 7.

MARTINSON, RUTH A., and HARRY SMALLENBURG: *Guidance in Elementary Schools*, Prentice-Hall, Inc., Englewood Cliffs, N.J., 1958, chap. 6.

MC DANIEL, HENRY B.: *Guidance in the Modern School*, The Dryden Press, Inc., New York, 1956, chaps. 8–10.

———, JOHN E. LALLAS, JAMES A. SAUM, JAMES L. GILMORE: *Readings in Guidance*, Holt, Rinehart and Winston, Inc., New York, 1959, chap. 5.

MORTENSEN, DONALD G., and ALLEN M. SCHMULLER: *Guidance in Today's Schools*, John Wiley & Sons, Inc., New York, 1959, chap. 7.

OHLSEN, MERLE M.: *Guidance Services in the Modern School*, Harcourt, Brace & World, Inc., New York, 1955, chaps. 7–9.

PETERS, HERMAN J., and GAIL F. FARWELL: *Guidance: A Developmental Approach*, Rand McNally & Company, Chicago, 1959, chap. 8.

SHERTZER, BRUCE, and HERMAN J. PETERS: *Guidance: Techniques for Individual Appraisal and Development*, The Macmillan Company, New York, 1965, chaps. 7, 8, and 11.

TRAXLER, ARTHUR E., and ROBERT D. NORTH: *Techniques of Guidance*, 3d. ed., Harper & Row, Publishers, Incorporated, New York, 1966, chaps. 5–11.

WILLEY, ROY DE VERL: *Guidance in Elementary Education*, Harper & Row, Publishers, Incorporated, New York, 1960, chap. 5.

——— and DEAN C. ANDREW: *Modern Methods and Techniques in Guidance*, Harper & Row, Publishers, Incorporated, New York, 1955, chaps. 7–10.

——— and MELVIN DUNN: *The Role of the Teacher in the Guidance Program*, McKnight & McKnight Publishing Company, Bloomington, Ill., 1964, chap. 12.

Journals

BARCLAY, JAMES R.: "The Attack on Testing and Counseling: An Examination and Reappraisal," *Personnel and Guidance Journal*, vol. 43, pp. 6–16, September, 1964.

BERDIE, RALPH F.: "Testing Programs and Counseling in the Schools," Sixty-second Yearbook of the National Society for the Study of Education 1963, vol. 62, part II, pp. 126–162.

BLIGH, HAROLD F.: "Trends in the Measurement of Education Achievement," *Review of Educational Research,* vol. 35, pp. 34–52, February, 1965.

COLEMAN, WILLIAM, and DOROTHY M. COLLETT: "Development and Application of Structured Tests of Personality," *Review of Educational Research,* vol. 29, pp. 57–72, February, 1959.

DOBBIN, J. E.: "Place of Testing in Guidance Services," *Virginia Journal of Education,* vol. 55, pp. 16–19, November, 1961.

ECKERSON, LOUISE O.: "Testing and Counseling," *School Life,* vol. 43, pp. 10–13, September, 1960.

FELDT, LEONARD S.: "Role of Testing in Guidance," *Educational Forum,* vol. 23, pp. 293–301, March, 1959.

FINDLEY, WARREN G.: "Purposes of School Testing Programs and Their Efficient Development," Sixty-second Yearbook of the National Society for the Study of Education, 1963, part II, pp. 1–27.

FLANAGAN, JOHN C.: "New Tool for Measuring Children's Behavior," *Elementary School Journal,* vol. 59, pp. 163–169, December, 1958.

GAIER, EUGENE L.: "Trends in the Measurement of Personality," *Review of Educational Research,* vol. 35, pp. 63–81, February, 1965.

GOSLIN, DAVID A.: "The Social Impact of Standardized Testing," *National Education Association Journal,* vol. 52, pp. 20–22, October, 1963.

GUILFORD, JOY P., BENJAMIN FRUCHTER, and PAUL H. KELLEY: "Development and Applications of Tests of Intellectual and Special Abilities," *Review of Educational Research,* vol. 29, pp. 26–41, February, 1959.

KIRK, BARBARA A.: "Extra Measurement Use of Tests in Counseling," *Personnel and Guidance Journal,* vol. 39, pp. 658–661, April, 1961.

KLAUSMEIER, HERBERT J.: "Identifying Children through Measurements," *Education,* vol. 80, pp. 167–171, November, 1959.

LORETAN, JOSEPH O.: "The Decline and Fall of Group Intelligence Testing," *Teachers College Record,* vol. 67, pp. 10–17, October, 1965.

LUNDY, CHARLES T., and BRUCE SHERTZER: "Making Test Data Useful," *Personnel and Guidance Journal,* vol. 42, pp. 62–63, September, 1963.

MC CALL, JOHN N.: "Trends in the Measurement of Vocational Interest," *Review of Educational Research,* vol. 35, pp. 53–62, February, 1965.

MERRIFIELD, PHILIP R.: "Trends in the Measurement of Special Abilities," *Review of Educational Research,* vol. 35, pp. 25–33, February, 1965.

MERWIN, JACK C., and others: "S.V.I.B. Machine Scoring Provided by a Test Scoring Agency," *Personnel and Guidance Journal,* vol. 43, pp. 665–668, March, 1965.

MILLER, CARROLL H.: "Guidance and Programs of Testing," *School Life,* vol. 42, pp. 18–20, September, 1959.

OHLSEN, MERLE M.: "Interpretation of Test Scores," Sixty-second Yearbook of the National Society for the Study of Education, 1963, part II, pp. 254–294.

PROFF, FRED C.: "The Use of Appraisal Data," *Review of Educational Research,* vol. 30, pp. 141–145, April, 1960.

ROBY, DONALD L.: "Learning About Pupils: Non-test Tools and Their Uses," *Teachers College Journal,* vol. 31, pp. 65–66, December, 1959.

TRAXLER, ARTHUR E., and ROBERT D. NORTH: "The Selection and Use of Tests in a School Testing Program," Sixty-second Yearbook of the National Society for the Study of Education, 1963, part II, pp. 211–231.

TYLER, RALPH W.: "The Impact of External Testing Programs," Sixty-second Yearbook of the National Society for the Study of Education, 1963, part II, pp. 193–210.

WELLMAN, FRANK E.: "Administration of the Testing Program," *School Life,* vol. 42, pp. 21–25, September, 1959.

WRIGHTSTONE, J. WAYNE: "The Relation of Testing Programs to Teaching and Learning," Sixty-second Yearbook of the National Society for the Study of Education, 1963, part II, pp. 45–61.

SEVEN

/THE COUNSELING SERVICE

The counseling service is the heart of the guidance program. Counseling provides students with opportunities to look objectively at their problems, gain insights from which intelligent action may be taken, plan logically for the future, and make personal gains in the self-actualization process. Problems become less formidable as possible solutions occur to the student. Self-confidence increases and doubts and apprehensions are dissipated as the student begins to see himself in a more realistic perspective and as he becomes better informed about his environment. The atmosphere of the counselor's office and the understanding reflected there encourage the student to face his problems and to give candid expression to his feelings.

The student's development is aided as he profits from the counseling experience. As he is challenged to increase his self-understanding and as his intellect is sharpened and his emotions properly utilized, a higher level of maturity is realized. Decisions are likely to be more logical and hold greater promise for success when the student has the benefit of the counselor's aid rather than having to rely entirely upon his own resources. The counselor gives his full attention to each student within a setting of privacy and concentration. Each problem is given careful consideration, plans are formulated, and a course of action is established.

Attention is given in this chapter to the nature and meaning of counseling. Criteria are enumerated which should be met if the activity is to be called counseling. The belief is expressed that counseling and related services designed to aid each individual child should be provided at all educational levels. The principal points of emphasis underlying three arbitrarily classified "schools" of counseling are enumerated.

The Nature of Counseling

The needs of young people and the demands of the times vigorously suggest the significance of counseling as a vital force in the lives of individuals. Current data indicate that benefits are gained from the counseling experience by a substantial number of young people. The benefits to be gained, however, are not always susceptible to present research methodology. Many problems are still encountered in this kind of research. Careful observation is therefore needed in order to note the degree to which students appear to profit from counseling.

Individual counseling and its meanings and place in the educational program are the focus of this section; group counseling is covered in Chapter 11.

The Meaning of Counseling

Since many people have assumed the title of counselor, if not its true role and responsibility, the term "counseling" has a variety of meanings to various individuals. The business counselor, economic adviser, real estate counselor, financial counselor, and academic adviser may indeed perform certain functions similar to those of the professional guidance counselor. However, the work of the guidance counselor is more restricted and is limited to certain functions and processes which are not the prerogatives of the businessman, the financial adviser, or even the academic adviser. There are other differences which will become apparent as counseling is further described and defined. A look at a few representative definitions may be helpful. Glanz [1] defines counseling as "an open-ended, face-to-face, problem solving situation within which a student, with professional assistance, can focus and begin to solve a problem or problems." Clinical or psychological counseling is defined [2] as a "process which takes place in a one-to-one relationship between an individual troubled by problems with which he cannot cope alone and a professional worker whose training and experience have qualified him to help others reach solutions to various types of personal difficulties." Arbuckle reviews several counseling definitions.[3] He then describes counseling [4] as a "human relationship—a warm relationship in which the counselor, fully and completely, without any ifs or buts, accepts the client as a worthy person. In this relationship of complete acceptance, the client can grow and develop, and come to use the strengths and capacities that are his, and to make decisions and choices that will be satisfactory to him, and thus to his fellows."

An adequate definition of counseling needs to be comprehensive if it is to include all the important elements and satisfy the counselor. He sees his work as including a number of functions and as providing a setting within which a student can gain the encouragement and understanding which will serve as an impetus toward greater self-realization and major accomplishment. To define such an activity or experience with its many complexities and ramifications is no easy task. The following definition should, however, serve the purposes of this text:

Counseling is both a process and a relationship. It is a process by which concerted attention is given by both counselor and counselee to the problems and concerns of the student in a setting of privacy, warmth, mutual acceptance, and confidentiality. As a process it utilizes appropriate tools and procedures which contribute to the fruitfulness of the experience. Counseling is also a relationship characterized by trust, confidence, and intimacy in which the student gains intellectual and emotional stability from which he can resolve difficulties, make plans, and realize greater self-fulfillment.

Rogers speaks of counseling as a relationship in which one of the parties has the intent of promoting the growth, development,

[1] Edward C. Glanz, *Foundations and Principles of Guidance*, Allyn and Bacon, Inc., Boston, 1964, p. 93.

[2] Milton E. Hahn and Malcolm S. MacLean, *Counseling Psychology*, 2d ed., McGraw-Hill Book Company, New York, 1955, p. 6.

[3] Dugald S. Arbuckle, *Counseling, Philosophy, Theory, and Practice*, Allyn and Bacon, Inc., Boston, 1965, pp. 63–70.

[4] *Ibid.*, p. 70.

maturity, and improved functioning of the other.[5] The quality of the relationship thus receives the major emphasis. It should also be noted that the success of that aspect of counseling regarded as a process also depends upon the quality of the relationship. Rogers also notes that it is the quality of the interpersonal encounter with the client in a wide variety of professional relationships which determines its effectiveness.[6] The quality of the relationship is of the greatest importance to the client-centered counselor. It is also important to all counselors, but the techniques used in achieving it may differ.

The importance of effective communication is stressed by Williamson and its meaning explained in an article published several years ago.[7] He states that [8] "Presently we are engaged in a search for theories to explain counseling processes and to identify the psychology of problem solving and anxiety-reducing processes . . . that is, we search for a theory of the way personality develops as the supporting foundation for counseling techniques." He notes that although these approaches have merit, there is still another way to delineate counseling and to identify its techniques: [9] "And this is the way of identifying *modes of communication* between counselor and counselee—conversing about optional value orientations in search of clarification of the student's question and confusion. . . . This is the basic content of counseling because it is *the* basic problem in human adjustment and development—organizing a way of life around an explicit system of values, beliefs, and life objectives." Techniques are obviously important to the counselor as he strives to effect a system of communication between himself and his client. This too may denote the concern of the counselor for the establishment of a strong, positive, relationship in which the client can grow and in which the communication techniques of the process facilitate his seeing alternative courses of action to be followed and possible solutions to his problems.

Related to the concepts of counseling as a relationship and the significance of communication is the proposal that the counselor is

[5] Carl R. Rogers, "The Characteristics of a Helping Relationship," *Personnel and Guidance Journal,* vol. 37, p. 6, September, 1958.

[6] Carl R. Rogers, "The Interpersonal Relationship: The Core of Guidance," *Harvard Education Review,* vol. 32, no. 4, p. 416, Fall, 1962.

[7] E. G. Williamson, "The Meaning of Communication in Counseling," *Personnel and Guidance Journal,* vol. 38, pp. 6–14, September, 1959.

[8] *Ibid.,* p. 6.

[9] *Ibid.,* p. 7.

also a technique.[10] "I refer to the counselor himself as a technique of counseling, not only what he does or says in the interview, but how he conducts himself and the manner of often unverbalized communication. I suggest that the style of living of the counselor himself is an extremely important and effective technique in counseling." Certainly the techniques of the counselor in developing the relationship with the client are a reflection of him as a person as well as a reflection of his familiarity with, and commitment to, a particular theory or system. The counselor will also capitalize on those particular elements of a theory or combination of theories which most adequately provide for his own self-expression and which are most likely to provide for him the greatest comfort and satisfaction. In this case, the particular techniques used are means by which the counselor works toward his need fulfillment and through which he expects to be of assistance to the client. The techniques, then, are means to ends.

A better understanding of counseling might also be gained by reviewing nine basic principles of counseling.[11] These principles emphasize the importance of counseling as a personal service designed to assist each individual student in accordance with his needs and aspirations.

Criteria for Counseling

An awareness of certain criteria and an adherence to them should be helpful as guides in determining whether a particular activity is indeed counseling or if it should receive some other designation. The frequent abuses or misuses of the term "counseling" might thus be reduced as the public and educators become better informed about this personal relationship and as it is subjected to careful, objective scrutiny. The following criteria provide a sound framework from which this evaluation may be made.

Qualifications and competence of the counselor.   The person doing the counseling must be a qualified, professional person. He should have received the necessary training and gained the required experiences to meet certification standards within his state. If certifica-

[10] E. G. Williamson, "The Counselor as Technique," *Personnel and Guidance Journal,* vol. 41, p. 108, October, 1962.
[11] See Jane Warters, *Techniques of Counseling,* 2d ed., McGraw-Hill Book Company, New York, 1964, pp. 10–14.

tion is not required in a particular state, the requirement of essential preparation should still prevail. Standards from other sources should also be considered. The American Personnel and Guidance Association and the American Psychological Association, Inc., provide such guides. A general standard for counselors in elementary and secondary schools is a minimum of a master's degree earned in appropriate courses, including a practicum, or the equivalent of the degree in course work. A second year of graduate study is, however, becoming more common as preparation for counseling positions and is strongly recommended by national study groups that have made an intensive study of counselor preparation.[12]

Adequate time allotments for counseling. Designated times for counseling sessions should be observed during which both participants are able to give their undivided attention to the counseling function. The incidental advisement, instruction, and directions that occur during the school day are also essential to the educational progress of a child.

Individual, personal consideration. Counseling is personal; its major concern is with just one person at a particular time. The teacher or counselor who attempts to teach or supervise a class and counsel a student simultaneously is probably failing at both. The undivided attention of counselor and counselee is mandatory in counseling.

Privacy. A setting of privacy, with the opportunity to explore and express feelings free from the inhibiting influence of curious observers, is most essential. A suitable office arrangement in which privacy can be maintained thus becomes obvious. This office should serve the counselor only and should not be used for any purpose which might encroach upon privacy.

Personal development of the individual. The development of the individual is a major aim of counseling and is another criterion by which the counseling activity is judged. This aim must take precedence over the secondary aims. Instruction is not without the same

[12] See John W. Loughary, Robert O. Stripling, and Paul W. Fitzgerald, *Counseling: A Growing Profession,* joint publication of the Association for Counselor Education and Supervision and American School Counselors Association, Divisions of the American Personnel and Guidance Association, Washington, D.C., 1965, p. 26.

goal, but the approaches and setting are different. Counseling must assist the individual toward greater maturity and increasing strengths and capabilities from which may come a more fruitful life.

Counseling Service at All Educational Levels

Counseling as herein defined and understood is a service for all students at all levels of education. Elementary schools, secondary schools, colleges, and universities must have organized counseling services if students are to utilize their potentialities more realistically. Traditionally, counseling has been regarded as a service for the secondary school. Individualized services and activities in the elementary school have not normally been looked upon as counseling. However, recent events provide encouragement to the many people who have deplored the lack of concern for providing counselors for the elementary school. The National Defense Education Act of 1958 was modified by the Eighty-eighth Congress in October, 1964, to include the training of counselors for public elementary schools and institutions of higher education under the Guidance and Counseling Institute Program of NDEA. Elementary schools, public junior colleges, and technical institutes become eligible for funds under the authorization of the state in this same act. Prior to this revision only secondary school counselors were eligible for training under this act.

The elementary school counselor functions as a child guidance, or child development, specialist and may bear such a title rather than be called a counselor. The nature of his work also differs somewhat from the usual work of the secondary school counselor. One difference is that he spends proportionately more time in working directly with teachers and parents than is the case with the secondary school counselor, who spends proportionately more time in actual counseling.

The arguments used in the past as justification for not providing counseling below the secondary level are fading rapidly. They are no longer tenable, if indeed they ever were. The points emphasized by the opponents of elementary school counseling might be summarized as follows: (1) vocational counseling has little part to play with elementary children; (2) the curriculum of the elementary school is less complex, thus reducing the need for aid in course selection; (3) sexual-social problems are less pronounced during the early years; (4) the incidence of delinquency is lower among elementary-age children; (5) the teacher and pupil already have a close personal relationship by virtue of the time spent together each day.

There are elements of truth in each of these statements, but in most cases they miss the point and fail to note the real purposes of counseling. For example, although the elementary child does not make a vocation selection this early in life, he can profit from the experience provided for him through an organized guidance program. True, too, are the statements about sexual-social problems and delinquency. However, the elementary years are the time to help youngsters develop proper attitudes about all aspects of life, thus helping them to avert potential problems and to be better prepared to handle any difficulties which might arise. The teacher pupil relationship should be close and warm, but this relationship is not a satisfactory substitute for the counseling relationship or for other activities found in the guidance service.

The Need for Counseling and Individualized Services

The fulfillment of personal needs by individuals is expedited by the aid and sustaining influence of a professional person appropriately trained and properly oriented to provide this aid. Societal expectations of, and demands upon, youngsters within the educational setting are constantly increasing. Frustrations, anxieties, and confusion occur as outgrowths of such a complex, dynamic, ever-changing and demanding society. These youngsters must have greater moral strength, greater competence, more unusual adaptive powers, and a stronger sense of commitment than their elders needed. The more complex and demanding life is, the greater becomes the need for counseling and other individualized services. Personal assistance is required in the modern world if adequate adjustments are to be made and if potentialities are to be discovered and developed.

Transition from home to school.　Individualized attention and services contribute to the smoothness and efficiency with which children make the transition from home to school. Secondary school youth have long since experienced the period of transition, but there still remain problems of cooperation and mutual understanding between home and school. Counseling opportunities for these youth result in a reduction of problems encountered and in a more hasty and satisfactory solution to the problems which do occur.

The immaturity and inexperience of children and youth. Because of their relative immaturity and lack of experience, youngsters of all ages need adult guidance and direction. Counseling aids young people to bridge the gaps between the expectations of home, school, and society and to develop their capabilities for fulfilling these expectations adequately.

Changing concepts about the human personality. With changing concepts and philosophies and an increased sensitivity to the individual has come the need for formal and incidental services structured to stimulate the individual toward greater achievements and to aid him in his development. The importance of the individual and the right of each person to maximum development and full realization within his particular limits has become a significant concept in modern education. The traditional approach in education is being altered to provide for a high degree of freedom, individuality, and the creative effort.

Benefits to be Gained from Counseling

Although it has been quite well established that there is a need for counseling services and despite some excellent research with encouraging findings and hopeful conclusions, more evidence is needed to support the hypothesis that most people do indeed profit from counseling. For example, Campbell states: [13] "There is an ever-increasing body of evidence to show that counseling is effective in changing behavior. While the changes are never dramatic . . . they are consistent and generally show that the counseled students make better grades, or are more comfortable with life, or have a more accurate perception of themselves, or, in general, score higher on whatever relevant criterion the counseling researcher has chosen." As Campbell presents a fascinating report on the apparent influence of counseling on students twenty-five years ago at the University of Minnesota, he notes [14] that there are certain criteria generally used for assessing progress and improvements of clients. These criteria include ". . . improvements in grades, higher frequency of graduation, more involvement in social activities, better progress in post-high school endeavors, better involuntary motor responses to a word association test, scores on adjustment inven-

[13] David P. Campbell, *The Results of Counseling: Twenty-Five Years Later*, W. B. Saunders Company, Philadelphia, 1965, p. 14.
[14] *Ibid.*, p. 14.

tories, changes in self-perception, and more accurate awareness of specific interests."

Declarations of gratitude to a counselor and expressions of greater satisfaction with oneself and greater ability to deal with life's problems on the part of people who have received counseling should not be overlooked as support for the counseling function. Results of research, although not always conclusive, are quite encouraging. There is reason to believe that with a better understanding of the counseling process by both the client and the counselor, and with the appearance of more competent counselors on the scene, the benefits gained from counseling will increase in quantity and quality.

Relationship of Counseling to Instruction

Are counseling and instruction essentially the same? How different are their aims? What elements characterize their differences—and their similarities? Since the role of the teacher in guidance is the subject of Chapter 3, in this section we will look briefly at the relationship between counseling and instruction.

Differences between counseling and teaching. Although not mutually exclusive, counseling and teaching are not the same. Each has its principal responsibilities, procedures, relationships, and anticipated outcomes. The teacher is a specialist in instructing students toward the attainment of academic knowledge and skills. His major aim is scholastic competence and academic achievement on the part of his students. The counselor is a specialist in conducting private interview or therapy sessions with individual students with the aim of greater personal competence on the part of each student counseled. Instruction takes place normally without benefit of formal counseling, and counseling occurs with little or no formal instruction. An exception is when the teacher does actual counseling with a student in a setting of privacy and in keeping with the other established requirements. The counselor too might devote some time to providing academic instruction. However, this would be done as a means by which the counseling relationship is to be enhanced, using instruction as a means to that end.

Misunderstandings sometimes occur when the teacher's role as a counselor is discussed. It is true that the teacher is not a counselor in the same sense that the designated counselor is. However, no one is in a more favorable position to develop a warm, close relationship with a child than the teacher. This relationship provides the foundation and the atmosphere from which the child may well profit. The teacher demonstrates his worth and effectiveness as he indicates his concern for the child. His attitude should convey warmth, encouragement, good will, and affection for the child. The *quality* of the relationship between the teacher and the child is the major consideration. The teacher should use any procedure, device, or technique which will contribute to the quality of this relationship, so long as it is consistent with his professional qualifications and in keeping with the ethics of the situation. Technical complex procedures are not necessary in these cases. What a teacher does as a part of his work with a child and as a reflection of his genuine interest in him is essentially the same as what good teachers have been doing for a long time.

Good teaching combined with competent counseling provide a combination of enriching, profitable experiences for students. Neither counseling nor teaching is to replace or duplicate the services of the other. Each has its unique responsibilities and opportunities for service, and each augments the other.

Contribution of counseling to the learning process. Teaching becomes more effective as students profit from the counseling relationship and gain insights and improved understandings which transfer to the classroom. The academic progress of a student is thwarted if he is emotionally disturbed or unduly concerned about personal matters. Aid in resolving his problems and planning courses of action results in achievement more truly representative of his ability and in the more efficient use of his time and energies. Causes of disturbances and apprehensions should be ascertained and either removed or dealt with satisfactorily. Behavior is more appropriate and attitudes of students are more positive within a classroom of well-adjusted, happy students. Good mental health is mandatory for effective learning.

Students are often stimulated by counseling and are motivated toward greater accomplishments. Counseling provides a setting for learning in which insights may be gained. Emotional barriers to learning may be minimized and judgments sharpened on what should be learned and retained and what should be discarded.

Concepts and Points of View

Concepts as to the true nature of counseling have varied considerably among educators, and to some extent among counselors themselves. The mental image of counseling has varied as people have relied upon their own experiences and notions. Disagreement and even some confusion, however, have to some extent been useful in providing the stimulus and the motivation for discussion, experimentation, and research. From these research activities have come additional knowledge and improved understanding.

Related to the conceptualization of counseling is the establishment of a philosophy, or point of view, about counseling. Counselor attitudes, skills, training, and experience and the like all have relevance to the counselor's philosophy of counseling. Methods and techniques employed by the counselor are an expression of his philosophy. This same philosophy determines the emphasis given to the concept of counseling as a relationship. A rather arbitrary classification of counseling techniques into three categories has emerged as the relative merits of counseling procedures have been considered: the directive, or clinical; the nondirective, or client-centered; and the eclectic. This classification suggests somewhat definite lines of distinction among these counseling approaches, but in fact no such clear demarcations exist. There are varying degrees of emphasis given to the techniques and viewpoints within the three categories but no actual hard-and-fast points of separation. However, since an awareness of the three approaches and some knowledge of their points of allegiance may make the counseling process more understandable, this classification is followed in this chapter. Hopefully, the end justifies the means. However, the novice should make no commitment to any particular view or philosophy until he is an experienced, knowledgeable counselor and thus able to see the merits and limitations of the various approaches. Since the quality of the relationship is more important than the utilization of any particular techniques, any approach used should be directed at developing and maintaining this relationship.

Some guides for the counselor, irrespective of philosophical commitment, are given below. Also, the general beliefs of the directive, client-centered, and eclectic approaches in counseling are reviewed, and reference is made to the more significant characteristics of each. The next logical step is for the student to make an intensive study of the major counseling theories. Such a study is not an appropriate subject for this text, however, and is left to other books.[15]

[15] See Buford Stefflre (ed.), *Theories of Counseling*, McGraw-Hill Book Company, New York, 1965.

Guides for the Counselor

Incumbent upon the counselor is the responsibility of becoming a highly competent, dependable, professional person. High competence presupposes and is dependent upon appropriate training at the graduate level, a variety of work and educational experiences, and essential personal qualities and characteristics. Thus, for the young person anticipating a career in counseling some cognizance of his responsibilities should result in more serious effort toward proper preparation. The practicing counselor too should recognize the importance of constant improvement in his counseling competence and see the need for continuous personal development.

A familiarity with counseling methods.   The counselor must be acquainted with and able to use professional methods and techniques. He has the prerogatives of utilizing the techniques he regards as most appropriate, but these rights increase rather than lessen his responsibility for knowing, understanding, and being able to use appropriate procedures. He chooses with care the techniques he uses and is able to do so because he knows enough about them to be able to make intelligent discriminations.

Superior self-understanding.   The counselor must have a more profound understanding of himself than perhaps any other professional person. He must be able to recognize and handle his own limitations and be equally aware of his capabilities and how best to capitalize on them for the benefit of others. The quality of his own personal adjustment is of first importance to his fitness to counsel others.

Client understanding.   Empathy, understanding, and concern are elements of great importance as the counselor seeks to provide a setting which is conducive to client growth. The perceptions of the client must be sensed and seen clearly by the counselor, who must then know how to capitalize on these perceptions for maximum progress.

Counselor comfort and congruence.   The counselor must be comfortable within the framework of the philosophical viewpoints he accepts and practices. The techniques used and the philosophy permeating the relationship are determined largely by the counselor himself. He must feel comfortable with his beliefs and methods and proceed with self-confidence, with faith in himself and his client, and with a firm belief in the efficacy of the counseling relationship.

Degrees of emphasis upon various elements. Elements which characterize the client-centered theory are not unlike elements which are important in the other theories or approaches. For example, the client-centered approach emphasizes the immediate situation as worthy of initial and concerted attention, and the counselor with the orientation of so-called directive counseling is also interested in the immediate situation. The counselor with the directive orientation, however, would give minimal attention to the immediate situation while looking to past events in his effort to be of help to the client.

Personal growth on the part of the client, to take another example, is a major aim of the client-centered technique. However, while the other counseling orientations also have client growth as an objective, they differ as to what procedures to use in order to realize this objective. Thus, whereas an outright acceptance or rejection of a particular element of one approach or another is generally not in keeping with what actually happens in counseling sessions, there are degrees of emphasis running the gamut from whole-hearted acceptance to firm rejection.

The Concept of Client-centered Counseling

Client-centered counseling had its origin with the early work of Carl Rogers [16] and has received considerable attention since that time. Stefflre includes the client-centered approach as one of four major theories of counseling.[17] The experiences of Carl Rogers and his contributions to the philosophy of counseling have probably done more to stimulate thinking, action, and the development of new approaches in counseling than any other person or concept. Any honest, serious study of counseling and psychotherapy should include thoughtful consideration of Rogers' thinking and proposals. Certainly, the same statement holds for an exploration of other views and philosophies and for considering the contributions of other authorities, irrespective of philosophical biases.

Rogers points out that there are certain characteristics of the client-centered psychotherapy: (1) the aim is to assist the individual to grow and gain his independence; (2) it places greater stress upon the emotional elements, endeavoring to work in the realm of feeling and emotion rather than to use an intellectual

[16] Carl R. Rogers, *Counseling and Psychotherapy*, Houghton Mifflin Company, Boston, 1942.
[17] *Op. cit.*

approach; (3) the immediate situation is the important consideration rather than concern about the past; (4) the therapeutic experience provides the opportunity for and promotes growth of the
client.[18] These points of emphasis are still fundamental to the
client-centered approach.

Characteristics of client-centered counseling. The major elements
which characterize client-centered counseling are briefly summarized below with no attempt to supply details. Additional reading
should prove helpful.[19]

1 The quality of the relationship between counselor and client
is of maximum importance. The *relationship* is the heart of
therapy. Progress realized by the client in therapy and the benefits gained depend to a high degree upon this relationship.
Although the devoutly committed client-centered counselor is
not likely to deviate from his procedures of reflecting feeling,
he might well take the view that the exact nature of the techniques is relatively minor—the relationship is the important
element.

2 There is an element of the subjective within this relationship.
This is inevitable, since the structuring is kept to a minimum
and there is considerable freedom for expressing feelings.
There is no mechanical, objective, routine set of procedures to
observe.

3 It is a theoretical construct which permits considerable freedom, exploration, and experimentation. The client-centered
theory is not a dogmatic system making unrealistic demands
upon its adherents.

4 The emotional aspects of the relationship are far more important than the intellectual. If one can work through his feelings
and gain the necessary emotional insights, the necessary intellectual insights will also occur. Feelings of the client are paramount, and the feelings of the counselor are equally significant
as they contribute to the relationship and stimulate client
growth.

5 The interaction within the relationship is the element which
provides the catharsis by which the client gains relief from his
guilt and other negative feelings and through which he gains
emotional strength upon which to build for greater future security. Client and counselor are thus engaged in an intimate,

[18] Rogers, *op. cit.* pp. 28–30.
[19] Two excellent sources are Dugald S. Arbuckle, *Pupil Personnel Services in American Schools,* Allyn and Bacon, Inc., Boston, 1962, pp. 169–189,
and Donald L. Grummon, in Stefflre, *op. cit.,* chap. 2.

emotionalized, therapeutic relationship with the potential for mutual benefits and with reciprocal responsibilities.

6   The immediate situation is the focus of attention, its accompanying feelings providing the fountain for expression. Historical events of the past and prognostications for the future receive little more than casual attention.

7   The counseling experience provides the opportunity for growth. The possibilities for maturing, improved stability, and better adjustment are increased as a person profits from, and grows as a result of, his experiences in this relationship.

8   Counselor responsibility is generally regarded as less than that of the directive counselor. The client assumes considerable responsibility for himself in therapy and in the decisions he makes. However, it should be noted that the difference might be in the nature of the responsibility rather than its quantity.

9   Giving advice, making interpretations, and diagnosing, as generally defined, have no place. Freedom of thought, immunity from coercion, and individual responsibility mark the client-centered approach. Advising, interpreting, and diagnosing limit the client's freedom and may threaten rather than aid his growth.

10   The relationship is warm, accepting, and permissive but is relatively narrow in its coverage, since it does not include guidance, imparting information, or advisement. Counseling is regarded as an activity distinct from the other educational, medical, or sociological services.

11   Both flexibility and limits characterize the client-centered approach. There is considerable freedom within the relationship, but the counselor believes in being consistent. He is not willing to deviate markedly from his beliefs or commitments and thus jeopardize his chances for an objective assessment of his counseling. Besides, the client-centered counselor believes in what he is doing and has faith in the outcome. He feels no impulse to change.

Clinical, or Directive, Counseling

Although the positions on particular elements in a counseling approach may vary among individual counselors within each method, for purposes of simplification and clarification the directive approach may be arbitrarily placed at the opposite end from the client-centered approach on a continuum representing different views on some points. This, however, might lead one to conclude that the directive approach either minimizes or entirely eliminates from its repertoire of techniques and theories the eleven elements of the client-centered method, a conclusion that would be somewhat inaccurate and therefore could lead to misunderstandings. For example, the client-centered approach emphasizes the immediate situation and the emotional aspects of the problem, while the directive stresses the past, the history of the problem, and the intellectual aspects. However, the directive technique is also interested in the present and in the feelings of the client. Not only are these differences a matter of degree, but also the goals of the two methods are essentially the same, even though the procedures for achieving them are different.

The following are some points of emphasis within the directive approach:

1 Considerable responsibility is assumed by the counselor. This is made manifest in the structuring he provides, the direction he gives, his activity in the relationship, and his sharing in the decisions and outcomes.

2 There is concern for techniques, procedures, and the systematic attack upon problems. Whereas in the client-centered approach procedures are incidental and almost ignored, the more directive counselor uses specified procedures as means for the attainment of anticipated goals.

3 Counseling tools such as test data, records, case histories, and various reports play an important part in the counseling effort. Objective data are used to improve client self-understanding and to serve as guides to the counselor in determining procedures to be used and decisions to be made.

4 Diagnosis is a major step in the therapeutic relationship. Possible causes of problems are determined, the significance of these causes in terms of the present status of the client is ascertained, and decisions are made for courses of action.

5 Interpretation is considered a responsibility, since the client depends upon the professional competence of the counselor for possible answers to his problems and for direction in dealing with them. The counselor interprets for the client to aid him in gaining intellectual insights and understandings from which future progress and growth can be realized.

6 Purposeful questions are posed by the counselor to stimulate the thinking of the client and to gain information. He has no compunctions about asking questions or noting for the client the implications of his answers. Counselor direction is given throughout, although there is client participation, as well.

7 The problem and its ramifications are considered with the calm objectivity of the scientist. The intellectual aspects of the problem, not the emotional, demand first attention. If the client is

emotional, the logical procedure is to help him gain emotional control so that he can more effectively utilize his intellectual capabilities.

8 Decisions reached are to a great extent those of the counselor, but with the aid and approval of the client. The counselor can justify maximum involvement here by stating that the essential preliminaries to a decision making have been covered adequately and thus a decision has been reached which is in reality a consensus of the client and the counselor.

9 Eclecticism plays a larger part in directive counseling than in the client-centered method. The directive counselor shifts back and forth from elements of one of these approaches to those of the other with greater freedom than does the client-centered counselor. He might, for example, reflect feeling much as the client-centered counselor does. The latter is not likely, however, to use diagnosis or interpretation.

10 Judgments of tools, instruments, and techniques to be used and decisions to be made are the prerogatives of the counselor. However, he is not likely to extend the making of judgments to judging people, moral values, or behavior.

Certain techniques or responses are generally regarded as off limits to all counselors, irrespective of orientation. Moral judgment is one of these, particularly if it involves preaching, moralizing, or coercing. Another is undue probing. Human dignity, integrity, and self-esteem must be respected and protected under all circumstances. Threatening, badgering, and extracting promises likewise have no place in therapy. Promoting one's own biases, extolling the virtues of any point of view, or soliciting an interest in any thing, person, or belief have no place within counseling. The intimacy, warmth, and permissiveness of the therapeutic relationship require that the counselor's behavior exemplify dignity, poise, integrity, and honor.

The Eclectic Approach

The eclectic approach to counseling is best characterized by its freedom to use whatever techniques or procedures seem to the counselor to be most appropriate at any particular time. It might utilize client-centered procedures at one time and follow the structured techniques of the directive counselor at another. The counselor with the eclectic approach also assumes the prerogatives of rejecting either or both of the other two approaches and using his own or of modifying the client-centered or the directive to suit his purposes. In the eclectic technique the counselor is not limited to any one operational viewpoint or method.

A word of caution to the counselor who regards himself as eclectic: Eclecticism assumes high-level competence and should never be used as a rationalization by the counselor for indiscriminate use or neglect of particular procedures advocated in other philosophies. The competent eclectic counselor is well acquainted with all the major theories or philosophies in counseling and uses this knowledge in choosing techniques and in the establishment of a positive working relationship with the client. A rejection of any philosophical framework is justified by the counselor if he has a better way to accomplish the tasks at hand. Incumbent upon him is the responsibility for knowing what he is rejecting, why he is rejecting it, and what will better serve his purposes.

Many counselors regard themselves as eclectic. This position is logical in view of the variety of individuals and personalities receiving counseling and the great range of problems requiring consideration. Many counselors hold in disfavor the relatively restricted areas of operation imposed respectively by the client-centered and the directive approaches and prefer a position of greater freedom and comfort on the continuum.

The client-centered and directive procedures and viewpoints are all open to the eclectic counselor but with greater freedom than to either the client-centered or directive counselor. He has not made the same commitment of allegiance, nor is he as concerned about being consistent.

A summary of the eclectic view may be helpful in clarifying relationships among the various approaches:

1 The methods used are justified by the counselor because of their appropriateness for both the client and the counselor. These methods may change from client to client or even with the same client.

2 Flexibility is characteristic, making a shifting of emphasis in techniques possible and in some cases desirable.

3 Freedom of choice and of expression is open to both counselor and client. Inhibiting influences and feelings of guilt by the client are minimized or eliminated.

4 Modification of methods is made in an effort to accommodate the client, and philosophical frameworks are adjusted to serve the purposes of the relationship.

5 Feelings of comfort are essential. Both people must feel good about what they are doing, experience mutual confidence, and have faith in the relationship.

6   Adaptations are made within the intellectual and emotional structure of the client as he makes an effort to capitalize on his best
resources. He utilizes the concepts of the best philosophies
available to him in bringing about desired changes in his behavior. The counselor, likewise, makes adaptations and adjustments.

Similarities are at once evident as the characteristics of the
client-centered, directive, and eclectic techniques are reviewed. The
overlap between points in some cases is so pronounced as to make
an exact differentiation almost impossible. This condition is not to
be abhorred, however, since the differences in philosophical viewpoints are those of degree rather than of characteristics. There are
certain views which should permeate all counseling encounters and
certain procedures which have a place in all counseling, irrespective
of one's orientation. These views and procedures, which are presented in the next chapter, are elements essential to any counseling
relationship but in no particular order and with varying degrees of
intensity.

SUMMARY/

The counseling service is the most essential of all the basic elements
of the guidance program. Within this activity students are assisted
in resolving their problems and aided in planning for the future.
Personal development is a major aim of this service. Students are
given the opportunity for free expression within a setting of privacy
and acceptance. Counseling is a professional service unique in the
nature of its activities and with established criteria by which its
status is assessed. Although it is both a process and a relationship,
emphasis is given to counseling as a relationship wherein the atmosphere of the setting itself provides for client development.

Many conditions within the society and within the nature of
youngsters make the need for counseling quite evident. The educational experiences of youngsters become more meaningful and
profitable as they benefit from this essential service.

The client-centered, directive (or clinical), and eclectic techniques in counseling represent varying views as to the degree of
direct participation by the counselor and the student. Each represents a position on a continuum, but none should be regarded as
distinct and completely separate from the other two. The concept of
the continuum is used for purposes of illustrating techniques and

to note how various counselors go about establishing a good working relationship.

PROBLEMS/

1   Why is counseling regarded as the "heart" of the guidance service? Explain how the other basic elements of the guidance service depend upon the counseling program.

2   Enumerate some of the major benefits to come from counseling. Suppose a student has no particular problems, is it possible for him nevertheless to benefit from the counseling experience? How? Can you justify the cost of using the counseling service for students who are getting along satisfactorily?

3   Define "counseling" as it is used in an educational or clinical setting. Point out the major differences between this kind of counseling and counseling as a term used in business circles.

4   Explain how counseling can be both a process and a relationship. It has been noted that it is possible for one or the other to receive the major emphasis; what would the view of the client-centered counselor be on this point? What would be the view of the clinically oriented, or more directive, type of counselor?

5   In what way does Williamson place importance on the counselor in the relationship? To what extent do you agree or disagree with Williamson? Defend your answer.

6   The chapter provides five criteria for counseling. Of what value are these criteria to people in training for counseling positions and for counselors currently involved in counseling?

7   Account for the fact that the counseling service has been limited to the secondary school and largely ignored at the elementary school level. What is the current thinking on this problem?

8   Note some conditions in society and in education which indicate the need for the counseling service. In which cases can counseling be of the greatest assistance?

9   Note some of the ways in which the typical student can profit from the counseling experience. How much is known about the benefits gained by students from counseling? What is needed?

10 Explain how counseling and teaching differ. What are some similarities or overlapping elements?

11 How can the teacher be of the greatest service to the counseling service? To what extent does the teacher conduct counseling sessions which would be consistent with the counseling criteria developed in this chapter?

12 What changes might be expected in a student's behavior if he is profiting from the counseling he is receiving from a qualified counselor? How does this help the teacher?

13 What are some of the advantages that may result from differing views as to the true nature of counseling? What are possible undesirable results?

14 What is the major responsibility of the counselor as he seeks to find his own philosophical position? Why is it difficult for the ill-prepared counselor to do this?

15 For purposes of review, note the most important characteristics of each of the categories of counseling concepts. What are the limitations inherent in this kind of classification? What are the strengths, or benefits?

Selected References

Textbooks

ARBUCKLE, DUGALD S.: *Pupil Personnel Services in American Schools*, Allyn and Bacon, Inc., Boston, 1962, chap. 5.

FROEHLICH, CLIFFORD P.: *Guidance Services in Schools*, 2d ed., McGraw-Hill Book Company, New York, 1958, chap. 10.

FULLMER, DANIEL W., and HAROLD W. BERNARD: *Counseling: Content and Process*, Science Research Associates, Inc., Chicago, 1964, chaps. 4, 5, 7.

GLANZ, EDWARD C.: *Foundations and Principles of Guidance*, Allyn and Bacon, Inc., Boston, 1964, chap. 5.

HUMPHREYS, J. ANTHONY, ARTHUR E. TRAXLER, and ROBERT D. NORTH: *Guidance Services*, Science Research Associates, Inc., Chicago, 1960, chap. 8.

HUTSON, PERCIVAL W.: *The Guidance Function in Education*, Appleton-Century-Crofts, Inc., New York, 1958, chaps. 15 and 16.

JOHNSON, MAURITZ, WILLIAM E. BUSAKER, and FRED Q. BOWMAN: *Junior High School Guidance*, Harper & Row, Publishers, Incorporated, New York, 1961, chap. 5.

JOHNSON, WALTER F., BUFORD STEFFLRE, and ROY A. EDELFELT: *Pupil Personnel and Guidance Services*, McGraw-Hill Book Company, New York, 1961, chap. 16.

KOWITZ, GERALD T., and NORMA G. KOWITZ: *Guidance in the Elementary Classroom*, McGraw-Hill Book Company, 1959, chap. 8.

LOUGHARY, JOHN W., ROBERT O. STRIPLING, and PAUL W. FITZGERALD: *Counseling: A Growing Profession,* joint publication of the Association for Counselor Education and Supervision and American School Counselors Association, Divisions of the American Personnel and Guidance Association, Washington, D.C., 1965.

MC DANIEL, HENRY B.: *Guidance in the Modern School,* The Dryden Press, Inc., New York, 1956, chap. 6.

——— and others: *Readings in Guidance,* Holt, Rinehart and Winston, Inc., New York, 1959, chaps. 8–10.

MC GOWAN, JOHN F., and LYLE D. SCHMIDT: *Counseling: Readings in Theory and Practice,* Holt, Rinehart and Winston, Inc., New York, 1962.

MILLER, FRANK W.: *Guidance Principles and Services,* Charles E. Merrill Books, Inc., Englewood Cliffs, N.J., 1961, chap. 6.

MORTENSEN, DONALD G., and ALLEN M. SCHMULLER: *Guidance in Today's Schools,* John Wiley & Sons, Inc., New York, 1959, chap. 12.

OHLSEN, MERLE M.: *Guidance Services in the Modern School,* Harcourt, Brace & World, Inc., New York, 1964, chaps. 12 and 13.

PETERS, HERMAN J., and others: *Counseling: Selected Readings,* Charles E. Merrill Books, Inc., Englewood Cliffs, N.J., 1962.

ROGERS, CARL R.: *Client-centered Therapy,* Houghton Mifflin Company, Boston, 1951.

SHERTZER, BRUCE, and HERMAN J. PETERS: *Guidance: Techniques for Individual Appraisal and Development,* The Macmillan Company, New York, 1965, chap. 3.

SMITH, GLENN E.: *Principles and Practices of the Guidance Program,* The Macmillan Company, New York, 1951, chap. 8.

STOOPS, EMERY, and GUNNAR L. WAHLQUIST: *Principles and Practices in Guidance,* McGraw-Hill Book Company, 1958, chap. 6.

TRAXLER, ARTHUR E., and ROBERT D. NORTH: *Techniques of Guidance,* 3d ed., Harper & Row, Publishers, Incorporated, New York, 1966, chap. 19.

WILLEY, ROY DE VERL, and DEAN C. ANDREW: *Modern Methods and Techniques in Guidance,* Harper & Row, Publishers, Incorporated, New York, 1955, chap. 14.

WILLIAMSON, E. G.: *Counseling Adolescents,* McGraw-Hill Book Company, New York, 1950.

WRENN, C. GILBERT: *The Counselor in a Changing World,* American Personnel and Guidance Association, Washington, D.C., 1962, chaps. 4 and 6.

Journals

ADAMS, J. F.: "Ethical Responsibilities in Counseling; Excerpts from Problems in Counseling: A Case Study Approach," *School and Society,* vol. 90, pp. 34–40, Jan. 27, 1962.

APPELL, MOREY L.: "Self-understanding for the Guidance Counselor," *Personnel and Guidance Journal,* vol. 42, pp. 143–148, October, 1963.

ARBUCKLE, DUGALD S.: "Counseling: Philosophy or Science?" *Personnel and Guidance Journal,* vol. 39, pp. 11–14, September, 1960.

———: "Existentialism in Counseling: The Humanist View," *Personnel and Guidance Journal,* vol. 43, pp. 558–567, February, 1965.

———: "Learning of Counseling: Process Not Product," *Journal of Counseling Psychology,* vol. 10, pp. 163–168, Summer, 1963.

BENTLEY, JOSEPH C.: "Role Theory in Counseling: A Problem in Definition," *Personnel and Guidance Journal*, vol. 44, pp. 11–17, September, 1965.

BERGSTEIN, HARRY B., and CLAUDE W. GRANT: "How Parents Perceive the Counselor's Role," *Personnel and Guidance Journal*, vol. 39, pp. 698–703, May, 1961.

BERNARD, HAROLD W.: "Socioeconomic Class and the School Counselor," *Theory into Practice*, vol. 2, pp. 17–23, 1963.

CHAPIN, ARTHUR B., DAVID E. CLOSSON, and JOHN P. LEMBO: "Career Counseling Builds Good Will," *Bulletin of the National Association of Secondary-school Principals*, vol. 44, pp. 63–67, September, 1960.

CLARK, CHARLES M.: "Confidentiality and the School Counselor," *Personnel and Guidance Journal*, vol. 43, pp. 482–484, January, 1965.

COLLINS, MILTON E.: "Place of Counseling in a Guidance Program," *Teachers College Journal*, vol. 31, pp. 62–63, December, 1959.

COMBS, ARTHUR W.: "Counseling as Learning," *Journal of Counseling Psychology*, vol. 1, no. 1, pp. 31–36, 1954.

COTTLE, WILLIAM C.: "Some Common Elements in Counseling," *Personnel and Guidance Journal*, vol. 32, pp. 4–8, September, 1953.

DREIFFUS, EDWARD A.: "The Counselor and Existentialism," *Personnel and Guidance Journal*, vol. 43, pp. 114–117, October, 1964.

ERICKSON, KENNETH A.: "Blueprint for Counseling Programs," *Phi Delta Kappan*, vol. 43, pp. 309–311, April, 1962.

FROEHLICH, CLIFFORD P.: "Stars, Parson, and Clients," *Personnel and Guidance Journal*, vol. 36, pp. 10–16, September, 1957.

GILBERT, MARY E.: "Counselor's Year in Review," *Personnel and Guidance Journal*, vol. 38, pp. 493–496, February, 1960.

HERR, EDWIN L.: "Field theory and Differential Press: Implications for Counseling," *Personnel and Guidance Journal*, vol. 43, pp. 586–590, February, 1965.

HOBBS, NICHOLAS: "Complete Counselor," *Personnel and Guidance Journal*, vol. 36, pp. 594–602, May, 1958.

KABACK, GOLDIE RUTH: "Who is the School Counselor?" *Education*, vol. 80, pp. 438–440, March, 1960.

KOILE, EARL A.: "Counseling Policies and Programs," *School Review*, vol. 69, no. 2, pp. 181–190, Summer, 1961.

LANDSMAN, TED: "Existentialism in Counseling: The Scientific View," *Personnel and Guidance Journal*, vol. 43, pp. 568–573, February, 1965.

LAYTON, WILBER L.: "Constructs and Communication in Counseling: A Limited Theory," *Journal of Counseling Psychology*, vol. 8, no. 1, pp. 3–6, Spring, 1961.

MILLER, CARROLL H.: "Defining the Role of the Counselor," *Education*, vol. 81, no. 4, pp. 198–201, December, 1960.

MINK, OSCAR G., and M. SGAN: "Does Counselor Approach Really Matter?" *Vocational Guidance Quarterly*, vol. 11, pp. 204–206, Spring, 1963.

NASH, PAUL: "Some Notes toward a Philosophy of School Counseling," *Personnel and Guidance Journal*, vol. 43, pp. 243–248, November, 1964.

NELSON, A. GORDON: "Dr. Conant and Program Counseling," *High School Journal*, vol. 43, pp. 139–142, January, 1960.

ROEBER, EDWARD C.: "Counseling Which Approach?" *Theory into Practice*, vol. 2, pp. 4–9, 1963.

ROGERS, CARL R.: "A Note on the Nature of Man," *Journal of Counseling Psychology*, vol. 4, pp. 199–203, 1957.

———: "Person or Science . . . ?" *The American Psychologist*, vol. 10, pp. 267–278, July, 1955.

SHOBEN, EDWARD J., JR.: "Counselor's Theory as Personal Trait," *Personnel and Guidance Journal*, vol. 40, pp. 617–621, March, 1962.

STILLER, ALFRED: "High School Guidance Counselor," *Bulletin of the National Association Secondary-school Principals*, Vol. 45, pp. 150–159, May, 1961.

TIEDEMAN, DAVID V., and FRANK L. FIELD: "Guidance: The Science of Purposeful Action Applied through Education," *Harvard Educational Review*, vol. 32, pp. 483–501, Fall, 1962.

VAUGHAN, RICHARD P.: "Existentialism in Counseling: The Religious View," *Personnel and Guidance Journal*, vol. 43, pp. 553–557, February, 1965.

VAN KAAM, ADRIAN: "Counseling from the Viewpoint of Existential Psychology," *Harvard Educational Review*, vol. 32, no. 4, p. 403, Fall, 1962.

WALKER, DONALD E.: "Carl Rogers and the Nature of Man," *Journal of Counseling Psychology*, vol. 3, no. 2, pp. 89–90, 1956.

WEITZ, H.: "Guidance as Behavior Change: With Comments by E. J. Shoben," *Personnel and Guidance Journal*, vol. 39, pp. 550–562, March, 1961.

WELCH, FRANK: "The High School Counselor," *Education*, vol. 82, pp. 332–335, February, 1962.

WILLIAMSON, E. G.: "Counseling in Developing Self-confidence," *Personnel and Guidance Journal*, vol. 34, pp. 398–404, March, 1956.

EIGHT

/COUNSELING AS AN INTEGRATION OF VARIOUS APPROACHES

Effective counseling is an outcome of the counselor's intensive study of the various views presented by recognized authorities and of his own dedication to self-understanding and self-improvement. Each counselor must develop for himself suitable techniques by which his effectiveness with his clients is enhanced. His study of the literature and of the work of other counselors bears fruit in new insights and improved skills. These efforts result in the establishment of a framework of concepts and guides from which he can operate. Differences in views between the counselor and his colleagues may be reconciled as he gains in competence and proves his effectiveness with students. Adaptations and modifications of approaches and procedures may be made as these differences are reconciled and as the counselor strengthens his own theoretical position through research findings and support from others. Among the questions he must ask himself in consolidating his views are "What theoretical position is best for me and my students?" "What procedures hold the greatest promise for success?" "How can I best improve my competence and skill?"

Possible answers to these and other pertinent questions may be found in the establishment and utilization of some common guidelines. A formulated framework of philosophies and methods on which to draw in his work is essential for every counselor. The typical school counselor recognizes the need for flexibility in his relationships, since he is working with a great number and variety of youngsters. He also regards extremes in attitudes and methods as undesirable, since they may contribute to the anxieties of youngsters, fail to provide the necessary opportunity for growth, or leave them with the feeling that no help was given.

Essential Elements in Counseling

Irrespective of a counselor's orientation or theory preference, there are certain components which characterize the counseling relationship. These components must be present to some degree in all cases. The success of the counseling then depends upon the quality of the relationship established and upon the thoroughness with which each of the essential elements is incorporated into this relationship.

There are also some real dangers associated with a hasty commitment to some one theory or point of view. The counselor preparation program should provide the prospective counselor with opportunities to become well acquainted with a number of theoretical views and conversant with the various issues. A premature alignment with some one theory will result in a narrowness of thought and action as unbecoming in the growing student as in the professional counselor. Practice must respect theory and depend upon it for aid in the establishment of principles of procedure, but theory should not dictate the details of practice. The counselor at all levels of professional competence and experience must constantly maintain an open mind and a seeking attitude. The counselor who has "arrived" in all probability has not come very far, nor is he likely to do so in the future.

Anticipating the Interview

The preparatory stage in counseling occurs prior to the actual contact. As the interview with the student is anticipated, certain preliminary and study procedures are observed. The efficiency with which the counseling is conducted and its resultant helpfulness to the student are determined to a great extent by the quality of these preliminary activities and the seriousness with which the counselor regards these functions.

A casual review of the cumulative folder, an inquiry directed to a teacher, or observations of a youngster in school may serve as preliminary ways of gaining information. If there is a substantial amount of information readily available, the counselor will need only to review and organize it for rapid and efficient use. If needed data are not available, steps may be taken to obtain them, either prior to the actual counseling or as activities associated with the counseling relationship. It is well for the counselor to become somewhat acquainted with the client prior to the interview, even though he still does not know what the client's problems are. Even the client-centered counselor will find the gaining of certain basic information about a student ahead of time to be advantageous rather than detrimental. Knowing too much about the student is not an issue here. The test of effectiveness is in the intelligence, maturity, and competence of the counselor demonstrated by his ability to use information properly and his capacity to minimize or eliminate biases. Delays or floundering are costly and embarrassing for counselor and student.

As basic information is obtained prior to the initial interview, only a review of the counselor's notes will be necessary as preparation for succeeding contacts. Although the counselor's concern is with the client's present and future rather than the past, he needs to know enough about the past to facilitate present adjustments and expedite plans for the future.

Developing a Positive Working Relationship

The development of a positive, warm, accepting working relationship between counselor and client is basic to all counseling, be it one interview or long-term therapy. The quality of the atmosphere within which the relationship is developed is a point of major consideration. Certain techniques of the counselor might contribute to counseling effectiveness, but these procedures are important only as they make a direct contribution to the relationship itself. A good working relationship is thus characterized by mutual (1) understanding, (2) acceptance, (3) respect, (4) confidence, (5) concern, and (6) faith in the future. A positive working relationship develops as counselor and client combine their efforts in a mutually satisfying experience. These desirable influences are essential to progress and should, therefore, be present early in therapy and throughout its total course.

Counseling theory or orientation determines to a degree the methods employed by the counselor, since counselors within the various theoretical structures have varying notions as to the appropriateness of certain procedures. However, techniques are used as means to ends and are important only as they contribute to the quality of the relationship. Indeed, an excellent relationship is regarded as an end from which more desirable adjustments and more logical decisions may be made. The ultimate objective is, of course, client growth and progress. This objective is most quickly realized and most satisfactorily maintained if the counseling reflects a warm, good relationship between counselor and client.

This relationship is, then, both a reflection and a determiner of the attitudes of the two participants. A positive attitude, which includes a willingness to make an effort to resolve problems, helps realize and maintain a strong relationship. Attitudes also improve as counselor and counselee experience feelings of satisfaction in the relationship and as worthwhile results become apparent.

Exploring Feelings and Attitudes

The opportunity for a free, uninhibited exploration of feelings and attitudes is an element of maximum significance in all counseling and therapy. The setting makes possible a concerted attack upon problems and candid expressions of concerns and beliefs. Logical, intelligent approaches to problem resolution and the attainment of insights are possible to perhaps a higher degree in counseling than in any other setting. The permissive atmosphere, unique structure, and counselor personality all contribute to a relationship and an experience with unusual growth potentiality.

There are many cases, however, within the school where students are concerned primarily with planning and decision making. In many instances they may be seeking information needed to carry out plans and decide on courses of action. Emotions are generally of less concern in these cases than is true with problems of a more personal and intimate nature. Even here, however, the connotative aspects of the problem and the verbal expressions of the student should be considered. The exploration of feelings and the free expression of emotions contribute to the student's ability to proceed with his plans with the benefit of new insights and increasing self-understanding. Self-appraisal techniques are developed and attitudes are modified during the early years when youngsters are flexible and still in the "process of becoming." The guidance provided and the opportunities made available through counseling make the entire developmental process of youth more enjoyable, challenging, meaningful, and fruitful.

Reviewing and Determining Present Status

Together, the counselor and client come to some determination as to the client's present status. To do this a brief review of the past may be desirable by which the conditions of the present come to have more significance. Also, as an understanding of current status is ascertained, the appropriate action for future progress becomes more apparent. Such questions as these may then be considered by the student as an effort is made to come to a clear understanding of where he is now and to decide what must be done for improvements:

1 What is the quality of my relationship with other people in my environment? Where do I stand? How do we get along?
2 Do I have the insight to note weaknesses in myself? What am I doing to improve myself?
3 Do I have the necessary resources and strength to make a ready adjustment to incidents and events in my life? Am I able to accept setbacks and disappointments with poise and with a degree of confidence which will make continued progress possible?
4 Am I evasive and prone to rationalization, or do I come to grips with critical problems and make an effort to resolve them? Does my behavior in the face of adversity indicate strength, and are my methods of handling situations usually adequate, or do I need to change?
5 Are my educational and vocational plans realistic? Am I aware of my strengths and limitations, and do I know how to capitalize on the former and minimize the latter?

These and other questions may serve as points from which to build the counseling relationship. As concerted attention is given to the matter of current status, possibilities for improved behavior become known, and better time utilization for self-improvement is achieved. These questions also suggest the importance of three conditions essential to any successful counseling: (1) careful, serious thought about oneself and his relationship to other people; (2) a willingness to work and commit one's energies to a goal of self-improvement and to problem resolution; and (3) an attitude of concern for the future from which appropriate plans are formulated.

Decisions are then made as to how to proceed in order to best utilize talents and abilities. Possible courses of action are determined as the relative merits of the alternatives are assessed. The student comes to see himself in a more realistic perspective and arrives at an objective realization of his true status within his environment.

Considering Existing Problems

An honest, straightforward self-appraisal is essential for the student as he works toward better self-understanding and as he considers courses of action for resolving his problems. Self-understanding and progress depend upon a student's facing his problems resolutely and upon his feelings of confidence for dealing with these problems as they occur. Counseling affords the student the opportunity to recognize incongruities in his life and to relegate each problem to its proper level of significance. The counseling session permits a careful consideration of concerns, attitudes, aspirations, frustrations, and plans. No other setting is comparable to that afforded by counseling. Here the student is able to give his undivided attention and full energies to matters of vital concern in a favorable atmosphere and with the aid and support of a professional person.

Counseling also has the inherent potential for being a profitable experience for most people even if no problem exists. Its usefulness extends beyond just a consideration of problems. Aid can be provided prior to or during the very early stages of the existence of problems. Possible failures, events, and indecision can be anticipated, and appropriate action initiated in order to avoid difficulties and disappointments. Thus counseling is for everyone, not just youngsters already facing serious difficulties.

Exploring Alternatives

Various alternative courses of action are generally available to a person as he seeks answers to his problems and as he plans for the future. Each alternative should be given careful consideration before it is discarded. This exploration of possibilities is accomplished within the counseling setting. Prior to making the final decisions client and counselor both suggest possibilities, and both give intelligent consideration to the various choices. Choices made under these favorable conditions are much more likely to be appropriate for the client than those made by student judgment only.

Giving careful consideration to alternatives is a more logical approach than the outright giving of advice and usually eliminates the need to give advice. Decisions are reached without it.

Making Decisions

Another essential element of counseling is arriving at a decision. This comes after a consideration of the problem and an exploration of the alternatives, which includes an anticipation of possible outcomes of any one choice. Merely making a decision is not enough. Judgments must be made in accordance with known facts and expected results.

Postponing a decision beyond a reasonable time creates new problems and retards progress. However, undue haste is equally undesirable, since it carries the risk of using poor judgment and making inappropriate decisions. Therefore many of the counseling activities serve as background experiences from which right choices are made at the most expedient time. Client and counselor can generally sense the best time to make the final choice, and they are able to strike a balance between haste and procrastination.

Postcounseling Contacts

Much of the genuine benefit to be gained from counseling and of the growth which eventually takes place actually occurs during the interval between interviews. The stimulation may come from the sessions, but the motivation, the improvement in behavior, and the increase in the student's confidence and maturity of his desires are to be used to advantage during the times when he is largely on his own.

The termination of counseling sessions should not constitute a permanent break from all contact with the student. The counselor needs to be aware of his progress and have some knowledge as to the appropriateness of the choices made and the effectiveness of the counseling. The student may also need additional help with his original problem or help with new problems.

The Counselor's Functions

The quality of the counseling relationship and the success with which the basic elements of the guidance services are carried out obviously depend upon the competence of the counselor. Appropriate professional training, personal characteristics, and background of work and educational experiences are all basic to the functions of the counselor. Unfortunately, too many school counselors do not meet the criteria of competence; the quality of their services is too often considerably below standard. A study of counselor functions should result in a stronger determination by counselors and those aspiring to be counselors to make a greater effort to prepare themselves adequately for the work they are to do. Improvement through dedication and concerted effort should be an aim of every professional counselor.

The counselor's major responsibility is, of course, counseling. However, the typical school counselor also has administrative and leadership responsibilities, functions with the pupil inventory system of guidance records and testing, obligations as a consultant for other professional people, and duties associated with evaluation and research. The size of the system, the number of counselors and their specific assignments, and the administrative structure of the school are all factors which help to determine the degree to which any one counselor assumes certain responsibilities. For example, a large school with a proportionately large counseling staff may so divide the labor as to permit areas of specialization for each counselor and by doing this make possible a greater time commitment to counseling without neglect of other important related functions. Although the tasks of the counselor may vary somewhat from school to school, there are basic functions of the counselor which should be essentially the same in all schools. These are enumerated and discussed in this section. The influence of the school's expectations of the counselor is also considered.

Expectations of the School

The counselor has a responsibility to himself and to the profession to give his best efforts to his functions and to protect himself against unrealistic and inappropriate demands upon his time and energies. Under the pressure and urgent demands incident to the operation of a school, the administrator may take advantage of the counselor's availability and relegate to him tasks which are not a part of the guidance service. This situation calls for a clarification of roles and an understanding as to the true function of the counselor. The expectations of the school should be in keeping with the responsibilities of the counselor as a professional person trained and committed to provide specialized services to the students in a school.

The expectations of the school to be met by the counselor may include the following:

1 The counselor should understand the educational process and should have a genuine commitment to education. His work with youngsters and with the staff should reflect this orientation and concern. Since he functions in an educational setting, he is an educator as well as a counselor.

2 He should be a highly competent person with the necessary skills and knowledge to work and perform effectively with students and teachers. He should be a source of information and a provider of specialized services not normally available elsewhere.

3 He should be available to students and the staff for the services he is prepared to provide. He is more than a member of the guidance team; he is the ranking authority on guidance and counseling procedure.

4 He has some responsibility for the personal welfare of each student. The school expects him to have and to demonstrate an interest in, and concern for, the welfare of others.

5 He should be constantly profiting from his experiences and professional study, and should bring his influence to bear in developing a stronger program of guidance services. Continuous improvement should be a goal.

Individualized Services

Services designed to provide aid and attention for each youngster include counseling, but they also include other activities which make possible contact between counselor and student, though with perhaps less formality than is characteristic of the counseling interview. Informal visits, casual observations in the classroom, and encouraging remarks at any appropriate time are examples of this individualized service. The teacher also shares in these activities but in a somewhat different manner because of his somewhat different relationship to the child and because of the heavy demands made upon him by his teaching functions. Individual attention is frequently given by the good teacher to each child, but this attention is generally motivated by the academic needs of the child. The counselor can assist in providing for other kinds of needs.

The time schedule of the counselor may be more flexible than that of the teacher, which makes it easier for him to give individual attention to a child. However, the daily schedule should include a specified period for counseling and other personal services, and should be relatively free of demands unrelated to his major functions as a counselor. Within the typical school a variety of tasks must be carried out. Administrative arrangements should provide for the performance of these tasks by secretaries, teaching assistants, and administrative aids. Unwarranted demands upon the energies of teachers and counselors should be kept to a minimum.

Administrative and Leadership Activities

Certain administrative and leadership functions associated with conducting a guidance program are the prerogatives and responsibilities of the counselor. The extent, nature, and degree of this responsibility depend upon the administrative structure under which the counselor functions. The director of pupil personnel services is, for example, primarily an administrative officer, while a head counselor's time is divided between leadership activities and counseling. A counselor functioning under a head counselor is relatively free of administrative duties and gives his full time to counseling and guidance activities.

Administrative functions of the counselor include the development and promotion of a cooperative effort with the school administration. It is most essential that counselors and administrators support and aid each other in a setting of mutual concern and effort. Leadership in in-service training activities is another counselor function. He takes the lead in structuring the guidance services, in enlisting the assistance of others, and in formulating plans for future action.

The coordination of all guidance activities in an effort to ensure their functioning efficiently and effectively is also a counselor responsibility. Duplication of effort is kept low, with all school personnel properly utilized and a plan of operation put into effect.

Services with Pupil Inventories

The pupil inventory includes guidance records and testing, and constitutes an area of activity which requires the services of the counselor. The cumulative records are maintained under his direc-

tion. He provides instructions and suggestions in the proper recording of data and in the effective utilization of all guidance records.
The program of standardized testing, with careful selection, administration, and interpretation of tests, is carried out under his leadership.

Teachers' meetings, in-service training sessions, and personal
contacts are all areas in which the counselor functions as a leader.
He provides instructions by which teachers are prepared to help
administer and interpret test results and by which they can make a
full utilization of the cumulative record. He also interprets recorded
data and test results to individual students and to student groups
organized for this purpose.

The Counselor as a Consultant and Resource Person

The counselor is a specialist in certain areas of human behavior
and is informed about possible procedures to use in aiding youngsters. He acts as a consultant and resource person to teachers, who
by virtue of this aid are better prepared, to assist students in the
classroom. As a result of insights and information gained in counseling sessions with the student the counselor is able to recommend
procedures to the teacher for bettering the circumstances of
students.

The self-understanding of both counselor and teacher is also
improved as a relationship of mutual aid and mutual dependence
is developed. The ability to establish and maintain a positive relationship with youngsters is enhanced as understandings are gained
and as skills are developed in the consultant relationship between
counselor and teacher. Teacher personality is a potent force in
bringing about changes in the attitudes and behavior of students.
Communication between teacher and student improves, understanding between the two is enhanced, and emotional capabilities
are strengthened as the teacher profits from his experiences with
the counselor. As a resource person, the only limits placed upon
the counselor are those of his own capabilities and of the ability of
the teacher to make appropriate applications of new insights into
his relationships with students.

The special competences of the counselor should be utilized
to the highest degree possible in accomplishing better student adjustment and in improving the classroom climate. His assistance should
be sought by teachers, and he should regard his professional asso-

ciation with teachers as providing many opportunities for bettering the educational experiences of students.

Conducting Evaluation Studies and Research

Continuous evaluation of the various guidance services is essential to its growth and improvement. Research must also receive due attention, and the counselor is the logical person to provide some leadership in initiating and conducting research activities. Evaluation includes such procedures as (1) the utilization of questionnaires and checklists by which information is obtained from students and teachers; (2) the recording of notes or brief anecdotes pertinent to the guidance service; (3) the making of surveys by which opinions and reactions of students and teachers are gained; (4) the noting of strengths and weaknesses in the program as they become evident; and (5) the solicitation of recommendations from all appropriate sources through which program improvements may be accomplished.

Research projects should be under way at all times. As appropriate data are gained from one study, from which conclusions may be drawn, another study should be launched. Most of these studies should be based upon local problems, but research with broader connotations should also be undertaken as time and conditions permit. The talents and services of others should be utilized in the research effort in order to accomplish needed research without neglecting students and other important activities.

A number of studies have been done in an attempt to determine the major tasks and functions of the counselor. A frequently encountered problem is one of finding counselors working at a number of different tasks which are only remotely related to the guidance program. Considerable confusion also prevails as to just what the functions of the counselor are. Some intensive efforts are being given to these and related problems in an effort to bring about greater clarification and to lend greater strength and impetus to the counselor's effectiveness.[1]

The Setting and Conditions for Counseling

The great potential counseling has for benefiting students can be realized to its highest degree only if the setting is appropriate and conditions are favorable. An atmosphere of quiet, comfort, and

---

[1] See C. Gilbert Wrenn, *The Counselor in a Changing World,* American Personnel and Guidance Association, Washington, D.C., 1962, chap. 5.

dignity is conducive to effective counseling. Noise, confusion, inter-ruptions, and general disorganization are so detrimental to the counseling relationship as to constitute a serious threat to its effec-tiveness.

The setting for counseling includes adequate office space stra-tegically located in the building, proper facilities to ensure comfort and to evoke student confidence, and the availability of appropriate materials and equipment. Other essential conditions are privacy, positive attitudes by all staff members toward counseling, an under-standing by staff and students of the counseling service, administra-tive support and encouragement, and an attitude of respect by students and faith in the efficacy of the counseling relationship. The following discussion enlarges upon the important factors asso-ciated with an appropriate setting and desirable conditions for counseling.

An Appropriate Setting

Suitable office space is a first requisite for effective counseling. The availability of space depends either upon the provisions made at the time the building was planned or upon the willingness of the administration to make offices available despite omissions in the original building plan. Adjustments in space utilization and minor modifications within the existing building will in many cases take care of this problem. Large offices might be made into two, or rooms with limited use might be divided for more economical space utili-zation. Imaginative, resourceful, dedicated people are often able to eliminate barriers. Buildings of more recent construction have in many cases provided counseling offices and other essentials, thus eliminating the need to scramble for, or compete with other services for, building space.

The strategic location of the counselors' offices is a second point for consideration. The location might be best determined by these two factors:

1 Their accessibility to students. They should be conveniently located to make it possible to reach them in a minimum of time.
2 Their location away from the main traffic of the school. An effort should be made to avoid the noise which ordinarily char-acterizes an area of entrance and exit. Separation from admin-istrative centers is also suggested. The location should be some distance from such facilities as lunchrooms, band rooms, and recreational or sports areas.

Proper facilities include appropriate furnishings, comfortable and attractive surroundings, and interesting and stimulating aesthetic appliances in the counselor's office. Ostentation, however, is neither essential nor desirable. The atmosphere of the interview, the quality of the relationship, and the attitude of the student toward counseling are influenced by the physical surroundings in which the counseling takes place.

A fourth point to consider in the setting for counseling is the availability of appropriate materials and equipment. These include the tools upon which successful personnel work depends. Adequate record forms properly used and maintained, information-service files of educational and vocational data, suitable standardized tests and inventories, test-interpretation forms, and appropriate books and magazines constitute some of these necessary materials. In addition to office and room furnishings equipment might include a tape recorder, record players, bulletin boards, a mobile cabinet for vocational literature, a typewriter, and duplicating facilities. If play therapy is used, the room in which it takes place must also be properly supplied with equipment and facilities. Other needs may become evident to the counselor as services are expanded and as the demand for aid is intensified.

Favorable Conditions for Counseling

There is no clear-cut distinction between an "appropriate setting" and "favorable conditions." However, the separation is made in order to permit emphasis upon various factors which are essential to effective counseling. The "setting" is regarded as having to do primarily with physical facilities, while "conditions" include the less tangible factors such as attitudes, cooperation, respect, and morale. These intangibles are just as essential to counseling success as the tangibles but are more difficult to identify and assess.

A first consideration as a condition for effective counseling is privacy. An intimate personal discussion of problems and concerns demands protection against interruptions, curious interlopers, and nerve-shattering confusion. An atmosphere of dignity and calm should prevail as a client gives verbal expression to his feelings and seeks answers to problems upon which future decisions rest. A client-counselor relationship characterized by tensions, suspicions, and inhibitions and intensified by lack of privacy is of no value and might indeed be harmful. This office should contain no clear windows through which the curious may stare, and should be located some distance from any source of noise. Secondly, the counselor must provide a system by which interruptions will not occur. Telephone calls, personal inquiries, and all other possible threats to privacy should be handled by a secretary outside the counselor's office.

Privacy will also be aided if the counselor's office provides for an exit other than the door leading into the waiting room or secretarial offices. This arrangement protects the student against any possible embarrassment which may occur because of his emotions following an interview. This arrangement may not be practical in view of space requirements, but the idea should be given consideration when plans are made for counseling offices.

Positive attitudes of all staff members toward the counseling function is another requisite for its success. A person's attitudes are manifest in his behavior. If teachers and administrators feel good about the counseling program and have confidence in it, their conduct will reflect this attitude. Conversely, a negative attitude will result in critical remarks and cynical references which can do real damage to the program and seriously jeopardize its future. An aim toward which everyone should work is the attainment of an atmosphere characterized by understanding, mutual effort, and appreciation.

A third condition of importance is a clear understanding by staff and students as to the true nature of counseling. Its nature, purposes, goals, and achievements should be known and understood by all school people. This highly important and perhaps idealistic attainment will not occur by chance. The efforts and dedication of staff and students are required to bring it about.

Administrative support and encouragement may well be the most important condition of all for a successful counseling program. The administration must provide for the necessary facilities, materials, and personnel, and it is responsible for the degree of importance given to the service within the school setting. For example, providing for interview time and other guidance activities in the daily schedule is a reflection of the administration's attitude and is a clue as to the kind of leadership and support the counseling program can expect. The best of counselors will be limited in their accomplishments without the necessary leadership and support of the administration. Such support will, on the other hand, go a long way in ensuring a strong program.

A fifth essential condition is an attitude of respect by students toward counseling and faith in it as a source of direction and encouragement. The realization of this condition also requires effort and planning in order to inform students and provide a high-quality service which evokes their faith and confidence. As benefits gained from counseling become known, praises for the service will be forthcoming, and as students profit from the counseling experience, their remarks will reflect this confidence.

Suggestions for Improving the Conditions for Counseling

Paramount to a successful counseling service is keeping students and faculty well informed about the nature of the counselor's work and positively inclined toward it. They must know something about how counseling is conducted, the role of both counselor and students, the reasons for following certain procedures and subscribing to basic counseling principles, how a good relationship is established, the benefits to be gained by students and teachers, and how the service can contribute to the total educational program. The more knowledgeable everyone is, the greater the possibilities become for personal growth by those who utilize the services. Everyone should be kept informed on the nature of activities currently being provided, and broad participation in program planning should be encouraged. Following are a few suggestions on procedures for the counselor to follow in keeping students and teachers informed:

1   Make periodic announcements. Such announcements should include information about the time and place to contact the counselor, and other essential information. They should be brief, informative, and dignified. The school paper, bulletin boards, and administrative channels of communication may be used for these purposes.
2   Make explanations to individuals as the opportunities present themselves or as questions are asked. The counselor might also visit classrooms periodically and make explanations and answer questions. This procedure also permits the students to become better acquainted with the counselor and with the service.
3   Arrange for sessions in classes or informal groups in which stories are told to illustrate a lesson or a point. Student tensions or apprehensions may be reduced through these experiences. This procedure has merit for both elementary- and secondary-age students; modifications may be made to suit various age groups.
4   Provide for announcements and brief skits in student assemblies by which the counseling service is called to the attention of the

students and faculty. These dramatizations may be humorous but should also be informative.

5 Provide for private orientation interviews. Both teacher and counselors may devote some time to this activity. Instruction given here will supplement information gained elsewhere, and it is helpful in clarifying problems and in assisting students toward a better understanding of the counseling process.

6 Capitalize on test-interpretation interviews to further student understanding of counseling. After the completion of a test or inventory, students are invited to come to the counselor for a review of the results. The student then profits from the information gained from the testing and also becomes better informed on the nature of counseling. These students may then be encouraged to return for additional counseling sessions.

7 Utilize audio-visual aids. These aids appeal to students and contribute to an understanding of other aspects of the guidance program as well as the counseling.

8 Capitalize on any available special activities. An attitude which is imaginative and resourceful can often lead to many interesting ways of accomplishing goals. If an idea seems to hold possibilities for results and is in harmony with logical thinking and is ethical, then it justifies consideration and use.

9 Provide services of high quality at all times. The best possible advertisement for counseling is the end product. The benefits gained by individuals will be noted and appreciated.

Kinds of Problems Experienced by Students

Students experience a variety of concerns during their school years. The counselor thus encounters a great range of problems as he works with many different children and youth. He must have unusual insights and possess the ability to perceive problems from the viewpoint of the student, rather than from his position as an observer. The challenge to the counselor is indeed formidable. He must be an unusually capable person with a background of intensive training and appropriate experiences.

Any classification of problems must be done arbitrarily and with the realization that such a procedure is an oversimplification of a rather complex situation. Normally, as a person experiences a problem or fails to fulfill his needs, a number of factors are contributing to his difficulties. Therefore, the arbitrary classification of his problem into a particular category is unrealistic. For example, a student may be unable to make up his mind as to what college to attend following high school. This may be an educational or a vocational problem and in all probability includes some elements of an emotional, family, or even financial problem. However, an awareness by the counselor of the kinds of problems that can be expected with students at various ages may be helpful to him in planning courses of action. The following major problem areas are therefore described:

1 Educational problems. Academic achievement, orientation, discipline, curricular choices, and educational planning are the typical problems encountered in this classification.

2 Social adjustment. Adjusting to, and getting along with, other people is an ever-challenging task. As such, it presents many possibilities for problems. Youngsters need help in developing social skills and in improving behavior.

3 Personal concerns, personality, and adjustment. Problems of a personal nature are usual occurrences with growing youth. These problems may appear to be relatively minor to an adult but are nevertheless important to the person experiencing them. For these youngsters to make a proper adjustment, they should be given personal attention.

4 Problems of home and family. Relationships in the home may lack harmony and thus be a source of concern to children. Counseling assistance may prove to be very helpful during these times. The family conditions themselves may not be changed, but the youngster may gain in maturity and understanding and consequently make a better adjustment to the home situation as it exists.

5 Emotional problems. Human emotions play a significant part in the lives of all people. Emotions influence learning. They may either facilitate or interfere with learning. Other aspects of life and behavior are also influenced by the emotions. For improvement in mental health youngsters need to be given help with problems which are having a detrimental effect on emotions.

6 The selection of a vocation. The concern of students in respect to the selection of a vocation usually becomes more pronounced and intensified with the passing years and as the time for a decision draws near. Adequate counseling and appropriate activities throughout the elementary and secondary years will result in a minimum of frustration, apprehension, and indecision for most youngsters. Wiser choices and more intelligent decisions should also result than would be true if the above aids were denied.

7 Problems of finances. An alert counselor is prepared to suggest possible solutions for minor financial problems. Or at least he can provide some direction in making plans to deal with the

situation. He should know of the availability of part-time jobs and of loan possibilities to see individuals through emergencies.

8 Health. The function of the counselor in matters of health includes identifying pupils in need of medical attention and then making referrals to appropriate personnel for attention and treatment.

Counselor Proficiency

It has already been emphasized that the competence of the counselor is basic to an effective counseling relationship. The quality of the assistance provided and its ultimate value to the client in the realization of growth and self-improvement is determined primarily by the counselor. The setting for counseling, and even the counseling experience, may appear to be very much the same for a number of students with a variety of counselors, and, indeed, the routine functions of these counselors may be quite similar. There are differences, however, in the quality of the experience and in the potential it holds for client growth. These differences are often attributable to varying proficiencies and skills demonstrated by the counselors. The highly competent counselor will realize encouraging results with his clients, while the incompetent or less proficient one may be of little or no help to his students. The implications are most obvious. The importance of having only highly proficient counselors functioning in the schools cannot be overemphasized. Better, more objective selection procedures and stronger counselor preparation programs not only are desirable but will be a must in the immediate future and in the years ahead.

There are many issues dealing with counselor education currently receiving attention.[2] Four major issues and areas of concern are noted below but without a detailed discussion of them.[3]

[2] The American Personnel and Guidance Association with certain of its divisions has given and is continuing to give considerable attention to this problem. Some excellent recommendations and guidelines have been developed by these groups.

[3] Some excellent sources of information on these and related problems are the following:

George E. Hill, *Management and Improvement of Guidance*, Appleton-Century-Crofts, Inc., New York, 1965. The American School Counselors Association's proposal for counselor education is found on pp. 386–388, the proposals of the Association for Counselor Education and Supervision are on pp. 393–405.

John W. Loughary, Robert O. Stripling, and Paul W. Fitzgerald, *Counseling: A Growing Profession*, joint publication of the Association for Counselor Education and Supervision and American School Counselors Association,

Nature of the Counselor's Preparation

The kind of counselor preparation program deemed desirable can be best determined by first arriving at some definite conclusion as to the nature of the tasks to be performed. So long as there is confusion as to the role and functions of the counselor, there will be confusion as to the kind of preparation he should receive. However, considerable progress has been made in both respects. Agreement is being reached as to the work of the counselor, and some excellent suggestions and guides are now being provided by both individuals and professional groups for the establishment of counselor preparation programs. These suggestions and standards include courses to be taken, experiences to be gained, and length of the training program.[4]

In addition to current demands, a projection into the future with an anticipation of educational and societal changes and advances should be made. Envisioning the work of the counselor several years hence will be helpful in planning the program of preparation for today. And since some rather glaring omissions and weaknesses characterize the preparation of many counselors of the present, firm steps in the direction of more substantial programs of counselor preparations are of the utmost importance.[5]

Broad areas of preparation currently receiving attention include: [6]

1   Psychology, including developmental and child psychology, personality, and group psychology.
2   Study of societal forces including courses in sociology, anthropology, economics, and international relations.
3   An understanding of basic educational philosophies and school curriculum.
4   Provision for essential applied technique courses in counseling, measurement, and occupational and educational information.

Divisions of the American Personnel and Guidance Association, Washington, D.C., 1965; chap. 2 by Robert O. Stripling is particularly appropriate.

C. Gilbert Wrenn, *The Counselor in a Changing World,* American Personnel and Guidance Association, Washington, D.C., 1962; chap. 7 deals with the professional preparation and personal qualities of the counselor.

[4] The American School Counselors Association (ASCA) and Association for Counselor Education and Supervision (ACES) studies and recommended standards are particularly helpful.

[5] C. Gilbert Wrenn, *op. cit.,* p. 164, reports a study in which a substantial number of counselors in a total of 1,200 had little or no work in academic areas of critical importance to the counselor.

[6] *Ibid.,* pp. 167–168.

This should be no more than one-fourth of the total graduate program.

5   Supervised experience in counseling and working with groups.
6   Research methods and newer techniques including computer programming.
7   An introduction to problems of ethical relationships and legal responsibilities.

Such a program suggests the importance of graduate study of two-year duration and some preparatory work at the undergraduate level, as well. Promising young people might be identified early and provisions made for them to take courses which would provide a background for the more intensive work at the graduate level.

Counselor Personality

The quality of the counselor both as a human being and as a professional person is of critical importance. It is his ability to establish and maintain a strong, warm, fruitful relationship with a client that determines his professional success and his effectiveness. Efforts have been and are still being made to determine just what these personal qualities are and to ascertain to what extent they are innate or dependent upon learning. A logical conclusion of the present is that these qualities are to a degree innate but that appropriate learning experiences also help people to develop these needed qualities. Their origin is not so important, but it is most essential that every counselor have the qualities and characteristics necessary to aid and influence positively the development of another person.

Experiences as Preparation for Counseling

Another controversial issue is whether or not the counselor should be required to be certified as a teacher and also have teaching experience prior to, or concurrently with, his counseling. There is no simple solution to this problem, but considerable thought is being given to it, and some interesting ideas are being developed. There is a definite trend in the direction of not requiring teacher certification of the counselor and likewise eliminating the teaching-experience requirement. However, many school people, administrators particularly, still hold to the view that the counselor should first of all be a teacher. Many counselors gain their positions from the teaching ranks. A number of factors need to be given careful consideration concerning this problem before a definite conclusion is reached. For example, the level of professional proficiency attained by the counselor should be a major determinant as to whether or not he should be a teacher. The higher this level of preparation is and the more specialized his work is as a clinician, the less logical the teaching preparation and experience becomes. On the other hand a counselor who is working closely with the teacher and the student in the conventional learning setting might be best prepared for his work by virtue of his preparation and experience as a teacher. Satisfactory solutions to these and other problems are being found as intelligent, dedicated people give concerted attention to them.

Certification for the Counselor

A problem closely allied with the other three discussed is one of appropriate certification standards for the counselor. Academic preparation, personal qualities, and experience must all be considered in arriving at suitable standards of certification. The following is a summary of current thinking:

1 An offering of appropriate courses at the graduate level based upon the anticipated functions of the counselor in the schools. He must be well prepared to do the work expected of him in a school setting.

2 A longer, more intensive program of training than that found in the typical master's degree program. A two-year graduate program is receiving strong support nationally.

3 An increase in opportunities for the candidate to engage in practicum and internship experiences under supervision. The second year of preparation will permit the strengthening of a candidate's preparation beyond what it has been with the typical one-year program.

4 Giving greater attention to the development of a preprofessional program at the undergraduate level. Appropriate course recommendations may be made for promising undergraduates who are looking forward to a career in counseling.

5 The identification of suitable work experiences for the candidate as requirements for full professional certification. Traditionally, teaching experience has been included here. The trend is toward requiring experiences more closely allied with counseling or to let the experience as a counselor fulfill the experience requirement for certification. In this case neither teaching certification nor teaching experience would be required of the counselor.

6   The establishment and strengthening of screening procedures and criteria for the admission of candidates to the counselor preparation program. These improvements will minimize the possibilities of unsuitable people becoming counselors. Historically, admission standards have been woefully inadequate.

7   Bolstering and building up the counselor education staffs in the universities. The shortage of highly competent college and university personnel for the preparation of counselors is only too well known by everyone concerned with counselor preparation programs.

These and other problems related to the preparation of counselors are receiving attention, and heartening progress is being made. Many state and local groups and committees are dedicating themselves to finding solutions to the most urgent problems and to making recommendations to national committees and to state legislatures. Progress is being achieved as actions are gradually replacing complaints.

SUMMARY/

The effectiveness of the counselor depends to a high degree upon his ability to develop a good working relationship with the client. This effectiveness is enhanced as the counselor is able to integrate the important elements of several counseling approaches, or philosophical viewpoints, logically into a conceptual framework within which he can function with confidence. Certain elements characterize the counseling relationship, and the counselor's effectiveness becomes evident when he is able to utilize these elements properly in his counseling.

The counselor has certain functions to perform. The nature of these functions should be in keeping with his professional preparation and congruent with the expectations of his profession. The success of the counseling program also depends upon an appropriate setting and upon suitable conditions. If these conditions are not favorable, appropriate action should be taken to correct them.

The proficiency of the counselor is basic to any successful program. He must have the personal qualities necessary and should have received academic training of the highest quality possible. He should also have appropriate educational and vocational experiences as preparation for his work and as requirements for professional certification.

PROBLEMS/

1   Would it be more beneficial to have a set of established techniques or procedures to serve as guides to the counselor rather than to leave him somewhat to his own resources? Defend your answer.

2   What resistance, if any, might you anticipate from counselors to the suggestion that certain elements are essential to all counseling irrespective of theory or philosophical commitment? How might counselors profit from knowledge of these elements?

3   Look at each of the "essential elements" discussed in problem 2 and note the possible weaknesses in each. Make some suggestions which may result in appropriate changes and improvements.

4   In looking at these elements for a second time, identify the points that may be strongly supported by a so-called client-centered counselor and those that may be most strongly supported by a more directive type of counselor.

5   If some disagreements occur between the counselor and the administration as to the nature of the counselor's duties and functions, what should be done? How can a counselor protect himself and the school against these misunderstandings? Why should he do so?

6   What are some logical expectations the school may have for the counselor? What are his major commitments to the school?

7   After deciding just what the major functions of the counselor are, note some implications that become immediately apparent. For example, what are the implications in regard to the training, experience, and general competence of the counselor?

8   Why are the conditions under which the counseling is to take place so important? What are some of the typical limitations encountered in the school? How might these be corrected?

9   Might it be helpful to the counselor to know essentially the nature of a student's problem when he seeks assistance? What differences might this make in the procedures the counselor may use?

10   Why is the competence of the counselor so critical? How can high-level competence on the part of all functioning counselors be attained?

11 Identify some groups at the national level which have provided considerable influence in upgrading the preparation of counselors. How can the work of these groups benefit the various states and the universities?

12 Enumerate some of the major areas of concern in counselor preparation programs. Note some major trends.

Selected References

Textbooks

ARBUCKLE, DUGALD S.: *Counseling: Philosophy, Theory and Practice*, Allyn and Bacon, Inc., Boston, 1965.

BRAMMER, LAWRENCE M., and EVERETT L. SHOSTROM: *Therapeutic Psychology*, Prentice-Hall, Inc., Englewood Cliffs, N.J., 1960.

BLOCHER, DONALD H.: *Developmental Counseling*, The Ronald Press Company, New York, 1966, chaps. 1 and 2.

BORDIN, EDWARD: *Psychological Counseling*, Appleton-Century-Crofts, Inc., New York, 1955.

FULLMER, DANIEL W., and HAROLD W. BERNARD: *Counseling: Content and Process*, Science Research Associates, Inc., Chicago, 1964, chaps. 6, 8, and 12.

HAHN, MILTON, E., and MALCOLM S. MAC LEAN: *Counseling Psychology*, 2d ed,. McGraw-Hill Book Company, New York, 1955.

LOUGHARY, JOHN W., ROBERT O. STRIPLING, and PAUL W. FITZGERALD: *Counseling: A Growing Profession*, joint publication of the Association for Counselor Education and Supervision and American School Counselors Association, Divisions of the American Personnel and Guidance Association, Washington, D.C., 1965.

OHLSEN, MERLE M.: *Guidance Services in the Modern School*, Harcourt, Brace & World, Inc., New York, 1964, chap. 4.

STEFFLRE, BUFORD (ed.): *Theories of Counseling*, McGraw-Hill Book Company, New York, 1965.

TYLER, LEONA: *The Work of the Counselor*, Appleton-Century-Crofts, Inc., New York, 1961.

WARTERS, JANE: *Techniques of Counseling*, 2d ed., McGraw-Hill Book Company, New York, 1954.

WRENN, C. GILBERT: *The Counselor in a Changing World*, American Personnel and Guidance Association, Washington, D.C., 1962, chaps. 5 and 7.

Journals

ARBUCKLE, DUGALD S.: "The Conflicting Functions of the School Counselor," *Counselor Education and Supervision*, vol. 1, pp. 54–59, Winter, 1961.

ASTOR, MARTIN H.: "Counselors Seek to Understand Themselves: A Philosophical Inquiry," *Personnel and Guidance Journal*, vol. 43, pp. 1029–1033, June, 1965.

BANK, DOROTHY J.: "In-service Training for Secondary School Counselors,"

National Association of Women Deans and Counselors Journal, vol. 26, pp. 10–14, June, 1963.

BOY, A. V.: "Are Counselors Counseling?" *Bulletin of the National Association of Secondary-school Principals*, vol. 42, pp. 160–161, September, 1958.

BRAYFIELD, ARTHUR H.: "Performance Is the Thing," *Journal of Counseling Psychology*, vol. 9, no. 1, p. 4, Spring, 1962.

BRIGANTE, THOMAS R.: "Clinical Counseling Psychologists Perceptions of Their Specialties," *Journal of Counseling Psychology*, vol. 9, no. 3, pp. 225–231, Fall, 1962.

CALLIS, ROBERT, PAUL C. POLMAUTIER, and EDWARD C. ROEBER: "Five Years of Research on Counseling," *Journal of Counseling Psychology*, vol. 4., no. 2, pp. 119–122, 1957.

COMBS, ARTHUR W., and DANIEL W. SOPER: "The Perceptual Organization of Effective Counselors," *Journal of Counseling Psychology*, vol. 10, pp. 222–226, Fall, 1963.

CORTALE, MICHAEL J.: "Counselors and Discipline," *Personnel and Guidance Journal*, vol. 39, pp. 349–351, January, 1961.

DRASGOW, JAMES, and ROBERT J. WALKER: "A Graphic Description of a Counseling Relationship," *Journal of Counseling Psychology*, vol. 7 no. 1, pp. 51–55, Spring, 1960.

DRESSEL, PAUL L.: "Counseling Caprices," *Personnel and Guidance Journal*, vol. 33, pp. 4–7, September, 1954.

FARWELL, GAIL F., and ANTHONY C. RICCIO: "Case Study: A Means of Introducing Guidance Services," *National Elementary Principal*, vol. 40, pp. 38–40, May, 1961.

FEDER, DANIEL D.: "Emerging Role of the Professional Personnel Worker," *Personnel Services in Education*, Fifty-eighth Yearbook of the National Society for the Study of Education, 1959, part II, pp. 181–209.

HEILBRUN, ALFRED B., JR.: "Counseling Readiness: A Treatment, Specific or General Factor?" *Journal of Counseling Psychology*, vol. 12, pp. 87–90, Spring, 1965.

———: "Psychological Factors Related to Counseling Readiness and Implications for Counseling Behavior," *Journal Counseling Psychology*, vol. 9, pp. 353–358, Winter, 1962.

HOYT, KENNETH B.: "What the School Has a Right to Expect of its Counselor," *Personnel and Guidance Journal*, vol. 40, pp. 129–133, October, 1961.

HUMMEL, RAYMOND C.: "Ego-counseling in Guidance: Concept and Method," *Harvard Educational Review*, vol. 32, pp. 463–482, Fall, 1962.

HUTSON, P. W.: "Views on Counselor Preparation," *Bulletin of the National Association of Secondary-school Principals*, vol. 47, no. 284, pp. 19–26, September, 1963.

JOHNSON, Y. O.: "Standardized Counseling Procedures," *Journal of Secondary Education*, vol. 40, pp. 320–324, November, 1965.

JOSLIN, LEEMAN C.: "Knowledge and Counseling Competence," *Personnel and Guidance Journal*, vol. 43, pp. 790–795, April, 1965.

KINZER, JOHN R.: "The Educated Counselor," *Journal of Counseling Psychology*, vol. 8, no. 1, pp. 14–16, Spring, 1961.

KLOPF, GORDON: "Design for Counselor Preparation," *National Association of Women Deans and Counselors Journal*, vol. 26, pp. 5–9, June, 1963.

KRUMBOLTZ, JOHN D.: "Behavioral Counseling: Rationale and Research,"

Personnel and Guidance Journal, vol. 44, no. 4, pp. 383–387, December, 1965.

———: "Parable of the Good Counselor," *Personnel and Guidance Journal*, vol. 43, pp. 118–126, October, 1964.

LINDEN, JAMES D., SHELLEY C. STONE, and BRUCE SHERTZER: "Development and Evaluation of an Inventory for Rating Counseling," *Personnel and Guidance Journal*, vol. 44, pp. 267–276, November, 1965.

MANN, KENNETH W.: "Religious Factors and Values in Counseling," *Journal of Counseling Psychology*, vol. 6, pp. 255–274, Winter, 1959.

MAZER, GILBERT E.: "The Factorial Dimensions of School Counselor Practices," *Journal of Counseling Psychology*, vol. 12, pp. 127–132, Summer, 1965.

MOWRER, O. HOBART: "Science, Sex, and Values," *Personnel and Guidance Journal*, vol. 42, pp. 746–753, April, 1964.

———: "'Sin,' the Lesser of Two Evils," *The American Psychologist*, vol. 15, pp. 301–304, May, 1960.

——— and others: "The Role of Sin in Psychotherapy," *Journal of Counseling Psychology*, vol. 7, no. 3, pp. 185–197, Fall, 1960.

OLSEN, LEROY C.: "Success for New Counselors," *Journal of Counseling Psychology*, vol. 10, pp. 350–355, Winter, 1963.

PARKER, CLYDE A.: "As a Clinician Thinks," *Journal of Counseling Psychology*, vol. 5, no. 4, pp. 253–261, 1958.

PATTERSON, C. H.: "Control, Conditioning, and Counseling," *Personnel and Guidance Journal*, vol. 41, pp. 680–686, April, 1963.

PEPINSKY, HAROLD B., and HENRY BOROW: "Automated Learning and the Counselor," *Journal of Counseling Psychology*, vol. 8, no. 3, pp. 272–277, 1961.

PERRONE, PHILIP A., MARY L. WEIKING, and ELWYN H. NAGEL: "The Counseling Function as Seen by Students, Parents and Teachers," *Journal of Counseling Psychology*, vol. 12, pp. 148–152, Summer, 1965.

PINE, GERALD J., and ANGELO V. BOY: "The Counselor and the Unmotivated Client," *Personnel and Guidance Journal*, vol. 44, no. 4, pp. 368–371, December, 1965.

POPPEN, W. A.: "Expectations of Junior High School Pupils for Counseling," *Journal of Educational Research*, vol. 58, pp. 358–361, April, 1965.

RAMSEY, GLENN V.: "Referral Task in Counseling," *Personnel and Guidance Journal*, vol. 40, pp. 443–447, January, 1962.

RICE, JOSEPH P., JR.: "Types of Problems Referred to a Central Guidance Agency at Different Grade Levels," *Personnel and Guidance Journal*, vol. 42, pp. 52–55, September, 1963.

ROBERTS, RALPH R.: "The Influence of Tape Recording on Counseling," *Journal of Counseling Psychology*, vol. 12, pp. 10–16, Spring, 1965.

ROBINSON, FRANCIS P.: "Cubist Approach to the Art of Counseling," *Personnel and Guidance Journal*, vol. 41, pp. 670–676, April, 1963.

SCHAL, BILL D.: "Counselor Listens to Johnny," *Catholic School Journal*, vol. 65, p. 75, September, 1965.

SCHMEDING, ROBERT W.: "Use of the Playback in the Counseling Situation," *Vocational Guidance Quarterly*, vol. 11, pp. 64–67, Autumn, 1962.

STEFFLRE, BUFORD, PAUL KING, and FRED LEAFGREN: "Characteristics of Counselors Judged Effective by Their Peers," *Journal of Counseling Psychology*, vol. 9, pp. 335–340, Winter, 1962

STONE, SHELLEY C., and BRUCE SHERTZER: "The Militant Counselor," *Personnel and Guidance Journal*, vol. 42, pp. 342–347, December, 1963.

STRIPLING, ROBERT O.: "School Counselor Preparation: The Key to Effective Guidance," *Theory into Practice*, vol. 2, pp. 33–38, 1963.

SUPER, D. E., and T. R. BRIGANTE: "Clinical and Counseling Psychologists Perceptions of Their Specialties," *Journal of Counseling Psychology*, vol. 9, pp. 225–231, Fall, 1962.

WALZ, GARY W., and EDWARD C. ROEBER: "Supervisors' Reactions to a Counseling Interview," *Counselor Education and Supervision*, vol. 2, pp. 2–7, Fall, 1962.

WASSON, ROBERT M., and R. WRAY STROWIG: "Professional Isolation and Counselor Role," *Personnel and Guidance Journal*, vol. 43, pp. 457–460, January, 1965.

WRENN, C. GILBERT: "Culturally Encapsulated Counselor," *Harvard Education Review*, vol. 32, pp. 444–449, Fall, 1962.

WRIGHT, C. W.: "Comparison of Individual and Multiple Counseling for Test Interpretation Interviews: With Comments by M. M. Ohlsen," *Journal of Counseling Psychology*, vol. 10, pp. 126–135, Summer, 1963.

NINE

/EDUCATIONAL AND VOCATIONAL INFORMATION SERVICE

The information service is an essential element in the guidance program, and it serves many useful functions for students. This service provides for the accumulation, display, and utilization of educational and vocational information for purposes of aiding students in making appropriate curricular choices and wise vocational plans.

An organized, systematic approach is needed by which pertinent information is made available to students. The information service fulfills this need. It provides youngsters with opportunities for educational and vocational exploratory activities through which they can identify areas of genuine interest and aptitude. New fields and possibilities are opened to them, and tentative selections are made as they become better informed about themselves and about the world of work. From incidental learning in the classroom students gain limited information about vocations, but this information should supplement and never supplant what may be gained under an organized service in the guidance program.

The importance of being well informed about the world of work can hardly be overestimated, since vocational decisions determine to a great extent the course of one's life. The startling technical and scientific advancements being made in our time have made it more important than ever that students be given some assistance in planning their careers. This phase of a student's education has been woefully neglected, as the predominant attitude has been one of leaving vocation selection to chance. The notion has prevailed that by some act of fate most people would eventually find a satisfactory work life for themselves. Leaving such an important matter to accident or incident makes little sense in the modern world. The guidance service provides the information from which intelligent planning and logical decisions may be made.

The nature of the information service will be discussed in this chapter in an attempt to show its role in the guidance program and as a part of education. Sources from which data and literature may be obtained will be identified. Major functions of the teacher and counselor are also reviewed.

The Nature of the Information Service

The activities of the information service are designed to assist students in learning more about their educational opportunities and in becoming acquainted with vocational possibilities. Files of pertinent literature are maintained. Bulletin-board displays are provided, university catalogs and training school literature are made available, and a variety of literature on personal and social topics is conveniently located for student use. Field trips, classroom and school projects, and related activities are encouraged as aids to young people in their preparation for a life commitment to a job or field of work.

Traditionally, vocational information used to receive the greatest emphasis. Educational information, however, has been added as an important part of the information service program. A third dimension to enter the picture is that of sociopsychological enlightenment. Awareness of the importance of human relationships has become more pronounced, resulting in a need for self-understanding and a greater sensitivity to other people. The information service is thus broadening to include considerably more data and activities than those associated with vocational guidance alone.

Just as the guidance service as a whole is designed to serve all levels in education, so, too, is the information service organized to serve students of all ages, including elementary school children. The nature of the activities conducted and of the materials used differs according to the age and experience levels of the students, but the principles underlying the service and the framework within which it operates are essentially the same. A broadening of a child's understanding of himself and of his world, while he is learning the basic skills, is a major objective of the elementary school. This objective can be realized through meaningful exploratory experiences throughout the early school years that pave the way for later decisions based on educational maturity.

Vocation Selection as a Developmental Process

For most people the comfort of choosing a natural, easy course in entering upon one's lifework, such as following in Dad's footsteps or accepting the first promising job opportunity that comes along, is a thing of the past. True, these are still the ways of a substantial number of young people. In most cases, however, the eventual selection of a vocation is merely one choice among many made during the process of growing up. Vocation selection is a part of the total developmental process. Many influences are brought to bear upon a person during his maturing years, and a variety of reactions are experienced by virtue of these influences. The decisiveness with which a person makes choices is a reflection of the quality of the environment in which he grew up and an indication of his adaptive and adjustment resources.

Many theories of vocational choice have appeared over the years.[1] These are useful as guides in attempting to determine what influences underlie a person's choices. However, the speculative aspects of some theories are quite evident, and sometimes the explanations given of why a person makes certain choices are relatively narrow and incomplete. The hard, real, factual circumstances of life should not be overlooked in attempting to determine why a person pursues one kind of work rather than another. Finances, friends, family, and other relevant circumstances cannot be ignored if logical explanations for choices are sought. There is also truth in Hill's statement that there is considerable agreement among theories.[2]

[1] See Robert Hoppock, *Occupational Information*, 2d ed, McGraw-Hill Book Company, New York, 1963, chap. 7, for a brief review of theories.

[2] George E. Hill, *Management and Improvement of Guidance*, Appleton-Century-Crofts, Inc., New York, 1965, p. 269.

Considering differences and points of agreement among theories, the development of a composite theory [3] from which the counselor may work is valid and emphasizes the concept that vocational preparation and selection are essential elements in a person's development . To put it another way, virtually all school experiences have some relevance for a student's development, including his choice of a vocation. Such a composite theory may also include some basic principle by which the counselor can function in his relationship with students.[4]

Purposes to Be Served

Each element of the guidance program serves certain purposes which in part are unique. Unless the appropriate activities and materials are provided, these purposes are never completely met. Plans are more readily made and more realistically adhered to as the influences of the various services of the guidance program are felt. The general aim of the informational service is the stimulation and direction of students toward wise educational and vocational decisions. Thus the principal purposes of this service include:

1   Developing student interests in the world of work and in the many activities used by people for earning a living.
2   Stimulating students to give careful consideration to the many educational and vocational possibilities open to them.
3   Providing experiences and a wholesome atmosphere by which healthy attitudes of respect for all kinds of useful work are developed.
4   Helping students make wise choices in educational experiences, by which personal development may be enhanced and adequate preparation realized for future experiences.
5   Providing information about the many opportunities open to young people in various colleges, universities, and technical training schools, among which choices may be made.
6   Providing a continuous program of experiences well integrated with the instructional program, experiences which provide strength and continuity for the total educational process.
7   Keeping to a minimum frustrations and indecisiveness and eliminating wasteful trial-and-error approaches in decision making.
8   Improving the self-understanding of young people from which a greater appreciation for other people may emerge.

[3] Hoppock, *op. cit.,* chap. 8.
[4] *Ibid.,* pp. 114–115.

As efforts are made by the school to bring these purposes to fulfillment, the long-term goals of vocational adjustment and success for all citizens become more realistically attainable. After purposes and goals have been established, the implementation of appropriate procedures becomes another challenge. The practical aspects of carrying out these procedures fall upon the school personnel. The principal, teacher, and counselor are all involved. The nature of the experiences provided must be in keeping with the maturity level of the students being accommodated and in harmony with the avowed purposes of the program.

Underlying these purposes is the assumption that students will gain information and understanding from which intelligent decisions can be made in terms of the anticipated future as well as the present. Trends and demands should be known sufficiently early, so that a student may plan his career accordingly. Exactness is still impossible, however, since highly accurate predictions about vocational innovations and work demands are extremely difficult to make. Information such as that quoted by Wrenn [5] from a 1960 U.S. Department of Labor bulletin, about certain trends in occupations and the needs for various workers, can be helpful. Here, for example, the percent of change in eight vocational categories from 1960 to 1970 is given. Professional and technical workers, will have increased by 41 percent during this period, while there will have been a reduction in farmers and farm workers of 17 percent. Substantial increases are noted in the remaining six categories.[6]

Aiding Students through Providing Information

Providing files of educational and vocational information for student use is certainly one function of the guidance service. Logical choices of careers depend upon the adequacy and quality of this information. This service is only one phase of the guidance program, however; it is a relatively simple one, and the counselor must not delude himself with the belief that he is doing his job merely by providing such information. Self-understanding on the part of the student is also essential to decision making, and it occurs as a part of the developmental process. Development is a continuous process in which growth is taking place, attitudes are being formed, a

[5] C. Gilbert Wrenn, *The Counselor in a Changing World*, American Personnel and Guidance Association, Washington, D.C., 1962, p. 20.
[6] *Ibid.*, p. 20.

self-concept is being developed, and aspirations are being solidified. Information provided at an appropriate time is useful to each student only as it contributes to this development. As self-understanding increases and a student is able to think with greater depth, by virtue of his increasing maturity and greater knowledge, he is better able to discriminate, make choices, and formulate plans which are logical in terms of his competence and potential, and which are in keeping with what will be expected of him in a particular vocation.

Research findings have made it possible to state with some confidence what happens in a person's vocational development. A considerable amount of research evidence has led to Hill's seven propositions on how youngsters develop in their thinking and choosing.[7] The thoroughness of Hill's work in his attempt to formulate some conclusions which might well serve as guides to all counselors is highly commendable. Support for the concept that vocation selection is a part of one's development and not an isolated event in one's life is very much in evidence. The implications for the total guidance service become quite evident as the counselor understands and accepts this concept. Preparing a student for the choices he will eventually make in his life is primarily a matter of providing him with a variety of enriching, satisfying, challenging, self-development-promoting experiences throughout all his school years. Paramount is the philosophy that a youngster must develop a high level of self-confidence, in which he will be relatively free of debilitating anxieties and handicapping inhibitions.

The information needed by the student can be gained from the guidance service, and considerable encouragement is also realized as the student engages in, and profits from, the experiences provided. The counselor may also be heartened by the statement [8] ". . . that the research on vocational development tends to reinforce, not weaken, one's confidence in the validity of the basic guidance learnings."

Choosing a Vocation

The actual choice of a vocation is, then, a result of many influences over a long period of time. The choice is not generally an abrupt, decision-making event, even under ideal circumstances fostered by

[7] *Op. cit.*, pp. 269–278.
[8] *Ibid.*, p. 278.

a strong guidance program. Decisions are made by the typical student concerning course offerings, majors and minors, extra-curricular activities, part-time jobs, and choices of friends, all of which have relevance for his life's work. Elements of chance, circumstances, family, and the economy of the times are also influencing factors. So many people find themselves working at a particular job without really knowing how they got there. By-chance elements should, however, be reduced or eliminated and replaced by a carefully conceived, well-organized plan for selecting and preparing for a vocation. The guidance service attempts to do this.

Ginzberg's theory of vocation selection is summarized in four major points. It includes some of the more "realistic" aspects of vocation selection and permanence of commitment. He notes that: [9]

1. Occupational choice is a development process which takes place over a period of some ten years.
2. The process is largely irreversible. . . .
3. The choice of an occupation ends in a compromise between interests, capacities, values, and opportunities.
4. There are three periods of occupational choice: the period of fantasy choice, governed largely by the wish to be an adult; the period of tentative choices, beginning at about age eleven, and determined largely by interest, then by capacities, and then by values; and the period of realistic choices, beginning at about age seventeen, in which exploratory, crystallization, and specification phases succeed each other.

Other theories are equally beneficial to the counselor and the student as they provide some structure for decision making. As suggested earlier in this chapter, a composite of theories is probably more useful than a strict adherence to any one theory. Guidelines are essential for intelligent planning, but flexibility within these guides is also necessary.[10]

[9] E. Ginzberg and others, *Occupational Choice: An Approach to General Theory*, Columbia University Press, New York, 1951, p. 196.

[10] For a review of some leading theories, see James F. Adams, *Counseling and Guidance: A Summary View*, The Macmillan Company, New York, 1965, pp. 207–227; also see Herman J. Peters and James C. Hansen, *Vocational Guidance and Career Development*, The Macmillan Company, New York, 1966, pp. 93–118.

Nature and Kinds of Activities

A variety of activities is possible within most schools by which the aims and purposes of the informational service may be accomplished. Resourceful, imaginative teachers and counselors experience no problems in determining what to do. The possibilities are almost without limit; but there are practical problems of administration and organization to be considered. Many of these activities are primarily exploratory, particularly at the elementary level, and they permit a variety of experiences with excellent potential for gaining insights and understandings about job selection. The intent is to encourage a broad exploration of many fields from which a sound foundation for future decisions may be established. Some typical or representative activities include:

1   Taking field trips to observe people at work and to note the nature of the work being performed
2   Utilizing audio-visual aids by which information can be brought to the attention of students
3   Subscribing to one of the commercial vocational information services from which packets of materials are received each month
4   Setting up files and shelves of educational and vocational information
5   Utilizing bulletin-board space for displaying posters and bulletins
6   Providing role-playing and dramatization experiences in which students learn about applying for a job, demonstrating tact in work relationships, or employing practices
7   Conducting classroom projects in which the tasks of real workers are simulated
8   Providing for some work experiences on a limited scale for selected students
9   Completing application forms for jobs as a classroom experience for purposes of learning correct procedures

Kinds of Information

Many kinds of information are available to the student in the information service. This variety of information includes answers to questions concerning colleges, technical training programs, and vocational schools, in addition to facts about his present school. Thus, planning for immediate and future decisions is possible and can be done more realistically. The principal kinds of information provided include:

1 The nature and extent of curricular and extracurricular offerings within the school
2 College catalogs, literature on technical and trade schools, and data on opportunities in the armed services
3 Information on job requirements, necessary qualifications of workers, how to obtain employment, and the nature of different types of work
4 Facts about specific advantages and disadvantages of vocations or jobs under consideration
5 Statistical data on employment prospects, number and kinds of workers needed, and future trends and expectations
6 Facts about promotion and advancement possibilities, salary expectations, and potential for satisfying personal needs
7 Guides on how to gain entrance to a field of work, what precautions to take, and how to utilize contacts and people currently employed in that area
8 Facts about labor union regulations, professional organization standards, and regulations governing workers in a particular field

Place of These Activities in the School Program

The services, activities, and materials provided and utilized in the information service are primarily the responsibility of the guidance program. However, many of these services should be handled as integral parts of the total school program. Guidance personnel and teachers need to work together in a cooperative effort to provide students with essential information and activities. The guidance service provides the leadership, direction, and materials, and instruction provides appropriate learning experiences and activities. Students profit from an educational program that wisely utilizes the capabilities of all staff members.

Sources of Information

There are many sources of excellent vocational information. This information is designed for use in the schools and is therefore written in an appropriate, interesting form. Some of these sources are noncommercial, such as the immediate community and government agencies. Commercial sources include companies dealing in guidance literature, audio-visual aids, periodicals, and business and industrial concerns. The alert teacher and counselor soon identify particular sources with the greatest potential for being helpful and capitalize on them accordingly.

Noncommercial Sources

The immediate community is an excellent source of information about job possibilities. Many young people remain within the community following school and are absorbed into its industrial, business, or agricultural endeavors. These people often overlook some of a community's more promising employment possibilities as they envision careers in distant places. Although it is true that some will move, the facts indicate that a substantial number will remain in the community in which they grew up. Teachers and counselors may also overlook community job possibilities as they plan with young people for college or vocational training programs following high school. The community also serves as a laboratory for tryout work experiences for youth while they are still in school or upon termination of formal schooling, and as a source of information for field trips and classroom study.

Government agencies at local, state, and national levels also provide schools with helpful data about employment trends and job possibilities. Literature is provided by some of these agencies free upon request, or for only a small charge.

Another noncommercial source of vocational information is the B'nai B'rith Vocational Service, with national headquarters at 1640 Rhode Island Avenue, NW, Washington, D.C., and branch offices in other cities.

Commercial Sources

Several commercial companies have done extensive pioneering and research in developing a variety of guidance materials for use in the schools and colleges. Their services are excellent, and the materials are informative and interesting. Among these companies are:

1   Careers, P.O. Box 522, Largo, Florida
2   Chronicle Guidance Service, Moravia, New York
3   Science Research Associates, Inc., 259 E. Erie St., Chicago 11, Illinois

These companies provide kits of materials which are sent monthly to their subscribers. A subscription to one of these services is a desirable beginning for the information service program. The program can be extended from this basic service to include data from other sources.

Industrial and business concerns issue literature of a vocational nature as a public service and as an advertising device. The information gained from these sources can be of great value if it is properly selected and utilized. This literature can be obtained by making a direct request to the company. Names and addresses of these business concerns are provided in the literature published by the commercial companies and organizations that handle guidance literature.

Periodicals contain advertisements of educational and vocational literature. These sources may be added to the files and made available to students. Periodicals often publish articles, too, of a vocational nature which may be utilized by students in their study of placement opportunities.

Audio-visual aids are now available in abundance and variety. Motion pictures, filmstrips, tapes, posters, and related materials are available at moderate costs. University film libraries constitute a major source of these materials. Some commercial companies and community agencies are also able to supply these aids.

Some Basic Publications

Certain publications are essential to the program as basic materials from which to work. Additions may be made as the needs of the program dictate. Some of these include the following:

1 *Occupational Outlook Handbook* (Bureau of Labor Statistics Bulletin 1450), published biennially by the Bureau of Labor Statistics of the U.S. Department of Labor, Washington, D.C., priced at $5 and obtainable from the Superintendent of Documents, Washington, D.C. 20402, or from certain regional offices of the Bureau of Labor Statistics

2 *Occupational Outlook Quarterly,* a periodical available for the yearly subscription price of $1.25, also from the Superintendent of Documents, Washington, D.C. 20402, or regional offices of the Bureau of Labor Statistics

3 *Dictionary of Occupational Titles* (DOT), vol. I, *Definitions of Titles,* and vol. II, and *Occupational Classification and Industry Index,* available from the Superintendent of Documents, Washington, D.C. 20402, at an approximate cost of $5 and $4.25 respectively

4 *The Vocational Guidance Quarterly,* published by the National Vocational Guidance Association, Washington, D.C., at $4 a year

From the commercial sources mentioned earlier subscriptions to monthly publications are available that provide occupational information. Obtaining such a subscription is one of the first things the counselor might do in establishing the service. These materials are attractive, well-organized for immediate use, and very informative for both student and counselor.

The intelligent utilization of these materials requires the interest and cooperative efforts of teacher and counselor. Many stimulating, informative activities may be conducted under the direction of the teacher. Basic academic skills are being learned by students as they concurrently gain information about the world of work. The teacher thus integrates into a meaningful learning experience academic knowledge, data, and information about vocational possibilities a more objective view of occupational opportunities. The next section outlines specific functions of the teacher and of the counselor, which, if properly performed, will result in a program of quality from which students of all ages and of various academic potentialities and aptitudes may profit.

Teacher and Counselor Functions

Both teacher and counselor have contributions to make and functions to perform in the information service, although the counselor heads the program. Some functions more logically belong with one or the other of these two people; in other cases, the responsibilities are shared. An attitude of cooperation and dedication to the service of young people is essential to the successful conduct of all aspects of this program. The teacher and the counselor unite their efforts, and each augments the work of the other in providing a program of services from which students receive directions and assistance in course selection and in decision making leading to vocational choices. Each student is given the necessary direction and assistance needed to make him a more independent, resourceful person capable of thinking clearly, of weighing the evidence logically, and of arriving at appropriate decisions.

Teacher Functions

The teacher's job is one of teaching and providing a setting in which learning takes place. With some of this learning the student becomes better informed about possible vocations and about himself. The typical classroom provides many opportunities for enriching class materials and experiences with activities related both to instruction and to the guidance program. For example, the teacher may:

1 Prepare bulletin-board displays of posters and appropriate vocational literature.
2 Call accumulated information to the attention of students and encourage its use.
3 Point out relationships of subjects being taught to various vocational opportunities and indicate how the study of certain subjects will help prepare a person for a profession or vocation.
4 Use vocational literature and data for assignments.
5 Conduct field trips and supervise study groups designed to become better acquainted with occupational information.
6 Invite community people to class for purposes of discussing sources of information and job opportunities in the area.

Counselor Functions

Although certain functions are carried out by staff members other than the counselor through common consent or through delegation of responsibility, the counselor is responsible for the conduct of the information service, just as he has major responsibilities associated with the other elements of the guidance program. Providing files and shelves of information is just one function of the counselor. The proper identification and utilization of these materials are essential if they are to serve their purposes. Therefore, it is particularly important that interviews be held with students for the purpose of answering questions, providing information, evaluating and interpreting data, and helping youngsters formulate plans. The counselor can also encourage the teacher to make use of information by integrating it with other instructional presentations and by regarding vocational data as sources of informative facts to be incorporated into classroom activities.

Teachers and students should be kept informed on the extent and nature of materials available and the procedures by which they may locate and utilize these materials. The counselor can provide leadership and direction by which materials are made accessible and kept in usable form.

Establishing suitable files. Appropriate files of vocational information must be established and maintained. The counselor may enlist the assistance of other staff members with this task, and he should be provided the necessary clerical assistance. Science Research Associates, Inc., Careers, and Chronicle Guidance Service have excellent filing plans, which are based on the *Dictionary of Occupational Titles,* for the proper numbering and filing of literature.

Some typical problems in establishing files may include:

1 The advisability of purchasing a complete filing system as compared with just the basic plan to which additions can be made
2 The location of the information files in the building
3 The persons to be responsible for the various tasks
4 The establishment of a system by which materials may be checked out
5 A system of clerical assistance by which materials are ordered and files maintained
6 The establishment of a system for encouraging the use of materials
7 Obtaining bulletin-board space and the facilities for maintaining appropriate displays

Solutions to these problems are found as each is met and dealt with by the school staff.

The counselor as a coworker and consultant.   The counselor is a coworker in the educational team but also serves in a more special capacity as a consultant. Teachers turn to him for help and suggestions in handling special problems encountered with students. He is also a resource person and gives teachers the benefit of his best professional judgment on matters of mutual concern. The counselor should keep the teacher informed on currently available literature and materials which may have value in both teaching and counseling. Contacts between counselor and teacher may be made by means of personal visits, written announcements, telephone calls, or prepared bulletins. The counselor can be helpful by taking the initiative in the selection of materials for classroom use, in pointing out uses to which they can be put, and in aiding with the interpretation of tests and other kinds of accumulated data.

Conducting lectures and demonstrations.   The counselor prepares and delivers lectures on special topics, conducts discussions, and demonstrates the use of materials or equipment. These activities may be provided for classes, student groups, teachers, or parent groups. He is the best-informed person on the staff on certain subjects, and his knowledge should be made available to all who can profit from his contributions.

Supplying and supervising an information service center.   The library of materials provided for use by teachers and students is the heart of the information service. This library includes the occupational information files, booklets and pamphlets on educational and vocational topics, college and training school catalogs, and related literature. The counselor provides the leadership in the accumulation, display, and utilization of these materials.

Teaching a course in occupations. A course in occupations is offered by some high schools, and the counselor in many cases is the logical person to teach this class. If a teacher asumes this responsibility, the counselor should work with him in providing the necessary materials.

Providing for vocational counseling. The counselor should give a substantial amount of the school day to counseling. Many problems reviewed by students with the counselor are directly related to the preparation for, or selection of, a vocation. Vocational counseling includes providing the student with information about the world of work, interpreting various kinds of data to him, and aiding him toward a better understanding of himself. Factual, intellectual, and emotional aspects of planning and decision making must all be considered and dealt with by the student and counselor.

Providing information and activities for social development. The counselor provides literature from which students can gain helpful information for social development. Appropriate social skills and the ability to work effectively with other people are essential to the success of every worker. The concern for human relationships has increased considerably in recent years, resulting in a substantial output of literature dealing with this vital subject. Opportunities for interaction and the development of social skills are provided through group guidance activities and through structured classroom experiences.

Conducting evaluation and follow-up studies. The information service should be subjected to constant evaluation, and follow-up activities should receive attention from the counselor. Evaluation involves a critical and objective view of the service in an attempt to determine its effectiveness and in order to make improvements. Some suggested procedures for evaluation are:

1   Ascertaining student and teacher opinions and reactions to the service by making personal contact and asking for candid reactions

2 Preparing and circulating questionnaires or checklists by which the judgments of students and faculty and their recommendations for improvements may be obtained

3 Conducting periodic evaluation studies in which criteria are used and ratings obtained on current practices

4 Inviting the participation of people outside the immediate staff to study and evaluate the program

SUMMARY/

The information service provides educational and vocational literature and activities designed to assist students in planning for vocational preparation and selection. The purposes of the information service can be used as guides in developing and conducting it. As these purposes are realized, students are better prepared to profit from the experiences provided within the school and are able to plan and choose more wisely among those educational and vocational opportunities through which personal ambitions may be satisfied. Since vocation selection is a part of the whole developmental process, appropriate activities are provided for students of all ages in keeping with their needs and designed to stimulate them toward greater efforts and a fuller realization of their potentialities.

Many sources of information are available to the school and files of pertinent data are maintained for student use. Both noncommercial and commercial agencies are sources of this information. Facts concerning the nature of various kinds of work, employment prospects, needed training, and related information are available from these agencies.

Some responsibilities are shared by the teacher and counselor, and others are assumed by one or the other. The teacher's activities are conducted primarily within the classroom as integral parts of instruction. The counselor's functions are more specialized and include specific services that he performs for the students and for teachers, as well. He is responsible for the total information service, including vocational counseling and the maintenance of information files. He is also a consultant to whom teachers can turn for aid, encouragement, and information. The success of the service depends to a high degree upon the competence of the counselor and the leadership he provides.

PROBLEMS/

1   The information service provides for meeting certain needs in the lives of students. Enumerate the most important of these.

2   Why is it so essential that a student be well informed about the world of work? Why is this more important now than ever before?

3   The information service is concerned with three kinds of information: vocational, educational, and sociopsychological. Explain the meaning of each of these, and note what the information service does to meet the needs of students in each area.

4   Explain the major functions of the elementary school in the information service. How does this program differ from the one designed for the secondary school?

5   What is the meaning of the term "exploratory experiences"? Note the principles which underlie these experiences.

6   What are the important implications associated with the statement that "vocational selection is a part of the development process"?

7   What are the benefits to be derived from having theories of vocation selection?

8   What is meant by a "composite theory"? How can the counselor capitalize upon this concept?

9   Note the major purposes of the information service. Which of these purposes might be the most difficult to accomplish?

10   What appear to be some of the most challenging problems currently? With which of these problems has research been most helpful? What are your recommendations for research for the immediate future?

11   Note the strengths and weaknesses in the suggested activities to be conducted. How might these be improved?

12   What basic information or publications should each counselor have?

13   In what ways are the functions of the teacher and of the counselor alike? How should they differ?

Selected References

Textbooks

ARBUCKLE, DUGALD S.: *Pupil Personnel Services in American Schools*, Allyn and Bacon, Inc., Boston, 1962, chap. 9.

BERNARD, HAROLD W., D. EVAN JAMES, and FRANKLIN R. ZERAN: *Guidance Services in Elementary Schools*, Chartwell House, New York, 1954, chap. 10.

COTTINGHAM, HAROLD F.: *Guidance in Elementary Schools*, McKnight & McKnight Publishing Company, Bloomington, Ill., 1956, chap. 10.

FROEHLICH, CLIFFORD P.: *Guidance Services in Schools*, McGraw-Hill Book Company, New York, 1958, chaps. 7 and 8.

GLANZ, EDWARD C.: *Foundations and Principles of Guidance*, Allyn and Bacon, Inc., Boston, 1964, chap. 10.

HUMPHREYS, J. ANTHONY, ARTHUR E. TRAXLER, and ROBERT D. NORTH: *Guidance Services*, Science Research Associates, Inc., Chicago, 1960, chap. 13.

JONES, ARTHUR J.: *Principles of Guidance and Pupil Personnel Work*, 5th ed., McGraw-Hill Book Company, New York, 1963, chap. 9.

MC DANIEL, HENRY B.: *Guidance in the Modern School*, The Dryden Press, Inc., New York, 1956, chaps. 11 and 12.

MILLER, FRANK W.: *Guidance Principles and Services*, Charles E. Merrill Books, Inc., Englewood Cliffs, N.J., 1961, chap. 7.

MORTENSEN, DONALD G., and ALLEN M. SCHMULLER: *Guidance in Today's Schools*, John Wiley & Sons, Inc., New York, 1959, chap. 13.

OHLSEN, MERLE M.: *Guidance Services in the Modern School*, Harcourt, Brace & World, Inc., New York, 1964, chap. 10.

SHERTZER, BRUCE, and HERMAN J. PETERS: *Guidance: Techniques for Individual Appraisal and Development*, The Macmillan Company, New York, 1965, chap. 12.

SMITH, GLENN E.: *Principles and Practices of the Guidance Program*, The Macmillan Company, New York, 1951, chap. 6.

STOOPS, EMERY, and GUNNAR L. WAHLQUIST: *Principles and Practices in Guidance*, McGraw-Hill Book Company, New York, 1958, chaps. 4 and 5.

WARTERS, JANE: *High School Personnel Work Today*, 2d ed., McGraw-Hill Book Company, New York, 1956, chap. 9.

WILLIAMSON, E. G.: *Vocational Counseling*, McGraw-Hill Book Company, New York, 1965, chaps. 2 and 3.

Books on Informational Services

BAER, MAX F., and EDWARD C. ROEBER: *Occupational Information*, Science Research Associates, Inc., Chicago, 1958.

BOROW, HENRY (ed.): *Man in a World at Work*, Houghton Mifflin Company, Boston, 1964.

HOPPOCK, ROBERT: *Occupational Information*, 2d ed., McGraw-Hill Book Company, New York, 1963.

NORRIS, WILLA, FRANKLIN R. ZERAN, and RAYMOND N. HATCH: *The Information Service in Guidance*, Rand McNally & Company, Chicago, 1960.

SHARTLE, CARROLL L.: *Occupational Information: Its Development and Application*, Prentice-Hall, Inc., Englewood Cliffs, N.J., 1959.

SUPER, DONALD E.: *The Psychology of Careers*, Harper & Row, Publishers, Incorporated, New York, 1957.

Journals

ANDERSON, THOMAS B., and LEROY C. OLSEN: "Congruence of Self and Ideal-self and Occupational Choices," *Personnel and Guidance Journal*, vol. 44, pp. 171–175, October, 1965.

BORDIN, EDWARD S.: "An Articulated Framework for Vocational Development," *Journal of Counseling Psychology*, vol. 10, no. 2, pp. 107–116, 1963.

BOYD, GERTRUDE A.: "Parents and Teachers Team Up to Give Prevocational Guidance," *Vocational Guidance Quarterly*, vol. 6, pp. 31–34, 1957.

CRITES, JOHN O.: "A Model for the Measurement of Vocational Maturity," *Journal of Counseling Psychology*, vol. 8, no. 3, pp. 255–259, 1961.

DU BATO, GEORGE S.: "Case Conference on Occupation," *Vocational Guidance Quarterly*, vol. 7, pp. 257–259, Summer, 1959.

FITZGERALD, PAUL W.: "Occupations Course Is a Fine Art," *Vocational Guidance Quarterly*, vol. 5, pp. 101–102, Spring, 1957.

GATES, CARROL F.: "Occupational Information Resources for Counseling," *Employment Security Review*, vol. 25, pp. 16–18, April, 1958.

GILKEY, MARGARET: "Vocational Guidance," *Educational Leadership*, vol. 22, pp. 497–504, April, 1965.

GUSTAD, JOHN W.: "Evaluation Interview in Vocational Counseling," *Personnel and Guidance Journal*, vol. 36, pp. 242–250, December, 1957.

HEWER, V. H.: "What Do Theories of Vocational Choice Mean to a Counselor?" *Journal of Counseling Psychology*, vol. 10, pp. 118–125, Summer, 1963.

HOLLAND, JOHN L., and ROBERT C. NICHOLS: "A Longitudinal Study of Change in Major Field of Study," *Personnel and Guidance Journal*, vol. 43, pp. 235–242, November, 1964.

HOPPOCK, ROBERT: "Best Books of 1958 on Vocational Guidance," *Bulletin of the National Association of Secondary-school Principals*, vol. 43, pp. 203–208, May, 1959.

KELLER, FRANKLIN J.: "Vocational Education and Guidance," Sixty-Fourth Yearbook of the National Society for the Study of Education, 1965, part I, pp. 135–167.

KRUMBOLTZ, JOHN D., and WADE W. SCHROEDER: "Promoting Career Planning through Reinforcement and Models," *Personnel and Guidance Journal*, vol. 44, pp. 19–25, September, 1965.

KUNTZ, JAMES E., and CLYDE T. JETTON: "Use and Appraisal of Occupational Literature by Secondary School Counselors," *Personnel and Guidance Journal*, vol. 37, pp. 441–443, February, 1959.

LERNER, LEON L.: " 'Occupationology' in the Education of Counselors," *Vocational Guidance Quarterly*, vol. 10, pp. 160–163, Spring, 1962.

MONTESANO, NICHOLAS, and HAROLD GEIST: "Differences in Occupational Choice between Ninth and Twelfth Grade Boys," *Personnel and Guidance Journal*, vol. 43, pp. 150–154, October, 1964.

ROBINSON, H. ALAN, RALPH P. CONNORS, and ANN H. ROBINSON: "Job Satisfaction Researchers of 1963," *Personnel and Guidance Journal*, vol. 43, pp. 360–366, December, 1964.

RUNDQUIST, RICHARD M., and ROBERT APOSTAL: "Occupational and Educational Information," *Review of Educational Research*, vol. 30, pp. 148–154, April, 1960.

SEGAL, STANLEY J.: "The Use of Clinical Techniques for Structuring Feedback in Vocational Counseling," *Personnel and Guidance Journal*, vol. 43, pp. 876–878, May, 1965.

STRAUSS, SAMUEL: "Career Choices of Scholars," *Personnel and Guidance Journal*, vol. 44, pp. 153–159, October, 1965.

SUPER, DONALD E.: "The Preliminary Appraisal in Vocational Counseling," *Personnel and Guidance Journal*, vol. 36, pp. 154–161, November, 1957.

VAIRO, P. D.: "Occupational Information: Need of American Youth," *Catholic Education Review*, vol. 63, pp. 468–470, October, 1963.

WATLEY, DONIVAN J.: "Time of Decision to Study Engineering," *Personnel and Guidance Journal*, vol. 44, pp. 63–67, September, 1965.

WILLIAMS, J. E.: "Changes in Self and Other Perceptions Following Brief Educational-Vocational Counseling," *Journal of Counseling Psychology*, vol. 9, no. 1, pp. 18–30, Spring, 1962.

TEN

/PLACEMENT AND FOLLOW-UP ACTIVITIES

Placement services and follow-up services are both essential to the guidance program. Educational and vocational placement activities provide students with assistance in choosing courses and in making decisions on job opportunities. The follow-up service ascertains the appropriateness of a course of action for each student after he embarks upon it. True, the functions of placement might be handled in one or more of the other basic areas of the guidance service, such as counseling and the information service, but it is preferable to treat placement as a separate activity in order to minimize the possibility of its being entirely neglected. However, exactly how this area is organized is not important so long as the services are provided.

Follow-up too must be given appropriate attention within the guidance service. It is sometimes considered a part of evaluation as an activity which includes research of various kinds. One of its major functions is the follow-up of former students, who serve as sources of information from which program improvements can be made. Thus the program is subjected to continuous appraisal in an effort to identify weaknesses and to gain data by which improvements can be made. These activities may be regarded as both follow-up and evaluation, but at the same time each constitutes a distinct area of activity within the guidance program.

The nature and purposes of the placement service in both educational and vocational placement are discussed in this chapter. The purposes of follow-up are also considered, and some suggestions for performing this service are given.

The Placement Service

Placement is a service within the guidance program designed to assist students in the selection of suitable courses or curricula, extra-class activities, and part-time or full-time employment. Expanding curricula offerings in the secondary schools, with more opportunities for choosing from a variety of courses, have given new importance to the need for knowing how to make logical choices. The placement service aids the student in making these decisions.

Placement at Elementary and Secondary Levels

Vocational placement as a direct service is of little use in the elementary school; however, educational placement is a matter of concern at all educational levels. Some freedom of course selection is enjoyed by secondary school youth, in contrast to elementary school youngsters, who generally follow a prescribed program of study. However, other educational placement functions are appropriate at the elementary as well as the secondary levels. These functions include such services as (1) providing youngsters with assistance by which a better adjustment might be made to school and to all curricular experiences; (2) providing curricula enrichment experiences within the classroom and making opportunities for children to work with youngsters in other rooms on certain projects, or in a variety of experiences; (3) providing youngsters with opportunities for group experiences in which they exchange ideas and achievements and through which they develop social skills; and (4) encouraging and permitting children to work under the supervision of teachers other than their immediate teacher. Both teachers and counselors contribute to these services and make these enrichment experiences possible.

Similar experiences but with appropriate modifications may be provided for secondary school youth. Guidance in the selection of appropriate courses results in better choices and more efficient time utilization. Encouragement toward participation in extraclass activities is also beneficial, particularly for the more timid youth who may be left out of important activities. Further, aid in finding part-time jobs and in vocational placement following high school is an essential part of placement in the secondary school. Finally, some guidance at this critical time in the life of a young person may mean the difference between wise choices and a life of satisfactory experiences and illogical choices with resulting frustration and unhappiness.

Purposes to Be Served through Placement

Placement functions contribute to the realization of educational and vocational goals. Since every activity should be able to justify its existence and the time and expenditure it requires, a closer look at placement purposes is appropriate.

Proper course and curriculum selection. As students are given personal attention and assistance in making logical, intelligent choices of courses and curricula at the appropriate time, by the counselor and teachers in an organized placement service, delays, disappointments, and inconveniences are minimized for the students. Also, as a result of the expedient handling of placement problems, there is less demand upon the time and energy of school personnel.

Extraclass-activities participation. Students may be encouraged to take part in social groups, clubs, athletics, speech, music, dramatics, and other activities of an appropriate nature. This kind of placement may be as important in a student's present and future life as academic choices. A student's interests, aspirations, and needs are ascertained through counseling and other personal contacts, and recommendations are made as to the kinds of activities that are likely to be interesting and beneficial to him. Referrals may then be made to appropriate staff members and the necessary steps taken to ensure the student's entry into, and success within, the activities of his choice.

Part-time employment. A number of teen-agers have an interest in obtaining part-time jobs by which they can earn money. In some cases such employment is a matter of necessity and may even be a deciding factor in a student's being able to stay in school. Other youngsters want to work just for the satisfaction and enjoyment to be gained. In either case the placement service can provide some assistance in locating suitable employment.

Full-time employment. A full-time job is generally needed by a student who leaves school before graduation or who seeks employment following graduation. One of the purposes of the placement service is to provide these students with the assistance they need in getting started in such a way that they will ultimately see their ambitions realized.

A logical selection of a vocation. A wise choice of a vocation is part of the developmental process of an individual. Rather than a single event, it is the result of many events that take place over a long period of time, including enriching school and other experiences, careful planning, and receiving the aid of interested teachers and counselors.

Decisions on appropriate training programs. Decisions for entering a particular program of training are made as students become acquainted with, and well informed about, the opportunities open to them. Students not going on to college may still need some specialized training for a job. The placement service may locate appropriate schools or training programs for them.

Educational Placement

Educational placement includes activities within the school and deals primarily with aiding youngsters in making logical choices of educational experiences. This kind of placement requires the participation of the teacher, counselor, and principal; all have particular functions to perform. A sympathetic understanding of the student and some awareness as to his needs are most essential in carrying out these services. The most important functions within educational placement include, as already noted, placement in appropriate educational curricula and courses, placement in extraclass activities, and vocational-training placement.

The specific procedures recommended here for a strong and successful educational placement program will vary in their appropriateness and usability from one school to another. Modifications or adjustments should be made to meet local needs and conditions.

1 Keep all information on course offerings up-to-date and immediately available for use with student groups and individuals. This must be done through the cooperative efforts of the staff members responsible for course offerings.

2 Develop a good working relationship with all staff members, and utilize their talents and knowledge in all phases of the placement service. Coordination is essential, as the counselor depends upon the teachers for information and assistance and upon the administration for the necessary leadership and facilities.

3 Conduct personal interviews with students in order to determine their needs and interests. Students also serve as a source of information which might be utilized in aiding other students. Their feelings or judgments about particular courses for example, or other school experiences may be of value to school personnel. Their intimate contacts with other students may also provide information useful to the counselor and teachers in their efforts to improve school conditions for all students.

4 Maintain a file on membership possibilities in clubs and other school organizations. A relatively simple clerical effort could result in the counselor's having at his fingertips information about school organizations which he might use in recommending affiliation with some of these groups. The counselor should know the requirements for membership in these groups, the nature of the activities, and opportunities for the students to take part in the activities.

5 Hold counseling sessions with individual students. Test and other data may be interpreted for students during these sessions and plans formulated for future action. A student will in this way be aided in attaining a more realistic appraisal of himself in relation to opportunities.

Other procedures will occur to the alert counselor as efforts are made to capitalize on the resources of the school and as concern for the welfare of students is transformed into action.

The attitude with which the students are approached and with which the various activities are conducted is just as important as the procedures themselves. Students appreciate a warm attitude of genuine interest on the part of counselors and teachers and generally reciprocate with enthusiasm and dedication. Their desire to plan wisely and choose carefully is bolstered and given clarity under the guidance and direction of a well-organized program.

Vocational Placement

Vocational placement refers to that phase of the placement service which is primarily concerned with (1) aiding students in obtaining part-time or full-time employment and (2) assisting students in gaining appropriate vocational training in order to prepare for job placement. It is directly concerned with making it possible for students to obtain employment or prepare for employment at the most suitable time and in accordance with individual needs.

Although making the ultimate choice of a job or program of training is an event taking relatively little time, the preparation for such choices takes place over a long period of time. Experiences with the educational system and under the guidance service help to prepare a youngster for the time when these decisions will be made —hence the importance of a strong program of personal service to all students during these years of growth and preparation. The decisions are not made during these early years, but the preparation for the decisions is taking place. Wise decisions are likely to follow an excellent program of preparation. Mistakes are to be expected if there has been no preparation or only preparation of poor quality.

Vocational placement activities under the direction of the counselor may be carried out in a variety of ways. However, the suggestions that follow may serve as guides in the promotion and development of the vocational placement service. Resourceful school people will think of many ways by which these suggested procedures may be implemented and will also develop devices of their own.

1   Maintain a card file on all students who have indicated a desire to find employment. Each card should contain the name of the student and the type of work he is seeking. The counselor can then contact the student when suitable opportunities become available.

2   Keep in contact with prospective employers, and maintain a card file containing pertinent information about job possibilities. These job possibilities can then be called to the attention of the students seeking work.

3   Hold periodic meetings with students interested in employment and those looking for suitable training opportunities. This procedure not only keeps students informed but also provides encouragement toward job placement or preparation for a vocation.

4   Hold termination interviews with all youth who leave school prior to graduation. Ascertain their status as to work opportuni-

ties, and provide the necessary assistance by which suitable job placement or training may be obtained.

5　Meet with all seniors early in the school year both in groups and in private sessions. Provide any needed aid or advisement to ensure a logical plan for the future.

6　Hold termination interviews with each high school senior, and determine the status of each in respect to educational or vocational placement following high school. The school should know just what each student plans to do, and the student should avail himself of the assistance the counseling service can provide.

7　Maintain appropriate files of vocational and educational literature, and make them accessible to students. Provide the students with aid in using these files. Teachers should encourage use of such files by their students.

8　Provide adequate bulletin-board space for the display of information about job and training opportunities. The dissemination of information to large numbers of students is possible with this procedure, thus reducing the time needed to keep students informed.

Some school people have the view that job placement is the function of the state and Federal placement agencies and not a school responsibility. These agencies do provide excellent service to people of a community both in job placement and in aiding employers to find qualified workers, but the nature of the placement service of these agencies and that of the school are quite different. The school has close contact with youngsters and is in a favorable position to provide needed aid at critical times. The school also has an interest in, and concern for, the total development of each youngster. Suitable educational or vocational placement is only one area of this concern. A more logical view is to regard the placement functions of the school and the services of employment offices as distinct, essential, supplementing agencies which can assist each other. Neither performs the same functions, and yet the services of both are needed. They are augmenting agencies, not competitors.

The Follow-up Services

The follow-up service is a basic element of the guidance program designed to provide information needed to assist youngsters in making a better adjustment to school, to a vocational training program, or to a job. As previously noted, the objectives of the guidance service itself, of which follow-up is just one part, include wholesome pupil development, satisfactory achievement, good adjustment, and wise choices on the part of all students within the school. Follow-up procedures provide information from which improvements in the school program may be made and by which students may be given needed assistance and encouragement. As data are obtained through follow-up procedures and utilized in making program improvements and in assisting present and former students toward a more fruitful life, everyone is benefited, and the school comes a little closer to fulfilling its obligations to students and to parents.

Educational, vocational, or job placement is merely one step and just one responsibility of the school. Ascertaining the wisdom of the choices made by learning how each person's choices are working out is also important. If errors in judgment have been made, they need to be identified early and steps taken to correct any situation that has turned out to be unpleasant for a student. Follow-up activities make possible the discovery of unwise choices, which in turn leads to corrective measures in the cases followed and insights that can be utilized in helping other youngsters avoid these pitfalls.

Follow-up activities have a place in the elementary school as well as in the secondary school. This topic will be explored briefly, along with giving consideration to the purposes of follow-up and some of the procedures for accomplishing these purposes.

Follow-up Services at All Educational Levels

Since follow-up services involve maintaining contact with all students in the various educational divisions of the school and with students in vocational training programs or in jobs, these services have a part to play and contributions to make at all educational levels. The particular procedures to be followed will of course depend upon the ages of the students and upon needs. The philosophy underlying follow-up as an important service is very much the same for any age level, and the principles to be observed in providing these activities are likewise the same.

Children in the elementary school follow a rather well-established pattern of activities within their classrooms. Most of the "placement" here is done in the class, under a teacher. The role of the counselor is minor in this area, although he provides other kinds of services for elementary children. Follow-up activities are also provided within the class but deal primarily with determining the academic progress of pupils and the appropriateness of various educational experiences. Follow-up involvement for the counselor includes maintaining contact with all pupils whom he has counseled and making certain that adequate adjustments are being made.

The secondary school is more specifically involved in follow-up as a guidance service than the elementary school. The activities are handled by the counselor in the high school, and more definite educational and vocational placements are made, with a resultant need for follow-up procedures. The follow-up service should be regarded by the school as an essential service whereby certain modifications will be made to meet the needs of students.

Purposes of the Follow-up Service

Better personal adjustment for the students, more satisfactory vocational experiences, and continuous educational progress are the ultimate aims of the follow-up service. The realization of the following more specific purposes of this service constitutes the major steps toward the fulfillment of its ultimate goals:

1   To ascertain the progress and status of students within the various classrooms, courses, and curricular areas. Just how each student is doing in his educational endeavors must be determined, and decisions must be made as to the kinds of help he might need.

2   To gain information which can be utilized in helping students make decisions and plan intelligently for the future. Important choices of educational pursuits and vocational aspirations should be made by virtue of available pertinent data. Continuous evaluation of progress and periodic assessment of decisions help to provide these necessary data.

3   To determine the appropriateness of decisions made prior to entry into a particular course of study or into some school activity outside the classroom. Follow-up makes possible a sound evaluation of decisions and courses of action.

4   To determine how well students are doing in part-time employment. A close check with these students should be maintained in order to avoid problems associated with neglecting their school work or of being exploited by employers.

5   To ascertain the job status and progress of former students who accepted employment upon leaving school. These individuals include those who withdrew prior to graduation and those who graduated. To follow through with these people for a few years after they have left school could result in suggestions for possible changes and improvements in their vocational endeavors.

6   To learn how former graduates are progressing in their college

work or vocational training programs. These sources of information are excellent for evaluating present curricular offerings and assessing the effectiveness of the guidance program.

7 To gain data which may identify weaknesses in the various phases of the school program. Continuous evaluation of all areas of the educational endeavor is essential to progress and improvement. Follow-up activities include a systematic approach in obtaining data and in presenting these data in usable form.

8 To conduct research on current problems and formulate conclusions from which essential modifications and additions may be made in the school's services. Problems are generally numerous. The researching of these problems should result in important findings which have immediate use in implementation.

Some Follow-up Procedures

The above and other purposes may be realized through the efficient conduct of the follow-up service. Exact ways of accomplishing these purposes probably do not exist. Imagination, resourcefulness, and interest on the part of staff members are the essential ingredients for progress. The particular procedures employed should be appropriate for existing conditions. Thus, the suggestions made in the following pages may be used as stated, or they may be modified to meet the needs and conditions of a particular school.

Conducting surveys of in-school youth. An occasional survey may be made to obtain data on the present educational status of each student. A determination may be then made as to which courses and extraclass activities are the most helpful to students. Possible instruments and techniques for conducting surveys are those discussed later in this chapter.

Conducting surveys on out-of-school youth. A survey of former students, both dropouts and graduates, should yield information of great value to the school for program improvements. These students may indicate, on the instruments provided, school subjects of the greatest and least worth to them and also which activities may have been most helpful in their development. Recommendations for changes and improvements in the school's services to students may be obtained. Care should be taken to separate the responses of graduates from those of dropouts. Concerted effort should be given to determining the reasons why the latter left school. The responses of these individuals can be extremely useful to those who are striving to bring about the changes needed to keep youth in school until graduation.

Providing for group conferences with students.   Group conferences provide a setting for the free expression of ideas and feelings concerning the school program. Criticisms and suggestions are invited from students in an atmosphere of friendliness and concern. Long-term planning is aided as program weaknesses and strengths are identified and as future needs are anticipated. Potential dropouts may be discovered in these group discussions, and all students can be aided in making plans for the future.

Holding conferences for staff members.   An organized conference of staff members makes possible a concerted attack upon existing problems and encourages cooperative effort toward improvements. One or two short conferences per year with all staff members may be adequate for accomplishing the tasks associated with the follow-up service. Problems may be aired, plans formulated, and recommendations expressed. Staff members are made more conscious of existing problems, and they are given information essential to their understanding of the school's services and programs. Improvements should result from such conferences.

Conducting workshops.   Workshops conducted for selected members of the faculty provide opportunities for the development and implementation of ideas and suggestions. Involvement of a number of teachers and counselors results in a stronger program of educational services.

Instruments and Techniques for Follow-up Activities

What are some of the instruments and techniques by which the procedures of the follow-up service can be carried out? As this question is answered, it will be helpful to keep in mind two important points:

1   There is no one instrument or technique for gaining information. Any one of several procedures, or combinations, may be used to advantage.
2   Procedures used for accomplishing one particular aim or purpose might be used with equal effectiveness in meeting other purposes.

Sound techniques are of use irrespective of the nature of the information being sought. The necessary adaptations and adjustments in techniques can be made as needed to accomplish the purposes of the follow-up activities.

Conducting interviews with individual students.   Follow-up information may be obtained in personal interviews with individual students. Student attitudes are ascertained as the students express themselves about various phases of the school program and about the counselors and teachers conducting the service. Recommendations might be made to the counselor for possible program improvements. The educational or vocational status of students and former students can be learned through these interviews. Suggestions might also be made by the counselor as to how the interviewer might proceed to achieve better results from the interview.

Using questionnaires.   Specific kinds of information are obtainable through the proper use of a questionnaire. The instrument provides space for responses to questions posed by the school. These responses constitute information which serves as a basis for making changes in current school programs and offerings. The questionnaire is especially valuable as a means of reaching people by mail and for obtaining spontaneous opinions and judgments.

Developing and utilizing checklists.   The checklist too may be useful for assessing attitudes, soliciting opinions, and gaining facts. It differs from the questionnaire in that the possible responses are included on the instrument and the respondent has only to indicate his choices. The checklist has the advantage of being easier to complete and taking less time. More people will respond to this instrument than to a questionnaire. It also permits the school to structure the items so that only essential data are gathered.

Soliciting written statements.   Current and former students can be encouraged to make written statements in which their reactions to the various school programs are expressed. Former students currently in college, in vocational training, or on jobs might be asked for candid statements about the school and how it helped or failed to help them. Although somewhat subjective, these responses have the advantage of being free, uninhibited reactions. Such statements from faculty members may also be helpful and may provide insights useful in aiding students. The amount of structuring to be included should be determined by the judgment of the school personnel making the study. Some structuring provides a framework for responses and results in the giving of essential information. Some freedom of responses should also be permitted.

Providing for group discussions. By means of group discussions and reports the participants are able to exchange ideas, note weaknesses in the program, and make recommendations for changes. While currently enrolled students are available for these activities, former students obviously are not, unless special arrangements for such meetings can be made. Some preparation might be made for these discussions by notifying participants as to their nature and use. More fruitful discussions may result than if no thought is given to the problem ahead of time. Group discussions yield a sampling of opinions, encourage personal contact and exchange, indicate a genuine interest on the part of the school, and suggest that improvements are always possible and generally needed.

SUMMARY/

Placement and follow-up services are essential to the guidance program of a school. The educational placement service helps students choose courses wisely, the vocational service helps them reach sound decisions as to obtaining employment, and the follow-up service gathers information about the ways these choices and decisions have worked out for the students.

The purposes to be served by the placement service include course and curriculum selection, participation in extraclass activities, placement in part-time employment while in school or full-time following school, vocation selection, and placement in appropriate training programs or colleges. Certain procedures are recommended by which these purposes can be fulfilled and by which the program of placement can be expedited.

Placement and follow-up activities are conducted at both the elementary and secondary levels, but with somewhat different objectives and with different techniques. The purposes of the follow-up service are essentially to evaluate the progress and status of students in the various educational endeavors and job activities and thereby to gain information needed for improving the educational offerings of the school. There are certain instruments and techniques by which these activities can be carried out.

PROBLEMS/

    1 Suppose a school had all the basic elements of a guidance program except placement. In what ways would the students of this school be neglected?

    2 What are some of the reasons for the apparent neglect of placement activities?

    3 Point out some essential differences between placement in the elementary school and placement at the secondary school level.

    4 What are some reasons for dividing placement into the two categories of educational and vocational?

    5 Enumerate the ways in which students are helped by a placement service in the school.

    6 What is the meaning of "follow-up services"? What are the benefits to be derived from this (*a*) by elementary school pupils, (*b*) by secondary school students, and (*c*) by the staff?

    7 List some of the procedures and activities of the follow-up program. Indicate in each instance the reasons for using the procedure.

    8 Explain the relationship between follow-up activities and research.

Selected References

Textbooks

FROEHLICH, CLIFFORD P.: *Guidance Services in Schools*, 2d ed., McGraw-Hill Book Company, New York, 1958, chap. 11.

HUMPHREYS, J. ANTHONY, ARTHUR E. TRAXLER, and ROBERT D. NORTH: *Guidance Services*, Science Research Associates, Inc., Chicago, 1960, chap. 10.

HUTSON, PERCIVAL W.: *The Guidance Function in Education*, Appleton-Century-Crofts, Inc., New York, 1958, chap. 17.

KOWITZ, GERALD T., and NORMA G. KOWITZ: *Guidance in the Elementary Classroom*, McGraw-Hill Book Company, New York, 1959, chap. 10.

OHLSEN, MERLE M.: *Guidance Services in the Modern School*, Harcourt, Brace & World, Inc., New York, 1964, chap. 12.

PETERS, HERMAN J., and GAIL F. FARWELL: *Guidance: A Developmental Approach*, Rand McNally & Company, Chicago, 1959, chaps. 16 and 17.

ROTHNEY, JOHN W. M.: *Guidance Practices and Results*, Harper & Row, Publishers, Incorporated, New York, 1958, chap. 4.

SMITH, GLENN E.: *Principles and Practices of the Guidance Program*, The Macmillan Company, New York, 1951, chaps. 8 and 9.

STOOPS, EMERY, and GUNNAR L. WAHLQUIST: *Principles and Practices in Guidance*, McGraw-Hill Book Company, New York, 1958, chaps. 7 and 8.

TRAXLER, ARTHUR E., and ROBERT D. NORTH: *Techniques of Guidance*, Harper & Row, Publishers, Incorporated, New York, 1966, chap. 17.

WILLEY, ROY DE VERL: *Guidance in Elementary Education*, Harper & Row, Publishers, Incorporated, New York, 1960, chap. 6.

—— and DEAN C. ANDREW: *Modern Methods and Techniques in Guidance*, Harper & Row, Publishers, Incorporated, New York, 1955, chap. 15.

Journals

HALL, L. G.: "A Gap in Our High School Program," *Bulletin of the National Association of Secondary-school Principals*, vol. 47, pp. 32–39, September, 1963.

O'NEILL, J. H.: "Follow Up Service in Guidance," *Catholic School Journal*, vol. 57, pp. 23–24, December, 1957.

WOOTTEN, RICHARD H., and FLORENCE M. WOOTTEN: "A Guidance-oriented Evaluation of a Student Survey," *Bulletin of the National Association of Secondary-school Principals*, vol. 47, pp. 58–77, September, 1963.

PART 3/

Related and augmenting activities

ELEVEN

/GROUP GUIDANCE ACTIVITIES

Many of the purposes to be served by a guidance program may be accomplished through the utilization of procedures which accommodate students in small groups. These group approaches are designed to supplement and augment the work of the counselor with individuals and the efforts of the teacher in instruction to make school experiences more meaningful and beneficial. Group guidance has a reciprocal relationship with other guidance activities, including the basic services of the pupil inventory, testing, counseling, information service, and placement and follow-up. Evaluation, research, multiple counseling, and related guidance activities also have a reciprocal relationship with group guidance. Each service aids and contributes to the other. Instruction too is benefited by the services of group guidance, and the learning capabilities of students are enhanced as insights are gained, social skills developed, and abilities more efficiently utilized. Although group guidance shares in a mutual exchange of information with other school activities and there is sometimes an overlap of service, it has unique features and characteristics.

Group experiences within the classroom under the direction of the teacher are designed primarily to facilitate learning. Group activities within the guidance service are conducted by the counselor with the principal aim of better personal adjustment. The significance of all group work is summarized in this statement: [1] "In the opinion of the authors, the importance of group work in counseling cannot be overestimated. Group work provides educators with an excellent way of determining a student's maturity level, his socioeconomic background, his value system, his attitudes, and his basic interpersonal behavior. Learning to be an adequate group member can be considered a major developmental task for the individual."

The present chapter explains the nature of group guidance and points out its distinguishing characteristics. The purposes of group guidance and the principles to be observed in conducting these activities are also established. The merits and limitations of group guidance are given and suggestions offered as to the counselor's qualifications. This is followed by a discussion on how to initiate and carry out group activities and how to select participants.

The Nature of Group Guidance Activities

The term "guidance" suggests an interest in the personal welfare of each individual being served. As we have seen, guidance activities have as their main objectives the educational, social, emotional, and psychological development of each youngster. Group guidance is that phase of the guidance service which provides youth with opportunities to share ideas and experiences with others within an organized setting under the direction of a competent counselor. Its purposes include giving and receiving information and providing an appropriate atmosphere for a free exchange of ideas and suggestions. It also provides the setting in which insights are gained, self-understanding is facilitated, growth and maturity are enhanced, logical decisions for action are made, and commitments to behavior changes are realized. Therapeutic benefits are realized and social skills developed in an environment that is both permissive and supportive. The ultimate goal is individual growth by each participant.

Group guidance includes those activities within the organization of a guidance program wherein several students meet, interact,

[1] Daniel W. Fullmer and Harold W. Bernard, *Counseling: Content and Process,* Science Research Associates, Inc., Chicago, 1964, p. 183.

gain information, share ideas, plan for the future, and make decisions. The possibilities for becoming better informed on a number of topics, for gaining new insights, for stimulating and assisting others, for developing social skills, for improving mental health, and for increasing achievements are many within group guidance.

Involvement in Activity

Group procedures permit and encourage active involvement by each student in the process. It is only through this involvement that lasting growth can take place. The small-group experience not only makes this involvement possible but depends upon high-level involvement for its existence. This experience, therefore, is not the same as participation in a class discussion, nor is it the same kind of activity as that experienced in counseling. The participant gives expression to his feelings, he verbalizes his ideas, he interacts with others, and he anticipates individual and group reaction both to his statements and to himself as a person. His behavior is a reflection of a new freedom not encountered elsewhere, and the exhilaration or anxiety or depression felt are reactions to a situation which provides a setting and offers challenges quite different from anything he has previously known. At least some of the growth he now experiences comes from his efforts to adjust, adapt, and contribute to the group.

Fullmer and Bernard note that *involvement in process* is the most important part of the counseling function, and that it is also important in group work.[2] This involvement includes more than just participation. Real emotions are involved. However, growth does not necessarily occur with the expression of an emotion. The force behind these feelings must be utilized in order for growth to occur.[3]

The Criteria for Group Guidance

Applying the criteria listed below is the soundest method of ascertaining whether an activity is bona fide group guidance. If the criteria are met, the activity may indeed be group guidance; if they are not met, a more appropriate designation should be used for the activity. For example, if the activity has a criterion of therapeutic benefits, it more logically belongs with group therapy than group

[2] *Ibid.*
[3] *Ibid.*, p. 184.

guidance. Some of the criteria listed here could, of course, be used in assessing other guidance activities, but not in the same combination or with the same emphasis.

1 Individual growth is a major objective. Although group members combine efforts in a common enterprise, each must profit individually from the experience.
2 Interaction between and among group members is essential. There is some independence of individual expression but also a dependence upon other group members. Unless this condition exists, the activity is not group guidance.
3 Usability and practicality are necessary. Functional possibilities must be present and new knowledge applied to a practical situation.
4 The potential for improvement and change must exist within each individual and within the group setting, and changes must eventually occur, even if accurate predictions are not made as to the nature or extent of personal growth to be realized by each group member.
5 A commonality of purposes must prevail. High-level involvement takes place as efforts are combined to gain information and as problems common to all are attacked.
6 Homogeneity of participants and concerns marks an effective group. The participants should possess personal characteristics to some degree common to all, and the focus of interaction should be on problems of mutual interest and concern.
7 Competent, qualified leadership must exist. Some structuring, organizing, and initiating are necessary. Considerable freedom exists within each group as it begins to function, but competent leadership is a primary requisite.
8 Organization as to time, place, topics, and information is essential.

Types of Group Guidance Activities

Group guidance activities include a variety of procedures by which all elements of the guidance service can be enhanced. Not only is group guidance an opportunity for interaction among participants, for the sharing of ideas and information, and for growth experience for the individual, but also there are therapeutic benefits as individual members gain new insights, clarify and come to a better understanding of their feelings, and improve self-understanding.

There are several kinds of group activities involving somewhat different approaches and having different major purposes.

Group instruction. Group instruction is a procedure within the classroom setting designed to further the learning process. Lecturing, class discussions, oral and written reports, and dramatizations are examples of teaching procedures. Group instruction is another. Its aim is to aid youngsters toward greater academic achievements and scholastic attainments. Its major purpose is not personal development as is the case with group guidance. Group instruction does not meet the criteria established earlier for group guidance. It is under the direction of the teacher and is conducted as a teaching technique. Although group guidance also involves instruction, it should be understood that the topics upon which information is given and shared are not the same, nor are the setting, atmosphere, leadership, and purposes the same. The previously established criteria should be helpful in noting these differences.

Group counseling. Terms such as "group guidance," "multiple counseling," and "group therapy" have normally been used in describing certain processes and activities taking place with a small number of participants. The term "group counseling" has not always been generally acceptable because of the apparent contradiction in the term. Counseling has generally been defined as a one-to-one relationship between a counselor and a client. The use of the word "group" may thus require a redefinition of counseling. However, "group counseling" is currently used in describing a kind of group activity, and the objections to its use have been answered satisfactorily. Of significance is this statement by Wright: [4] "In the studies reviewed, the use of the term *group counseling* exceeded significantly the references to *multiple counseling*, although the terms were generally considered interchangeable as distinguishable from group guidance." Perhaps more people feel comfortable with the term "group counseling" than with "multiple counseling," and the term is probably a more accurate description of the activity being sponsored. Ohlsen [5] makes a distinction between group counseling and group work and notes that the use of the terms "group counseling" or "group therapy" depends upon the preference of the author.

> When speaking of the group relations and group objectives briefly sketched above, some writers use the term group counseling while others prefer group

[4] E. Wayne Wright, "Group Procedures," *Review of Educational Research,* vol. 33, pp. 205–206, April, 1963.

[5] Merle M. Ohlsen, *Guidance: An Introduction,* Harcourt, Brace & World, Inc., New York, 1955, p. 295.

therapy. Though there are different levels of counseling which are a function of the counselor's or therapist's skills, writers' disagreement over the name for the process is not worth quibbling about here. It is important, however, that we discriminate between group counseling on the one hand and group work on the other. Group counseling is concerned with an individual's personal problems . . . ; while group work . . . places greater emphasis on social issues and the imparting of information.

Arbuckle, on the other hand, objects to the use of the term "group counseling" and notes that [6] "When Ohlsen . . . refers to group counseling . . . he is obviously describing group therapy as it is envisaged in this book, not group guidance." Arbuckle makes his major distinction between group guidance and group therapy. He gives ten major characteristics of each.[7] Therefore, one might conclude that he would place "group counseling," if he used the term at all, under "group guidance." Bennett suggests that the term "group counseling" has become very popular and that practices under this name have been used rather widely in school systems.[8] Certainly the use of group activities within the schools has increased, and varying degrees of success have been observed. However, not all these group counseling activities meet the criteria or standards by which such activities are evaluated. A logical assumption is that some of these group sessions belong most logically with group instruction or under some designation other than group counseling.

Group counseling is an activity conducted within the guidance program of an educational institution in which three to eight students are accommodated in counseling sessions under the direction of a qualified counselor. In this case the major distinction made between counseling and group counseling is in the number of participants. All other conditions are essentially the same.

Multiple counseling. Multiple counseling, for all practical purposes, may be regarded as essentially the same as group counseling. It is described as an activity conducted for the benefit of individual students within a small-group setting under the direction of a qualified counselor, with the personal growth of the participants as

[6] Dugald S. Arbuckle, *Guidance and Counseling in the Classroom,* Allyn and Bacon, Inc., Boston, 1957, pp. 329–330.

[7] *Ibid.,* pp. 328–329.

[8] Margaret E. Bennett, *Guidance and Counseling in Groups,* 2d ed., McGraw-Hill Book Company, New York, 1963, p. 136.

its major objective. It involves the utilization of known counseling techniques with small groups of individuals. The two terms might be used in describing counseling sessions in which there are several participants. A somewhat arbitrary position of this text is that group counseling and multiple counseling might differ from each other in two respects:

1   Group counseling is somewhat narrower in its purposes and coverage of topics. The problems discussed and matters of concern are generally of the kind given consideration in a guidance service. The problems are personal but may not have the same depth, nor are they pursued with the same intensity, as those in multiple counseling.
2   A number of students can take part in group counseling without necessarily receiving individual counseling. Profitable experiences may be had by students of all ages in a group setting with or without the accompanying individual counseling, desirable as the combination may be.

Driver states that [9] "The multiple counseling method . . . uses a small-group discussion activity as the learning medium for personal growth of participants, conjunctive with individual counseling by the group leaders." In describing the multiple counseling method she states that [10] "The group structure and discussion content depends upon the needs of the group and the type of leadership. The project may be a human relations or personal development course; it may be group or vocational guidance; it may be group therapy or psychotherapy." She further notes that the extent and depth of the counseling given depend upon the qualifications of the leader.[11] Group counseling or multiple counseling do not normally include psychotherapy as they are used in the school setting. Group guidance activities in the school do not meet the criteria for group therapy and should not be given this designation. However, "therapeutic" benefits may accrue to the participants with the group—irrespective of title. A logical view is that counseling and psychotherapy differ essentially in depth and length of treatment, degree of seriousness of the problem, and qualifications of the counselor. A hard-and-fast line of distinction between the two is not necessary, however, if the counselor or therapist is qualified.

Clifford Froehlich has referred to multiple counseling as a con-

[9] Helen Irene Driver, *Counseling and Learning through Small-group Discussion*, Monona Publications, Madison, Wis., 1958, p. 19.
[10] *Ibid.*, p. 27.
[11] *Ibid.*

cept of counseling and an experimental technique.[12] Since it is experimental, an attitude of inquiry should prevail as it is used. There is far more to be learned about multiple counseling than is presently known. In discussing when to use multiple counseling, Wright notes that it has value for achieving most of the goals of individual counseling and that it can often be more efficient than, and comparable in effectiveness to, individual counseling.[13] He also states that many similarities exist between individual and group counseling and hence there is the need for the counselor to identify the procedures he has found successful in individual counseling and then use them appropriately with groups.[14]

The possibilities for the use of group procedures in the educational setting at elementary and secondary school and college levels are many. Competent leadership and enthusiastic participants can make group guidance techniques most valuable in aiding young people in their development. The future should bring considerable expansion, progress, and research in this area.

Group therapy. The term "group therapy" belongs primarily to activity associated with the field of psychotherapy. It can be used to describe activities in an educational setting only under one of two conditions: (1) where an awareness prevails among the participants that it is a borrowed term and that "group counseling" or "multiple counseling" may be a more appropriate designation for the activity, or (2) where the essential criteria are met whereby "group therapy" can be considered the most appropriate term. These criteria should include a qualified counseling psychologist, clinician, or psychiatrist and a structure which permits emotional problems to be treated with depth and intensity over a period of time. Unless a school district provides the necessary facilities and personnel for such clinical services, a reasonable assumption is that the group activities being conducted are not truly group therapy. However, the term is included in this discussion for purposes of noting the major characteristics of the different group techniques in a guidance service and to encourage schools to provide such services both as a preventive measure and as treatment for youngsters with more serious emotional problems.

[12] Clifford P. Froehlich, "Multiple Counseling: A Research Proposal," unpublished manuscript, University of California at Berkeley, Berkeley, Calif.
[13] E. Wayne Wright, "Multiple Counseling: Why? When? How?" *Personnel and Guidance Journal*, vol. 37, pp. 551–557, 1959.
[14] *Ibid.*, p. 557.

Group therapy might be described as a psychological service afforded several individuals experiencing emotional problems within a setting which permits a free, uninhibited expression of feelings and interaction among group members under the direction of a qualified clinician. The characteristics of group therapy, listed below, may also be appropriate for each of the other group techniques; the differences are those of degree.

1   The person's feelings are of paramount importance. How he feels about the problem may be more important than the problem itself.
2   Considerable freedom is permitted, with few restrictions other than those the group might impose either directly or by implication.
3   Size of the group is limited to about five or six members, to permit considerable opportunity for expression and interchange.
4   The growth of the individual is a major aim. He is more important than the group. The group technique is merely a means to this end.
5   Although complete agreement may not be achieved and furthermore is not necessary, each member must be accepted by the others and must receive their encouragement and support.

Since 1934 Slavson has used group therapy as a method of psychotherapy in New York City under the Jewish Board of Guardians. This board is a social service agency that provides child guidance service to children with personality problems.[15] Slavson's work is conducted within a clinical setting, with qualified clinicians and psychiatrists working with children who are experiencing rather serious emotional disturbances.

Slavson states that grouping, as a social phenomenon, is not an invention but has its roots in nature. Groupings are essential to man's psychological and spiritual life, and man consciously uses groups for personality enhancement.[16] He also notes that true psychotherapy differs from guidance or counseling and can be effective "only through the process of emotional regression and reliving of traumatic feelings and memories of the past."[17]

School officials should consider the possibilities of providing some group therapy service. Matters of cost, facilities, and personnel cannot be ignored; however, providing clinical services within the

[15] S. R. Slavson, *An Introduction to Group Therapy,* International Universities Press, Inc., New York, 1954, preface.
[16] S. R. Slavson, *A Textbook in Analytic Group Psychotherapy,* International Universities Press, Inc., New York, 1964, p. 7.
[17] *Ibid.,* p. 37.

structure of a school district is preferable to having to rely upon outside agencies.

Purposes to Be Served through Group
Guidance Procedures

Group guidance does not stand alone as a separate service but is a means by which the basic elements of the guidance program can be carried out more economically, efficiently, and effectively. It is a technique by which students can be aided in their progress and development. Group guidance activities supplement other activities and add to their strength and meaning; they do not supplant anything. Although several studies have attempted to determine the relative merits of individual and group counseling, there is nothing to be gained by assuming that one is a substitute for the other. Nor is any form of group guidance to be used as a substitute for some other essential activity in the guidance service. As Wright has stated,[18] "The mounting research evidence in support of group counseling cannot be ignored. However, the distinctive merits of group counseling as compared with individual counseling are still inconclusive." Since they both have a place in the guidance service, perhaps the evidence should remain "inconclusive."

A summary of the purposes of group guidance might include the following items:

1   To make it possible for students to experience support and understanding on the part of other students. Strength is gained and self-confidence improves as participants realize that other people have similar problems and as they are able to give and receive support.

2   To allow each student to derive personal benefits from the interaction taking place with others. The student may benefit even more or in a different way than in private contacts with a counselor.

3   To identify students needing additional assistance. An observant counselor is able to spot individuals who are in apparent need of personal assistance.

4   To promote a readiness for individual counseling. Group experiences often result in an increased desire to seek counseling and in more maturity with which to profit from it.

5   To help develop social skills. Actual experience in social interaction, verbal exchanges, and shared planning is gained in

[18] "Group Procedures," p. 211.

groups. Learning is facilitated and behavior improved as a result of practical experiences in socializing.

6 To provide for therapeutic benefits, new insights, and better adjustment. Although the sessions are not group therapy sessions as such, the experiences yield genuine therapeutic benefits.

7 To increase counselor contact with a large number of students. Timidity may be overcome, inhibitions reduced, and attitudes improved as students become acquainted with their counselor. The counselor is thus aware of more students and their problems and is better prepared to be of service to them.

8 To contribute to feelings of security and self-confidence of young people. Youngsters feel more secure as they are able to gain status with their peers and as they experience the satisfaction of being a friend and having friends. Self-confidence improves as social skills develop and as youngsters are able to feel and take pride in their personal worthiness.

9 To provide opportunities for orientation to the counseling function. The reluctance to seek counseling may be reduced or eliminated as a student becomes acquainted with a counselor in the group setting and as his apprehensions and doubts are dissipated in a pleasant experience with counselor and peers.

10 To integrate the various educational experiences and provide the structure necessary for maximum benefits to be gained. Many of the school's activities become more meaningful to students, and a more harmonious relationship is realized among all elements of the school program as problems are discussed and procedures clarified.

11 To reduce tensions and anxieties of students and replace worry with action. Frank discussions within a friendly, accepting environment and the formulation of courses of action often result in fewer worries and a more energetic pursuit of work to be done.

12 To contribute to the efficiency of the counselor and the teacher in carrying out their tasks. Service to many students can be increased and its quality improved by working with several students in organized groups.

How well the major purposes of group guidance are realized is determined to some degree by the quality of the service itself. An important phase of the program is the initial stage in which action is begun. Some important aspects of this initial stage are considered in the next section.

Initiating Group Activities

The total guidance service depends upon group activities for the dissemination of information as well as for providing students with experiences which make their schooling more meaningful. Although there is no set formula for getting group activities started, suggestions will be given later in the chapter for satisfactorily putting these activities into action.

Problems and Deterrents to Progress

If the staff is aware of the usual problems and pitfalls that confront the typical school in initiating and carrying out group guidance activities, they will be able to take appropriate action to avoid these possible deterrents to progress or to deal with them as they occur.

The problems ordinarily encountered in the conduct of group guidance activities are not unlike the problems experienced in carrying out other activities in the school program. Any service to students requires planning and an intelligent, informed approach in order to proceed with efficiency. The following is a list of some of the usual deterrents to the initiation of group activities.

1   Disagreement within the staff as to the form and nature of the service to be provided. A teaching and counseling staff usually represents a variety of backgrounds, orientations, and biases. Full agreement is not likely to occur immediately as to the place of group guidance in the school program.
2   Difficulty in finding the time for group activities within the school day. Heavy demands are made upon time with many activities clamoring for a substantial portion of the school day. Unless plans are made carefully, some essential activities will be neglected.
3   Diversity of opinions as to the structure of groups and the kinds of problems or topics to be dealt with.
4   Difficulty in providing competent leadership for conducting group sessions. The school counselor should be qualified and willing to assume the leadership of these sessions. Additional help may be necessary, however.
5   Problems in coordinating group activities with other phases of the guidance service and educational program. No one service can function without the cooperation of others. A cooperative working relationship among group guidance and other phases of the guidance program, particularly counseling, and a clear understanding as to the major purposes of each

service and its contribution to each of the other services are essential for effective operation. The total program of activities must be viewed and each activity seen in its proper perspective.

6 Lack of broad support within the school and the community. Enthusiasm and competence of a few people will not do the job. The school as a whole, and especially its teachers, must be in agreement with the total program, and the community too should be informed and cooperative.

7 Difficulty in obtaining necessary facilities and materials. Very little beyond the necessities of the usual school program in facilities or materials is required; however, even the bare minimum may be hard to obtain in some schools.

8 Lack of adequate instructions for teachers in the use of group procedures in their classrooms. Plans to supply such instruction must be formulated and carried out.

9 Lack of differentiation between guidance activities and instruction. Although there may be some overlap between these two activities, their differences should be understood, and practices should reflect this understanding.

The resolution of these and other problems will require intelligent consideration during the early stages of establishing the group guidance program.

Suggestions for Handling Problems

Many problems will be eliminated or minimized if careful thought is given to organizing and preparing for group guidance activities. A first consideration is to determine the purposes to be served by the program. These purposes may then be used as guides in establishing all the elements of the program and in following through with the various services to be provided. The counselor may arbitrarily develop a list of essential purposes of group guidance, or he may solicit the assistance of others in developing these guidelines. The latter procedure has these two principal advantages: (1) the final list will reflect the thinking and contributions of several people, and (2) the solicitation of contributions brings about involvement, which in turn stimulates people toward greater interest in the project. Following are some suggestions to the school personnel on how to obtain this help in establishing guidelines from various sources:

1 Ask faculty members for suggestions as to the major purposes of the group guidance program. These queries might be made

through written communications, by personal contacts, or in faculty meetings.

2 Request the appointment of a committee whose task it would be to prepare statements on the purposes to be served. This committee might represent various segments of the faculty from which sources further suggestions might in turn be received.

3 Have the counselor assume the responsibility for preparing the initial list, and then submit it to the rest of the staff for recommended changes.

4 Utilize the sources given in textbooks and journals for gaining ideas to be incorporated in the list. These need not be used verbatim, but they may suggest items to be included.

5 Make a survey of the students, and from this determine the major problems of students. Decisions may then be made as to which problems may be handled adequately by means of group procedures.

6 Solicit the reactions and suggestions of parents through a prepared questionnaire or checklist on which the parents can indicate the major problems of their youngsters and thus aid the school in identifying both problem areas and particular youngsters with these problems.

7 Utilize the resources of accessible colleges, including the help of appropriate professors. Colleges can be a source of technical assistance as well as ideas and suggestions.

The above suggestions can be used in various combinations. Exact procedures are not so important so long as those adopted have the support of the staff.

Kinds of Problems Considered by Groups

No distinction need be made between the kinds of problems handled in individual counseling and those dealt with in group counseling. In some cases, particularly if the group procedures being used are those of multiple counseling, students participate in both individual and group counseling sessions. However, group procedures lend themselves better to some problems than to others, and the same is true of individual counseling. Those problems that may be advantageously dealt with in groups can be arbitrarily classified as follows:

1 Vocational problems. Group procedures are often very helpful in assisting young people to a better understanding of the vocational possibilities open to them. Information may be made

available to the group by the counselor, information gathered by group members may be shared, and questions of group members may be answered. Sources of data may be identified and students given directions on how to locate and use these data.

2 Educational problems. Many problems encountered by students are directly or indirectly related to their educational programs. Since students have similar concerns and need the same information that everyone generally requires, group procedures are highly appropriate in that they provide the most help in a limited amount of time.

3 Social adjustment. Group work provides the opportunity for participation, interaction, and practice in developing social skills. Many youngsters feel tense, lack self-confidence, and generally feel inadequate in their peer relationships. Participation with others in a cooperative, shared relationship reduces tensions and helps develop self-confidence. With improved social skills come stronger feelings of adequacy and competence.

4 Personality problems. Related to social adjustment is the problem of personality development. Insights may be gained as youngsters discuss freely their problems with others experiencing similar concerns. The seriousness of the problem would need to be considered before deciding on the nature of the help to be given. Group therapy, rather than the more typical group procedures, may be in order for students with more serious problems. Youngsters with the usual personality problems can obtain help in properly organized groups.

5 Test interpretation. Data on student aptitudes, interests, and achievement are gained from the testing service. These data can be interpreted for students and the major implications called to their attention quickly and efficiently within organized groups.

It is to be emphasized, however, that there is really no clear-cut limit on the kinds of problems to be considered in groups, nor do the concerns of young people fall into neatly divided categories. Nor is it necessary to determine exactly the nature of the problems besetting students at any one time. The creation of a strong, positive, relationship within a climate which is conducive to individual progress and growth is the key to problem resolution.

The Selection of Participants

Some thought should be given to the selection of students to participate in group activities. While the involvement of all students in these activities would be most desirable, there are practical, administrative problems to consider. Appropriate facilities, leadership personnel, and time are some of the problems encountered. Since the impracticability of a broad, inclusive program of group guidance during the initial stages is quite obvious, it is well to consider establishing a somewhat limited program with the potential for expansion.

Three basic assumptions might be made at the outset:

1   Many of the group activities at the elementary school level will be for purposes of instruction, rather than for guidance. The latter is possible and desirable but is not likely to take place immediately on a very wide scale. Some of the benefits of group guidance will be experienced in these groups even though the purpose is instruction.

2   Some students are in greater need of assistance than others and should be given priority. Once these students are identified, opportunities for participation should be provided. As the program is expanded, other students may also be brought in.

3   Certain limitations of time, personnel, and facilities exist in every school. These problems should be faced realistically, improvements made where possible, and appropriate adjustments made in order to realize maximum benefit from the school's strengths and to minimize the limitations.

Criteria for selection.   A guide by which participants may be selected might be in the form of criteria such as the following:

1   Age. The school must provide these experiences for the older students first on the assumption that the younger ones will have opportunities later. Also, a child should be old enough to assume his responsibilities as a group member.

2   Maturity. Some degree of maturity is necessary in order for a person to gain insights and to benefit from the group experiences.

3   Need. In view of the limitations imposed by existing conditions, participants should be selected on the basis of need for the kinds of help that group procedures can provide.

4   Intelligence. Certain precautions would of course have to be taken in order to avoid unfair discrimination against the less gifted. However, a degree of intellectual competence is necessary for a person to profit from the interaction in a group. A student's problems might in fact be intensified rather than alleviated if he is not equal to the task.

5   Time. A student should have adequate time free of other school responsibilities in order to take part in group work.

6 Homogeneity. There should be some degree of homogeneity within each operating group, both as to participants and the nature of the problems being considered.

These or similar criteria can be sufficient for organizing groups and beginning the sessions. Modifications may be made later, as the situation may demand. Members may be added or dropped, or members of different groups may exchange places. The group leadership may also change periodically, and the topics being discussed may be changed.

Group size. In selecting participants personnel should carefully consider the sizes of the groups. Once size has been determined, the number of active groups can be anticipated. The advantages and disadvantages of the group that is too small or the one that is too large are most likely evident to the teacher or counselor. The immediate purposes to be served also serve as a guide in determining group size. For example, if maximum individual participation and interaction is a major purpose, the groups should be kept quite small. If a broad exchange of information is the purpose, larger groups would be desirable. As a general guide, a group of three is generally too small, while nine are too many. Groups of five to seven are regarded as being of appropriate size for most activities taking place under group guidance.

Forming the groups. Groups may be formed in several ways: (1) the counselor may make the assignments either on the basis of homogeneity or arbitrarily; (2) participants may be given a choice of groups; (3) group members may be selected by chance; (4) students may be asked to indicate a problem area they would like to discuss and the group then formed according to these problems. There are other methods for organizing the groups. Exactly who is in the group is not a major consideration initially. The important thing is to get under way and then make the necessary modifications.

Groups in Action

Once appropriate plans have been made and the organizational pattern to be followed has been established, the actual work of the groups can be undertaken. The purposes established earlier in regard to starting a group may be used also as guides in conducting the activities of the group session. The separate groups will vary, each with its particular personality and unique qualities; freedom and flexibility are therefore needed in order that each group's activities may be of the greatest possible benefit to its members.

Kinds of Groups

Although the groups will change in membership, procedures, and results, kinds of groups to be organized may be classified as follows:

1 Groups supplementing the classroom. Problems may arise as a part of the classroom situation to which more time and attention should be given than is possible in the classroom. These problems may be handled in group sessions; the benefits gained will result in an improved classroom environment.

2 Information-giving sessions. Certain aspects of the guidance program may be expedited by providing small groups of students with essential information. Individual questions may be answered and vague ideas clarified.

3 Course-planning sessions. Instead of leaving each student to his own devices and errors, groups are organized in which members provide assistance to one another in planning courses and other school activities.

4 College and other post-high school planning sessions. Together with other students who have similar aspirations, each student can plan for his future by obtaining ideas and information from others, and in so doing gain some new insights and understandings.

5 Vocation-planning sessions. These sessions can be for students seeking part-time employment while in school and for those looking forward to employment following graduation.

6 Test-interpretation groups. Following the testing experiences everyone should have the opportunity to review the results of his tests. Limited staff may make individual interviews impossible. Considerable general information can be provided in group sessions from which students may draw their own profile sheets, have their questions answered, and come to an understanding as to the meaning and significance of their individual profiles.

7 Multiple counseling groups. In these groups, problems of the members are discussed freely in a highly permissive atmosphere. Procedures here are similar to those used in individual counseling, the major difference being the number of participants.

8 Group therapy. This is similar to multiple counseling but is distinguished from it by the intensity and seriousness of the problem and the professional qualifications of the person conducting the session.

The above classification of groups suggests that the content of group guidance is different from that of classroom instruction and that the procedures used may also differ somewhat.[19] Although there are elements common to both, each represents a separate area of activity. Everyone involved should be clear as to the purposes of the groups and the accomplishments anticipated.

The Group as a Relationship

The group constitutes a human relationship between and among several people, just as counseling is a relationship between counselor and client. The quality of the relationship is a major determinant of the success of the group and fruitfulness of the experience. Group members interact in many ways, some of which are tangible and observable while others are of an emotional nature. Gestures, words, and bodily movement are all observable. Reactions of group members to these gestures and expressions may also be discernible. The intangible qualities have as much influence and effect as the tangible forces. The presence of these forces and their impact upon others can be presumed from the reactions of other group members. Although the message may be so subtle as to escape the notice of the casual observer, it may be very obvious to one or more of the group members.

The therapeutic benefits to come from group guidance depend upon the interaction of group members and upon the strength of the relationship itself. Words are the only tools by which feelings are expressed and ideas conveyed; hence the need for the ability to verbalize. Also required are the ability to interpret properly another person's expressions and a sensitivity which permits understanding even when the verbal expressions are inadequate. Guidance groups provide opportunities for free expression and for learning from others. The benefits to be gained depend upon a relationship of high quality which provides the setting in which growth can take place.

Guiding Principles for Group Activities

There is no one way to conduct group activities, nor is there a set of rules to be followed. On the contrary, flexibility, spontaneity, and resourcefulness are the key to successful group guidance. The

[19] Goldman speaks of the content and process of group guidance and outlines levels of activities which characterize the various groups in guidance and in instruction. Leo Goldman, "Group Guidance: Content and Process," *Personnel and Guidance Journal,* vol. 40, pp. 518–522, February, 1962.

members of the groups often provide the impetus and the direction for the action that takes place. This kind of freedom however, presupposes a framework within which it is possible to achieve goals and to profit from the experiences. In other words, there is flexibility, but there is also direction. The two supplement each other.

The framework which provides the direction for the conduct of group activities consists of a set of guiding principles which must be developed from individual thought and which therefore reflect the beliefs and biases of the person who develops them. There is no one set of principles, just as there is no one set of procedures. The following suggested principles, however, should lend direction to any program of group guidance:

1   An atmosphere of warmth, mutual acceptance, and permissiveness must prevail. Each participant should be held in high esteem by the others and should be made to feel he is an important, worthy group member. Disagreements may occur, but these need not violate the principle of mutual esteem and acceptance. Dissent might even contribute to feelings of importance as participants gain confidence from their experiences in giving verbal expression to beliefs.

2   A strong, positive working relationship should characterize the group. Although growth of the individual is a major aim of the group, the occasional subordination of the wishes of one member in deference to the welfare of the group is in order.

3   Adequate and appropriate preparations for the group activities will help ensure their success. Failure to prepare properly reduces the effectiveness of the experience and may result in its being a waste of time. Some preliminary experiences may be needed to orient a person to the group process and to prepare him for the more intimate relationship of the group. The less experienced the participants, the greater the need for preliminary and orientation activities. The nature of the preliminary experiences needed can be determined by the counselor who has been able to observe the readiness level of the various individuals for participation in the group.

4   The general climate of the group should not only enhance the self-esteem of all members but should also protect the feelings of each person. The quality of the leadership and appropriateness of the setting are among the key factors in developing a positive climate. Coddling members and evading issues are not suggested here, nor are they necessary to protect and bolster the self-esteem of participants, but growth of an individual comes with increasing self-confidence, whereas threat hinders growth.

5   The problems to be considered should originate with the group members. Involvement, concern, and participation are essential for progress and will exist if a person is genuinely interested in the issues and aware of his own needs. A topic with only a remote relationship to a person's own problems will evoke little or no response from that individual. Problems for discussion may therefore constitute the major criterion for the selection of group members, resulting in a group membership which is homogeneous in respect to the nature of the specific problems to be attacked.

6   Broad, unimpeded, candid participation by all group members may be encouraged through subtle but effective techniques utilized by the counselor and the group members. A certain unrestrained, uninhibited, dynamic, vigorous action must characterize each group.

7   The counselor should have some knowledge of group members —of their qualities, characteristics, and needs. Appropriate assignments of students to groups, the structuring of the group experiences, and the general conduct of the group activities all depend upon the counselor's familiarity with students and his sensitivity to their feelings and needs.

Other guidelines will occur to the counselor as he works with students in groups and as he notes weaknesses in the program and becomes aware of limitations in group procedures. As his wisdom and understanding improve, the quality of group guidance activities should also improve. He profits from his experiences and capitalizes on existing conditions for a gradual strengthening of the group guidance program.

Qualifications of the Counselor for Group Guidance

The person responsible for conducting guidance activities within the school should be well qualified in training, experience, and personal characteristics. Satisfactory shortcuts to the attainment of skills and competences in any endeavor do not exist. The person who anticipates a professional position in which he renders service to others must plan to commit himself to the task of preparation and must make the necessary sacrifices of time, effort, and money to achieve this objective.

The qualifications of the person doing group guidance work are essentially the same as those of a counselor. Appropriate educational experiences are necessary and at least the minimum standards for certification must be met. Training beyond the minimum is highly recommended for the counselor who engages in any form of group guidance. The typical counselor may qualify for the counselor's certificate and still have received very little training in the group processes. The establishment of a two-year graduate program for training counselors will permit a broader coverage of courses and more intensive training. Appropriate courses in the group processes may then be taken. The typical one-year graduate program does not provide sufficient time to cover more than the bare essentials of counselor preparation.

The educational preparation of the counselor should include some intensive work in group guidance techniques. Training in group techniques presupposes a background and an understanding of guidance work and of counseling and extends the counselor's preparation beyond this level into the technical aspects of conducting group functions.

Experience requirements are also essentially the same as for counseling, except that direct experience in supervising group guidance work is desirable. Some experience in an educational setting is also expected. This experience might be teaching, counseling, or clinical work. Most counselors are currently certified as teachers; however, such certification or experience may not be required of the counselor in the future.

Participation in group work by the counselor is a valuable part of his training. Two writers with considerable experience in the preparation of counselors describe the experiences provided for their NDEA enrollees.[20] As these people become highly involved in the group processes, they react in various ways to their experiences. "The aim of these processes is to raise the participants to a *higher level of maturity*." [21] These writers note that a person goes through the process of maturing every time he enters a new situation.[22] Hopefully, however, the situation is so planned as to permit and stimulate growth on the part of all participants rather than just to make a new situation for the sake of putting someone in it. It becomes evident that a variety of appropriate experiences will serve the counselor in training to advantage.

The following is a description of some of the traits of the counselor in training who is well qualified to prepare himself for working with groups:

[20] Fullmer and Bernard, *op. cit.*, pp. 191–205. Enrollee reactions to group experiences are reported in diaries kept by the students.

[21] *Ibid.*, p. 193.

[22] *Ibid.*

1   He has the ability to arouse interests and to stimulate people to productive action. He evokes the confidence and trust of others.
2   He is proficient in organizing groups for effective action. This proficiency is apparent in all his relationships with students and other staff members.
3   His knowledge of guidance functions, the educational process, and of people is unusually strong, making it possible for him to anticipate and provide for the needs of individuals.
4   He is observant and sensitive, and is able to note the general tone and quality of various groups. He is able to foresee results within the various groups, thus making it possible to effect changes that are needed.
5   He is highly resourceful, flexible, and alert. He is able to capitalize on existing resources and to create new materials or develop new procedures as the situation may require.
6   He is imaginative in the identification and selection of possible topics for discussion and in his manipulation of groups for greater productivity.
7   His empathy for all members is especially sharp and apparent. His guiding and directing tactics are motivated by his genuine concern for group members.
8   He is adept at locating needed materials, quick to identify critical issues, and able to assist others in the effective utilization of materials and ideas.
9   His dedication to people's welfare and to the guidance effort is unusually strong. He regards working with people and assisting them in their development as a spiritual and emotional commitment, not just as a job.
10   He is prompt and efficient in his work. He plans his work carefully and executes these plans with dispatch and enthusiasm.

The number and scope of counselor characteristics desirable for group work are greater than this brief listing indicates. However, the above traits may be considered representative. Some of these competences are the result of training or experience, while others are personal qualities of the individual.

Evaluation of Group Sessions

The activities taking place under group guidance should be subjected to constant scrutiny and evaluation. There should also be a periodic, organized evaluation by which the effectiveness of the program as a whole may be determined. In the first instance various observational procedures may be used by the counselor, and teachers may also note behavior changes in students. General impressions will be gained by the staff members as they observe students in action and as they hear student comments about the activities. The obtaining of helpful information may thus be a concomitant of the group guidance activities.

The organized evaluation should be accomplished through the utilization of prepared instruments and a more formal approach for gaining information. Since evaluation can be accomplished through the utilization of a variety of procedures, there is no need to suggest any one way for it to be done. If constant improvement is desired, the resourceful staff will have no problems in agreeing upon procedures or instruments to be used. Questionnaires and checklists may be utilized for gaining both student and staff reactions to the program. Again, the particular nature of the instrument is not important so long as it provides information that can be used to make improvements.

The objectives of the group guidance service can be used as guides in preparing the instrument. For example, items such as the following might be included on a check sheet:

1 Extent to which objectives were realized
2 Quality and extent of benefits gained from the experience
3 Degree of participation by group members
4 Quality and extent of new insights gained
5 Atmosphere: positive and favorable, spirit of cooperativeness, absence of friction and negativism

in such a way that students could respond with any one of five different ratings:

4—Excellent: attained to a high degree
3—Good: satisfactory attainment
2—Fair: could have been better
1—Poor: condition was not realized
0—Negative: more harm than good resulted

SUMMARY/

Group guidance activities are intended to augment the total guidance program. Many concerns and problems of students can be dealt with in a small-group setting. Group guidance activities must meet certain criteria in order to be so classified. The objective of individual growth by participants must prevail and be realized. Group instruction is a teaching procedure and therefore does not meet the criteria for group guidance.

"Group counseling," "multiple counseling," and "group therapy" are terms used to describe the major activities under group guidance. Groups for disseminating information may also be organized but are conducted with a somewhat different emphasis from that of the above groups. Specific purposes are served through these various group activities.

Problems and difficulties are sometimes encountered in initiating and carrying out group activities. These problems can generally be handled or avoided as the staff makes an effort to provide for the needs of students through the group-experience approach. The number of students to take part at any one time, organization of the groups, objectives, and other considerations can be dealt with as alert, interested counselors and students cooperate in a mutually beneficial endeavor. The chances for successful experiences are also greater as guiding principles are observed. Students profit from group activities by gaining information from others, experiencing insights, and gaining strength through intimate association with peers.

The improvements made in the group guidance services may well depend upon the quality of the evaluation taking place. Weaknesses are identified through systematic appraisal, and the way is thus opened for program betterment.

PROBLEMS/

1 The guidance program has certain purposes to be met. How can group guidance contribute to these purposes? In what areas is group guidance particularly effective?

2 How can group guidance contribute to the total educational process? Explain the relationship between group guidance and the educational endeavor.

3 What kinds of useful information might the school gain about students through the use of group activities? Might this same information be gained elsewhere? Where? How?

4 Define group guidance. Explain how it might function in the typical school. What differences might be noted between group guidance work at the elementary school level and at the secondary school level?

5 Why is high-level involvement so important in group work? What is involvement supposed to accomplish? How might the counselor promote this kind of involvement?

6 Define and/or give illustrations of each of the following: group guidance, group instruction, group counseling, multiple counseling, group therapy.

7 How does Slavson's work in group therapy differ from group work in the typical school? What have Slavson's greatest contributions been?

8 Make a statement of evaluation for each of the twelve purposes of group guidance. Note the strengths and weaknesses of each statement.

9 Why is it so important that adequate preparation be made for the establishment of group guidance activities? What are some major problems to be overcome? What guides might be used in avoiding or resolving these problems?

10 What kinds of problems appear to be most suitable for consideration in groups? What kinds of problems might be dealt with best in some other setting? Does the nature of the individual's personality have any bearing on what approach might be best for him? Explain.

11 Defend the view that the school should provide for a variety of group experiences. What should determine the nature of the group and how it is conducted? Should there always be a purpose?

12 The "group as a relationship" means what? How important is the quality of this relationship? How can this relationship be improved once the group is in action?

13 Presumably the school counselor or some other personnel specialist will initiate and conduct group sessions. Describe this person as to training experience, and personality.

14 Why should the program of group guidance be evaluated? How might periodic evaluation be accomplished?

Selected References

Textbooks
ARBUCKLE, DUGALD S.: *Pupil Personnel Services in American Schools,* Allyn and Bacon, Inc., Boston, 1962, chap. 10.

BENNETT, MARGARET E.: *Guidance and Counseling in Groups,* 2d ed., McGraw-Hill Book Company, New York, 1963.

BERNARD, HAROLD W., E. EVAN JAMES, and FRANKLIN R. ZERAN: *Guidance Services in Elementary Schools,* Chartwell House, New York, 1954, chap. 13.

DRIVER, HELEN I.: *Counseling and Learning through Small-group Discussion,* Monona Publications, Madison, Wis., 1958.

FULLMER, DANIEL W., and HAROLD W. BERNARD: *Counseling: Content and Process,* Science Research Associates, Inc., Chicago, 1964, chap. 9.

GLANZ, EDWARD C.: *Foundations and Principles of Guidance,* Allyn and Bacon, Inc., Boston, 1964, chap. 7.

HUMPHREYS, J. ANTHONY, ARTHUR E. TRAXLER, and ROBERT D. NORTH: *Guidance Services,* Science Research Associates, Inc., Chicago, 1960, chap. 9.

JOHNSTON, EDGAR G., MILDRED PETERS, and WILLIAM EVRAIFF: *The Role of the Teacher in Guidance,* Prentice-Hall, Inc., Englewood Cliffs, N.J., 1959, chap. 17.

KEMP, C. GRATTON: *Perspectives on the Group Process,* Houghton Mifflin Company, Boston, 1964.

LIFTON, WALTER M.: *Working with Groups,* John Wiley & Sons, Inc., New York, 1961.

MARTINSON, RUTH A., and HARRY SMALLENBURG: *Guidance in Elementary Schools,* Prentice-Hall, Inc, Englewood Cliffs, N.J., 1958, chap. 5

MC DANIEL, HENRY B.: *Guidance in the Modern School,* The Dryden Press, Inc., New York, 1956, chap. 15.

————, JOHN E. LALLAS, JAMES A. SAUM, and JAMES L. GILMORE: *Readings in Guidance,* Holt, Rinehart and Winston, Inc., New York, 1959, chap. 12.

MILLER, FRANK W.: *Guidance Principles and Services,* Charles E. Merrill Books, Inc., Englewood Cliffs, N.J., 1961, pp. 341–345.

MORTENSEN, DONALD G., and ALLEN M. SCHMULLER: *Guidance in Today's Schools,* John Wiley & Sons, Inc., New York, 1959, chap. 10.

OHLSEN, MERLE M.: *Guidance Services in the Modern School,* Harcourt, Brace & World, Inc., New York, 1964, chap. 11.

PETERS, HERMAN J., and GAIL F. FARWELL: *Guidance: A Developmental Approach,* Rand McNally & Company, Chicago, 1959, chap. 9.

SHERTZER, BRUCE, and HERMAN J. PETERS: *Guidance: Techniques for Individual Appraisal and Development,* The Macmillan Company, New York, 1965, chap. 4.

SLAVSON, S. R.: *An Introduction to Group Therapy,* International Universities Press, Inc., New York, 1964.

————: *A Textbook in Analytic Group Psychotherapy,* International Universities Press, Inc., New York, 1964.

TRAXLER, ARTHUR E., and ROBERT D. NORTH: *Techniques of Guidance,* 3d ed., Harper & Row, Publishers, Incorporated, New York, 1966, chap. 20.

WARTERS, JANE: *High School Personnel Work Today,* 2d ed., McGraw-Hill Book Company, New York, 1956, chap. 11.

WILLEY, ROY DE VERL: *Guidance in Elementary Education,* Harper & Row Publishers, Incorporated, New York, 1960, chap. 8.

————, and DEAN C. ANDREW: *Modern Methods and Techniques in Guidance,* Harper & Row, Publishers, Incorporated, New York, 1955, chaps. 19 and 20.

Journals

ALEXANDER, EUGENE D.: "School Centered Play-therapy Program," *Personnel and Guidance Journal,* vol. 43, pp. 256–261, November, 1964.

BECK, R. R.: "Group Guidance," *National Education Association Journal,* vol. 48, pp. 22–23, January, 1959.

BELL, D. T.: "Group Guidance in Eighth Grade," *Clearing House,* vol. 39, pp. 81–84, October, 1964.

BONNEY, WARREN C., and WALTER J. FOLEY: "Transition Stage in Group Counseling in Terms of Congruence Theory," *Journal of Counseling Psychology,* vol. 10, pp. 136–138, Summer, 1963.

BUTLER, KATHRINE M.: "Home Room: A Greatly Needed Guidance Device," *School Activities,* vol. 32, pp. 183–185, February, 1961.

DRIVER, HELEN I.: "Small Group Discussion," *Personnel and Guidance Journal,* vol. 31, pp. 173–175, December, 1952.

FROEHLICH, CLIFFORD P.: "Must Counseling Be Individual?" *Educational and Psychological Measurement,* vol. 18, no. 4, pp. 681–689, Winter, 1958.

JESSEE, BILL E., and ROBERT A. HEIMANN: "The Effects of Counseling and Group Guidance on the Vocational Maturity of Ninth Grade Boys," *The Journal of Educational Research,* vol. 59, pp. 68–72, October, 1965.

KEMP, C. GRATTON: "Behaviors in Group Guidance and Group Counseling," *Journal of Counseling Psychology,* vol. 10, pp. 373–377, Winter, 1963.

KINZER, J. R.: "Evaluation of a Group Counseling Procedure," *Journal of Counseling Psychology,* vol. 11, pp. 152–159, Summer, 1964.

LANGHANS, ELIZABETH: "Group Guidance and the Orientation Class," *California Journal of Secondary Education,* vol. 32, pp. 271–272, May, 1957.

MINK, OSCAR G.: "Multiple Counseling with Underachieving Junior High School Pupils of Bright, Normal, and Higher Ability," *Journal of Educational Research,* vol. 58, pp. 31–34, September, 1964.

PEPINSKY, H. B., JOHN D. KRUMBOLTZ, and CARL E. THORESEN: "Effect of Behavioral Counseling in Group and Individual Settings on Information-seeking Behavior: With Comment," *Journal of Counseling Psychology,* vol. 11, pp. 324–335, Winter, 1964.

RICCIO, ANTHONY C.: "Group Guidance: A Step Toward the Core," *Educational Administration and Supervision,* vol. 44, pp. 1–9, January, 1958.

ROBINETT, DONALD W., and WARREN K. WAITE: "Voluntary Group Counseling in a Junior High School," *California Journal of Secondary Education,* vol. 39, pp. 226–229, May, 1964.

WINBORN, B., and K. A. MARONEY: "Effectiveness of Short-term Group Guidance with a Group of Transfer Students Admitted on Academic Probation," *Educational Research,* vol. 58, pp. 463–465, July, 1965.

WOAL, S. THEODORE: "Project in Group Counseling in a Junior High School," *Personnel and Guidance Journal,* vol. 42, pp. 611–613, February, 1964.

WRIGHT, RALPH E., and ALICE GORMAN: "Group Guidance Programs," *Illinois Education,* vol. 46, pp. 131–132, December, 1957.

TWELVE

/ORGANIZING AND ADMINISTERING THE GUIDANCE SERVICE

The guidance service, like any other phase of the educational program, requires initial planning, a structure upon which to build, dedication by staff members, and a commitment of the school to the concept of service to young people. The aim of maximum student development can be fulfilled as careful, serious attention is given to organizing the guidance service and as appropriate action is taken to keep it functioning properly. To achieve this the best efforts of the administration, counseling staff, and teachers are required. A firm belief by the school, both the educators and the students, in the guidance service as a power for good in the lives of young people is most essential for the establishment of the program. Its effectiveness with students depends upon the insights, knowledge, and skills of the school staff.

A sound organizational structure will lead to fruitful educational experiences for each student by which he might grow. To this end the administration provides leadership and facilities, and the teaching and counseling staffs assume their appropriate roles and responsibilities.

Flexibility and freedom should also characterize the program, but within the framework agreed upon. A commitment to an organizational pattern actually permits greater freedom, and certainly more effective action, than would exist in an unstructured setting.

This chapter stresses the importance of system, organization, and structure by noting the advantages to be gained from them. The classification of services and patterns of organization are also discussed. Common problems encountered in organizing the guidance service are pointed out, and suggestions are given on how to deal with them. The functions of the various staff members are identified. Attention is given to the actual administration of the guidance service in relation to the guidance philosophy, and suggestions are made on how to proceed in conducting the service.

Organization and Structure in the Guidance Service

The plea for an organized program for providing the specialized services of guidance is based upon three basic assumptions: (1) the quality of these services is contingent upon organization; (2) efficiency in use of time, resources, and personnel in providing the essential activities for students can be maintained and improved more readily; (3) the experiences gained by students, their exposure to ideas and information, and their association with the counselor will be meaningful and profitable. The organization must be functional, understood and agreed upon by staff members, and sufficiently inclusive in its coverage with a potential for expansion, and it must involve individual as well as collective effort. Duplication of functions and of resources is kept to a minimum through careful planning. Confusion, disappointment, and frustration by staff members and students can be avoided or replaced with confidence and enthusiasm as purposes are understood and responsibilities assumed.

The structure of the program provides the guidelines within which to work, but there is no established pattern to be superimposed upon a school. Each program should be developed with the strengths, weaknesses, needs, and resources of the school and the community in mind. The processes of implementation and fruitful action should be in evidence each year as needed adjustments are made in the program.

Guides to the Attainment of Structure

An appropriate functional service is seldom a matter of chance. Considerable thought and effort are prerequisites to any good service. The guides observed in developing the program are philosophical and attitudinal as well as specific. The following items may serve as guides in the development of an organization under which students will be aided:

1   There must be agreement among staff members as to the aims and purposes of the guidance service. A "guidance" philosophy and a dedication to the concept of service to others must prevail throughout the school.
2   The school staff must be knowledgeable and well-informed. Not all need be specialists in pupil personnel work, but all should be highly professional, skilled academicians with the ability to teach and to influence positively all youth in the school. Expectations extend beyond their academic areas to include a knowledge of children—of their development and needs.
3   A highly competent, skillful staff of guidance workers must be provided through careful screening at the time of employment coupled with in-service training opportunities.
4   There must be a commitment by the administration to the guidance service and a demonstration of faith in it by providing adequate funds and facilities.
5   A sense of permanence and long-term planning should prevail. The guidance service is developed for the years ahead as well as for the current year. Improvements should be anticipated, planned for, and effected.

Advantages of an Organized Program

A well-organized program of services is more economical to operate and more fruitful than a program conducted without a systematic approach. If left to chance the program seldom goes beyond the first stage, and its goals are even more rarely realized. The advantages of a strong organization may thus be stated in terms of specific benefits as outlined here:

1   The needs of students can be more accurately determined. There is less guessing and more factual information upon which to base decisions.
2   More students can be accommodated in less time and with

fewer personnel. Economy is a factor in most schools, necessitating efficiency in operation.

3   Duplication of effort is avoided or kept to a minimum. Each staff member knows his responsibilities and is able to develop his activities to their maximum. A change in assignments is also possible in order to capitalize on the strengths and interests of various staff members.

4   Roles and obligations are more readily assumed by staff members as they understand the nature of these obligations. A well-defined structure provides a clear-cut picture of the whole program and makes it possible for each person to see his role and its relationship to the total picture.

5   Interest is greater among the staff and the students and enthusiasm more pronounced within a program that carries a promise for success. Efforts are given more freely when the course is well outlined and the benefits to be gained become apparent.

6   Existing facilities can be utilized more efficiently as needs are anticipated by the staff. There is less waste of resources and more economical use made of all facilities.

7   Students are better informed about the guidance service and are more aware of its purposes. Greater utilization of the services is possible as students are apprised of the activities and are able to see the importance of these services in improving their own lives.

8   A more efficient coordination of all guidance activities is possible. The program structure identifies areas of activity and fixes responsibility with staff members, making coordination possible.

9   Competent guidance personnel and teachers are more readily obtained and retained when there is system and strength in a program and when it has promise for success. Professional people dislike uncertainty and chaos and avoid situations which are frustrating and nonproductive.

10 The objectives of the school and of the guidance service are more readily attainable, and the task of deciding upon and carrying out certain functions is simplified.

Classification of Services

There is merit in determining the exact services to be included in the guidance program prior to its initiation. Considerable overlap occurs among services, but this tends to emphasize the need for specificity in services in order to avoid omissions and to make certain that the necessary structure exists. These services can then be developed at whatever rate circumstances permit and in accordance with the most pressing needs of the school.

The various guidance activities also depend upon the existence of other services. For example, counseling depends upon the availability of information gained about pupils and properly recorded as a part of the pupil inventory. So as the program is developed, thought should be given to all elements of the program, but with the realization that some elements may have to be delayed for a time while others are being started. Ultimately, the total program with all services will be under way.

During the initial stages of program development a first step is to survey the present situation and determine which services should be initiated immediately. It is also well to capitalize on strengths currently existing in the school. Full use should be made of all existing programs, materials, and personnel. The same idea holds when personnel changes occur in a school. It is uneconomical and illogical to ignore everything that has been accomplished earlier by other staff members and organize the program according to the whims of new personnel. There should be sufficient time taken to make program changes and to initiate action. During this time all previous accomplishments and program arrangements should be properly utilized.

Complete agreement as to the essential services to be included in the guidance program has not always been reached. For example, the U.S. Office of Education called a conference in 1951, for purposes of determining the nature and titles of services to be included. These were child accounting and attendance, orientation, counseling services, clinical services, individual analysis, health services, home-community-school services, occupational and educational information services, and placement and follow-up.[1] Some of these services are the responsibility of the administration and are not currently recognized as elements of the guidance program. Frank L. Sievers of the U.S. Office of Education identified in 1959 the services of analysis, information, orientation, counseling, and placement.[2] The present text includes as the major services of the guidance program the pupil inventory (record system), testing, counseling, information service, placement, and follow-up.

[1] C. Gilbert Wrenn, *The Counselor in a Changing World*, American Personnel and Guidance Association, Washington, D.C., 1962, p. 139.
[2] *Ibid.*, p. 138.

Patterns of Organization

The organizational pattern used in a particular school should capitalize upon current conditions within that school. For purposes of clarification and operational efficiency, a graph should be prepared which shows the line and staff relationships between and among various staff members. This graph can be simple and still show the services to be provided and the responsibilities of the various staff members.

In preparing this graph, four different kinds of lines might be used to indicate the nature of the relationship of a particular service to other services:

1   A solid line might indicate line of authority. The principal, as the head of the school, is placed over the head counselor or director of guidance services in a direct line of authority relationship. Other counselors may then be placed under the head counselor and thus continue the line of authority.

2   A broken line might indicate a cooperative relationship between two services. Such a line might be used between the counselors and other special school personnel, such as the school nurse or the social worker.

3   A broken line with dots might denote a consultant relationship. This relationship may exist between teacher and counselor, or between the counselor and another professional person, such as a psychiatrist.

4   A dotted line might denote a referral resource. Guidance clinics, hospitals, or physicians are in this classification. This procedure makes the roles of the various participants more meaningful. Less confusion and inefficiency occur when such a guide is utilized by everyone.

Principles of Organization

Basic to education itself is the belief that everyone should have the opportunity to pursue an education so far as his talents and resources will permit. A basic principle of the guidance service is that every child should have the opportunity to benefit from the experiences and directions provided. The organized program of guidance services thus depends upon an adherence to some basic principles which serve as guides in establishing and conducting the guidance service. The techniques and tools used and the activities provided are chosen in accordance with these established principles, all of which have a close relationship to the goals of the total program. Principles developed for the guidance service may thus be used as guides throughout all stages of the establishment of the guidance service and throughout the duration of the program as it is administered, evaluated, and improved. Such principles are included in Chapter 1 of this text.[3, 4] The following are some broad organizational principles:

1   Capitalize on the strengths and existing conditions within the currently established educational program.
2   Anticipate changes in education, and organize the guidance program to permit flexibility and rapid change.
3   Continue to emphasize the concept that student needs constitute the focal point for the initiation and continuation of all activities and services.
4   Realize that prevention is the first concern of the guidance service, and that each phase of the guidance service should be designed with this in mind.
5   Provide for the treatment or referral of all students in need of special help, and realize that satisfactory adjustment to the typical school program is difficult and sometimes impossible for certain children.
6   Make an intelligent and efficient utilization of the resources of guidance materials currently available to schools through various agencies and companies.
7   Design all services to promote the increasing independence of each student and his continuous growth and progress.
8   Capitalize upon the abilities of various staff members, community agencies, parents, and students in organizing and carrying out the various functions of the program.

These principles are intended as representative of perhaps a hundred more that could be stated.

The Initiation of Action

Appropriate action for the initiation, establishment, and conduct of the guidance service depend upon strong leadership within the school. While the responsibilities for this leadership ultimately rest with the head administrative officer of the school, he delegates certain responsibilities to other staff members. Some involvement by all staff members is essential to the success of the program; how-

[3] Some representative principles for the guidance service itself are given in H. Fred Heisner, "Point 10 Program for Guidance," *School Executive*, vol. 78, pp. 66–67, May, 1959.

[4] An often-quoted list is found in Arthur J. Jones, *Principles of Guidance*, McGraw-Hill Book Company, New York, 1951, pp. 507–508.

ever, the degree of involvement and the quality of the contributions will be affected by the leadership exemplified by those in positions of authority.

The organizational structure for the guidance service can be strengthened through a careful consideration of existing or anticipated problems. A list is given below of the kinds of problems to be considered in getting the program under way. Suggestions are also made on how to handle these and related problems. The functions of the various school personnel are then reviewed, and suggestions are made in a later section on how to keep the program moving.

Some Preliminary Problems

The quality of the various services depends upon the ability of the staff to anticipate, avoid, and resolve problems which, if not considered early in the program, may seriously hamper progress. Discouragement and disillusionment by staff members should be avoided and every effort made to ensure an optimistic, enthusiastic start. The action to be taken and the benefits to be expected depend upon the answers to such questions as the following: [5]

1 What are the attitudes and general philosophy of the school and the community toward guidance?
2 What are the specific objectives of the guidance service? What should be accomplished?
3 What are the needs of the students, the school, and the community which might be served by the guidance program?
4 How is the program to be financed? What are the sources of revenue and the approximate costs to be met?
5 What is the extent of present facilities and materials, and what will be required?
6 What are immediate personnel needs? Is there need for additional staff? To what extent can the present staff be utilized?
7 How will the various services of the program be coordinated, and what division of responsibility can accomplish this?
8 What pattern of organization should be used?
9 How might essential information be disseminated to the various staff members?

[5] Some causes of difficulty in the organization of the pupil personnel program are noted and discussed by Dugald S. Arbuckle in his *Pupil Personnel Services in American Schools,* Allyn and Bacon, Inc., Boston, 1962. Another interesting source is Bruce Shertzer and Shelley C. Stone, "Administration Deterrents to Effective Guidance Programs," *Education Digest,* vol. 29, pp. 40–43, October, 1963.

10 How might the community resources be utilized, and how might community people be used in planning and conducting the program?

11 What is the nature and extent of the resources within the community? Which can be depended upon to be of assistance?

12 What is the size of the school or district to be included in the service? What grade levels are to be served?

13 To what extent can teachers take part in the guidance program? How much time can be given to specific guidance activities?

14 What procedures might be used for informing school personnel and the community about the guidance service? How can support and interest be solicited?

15 How might students be kept informed about what is happening and how their aid might be utilized in initiating and keeping the services moving?

Other problems of equal importance will need to be considered in the development of the guidance service. As these problems are solved, the guidance service will benefit, and new avenues of assistance and strength will be found.

Getting Under Way

The organization of the guidance service takes considerable planning prior to the initiation of the activities of the service. The director of the pupil personnel services has the major responsibility for this early planning, but he should capitalize on the contributions of other staff members. After the preliminaries have been accomplished, the means by which the major services can be conducted should become apparent. The director may then provide the necessary leadership to get the services under way. The framework of the guidance service should have been established, and the various staff members should be informed on the present status of the program and should know what their roles are to be. The implementation of the activities is the next challenge. This can be accomplished quite readily if the staff under strong leadership will (1) survey the present situation and proceed accordingly, (2) make intelligent use of all existing resources, (3) determine the immediate objectives to be realized, and (4) proceed in the development of each major service of the guidance program systematically and with dispatch under a solid, well-structured outline for action.

Once the principal has initiated action, made needed resources available, and delegated responsibility, the head counselor or director of the guidance service will assume a leadership role. He will, then, follow through on the four procedures suggested above.

Surveying the present situation. As the guidance director surveys the school, he will attempt to determine the current status of a number of services and will also identify staff members who are currently involved in guidance activities or those who are capable and willing to assist. This survey will also result in tentative answers to the preliminary problems posed earlier. Greater efficiency in program management can be expected as each staff member assumes his rightful role and becomes aware of his functions and responsibilities in the program.

Utilizing all available resources. In addition to the materials and personnel of the school, the community also provides resource materials and resource people. The program can be strengthened as these sources are properly used. Community support can be gained by maintaining contact with these people and by enlisting their assistance. Procedures for accomplishing this objective might include the following:

1 The guidance staff can prepare and mail bulletins to parents and other community resource individuals. These bulletins will keep parents informed on what is taking place and might also serve as a device for obtaining their suggestions and ideas.

2 School visits by parents might be encouraged. An informative program of activities should be provided which would be helpful and of interest. These visits permit an informal appraisal of the school program and promote a better understanding between parents and school personnel.

3 Evening discussion groups for school personnel and parents might be provided, with problems of mutual interest and concern as their focus. These group meetings would serve as information-giving sessions and as means for the expression of ideas.

4 Planning committees of teachers and parents might be organized, permitting the development of ideas from which action might be taken.

5 Contacts should be maintained with community leaders. Guidance personnel might solicit their assistance and encourage their active participation in the program. Telephone calls, letters, notes, and personal visits are suitable devices for improving these relationships.

Determining objectives to be accomplished.   Guidance personnel, in cooperation with teachers and administrators, need to determine during the initial stages of the program development just what the objectives should be. The ultimate effectiveness of the program depends upon the quality of these objectives and the degree to which they are realized. The total educational program should be considered at this time, since the objectives of the guidance service should also be the objectives of the total school program.

Objectives are often stated in the abstract and are sometimes rather vaguely expressed. A realistic and clear approach to the statement of the objectives should result in a practical program with great possibilities for success. One approach is to pose questions about which a school has some concern and from these to develop appropriate aims. Such questions might include the following:

1   What are the needs of our students in respect to educational, vocational, and personal adjustment?
2   What does the school hope to accomplish in preparing students for good citizenship in their communities?
3   What are the dominant educational philosophies of the school?
4   How will a knowledge of the backgrounds of our students help us in developing an educational program most appropriate for them?
5   What are the vocational possibilities for our students? What can we anticipate in respect to vocational training and selection by our students?
6   What are the vocational trends in today's world, and how might we prepare our students to make wise choices?
7   What are the demands and expectations of the community in respect to its young people?
8   What are the responsibilities of the school in the prevention of misbehavior and maladjustments?
9   What is the relationship of the typical school program to the promotion of good mental health?

Providing for a solid structure as a basis for action.   The speed and efficiency with which the program develops and becomes prepared to render service depend upon the organizational structure upon which it is built. It is also possible to move too fast and thereby jeopardize rather than strengthen the program. Progress should come as a result of careful, deliberate planning and never at the expense of stability and permanence. Enthusiasm can soon turn to apathy if anticipated results do not materialize. Efforts should be made to stabilize gains and to reinforce positive aspects of the service, rather than to emphasize speed for its sake alone. Planning must have long-term connotations. The spectacular, sensational elements of program development should be avoided if they have nothing to offer to its permanence and future.

Although it is wise to make haste slowly, time alone will not take care of organizational problems. To expect it to do so is likely to result in too little effort and commensurately meager results. The initial stages of program development do require considerable effort, even though the results may be far less noticeable at that stage than later on when these early efforts begin to yield results.

Functions of Staff Members

The typical school makes demands upon the time and talents of its personnel somewhat beyond the major functions of the position for which the person was employed. The teacher, for example, is involved in activities other than instructing students. The guidance personnel, supervisors, and administrators also expect and generally welcome opportunities for providing services beyond their immediate and major role. The nature of these secondary functions varies considerably within and among schools, since the abilities and interests of individual staff members determine where each may direct his energies. The major functions are, however, more clear-cut, and there is a general understanding as to just what duties each person will be performing.

This section is concerned with the roles of the staff members under the guidance service, particularly as these functions relate to the organization and administration of the guidance service. The functions described for the guidance director and for the counselor are major, or primary, roles. Any tasks they perform outside the guidance service are secondary functions. For teachers and administrators, on the other hand, functions under the guidance service are secondary. The teamwork approach makes possible this broad participation by all staff members at the same time that it permits specialization whereby each person can make his best contribution.

The Guidance Director

The duties of the guidance director vary somewhat, depending upon whether he is serving in a relatively small school or district or whether he is the director of pupil personnel services in a district large enough to employ a variety of specialists. In the first case, he may be the head counselor or the only counselor, while in the second case his position is primarily administrative. And there is a variety of positions between these two. The breadth and nature of his work, then, are determined by the size of the school or district, the availability of other special personnel, and the competence of the director. The director of the pupil personnel service will likely perform or supervise the performance of duties such as the following: [6] (1) health services, (2) attendance, (3) educational and vocational placement, (4) pupil records, (5) testing, (6) research, (7) study and revision of the curriculum, (8) mental health, (9) utilization of community agencies, (10) work-education experiences, and (11) evaluation.

This broad coverage suggested by Barry puts the director in a position of administrative authority and responsibility. He provides leadership and supervision in getting the work accomplished by other people, whereas the director in a small school may be the one who actually performs the work. Barry also discusses the director in the role of a "subordinate" responsible to a higher authority and in the major roles of "executive head," "consultant," and "coordinator." [7] The guidance director has a challenging task if he is to do justice to his many responsibilities.

In the following paragraphs the major responsibilities of the guidance director are stated as broad principles that can serve as guides irrespective of the size of the district. These statements may also be regarded as elements within concepts, which in turn reflect the philosophy of the school.

Stimulating the interests of other staff members. The guidance director should have as a major objective the interests and enthusiasm of other staff members. The success of the program depends upon this participation. The arousal of interests might be accomplished through brief announcements and demonstrations in faculty meetings. The faculty is kept informed on the progress of the program, recommendations for improvements are made, and suggestions solicited. A problem case might be reviewed, showing how personal assistance has been of help to some youngster.

[6] For a more detailed discussion of these or similar duties see Robert E. Barry, "Pupil Personnel Services," *Education*, vol. 82, pp. 327–331, February, 1962. Reprinted by permission of the publisher, The Bobbs-Merrill Company, Inc.

[7] *Ibid.*, pp. 329–331.

Soliciting the participation of students. As the guidance director is able to gain the participation of the students in various phases of the program, the guidance interests of the entire school improve. Everyone is interested in himself and in his own personal development, and will capitalize on the opportunities to enhance his own progress. The procedures used for providing such opportunities should be in keeping with the philosophy of the school and should dignify the guidance service, rather than disparage it. Dramatizations, for example, appeal to youngsters and so might be used to advantage in calling the guidance service to the attention of the students. The cooperation of the drama teacher is necessary when programs are prepared for presentation in student assemblies or for community groups. Interesting, eye-catching bulletin-board displays can convey a dynamic message. The school newspaper is likewise an excellent medium for reporting events associated with the guidance service and for announcing forthcoming activities. Student planning committees may also be organized and used in promoting the guidance program.

Planning each phase carefully. The director will have help in planning the program, but he will need to take the initiative in making certain that each necessary part of the program is planned for and receives appropriate attention. Needs of the greatest urgency should be determined early and then the necessary action taken to meet these needs. Other phases of the program may then be developed as time can be spared from the services currently under way.

Keeping well informed on educational trends. The guidance director is an academician as well as a practitioner. He is a well-informed, scholarly person but also one who is able to foresee the practical application possibilities for his knowledge. He should be adaptable and able to capitalize on existing conditions and current trends for the betterment of the guidance service he heads. One way to accomplish this is to develop a good library of guidance materials and to encourage their use with the staff. This library may include appropriate professional periodicals and books, and it might also include prepared bibliographies of references to be found elsewhere. Also, the guidance director might arrange to have staff members meet together in seminars for purposes of intellectual stimulation and exchange of information. Professional and academic competence should be the goal of the entire guidance staff but particularly of the person whose leadership determines the quality of the program.

Seeking the advice and recommendations of others. Other people within the school and community can be of assistance through their suggestions and participation. The suggestions of these people serve two principal purposes: (1) many of their ideas will be well worth adopting, and (2) their interest in the guidance service will be stimulated. The director should make it clear to these individuals that their support and suggestions are needed and that their roles are vital in the success of the guidance service. Suggestions can be obtained by means of personal contacts, notes or letters, or telephone calls. The tact, consideration, and respect shown by the guidance personnel to community people will be instrumental in obtaining community support and participation. Guidance people must be genuine and honest in their solicitation of aid and should demonstrate their sincerity by honoring and implementing suggestions and services of both school and community people.

Utilizing community and school resources. The people of the community comprise one of the resources available to the school. Others that should be used include the business, industrial, and manufacturing concerns, service clubs, community social and cultural organizations, and churches. These organizations will in most cases assist the school and its guidance service if asked to do so. Everyone is interested in the welfare of the youth within a community, and cooperative efforts can generally be elicited if competent leadership provides the necessary directions. Publicizing the program through local news media keeps the public informed on what is taking place and will also make possible the enlistment of participation from a variety of sources. Study tours and group field trips to plants, factories, and business concerns provide excellent educational opportunities for students; such projects also help maintain contact with community leaders who can be useful to the school.

Keeping parents, teachers, and students informed. The guidance director should make certain that appropriate information is made available to parents and that they are constantly aware of the program and the accomplishments being made by the guidance service. The task of keeping teachers and students informed is somewhat easier for the director, since he has immediate contact with them. Therefore, the devices used to make appropriate information available may vary, depending upon the individuals to be reached and the purpose of the communication. Periodic bulletins highlighting the progress of the program might be used. Announcements

placed on the bulletin boards, reports in assemblies or other gather-
ings, announcements over the intercommunication system, dramatizations at PTA meetings, letters, and phone calls are all means by
which everyone is given the opportunity to learn about the guidance
program.

Having the school placed on mailing lists.   There is an abundance
of literature and materials currently available for use by the guidance service. The director should make certain that these sources
are properly utilized and that the school is on the mailing lists of
these companies. Chronicle Guidance Service, Science Research Associates, Inc., and Careers (see Chapter 9 for addresses) are all
excellent, reputable companies with an interest in providing the
right materials for the school's guidance service. A postcard request
is all that is necessary to obtain the assistance of these and other
companies.

Planning for necessary personnel and facilities.   The efforts of the
guidance director must be coordinated with those of the administration in order to avoid duplications and to provide most economically the necessary materials and personnel. The director must
have accurate information as to present and anticipated needs of
the program, and should make this information available to the
administration as budgetary plans are formulated. To this purpose
the guidance director may (1) submit anticipated budgetary needs
to the administration well in advance, (2) maintain organized files
of test catalogs, record forms, periodicals, books, and other professional materials and equipment, (3) report personnel needs a year
or more before possible employment date and keep in touch with
promising prospective candidates for positions, (4) survey the building and all facilities and thereby know the potential uses of various
rooms or parts of the building.
    Besides the specific procedures that the director of the guid-
ance service may follow and the tasks he may perform in his leadership role, still more is required of him. The impression he makes
upon other staff members both as a person and as a professional
worker is important. He must be the kind of person who evokes the
respect and confidence of others, since the success of the program
is highly dependent upon the favorable feelings and reactions of
other staff members toward him. Student attitudes about the guidance service and the person heading it are also of critical importance for its success.

The Counselor

The counselor may also be the director of guidance, a counselor under the direction of the director, or one of several counselors, one of whom may act as the head counselor. The administrative arrangement of the program within the school determines the status and role of each counselor. Since guidance personnel are performing identical or similar functions with precisely the same aims, an attempt at a distinction in roles between the head counselor, or guidance director, and the counselor may serve no particular purpose. The director is the administrative head but may also perform many of the functions of the counselor. An exception is in the case of the director of pupil personnel services in a large district. The counselor also performs many of the functions outlined above under the duties of the guidance director.

As Wrenn notes, the counselor is a generalist and a specialist: [8]

> (*a*) The counselor is a generalist in the sense of his being widely available to the total school population. . . . He is a generalist also in the sense that he should be acquainted with the complete scope of school referral resources and know how these might be utilized. . . . (*b*) The counselor is a specialist in his specific knowledge of the student and in his ability to relate himself effectively to the student. . . . He is a specialist in the collation and interpretation of information about individual students and student populations. . . .

He also points out four specific responsibilities of the counselor as: [9]

> (*a*) Counseling with students. . . . (*b*) Consulting with staff and parents. . . . (*c*) Studying changes in the character of the student population. . . . (*d*) Performing a liaison function between other school and community counseling resources and facilitating their use by teachers and students.

In a more recent report Wrenn notes: [10]

> I have changed my thinking a little bit since the writing of the report. I would now describe the functions of the counselor in three divisions: (1) serving in a help-

[8] Wrenn, *op. cit.*, p. 142.
[9] *Ibid.*, p. 141.
[10] C. Gilbert Wrenn, "The Counselor in a Changing World Revisited," *The Teachers College Journal*, vol. 35, no. 6, p. 208, May, 1964.

ing relationship to students, parents, and teachers; (2) coordinating and developing certain guidance services; and (3) serving as a cooperative member of an educational team with team responsibilities.

The following discussion describes the major role of the counselor as both a specialist in counseling and a person with leadership responsibilities for the total guidance service. How much time he gives to counseling and related guidance activities and how much of his work is of an administrative or leadership nature depends upon his specific assignment within the guidance service.

Student counseling. The major function of the counselor is to counsel students. In the organizational phases of the guidance service he may devote more time to preparing the school and the students for the counseling experience than in actual counseling. Upon the successful completion of the preliminary work of establishing a structure within which the service can operate, he will devote a considerable part of each day to counseling.

Working closely with teachers. The association between counselor and teacher should be characterized by mutual confidence and respect. The efforts and contributions of both are essential, and the effectiveness of the educational process depends at least to a degree upon the quality of the teacher-counselor relationship. The strength and quality of the organizational pattern depend upon an understanding on the part of the teacher and counselor as to the purposes and goals of the guidance service and their insight into what must be done to accomplish these goals.

Aiding in the development of all phases of the service. The counselor should be involved to some degree in virtually all phases of the guidance service. To some degree specialization is possible, which permits the work load be shared with other counselors. However, guidance functions of all kinds are the counselor's primary responsibilities, and he has a role to play in each phase of the guidance service. The size of the counseling staff and the number of students being served help to determine just how widely each counselor will extend his activity and how much specialization is possible. If the school has but one counselor, obviously his activities will be numerous. A multiple staff will permit a logical division of responsibilities among the counselors. The intensity of the counselor's participation may be greater during the initial stages of the program's establishment. Once the service is under way, the demands of leadership may be lessened, making possible a delegation of responsibility to other people. Establishing the framework and getting through the preliminaries are often more demanding than keeping the service going after it is established.

The Teacher

The teacher's ideas, suggestions, and aid are essential throughout all phases of the program's establishment and development. He is in on the planning, the application and establishment of principles, the accumulation and utilization of data, and the founding of a good working relationship with students. Where the director and the counselors provide the leadership and the professional direction for establishing and conducting the service, the teacher provides many of the ideas and the means by which the various phases of the program are implemented. Many of the teacher's activities are prompted by his interest in the personal well-being of a student, and the quality of the relationship between teacher and student depends upon the philosophy, values, and attitudes of the teacher as they relate to the guidance function. Much of the teacher's influence is therefore subtle and unobservable but no less important than the more tangible, dynamic activities of the counselor. A clear-cut line of distinction between the role of instructor and of the guidance worker is not necessary for the teacher so long as he is providing appropriate learning experiences and aiding young people in their personal development.

Effective teaching. It is through superior teaching that the teacher makes his greatest contribution to the guidance service. As each child finds his classroom experiences to be interesting, challenging, and enjoyable, serious problems are less likely to occur. The teacher can aid in allaying fears of children, reducing anxieties, and avoiding frustrations. Positive mental health is fostered in an environment of warmth, acceptance, and wholesome stimulation.

Noting vocational possibilities of various subject areas. Each teacher should know and be concerned about the vocational possibilities of each subject and relate classroom activities to the world of work. Students can be shown how their interests and aptitudes can be developed, and the relevance of school subjects in career planning can be explained.

Demonstrating a genuine interest in students. The teacher makes another major contribution in showing his interest in the welfare of each student. The student's adjustment to school, his personal welfare, his attitudes, his state of happiness should all be the concern of the teacher. If the teacher is aware of needs and is sincerely willing to assist youngsters he can do much to help them by demonstrating his concern. This interest must be genuine and should reflect accurately the integrity of the teacher in his relationships with pupils.

Encouraging high academic achievement. The teacher can encourage each student to give each task his best efforts. Opportunities for the best achievement possible should be provided, and each person can be directed in efficient time and energy utilization. The quest for knowledge and for self-improvement can become attainable goals under the tutelage of a dynamic, genuine, dedicated teacher.

Serving on planning committees. Many of the teacher's activities put him in close contact with the student, making personal supervision possible. The teacher can also give support to the guidance service by performing functions such as serving on planning committees, leading group discussions, and giving lectures on pertinent topics to parent-teacher and student groups. The teacher's functions should not be burdensome or time-consuming, but they should permit the full utilization of his capabilities.

Holding individual conferences with students. The teacher may meet with each student periodically for purposes of resolving any existing problems or misunderstandings and to evaluate current progress and make plans for the future. Improved communication between teacher and student is an immediate aim of this activity, and student growth is the ultimate aim.

Providing anecdotal data. The close, personal, relationship between teacher and student provides the opportunity for the teacher to gain information and arrive at understandings about a student which can be used for guidance purposes. Brief anecdotes prepared by the teacher about significant student behavior may be useful to other professional people. The anticipation and preparation of anecdotal material also make the teacher more cognizant of a youngster's problems.

Assisting with the pupil inventory. The teacher helps provide an adequate system for the accumulation and reporting of important information. The teacher also assists in the usual activities of the testing program. He has a voice in the selection of tests, and he is instrumental in orienting pupils to the testing experience. Interpretation of test results to pupils under limited circumstances is also done by the teacher.

Making student referrals. The success of the counseling service depends upon the alertness of the teacher in identifying students who can profit from the counseling experience and upon his taking the initiative in making referrals to the counselor. The teacher is also able to provide the counselor with information about a student which may strengthen the counseling relationship and facilitate the students' growth and adjustment.

The Administrator

The administrator determines the destiny of the guidance service by his attitude toward it. If he sees it as having the potential for aiding youngsters in their development and decision making, chances are good that the service will flourish. In a school without this strong leadership, the service is not likely to progress, although other favorable factors may exist. Linked with his philosophy and attitudes are the specific functions he performs in providing for the resources and personnel upon which the program depends. Some of these specific functions are reviewed here.

The principal's role may be classified into three major categories: (1) his role as the chief administrative officer, (2) his role as coordinator of all school services, and (3) his role as a public relations man.[11] All his major functions may be covered under one or another of these categories.

Closely related to adequate role fulfillment by the administrator is his ability to recognize and handle problems associated with conducting the guidance program.[12] These administrative problems have been summarized by Max Gabbert.[13]

[11] A similar classification of roles is given by DeVries in his discussion of the role of the elementary school principal. He writes of (1) the administrative role, (2) the supervisory role, and (3) the public relations role. Robert DeVries, "Principal's Responsibility in the Guidance Program," *National Elementary Principal*, vol. 43, pp. 47–49, April, 1964.

[12] Many of these problems are covered in a symposium: John C. Hill, Max Gabbert, Donald A. Dake, and Glen Bretz, "Administrative Problems in Guidance," *The Teachers College Journal*, vol. 35, no. 6, pp. 221–223, May, 1964.

[13] *Ibid.*, p. 222

1   Problems of communication between the counselor and his administrative superiors. . . .
2   Problems in relation to faculty understanding of the guidance services. . . .
3   Problems relating to community understanding of the guidance services. . . .
4   Problems relating to financing the guidance services. . . .

Evidently, schools need administrators with the vision to see the problems, the ability to find solutions to them, and leadership qualities through which they carry out their roles.

The administrative role.   The administrator delegates responsibility to others for carrying out the functions of the guidance service. For example, he delegates to the director of the guidance or pupil personnel services the authority to carry out and implement school policies relevant to the guidance service. The director may in turn delegate responsibility and make assignments.

The principal also provides for an administrative framework from which all school services and activities receive their support and direction. Budgetary planning is another important administrative function upon which the guidance service depends. Appropriate plans must be made for acquiring funds and for intelligent expenditures. The morale of personnel and students depends upon the adequate provision of materials and personnel.

The selection of new personnel for the staff is an opportunity for the principal to strengthen the guidance service. His recommendations should include those individuals with the greatest competence for rendering superior service to the students.

The coordinating role.   The principal coordinates all school functions in order that the maximum good may be realized from each service and superior performance from each staff member. He arranges for essential services and makes certain that each is efficiently conducted.

Time allocation for guidance functions is also an essential function. The need for a careful scheduling of all events in the school day is obvious. Functions and activities of the guidance program are included in this schedule.

Committee and job assignments are also handled by the principal as he determines how each person can best serve the total effort. As specific assignments are made and each person knows what his responsibilities are to be, the service operates with greater efficiency.

The coordinating function of the principal includes providing for and supporting programs of training. Activities designed to improve the professional competence of the staff are essential to the continuous progress of the program.

The public relations role. The school serves the public and in turn depends upon the public for support. Keeping the public informed on current school activities, goals, and progress is of the greatest importance. The principal takes the initiative in establishing a system for establishing and maintaining favorable public relations. The usual communications media of the community are utilized in bringing information to the public.

He arranges for study groups, takes part in community activities, and sponsors or lends his support to a variety of activities designed to promote the cooperative spirit between school and community.

Fulfilling Functions and Responsibilities

Thus, as the director of the services, the counselor, the teacher, and the administrator each assumes his rightful role and takes the initiative in meeting all appropriate responsibilities, the guidance program flourishes. Each of these key people either performs a function himself or delegates the responsibility to another person, who then follows through. Permeating the total program is an attitude and spirit of cooperation and dedication, with each person performing the tasks most appropriate to his capabilities and each lending his support to the activities of the other staff members.

Conducting the Guidance Service

Conducting the guidance service involves reemphasizing the sound educational philosophy which must undergird each activity. Some promotional activities are essential in getting the program under way and in keeping it moving. Some selling may be necessary to combat any existing traditional views which resist progress of any kind. Some instruction is necessary too, in order that staff members may contribute more to the program through better preparation and increased knowledge. Closely allied with the philosophy of the school are the procedures developed and utilized for the promotion of the guidance service.

A Philosophy Which Exalts Guidance

If the prevailing views of the school are positively oriented toward the guidance program as an essential school service, the program will thrive. Attitudes of apathy or indifference will, on the other hand, retard any possible progress. The philosophical views discussed below are a sampling of the attitudes that are the keys to action.

A faith in the guidance service. Nothing will have greater influence in the promotion of ideas or in initiating action than a strong, fundamental, belief in these ideas. The conviction that the fulfillment of guidance service goals will add to the richness of a young person's life, belief in the guidance service as a means for stimulating and aiding students, and a faith in its possibilities for good constitute powerful forces which inevitably produce action and progress.

Strong confidence in the educational process must also characterize the thinking of all school people. Agreement must be reached as to the purposes of education and a unified effort generated through which these purposes can be fulfilled. The guidance service is only one of many educational activities and is indeed a subtle influence in virtually everything that takes place. All aspects of the educational program are strengthened through an overlapping, reciprocal relationship among all phases of the total program.

An acceptance of differing points of view. Guidance personnel must be the personification of patience in their relationships with others. They must be kind, accepting, and warm, irrespective of possible differences in beliefs. The guidance program is often judged by the quality of the personnel who represent it; thus it is of paramount importance that counselors be well-liked, respected, and accepted by other staff members. Wrenn outlines three characteristics of the counselor: [14]

> (1) Humility in the face of enormous ignorance. "How little I know, how very little I know! So I must be humble in the face of new evidence, new information, new insights that come almost day by day."
>
> (2) Compassion for the world and each person in it needing love. "I must carry the love of God into some kind of relationship with human beings. . . ."

[14] Wrenn, "The Counselor in a Changing World Revisited," p. 211.

(3) Courage. "I must have courage to face the fact that I shall always seek though I may never completely find. It takes a lot of courage to say, 'I'll never get there, but I am on the way all of my life.'"

The achievement of these goals is not readily attained by even the most sincere counselor, but they might well serve him as guides in a conscientious effort toward self-improvement and his striving to be of assistance to others.

Mutual confidence among staff members. Underlying the successful guidance program is an attitude of confidence in other staff members demonstrated by each person on that staff. In order to justify this confidence, each person must be imbued with a desire to improve himself. Personal and professional growth is essential to effective educational services for students. Each professional person, then, believes in his immediate coworkers, respects their judgment, and profits from their influences. This includes the teacher with other teachers, and the counselor with other counselors. This concept also applies to confidence in other workers with different assignments, such as the counselor in his associations with the teacher.

Procedures for Promoting the Guidance Service

The philosophical aspects of the guidance service have been reviewed in an attempt to show their importance in establishing and developing the guidance program. These philosophies are reflected in, and provide the framework and impetus for the formulation of, procedures for carrying out this work. Such procedures, described in the pages that follow, will need some modifications to meet local conditions. It should also be noted that the particular persons for carrying out these procedures are not identified. The procedures are accomplished through a cooperative effort of all staff members, under the leadership of the school's administrative personnel.

Encouraging and promoting cooperative effort. Greater interest is shown in an activity and more enthusiasm is demonstrated when there is broad participation. The spirit of fellowship and camaraderie which accompanies an effort makes the activity more enjoyable, and productivity is increased. Greater involvement is accomplished as ideas and suggestions are solicited from all staff members. They may not all have contributions to make, but the desirable objective of involvement is being realized. Teachers can be made to feel that their roles in the educational process and in the guidance service are vital to its success.

Providing for professional improvements. Being well informed about a school service is often the answer to prejudices and resistance. Opportunities for participation in seminars, planning groups, discussions, and other in-service training activities will contribute to the education of staff members. Enrollment in university classes offered through extension services and attendance at summer schools offer a second means for improving faculty competences and understandings. These opportunities make it possible for staff members to develop a positive attitude toward the guidance service and to become better acquainted with its function.

Encouraging and providing for research activities. Objective evidence upon which to base decisions for program changes and by which to draw conclusions is often lacking in the typical school. The structure of activities should provide for involvement in research. Faculty members can be encouraged to take part in studies by providing them with the time and facilities and by assigning appropriate people to these projects. A scientific attitude on the part of staff members results in more logical approaches to problem solution and contributes to the professional improvement of staff members.

Initiating parent contacts. Parental support and cooperative assistance is generally forthcoming if parents are kept informed and are able to see how their children will be benefited. Occasional home visits by teachers may be possible; they should be encouraged and actually provided for periodically. Study and discussion groups bring parents and teachers together and make possible a stimulating exchange of ideas leading to improvements in the guidance service.

Promoting community projects related to guidance. Most communities provide school people with considerable opportunity for participation in projects related to the needs and welfare of children. The school may also take the initiative in such projects if the community does not do so. The cooperation of school and community in improving the educational opportunities of youngsters is a worthy objective, and every effort should be made to achieve it. Service clubs often provide programs of assistance for children and youth within a community. These programs can be improved through school-community cooperation.

Soliciting the assistance of influential people.   Capable, influential people can be of help in stimulating others toward an interest in the school's activities and can give impetus to the growth and importance of the guidance service. The school should capitalize on the potential these people have for aiding in the promotion and conduct of the various school programs. Everyone who responds should be brought into the program. However, the interest and aid of established community leaders in particular should be sought, since their influence can be paramount in bringing about a strong guidance program.

Capitalizing on all opportunities for promoting the guidance service.   Alert personnel workers will see many opportunities for action in the interest of the guidance service. Lectures, demonstrations, workshops, and personal contacts all have merit and should be utilized as a means by which teacher, parent, and community groups can be made aware of the guidance program and by which they can become better informed about its functions.

The various communications media available in the community should also be utilized in publicizing the school's program and in enlisting the interest and help of community members.

SUMMARY/

The guidance service can become effective only if it is properly organized and efficiently administered. It will flourish as it receives the appropriate attention of the administration, teachers, and counselors; it will be ineffective if the organization and the administration of the guidance service are left to chance. Structure, organization, and a sound philosophy are essential in conducting the activities.

Initiatory action may include a consideration of preliminary problems the resolution of which will facilitate the establishment of an organized program of guidance services. Certain procedures may then be followed by which the program can be started.

An effective program depends upon the competent leadership and service functions of the various staff members. The guidance director has the responsibility for getting the various guidance activities under way and for utilizing all available resources and personnel. The counselor shares responsibilities with the director but devotes a major part of his time to student counseling and to related guidance activities. The teacher too has a part in the guidance service and makes his contributions felt through effective teaching and specific responsibilities within the guidance service. The attitude shown, participation given, and leadership demonstrated by the administrator constitute the key factors in the strength and success of the guidance program. He delegates responsibility, encourages action, and provides for the necessary personnel and funds. The participation and contributions of all school personnel are essential to the success of the guidance service.

In conducting the activities of the guidance program a positive philosophy and a strong belief in the guidance service must prevail among the staff. The actions of these staff members should exemplify the faith and confidence they have in the guidance function. Specific procedures may also be followed in promoting the guidance program within the school and the community. Local interest and support are essential to the development and progress of the program, and parents and community leaders should be encouraged to participate, and their abilities should be properly utilized.

PROBLEMS/

1   A successful guidance program depends upon a number of conditions and factors within the school. Identify these and point out why they are important to the guidance program.

2   A strong organizational pattern is merely a means to an end. What is the end, or the aim, of the guidance service?

3   The attainment of a sound structure may be an immediate goal, but it does not just happen. Review the guides to this structure as given in the chapter, and make a statement in support of each.

4   How might the school go about determining which of the basic elements of the guidance service should receive first attention? What is the next logical step to follow in the establishment of one of the elements?

5   There is no one pattern of organization, but each school should establish a suitable pattern for itself. Why?

6 In the chapter eight principles of organization are listed. See how many of these you can recall. Return to the chapter and add two or more principles to this list.

7 Note the advantages to come from looking at, and seeking answers to, certain problems prior to the actual initiation of the program.

8 How might the school go about finding answers to these problems?

9 If the various staff members have their unique functions in the guidance service but also share functions with other staff members, show how appropriate distinctions can be made in order to avoid confusion and duplication.

10 Identify the major work of each of the following by providing some broad, inclusive statements by which the work of each is described: (*a*) guidance director; (*b*) the counselor; (*c*) the teacher; and (*d*) the administrator.

11 What does a philosophy have to do with organizing and conducting the guidance service? What does the term mean? How does a school arrive at a "philosophy"?

12 Why is it necessary to "promote" the service? What guides can you give for accomplishing this?

Selected References

Textbooks

ANDREW, DEAN C., and LESTER N. DOWNING: *120 Readings in Guidance*, University of Nebraska Press, Lincoln, Nebr., 1955, pp. 247–276.

ARBUCKLE, DUGALD S.: *Pupil Personnel Services in American Schools*, Allyn and Bacon, Inc., Boston, 1962, chap. 11.

BARR, JOHN A.: *The Elementary Teacher and Guidance*, Holt, Rinehart and Winston, Inc., New York, 1958, chap. 20.

COTTINGHAM, HAROLD F.: *Guidance in Elementary Schools*, McKnight & McKnight Publishing Company, Bloomington, Ill., 1956, chaps. 11–13.

FARWELL, GAIL F., and HERMAN J. PETERS: *Guidance Readings for Counselors*, Rand McNally & Company, Chicago, 1960, chap. 8.

FROEHLICH, CLIFFORD P.: *Guidance Services in Schools*, McGraw-Hill Book Company, New York, 1958, chap. 4.

GLANZ, EDWARD C.: *Foundations and Principles of Guidance*, Allyn and Bacon, Inc., Boston, 1964, chap. 12.

HUMPHREYS, J. ANTHONY, ARTHUR E. TRAXLER, and ROBERT D. NORTH: *Guidance Services*, Science Research Associates, Inc., Chicago, 1960, chaps. 16 and 17.

HUTSON, PERCIVAL W.: *The Guidance Function in Education,* Appleton-Century-Crofts, Inc., New York, 1958, chap. 18.

JONES, ARTHUR J.: *Principles of Guidance and Pupil Personnel Work,* 5th ed., McGraw-Hill Book Company, New York, 1963, chap. 10.

KOWITZ, GERALD T., and NORMA G. KOWITZ: *Guidance in the Elementary Classroom,* McGraw-Hill Book Company, New York, 1959, part 3.

MC DANIEL, HENRY B., JOHN E. LALLAS, JAMES A. SAUM, and JAMES L. GILMORE: *Readings in Guidance,* Holt, Rinehart and Winston, Inc., New York, 1959, chap. 2.

MATHEWSON, ROBERT HENDRY: *Guidance Policy and Practice,* Harper & Row, Publishers, Incorporated, New York, 1955, chap. 13.

MILLER, FRANK W.: *Guidance Principles and Services,* Charles E. Merrill Books, Inc., Englewood Cliffs, N.J., 1961, chap. 2.

MORTENSEN, DONALD G., and ALLEN M. SCHMULLER: *Guidance in Today's Schools,* John Wiley & Sons, Inc., New York, 1959, chap. 3.

OHLSEN, MERLE M.: *Guidance Services in the Modern School,* Harcourt, Brace & World, Inc., New York, 1964, chap. 16.

PETERS, HERMAN J., and GAIL F. FARWELL: *Guidance: A Developmental Approach,* Rand McNally & Company, Chicago, 1959, chap. 14.

STOOPS, EMERY, and GUNNAR L. WAHLQUIST: *Principles and Practices in Guidance,* McGraw-Hill Book Company, New York, 1958, chap. 9.

TRAXLER, ARTHUR E., and ROBERT D. NORTH: *Techniques of Guidance,* 3d ed., Harper & Row, Publishers, Incorporated, New York, 1966, chap. 2.

WARTERS, JANE: *High School Personnel Work Today,* 2d ed., McGraw-Hill Book Company, New York, 1956, chap. 13.

WILLEY, ROY DE VERL, and DEAN C. ANDREW: *Modern Methods and Techniques in Guidance,* Harper & Row, Publishers, Incorporated, New York, 1955, chap. 4.

WRENN, C. GILBERT: *The Counselor in a Changing World,* American Personnel and Guidance Association, Washington, D.C., 1962, chap. 6.

Journals

BISH, HUGH, and J. A. DORFF: "How Best to Organize Guidance and Counseling Services for Students in the Senior High School," *Bulletin of the National Association of Secondary-school Principals,* vol. 44, pp. 170–173, April, 1960.

CALIA, VINCENT F.: "Organization Theory and Research: Some Implications for Guidance Programs," *Personnel and Guidance Journal,* vol. 43, pp. 757–763, April, 1965.

DEMEKE, HOWARD J.: "Low Cost to Better Guidance in the Elementary Grades," *School Management,* vol. 5, pp. 41–43, August, 1961.

DIAMOND, H. J.: "Reorganizing Our Pupil Personnel Program," *High Points,* vol. 43, pp. 49–51, June, 1961.

DUGAN, WILLIS E.: "Organization and Administration of Guidance Services," *Review of Educational Research,* vol. 30, pp. 105–114, April, 1960.

ERICKSON, CLIFFORD E., and RAYMOND N. HATCH: "Principles for Programming Personnel Services," *Personnel Services in Education,* Fifty-Eighth Yearbook of the National Society for the Study of Education, 1959, part II, pp. 85–102.

FARWELL, GAIL F.: "Continuity in the Guidance Programs," *Educational Leadership,* vol. 18, pp. 338–342, March, 1961.

FILBECK, ROBERT W.: "Perceptions of Appropriateness of Counselor Behavior: A Comparison of Counselors and Principals," *Personnel and Guidance Journal*, vol. 43, pp. 891–896, May, 1965.

FUSCO, G. C.: "Pupil Personnel Service Programs: Organization and Administration," *School Life*, vol. 44, pp. 28–30, September, 1961.

GIRERINGER, J.: "Workable Guidance Program," *School and Community*, vol. 46, pp. 10–11, January, 1960.

GLANZ, EDWARD C.: "Emerging Concepts and Patterns of Guidance in American Education," *Personnel and Guidance Journal*, vol. 40, pp. 259–265, November, 1961.

HOPKINS, R. P.: "Critical Problems in Pupil Personnel Administration," *Personnel and Guidance Journal*, vol. 40, pp. 240–246, November, 1961.

JOHNSON, Y. O.: "Standardizing Counseling Procedures," *Journal of Secondary Education*, vol. 40, pp. 320–324, November, 1965.

KAUFFMAN, J. F.: "Student Personnel Administration," *Educational Record*, vol. 45, pp. 291–298, Summer, 1964.

LINSLEY, GEORGE H.: "Small Elementary District has Successful Guidance Service," *California Education*, vol. 1, p. 11, April, 1964.

MC CABE, EARL N.: "Missing Word in Guidance," *Bulletin of the National Association of Secondary-school Principals*, vol. 47, pp. 89–93, September, 1963.

NANCARROW, JAMES E.: "Guidance Means Help," *Bulletin of the National Association of Secondary-school Principals*, vol. 45, pp. 1–5, May, 1961.

NUNLEY, JOE E.: "Initiating a Guidance Program," *Clearing House*, vol. 37, pp. 269–271, January, 1963.

OLSEN, LEROY C.: "In-service Guidance Training," *Bulletin of the National Association of Secondary-school Principals*, vol. 47, pp. 78–85, September, 1963.

———: "Responsibilities of the Board of Education and the Administrator in the Guidance Program," *Bulletin of the National Association of Secondary-school Principals*, vol. 46, pp. 24–27, November, 1962.

PAUL, HENRY A.: "Outline of High School Guidance," *Catholic School Journal*, vol. 62, pp. 45–48, May, 1962.

PETERS, HERMAN J., and JAMES B. HECK: "Essential Readings in Guidance," *Bulletin of the National Association of Secondary-school Principals*, vol. 47, pp. 99–102, September, 1963.

——— and ———: "Guidance Bookshelf," *Bulletin of the National Association of Secondary-school Principals*, vol. 45, pp. 59–61, May, 1961.

PHILLIPS, FLORENCE A.: "Role of Parents in a High School Guidance Program," *Personnel and Guidance Journal*, vol. 41, pp. 269–270, November, 1962.

PULLEN, MILTON V.: "When There Are No Guidance Specialists: Guidelines for Principals," *National Elementary Principal*, vol. 43, pp. 19–21, April, 1964.

REED, HAROLD J., and BUFORD STEFFLRE: "Elementary and Secondary School Programs: Organization and Administration of Guidance Services," *Review of Educational Research*, vol. 33, pp. 152–156, April, 1963.

SAMLER, JOSEPH: "The Counseling Service in the Administrative Setting: Problems and Possible Solutions," *Personnel and Guidance Journal*, vol. 44, no. 7, pp. 715–722, March, 1966.

SHAW, MERVILLE C., and JOHN K. TUEL: "A Focus for Public School Guidance

Programs: A Model and Proposal," *Personnel and Guidance Journal*, vol. 44, no. 8, pp. 824–830, April, 1966.

SHOBEN, EDWARD J., JR.: "The Counseling Experience as Personal Development," *Personnel and Guidance Journal*, vol. 44, pp. 224–230, November, 1965.

SPEARS, MACK J., and THOMAS J. JENKINS: "How Can We Make the Best Use of the Time and Energies of the Guidance Counselors We Now Have?" *Bulletin of the National Association of Secondary-school Principals*, vol. 45, pp. 302–307, April, 1961.

WYLIE, BRUCE A.: "Administrative Support of Key Guidance Dimensions," *Bulletin of the National Association of Secondary-school Principals*, vol. 46, pp. 96–98, November, 1962.

THIRTEEN

/MENTAL HEALTH AND THE GUIDANCE PROGRAM

We have seen that the major commitment of the guidance service is the personal welfare and emotional well-being of each person in the school. The total educational program reflects this concern and the awareness that emotional stability is favorable to the learning experiences of youngsters. The learning process for each child may be facilitated or impeded by the state of his mental health. The happy, well-adjusted, self-confident child learns more readily and is better prepared to utilize his knowledge and skills than the child who is handicapped by tensions, anxieties, and frustrations. Although considerable progress is being made in both prevention and remediation of emotional disturbances, the problems continue to persist, and the task is without end.

The matter of mental health is of vital concern to many other agencies at all governmental levels. The responsibilities for the promotion of good mental health are shared by many groups and by individuals representing these groups. Just as maladjustments and disturbances have their sources in a variety of causes, so, too, should there be expressions of interest and remedial action by a number of agencies.

While continued strengthening of cooperative effort among all the appropriate agencies is essential for the improvement of mental health of all citizens, the school is the major instrumentality for the promotion of good mental health. A number of factors support this contention: The school has the advantage of time spent with youngsters during which preventive measures may be taken. There exists an organized program of educational activities in which a variety of supervised experiences is enjoyed. Professional personnel are available within the school, and youngsters thus have opportunities for instruction and aid in development. Early identification of youngsters experiencing difficulties is possible, and appropriate action may be taken for assistance or treatment.

The school recognizes its responsibility in the promotion of favorable mental health, and efforts are made to meet this responsibility. Harris notes in this regard that the idea has prevailed for a long time that the school is responsible for fostering the mental and physical health of the child as well as his intellectual development.[1] He goes on to say,[2] "It is recognized widely that mental illness in adults develops from roots in childhood maladjustments and that preventive action during childhood is both more satisfactory and less expensive than intensive treatment for adults." Education itself has a commitment to the total development and welfare of each child, and the guidance service is instrumental in bringing this commitment to fruition.

It is the purpose of this chapter to show the relationship between the guidance service and the promotion of good mental health. The organization, facilities, and personnel of this service make the fostering of a positive environment for learning possible. Areas of concern are identified and suggestions given on how to determine a child's "mental health" status. The aims of guidance and the procedures for accomplishing these aims are reviewed. The role of the teacher is explained, and the major functions of the counselor are described. The importance of a close working relationship between teacher and counselor is emphasized throughout the chapter.

[1] Albert J. Harris, "Mental Health Clinic in Teacher Education," *Journal of Teacher Education*, vol. 12, p. 417, December, 1961.
[2] *Ibid.*

Responsibilities of the Guidance Service for Mental Health

If the guidance service is to assume its rightful place and its responsibilities for bettering school conditions in the interest of the good mental health of children, it must make known the nature of its position and responsibilities. Its position is one of several services within the school setting, all of which have an interest in the development and well-being of each student. Its responsibilities encompass providing the basic elements of a guidance program for all students and, more specifically, identifying youngsters in need of special help and either providing this aid or locating a suitable agency that can provide it.

A better understanding of human behavior is needed in order to provide more adequately for the development of children. Progress is being realized, however, and the current level of knowledge about behavior is sufficient that explanations for particular conduct by a child can generally be made, although some speculation may still be inevitable.

The traditional view of blaming the child for his uncooperative attitudes or placing the responsibility with the inadequacies of the home is no longer tenable. True, these factors do have influence upon the child and determine to a degree the kind of a person he will be in school. But they also oversimplify a very complex phenomenon—human behavior. Such oversimplification tends to ignore the concept that there are good reasons underlying all behavior and that if these reasons, or causes, are understood by adults, the child can be aided in improving his behavior.

Robert L. Anderson notes one of the problems of the past and also points up a present weakness in the schools with the following statement: [3]

> Twenty years ago teachers emphasized one of two reasons for a child having difficulties in school. He was either a victim of a low I.Q. or he was lazy. Today another explanation has been added and often replaces the other two. He is emotionally disturbed. While the diagnosis is sometimes correct, only a few questions need to be asked to discover that teachers and administrators alike are ill-informed regarding manifestation of symptoms, causation of the condition, and application of therapeutic practices.

Counselors too are in many cases relatively ill informed about the causes and treatment of maladjustments. The challenge for

[3] Robert L. Anderson, "Stressing Mental Health Programs in Public Schools," *Michigan Education Journal*, vol. 39, p. 468, March, 1962.

school personnel to become better informed and to make a greater effort to improve the educational climate of all youngsters is a formidable one. The guidance service can rightfully take the lead toward the realization of this aim.

Anderson stresses that teachers, administrators, and counselors need to be better informed on matters of mental health. He notes that 25 percent of school-age children may be classified as either moderately or seriously maladjusted. This figure represents a median percentage from thirteen studies showing a range from 10 to 50 percent.[4]

Areas of Concern

One approach for improving mental health conditions in the school is to note the problems of major concern to students. This can be done by enumerating the conditions and status of each student in respect to his current welfare and possibilities for improvement. The guidance service then initiates action by determining the nature of these student concerns, after which action can be taken to assist each student in meeting his problems.

The following outline might be used as a guide in determining the general status of any one student or a group of students:

1 The general quality of schoolwork. Is his achievement record of sufficient quality in terms of existing conditions and his capabilities?

2 His aptitude for schoolwork. Are his capabilities such that schoolwork is difficult or relatively easy for him? How great is the discrepancy between his ability and his performance?

3 His feelings and attitudes toward school. Are his feelings and attitudes toward school favorable and positive, or does he harbor resentments and negative feelings?

4 His feelings about his home. Does he feel that his home is helpful to him and that he can depend upon his home for support and direction?

5 Quality of the relationship with family members. Does he get along well with others in the family? What are his attitudes toward parents and siblings?

6 Nature and quality of relationships with friends and associates. Does he have some close friends? Does he gain emotional satisfaction from his associations with others?

7 Quality of the pupil-teacher relationship. Does he like and en-

----

[4] *Ibid.*, quoted from L. Kaplan, *Mental Health and Human Relations in Education*, Harper & Row, Publishers, Incorporated, New York, 1959.

joy his teachers? Does he feel comfortable with them? Are his attitudes toward them positive and realistic?

8   Quality of general health. Is he free of handicaps? If not, has he made the necessary adjustments?

9   The state of his emotional health. Is he even-tempered, flexible, and able to maintain a sense of humor? Does he feel adequate? Is he able to tolerate frustrations?

10   Nature and quality of plans for the future. What planning has he done? How realistic are his plans? What kind of help might he use most advantageously at this time?

As the counselor gives careful consideration to each of these areas of concern, he gains a better understanding of the current status of each student and is better prepared to move ahead with plans for remedy and aid. A "shotgun" approach including a number of activities for all students, with the hope that some may be beneficial for at least a few students, is inefficient and often disappointing. A more logical approach is to determine the status of each student and thus open the way for specific action by which he may be helped.

Identifying specific problems.   The preceding outline should be helpful in determining the general status of a child, but more specific information, including a pinpointing of specific problems, is needed in order to be able to help him. Instruments—checklists, inventories, and the like—designed for this purpose may prove helpful, particularly when used in conjunction with activities such as teacher observations, counseling, informal visits, class activity, and home visits.[5] Once problem areas are identified, appropriate procedures for coping with these problems and for preventing new problems may be developed and carried out.

There are broad problem areas, each of which contains a number of minor elements. For example, Arbuckle identifies four major areas of concern and then discusses each in some detail: [6] (1) The struggle for self acceptance as a never-ending struggle of the child . . . . (2) The adventure of going to school with its attending problems . . . . (3) Entering the adult world of work . . . and (4) The problems associated with one's developing body,

[5] Two such instruments are the Mooney Problem Checklist, by Ross L. Mooney, published by the Psychological Corporation, New York, (see Appendix A for address), and the SRA Youth Inventory, by H. H. Remmers and Benjamin Shimberg, Science Research Associates, Inc., Chicago.

[6] Dugald S. Arbuckle, *Pupil Personnel Services in American Schools,* Allyn and Bacon, Inc., Boston, 1962, pp. 54–70.

with its needs and demands, and the conflicts often encountered with society and the culture. . . . An awareness by teachers and counselors that students do experience frustrations and anxieties should result in a more effective educational program through which needed aid and encouragement can be provided at the critical times in each child's life.[7]

Needs of children and youth. Any program designed to assist youngsters in their emotional development must consider the needs of these young people. Obviously, this is a very broad topic. The intent here is to stress the fact that certain basic needs do exist, that their fulfillment contributes to emotional stability and appropriate development, and that their unfulfillment brings frustration and a thwarting of development.

Willey and Dunn note that teacher understanding of the child is important for his emotional welfare. The child has certain basic needs which are related to his having feelings of success.[8] As these needs are adequately met, good adjustment follows. The thwarting of these needs contributes to maladjustment. "A lack of any human need results in an upset of equilibrium causing (or constituting) a condition of stress. Once subjected to stress, the basic reaction fits into a general pattern of resistance and adaptation. . . ."[9] It is the intent of the guidance program to minimize both frustrations and the need for adaptations.

General Aims of Guidance in Mental Health

A major aim of guidance is to make the best use possible of each child's potential, to aid him toward the greatest possible accomplishment commensurate with his potentialities. For this aim to be realized there must be a minimization of factors which constitute any kind of threat to the full development possibilities of each child. The guidance service therefore attempts to provide the necessary structure and environment for protection of youngsters against unwarranted drains upon their energies and emotional resources.

Woolcock states that good mental health should be a first goal

[7] Also concerned with problems of the child is Dorothy Rogers, *Mental Hygiene in Elementary Education,* Houghton Mifflin Company, Boston, 1957, chap. 9.

[8] Roy DeVerl Willey and Melvin Dunn, *The Role of the Teacher in the Guidance Program,* McKnight & McKnight Publishing Company, Bloomington, Ill., 1964, chap. 9.

[9] *Ibid.,* p. 185.

in education and that it implies satisfying relations with others as well as freedom from guilt and nervous tensions, anxieties, and fears.[10] Certainly good mental health must be a first goal; otherwise many other worthy goals can never be reached.

Since the principal reason for a child's presence in school is to learn, everything done by the school to facilitate learning should reflect its concern for the learner's readiness for these experiences. Basic to this readiness is the emotional stability which permits the full utilization of the learner's powers. There is a reciprocal relationship between learning efficiency and good mental health, with some very important implications for the school. "Just as the school's efficiency in enabling a child to master his environment affects mental health, so a child's mental health alters his ability to learn." [11] The design of the educational program should thus provide for a comfortable, stimulating, profitable, learning environment and for conditions which are conducive to the emotional well-being of the learner.

Preventing dropouts. Certainly, the school has a number of worthy aims by which the life of each child is to be bettered and his development enhanced. One broad aim is to make the educational offering so enticing that not only will the youngster make satisfactory progress but the school will be his first choice as the best place to be. Unfortunately, this is not always the case, and escape from the school is joyfully anticipated by too many students. The guidance service plays a key role in the prevention of dropouts through early identification, treatment, and environment manipulation. Millard notes that the spiraling rate of dropouts is a matter for great concern, ". . . that such waste in human resources is indefensible; and that salvaging this precious resource is a challenging and urgent task for education, and one in which mental health has a vital interest." [12] He suggests that community resources and agencies can be helpful in reducing this problem, but it is the school's resources which are of the greatest importance, and specifically its mental health services. The school can observe and understand the sequence of events which normally lead to leaving school.[13]

[10] C. W. Woolcock, "Mental Health Aspects of the Gifted and Talented," *Bulletin of the National Association of Secondary-school Principals,* vol. 45, p. 63, November, 1961.

[11] Fritz Redl and William W. Wattenberg, *Mental Hygiene in Teaching,* Harcourt, Brace & World, Inc., New York, 1959, p. 205.

[12] Thomas L. Millard, "Some Clinical Notes on Dropouts," *Journal of Secondary Education,* vol. 39, p. 343, December, 1964.

[13] *Ibid.*

Satisfactory academic achievement.   Satisfaction with oneself and pride in accomplishments are certainly essential to the mental health of the student. Pride in accomplishments provides the stimulation and motivation from which continued successes will inevitably occur. Feelings of despair and discouragement, on the other hand, result in a reduction of effort and in low motivation. Good mental health, then, contributes to achievement and is in turn affected by achievement. A positive attitude by the school toward individual achievement and the realization that achievement is an individual matter, not one of competition with others, are essential for the good mental health of the student and for his realizing satisfactory achievement. Strom laments the condition which makes the gaining of grades a highly competitive, frustrating experience and stresses the importance of individuality as a criterion for grading. Individual achievement should be based on personal progress, and to do otherwise is to perpetuate a fraud upon students.[14]

Specific Aims of Guidance and Procedures for Fulfilling Them

Both the general and specific aims of the guidance service for promoting good mental health have a place in the educational scheme. These aims are broad and have far-reaching implications. The prevention of dropouts and satisfying academic achievement are only representative of these aims. Likewise, the aims outlined in this section and the suggestions for fulfilling them are merely representative. The suggested procedures may be modified to accommodate a particular school. There is nothing final or ultimate about any of these aims or procedures.

Supplementing the educational services.   The guidance program aids the educational program as a whole; it furnishes leadership and some organized procedures by which the total educational experiences of students may become more meaningful. This supplementing influence lends strength to the educational offering, broadens the opportunities for activities, and provides for enrichment experiences. Procedures to be used by guidance personnel for fulfilling these aims include the following:

1   Work closely with teachers in a cooperative effort to provide the most wholesome classroom environment possible, by means of

[14] Robert D. Strom, "Academic Achievement and Mental Health," *Journal of Secondary Education,* vol. 79, pp. 348–355, December, 1964.

    classroom visits, personal conferences with teachers, and suggestions for improving the classroom climate.

2   Maintain a close working relationship with the administration. Information may be gained on individual students and impending problems or difficulties. The administrative framework of the school may also be improved in relation to providing for the needs of students.

3   Be alert as to the availability of extraclass activities for students. Work with teachers who have the responsibility for supervising these activities, and solicit their help in encouraging the youngsters who need these experiences to take part.

4   Be available as friendly advisers, consultants, and coworkers in furthering the work of the school. Counselors can lend aid, provide information, and make suggestions for program improvements. Their availability, interest, and concern can provide a boost to the morale of the whole staff as well as improve the technical efficiency with which tasks are accomplished.

5   Make all counseling and personal contacts with students as effective as possible. Counseling time is valuable, and the influence it has upon students can have far-reaching effects. Students should be encouraged to give school their best efforts, and aid should be provided at times of stress or undue pressures.

Emphasizing prevention in avoiding serious problems.   Early detection, diagnosis, and treatment are most essential in a program of prevention. Teachers are in a good position to observe and identify children in need of special consideration or help. The counselor's value in prevention is determined by the ability of the teacher to capitalize on his capabilities. This is an example of the need for a good working relationship between the teacher and the counselor in order to utilize fully the resources of both. Techniques for strengthening the program of prevention may thus include the following procedures for the counseling staff:

1   Provide all students with opportunities for counseling interviews. Problems may thus be resolved as they occur, and in some cases the problems can be avoided.

2   Make periodic visits to the classrooms, and observe students in this setting. An alert counselor will note significant behavior by students and will gain information which will be helpful in his counseling and of equal value as he confers with the teacher on student problems.

3   Hold conferences with teachers both in groups and individually. Many purposes underlie this procedure, the most important of which is to make instructional activities as meaningful, inter-

esting, and purposeful as possible for students. An interested, motivated, enthusiastic person is not likely to become maladjusted or lack the resources to deal with his problems. Effective teaching by a competent, friendly, personable teacher creates an atmosphere in which children feel comfortable, and in which anxieties are kept to a minimum.

4   Utilize the referral resources of the school and the community. Other people within the school can often be of significant help to students. Their capabilities should be utilized as their assistance is solicited in aiding students. Community agencies and individuals may also provide information and assistance as referrals are made to them and as their help is requested.

5   Be alert and observant at all times, and identify students whose behavior may suggest symptoms of developing problems. Both counselors and teachers should make these observations and exchange ideas and information. They can then take appropriate action to avoid the development of more serious problems.

Providing appropriate diagnostic services.   Another aim of the guidance service is to make certain that needed diagnostic services are provided. Diagnosis is as essential to prevention as it is to treatment. Both detection and diagnosis depend upon the alertness and cooperation of all staff members. The guidance service, however, takes the initiative in providing the leadership, establishing the functions, and making certain that the necessary activities are carried out. The procedures of the diagnostic function might include the following:

1   Analyze and synthesize background data which may have relevance for the accurate appraisal of a child. These data should be reported simply and clearly for efficient and accurate interpretation and use.

2   Provide leadership in making case studies. Findings from these studies should be carefully reviewed, major points discussed with teachers, and decisions made by the people concerned on courses of action to follow.

3   Solicit the assistance of other specialists, and capitalize on their suggestions for improving conditions for children in the school.

4   Conduct fact-finding interviews with students for purposes of gaining information which may provide clues to possible problems. These interviews also stimulate students to plan more carefully for the future.

5   Provide appropriate counseling for students in an effort to resolve problems as they occur. Therapy of a more intensive nature may be needed by some students. This should be provided

either by a qualified person on the school staff or by referral to an outside source of professional help.

6 Administer appropriate tests at times when the availability of objective data will result in a better understanding of the student by the counselor.

Promoting conditions conducive to good mental health. Many problems involving frustrations, anxieties, and possible maladjustments may be avoided through an atmosphere of calm and reason. Students who may be disturbed by confusion, pressures, and disorganization may otherwise be relaxed and able to perform efficiently in a favorable environment. These favorable conditions can be provided by competent, well-informed, sensitive teachers and counselors. Certain procedures will be helpful, such as the ones listed below, but the existence of a wholesome, favorable environment also depends upon the positive attitudes of the staff. An attractive, appealing atmosphere is as much a result of attitudes as it is of techniques.

1 Providing a permissive, relaxed, wholesome, stimulating classroom environment. Such an atmosphere is created by the teacher of each class, but the counselor can help develop and maintain it. Appropriate freedom is essential here, but so are the appropriate limits and standards of conduct.

2 Identifying and correcting conditions which cause students anxiety and worries.

3 Encouraging students to utilize the services of the counselors. Rather free access to the counselor's office upon occasions, in addition to the formal scheduling of interviews, should be permitted.

4 Providing opportunities for broad participation in group activities. These may include informal, socializing groups, group guidance activities, and organized groups within the classroom.

5 Encouraging socializing experiences and providing opportunities for the development of leadership abilities. Considerable socializing occurs among young people with little direction. However, organized experiences under competent leadership is very beneficial for all participants.

Encouraging an attitude of wholesome self-acceptance among pupils. Pupils need to feel good about all aspects of their lives. Positive feelings are essential to the mental health and emotional balance of all people. Many children attain wholesome attitudes when the school environment is conducive to them. Teachers and counselors can contribute to this desirable atmosphere by being genuinely interested in youngsters and by providing the necessary professional services. A pupil's increasing self-confidence and positive self-esteem stem from a favorable environment. A concomitant of improved self-confidence is the ability of a child to accept himself and therefore live with himself more harmoniously. Weaknesses in self are recognized by the well-adjusted child as challenges for self-improvement, not as threats. Strengths are identified and utilized for purposes of self-enhancement. A pupil's tolerance level is high and therefore adequate for meeting daily frustrations when he has self-confidence and is able to accept himself as a worthy, competent person.

There are no exact techniques by which the aim of pupil self-acceptance, any more than other aims, can be reached, but procedures such as those suggested below may stimulate teachers and counselors toward the development of attitudes of greater concern for the welfare of each youngster.

1 Providing strong, meritorious teaching at all educational levels with all students. The responsibility for highest-quality teaching rests with the administration as it selects teachers for positions and provides the leadership for their improvement on the job. Excellent teaching is the means by which many problems can be averted and is the factor most likely to provide the greatest aid to a pupil in self-improvement and self-acceptance.
2 Making available suitable informative written matter from which students can become better informed on personality development and on problems of adjustment. Many student anxieties are reflections of their own naïveté.
3 Providing for occasional discussions of problems and concerns within the classroom or under the counselor's supervision. Information may be gained, attitudes improved, and therapeutic benefits derived from these experiences.
4 Providing students with appropriate counseling or therapeutic help at times of need. Early attention is critical, since detection and treatment will often resolve a problem promptly or may avert additional problems.

Ascertaining the causes of emotional problems. As the existence of emotional difficulties becomes apparent to the school staff, action is immediately called for. Of critical importance at these times is the determination of possible causes of the difficulties. Since pupil development is a major concern of the guidance service, the existence of any deterrent to this development immediately becomes a matter requiring the attention of guidance personnel. As possible causes are determined, appropriate measures may be taken for appropriate treatment and for the alleviation of the causative and precipitating circumstances. Teachers and counselors may determine the causes by one or more of several possible procedures:

1   Observe the child in the classroom and on the playground. Become acquainted with his behavior under a variety of conditions and draw some conclusions about his emotional status as evidenced by symptoms.

2   Maintain close contact with the child being studied, by means of casual, informal visits and conversations. The child should not be made to feel that he is an object of special study, but he should be aware of the school's interest in his welfare.

3   Make a case study in which needed information is accumulated and analyzed. The breadth and intensity of such a study should be determined by local conditions and by the urgency of the problem. Decisions may then be reached and courses of action outlined.

4   Utilize the resources of other agencies and professional people. Time may be saved and the quality of the service enhanced as the judgments of other people are solicited.

There are many ways by which children may be studied and aided in their development.[15] The guidance service aims to provide the leadership and the resources for accomplishing this important work.

Counselor and Teacher Roles in Mental Health Services

Virtually all activities within the school have the potential for influencing positively or negatively the emotional status of each child. Therefore, the effect on the emotional welfare of children should be a major criterion when planning the various educational experiences. Mental health is a responsibility of all school personnel— teacher, counselor, and administrator—and it requires the attention, participation, and unique contributions of each. By acting according to this principle the teacher and counselor can be of broader assistance to students.

In addition to the specific services provided by each, the cooperative efforts of the teacher and the counselor should result in a more favorable school environment for all students. Although the counselor's major aim is the personal development of each student whereas academic achievement is the teacher's main ob-

[15] See Dorothy Rogers, *op. cit.*, chaps. 11 and 12.

jective, there is considerable overlap between these two principal objectives that increases the need for a strong working relationship between counselor and teacher. In this section we look at the major responsibilities of each to the mental health program and consider their roles as coproducers.

Counselor-Teacher Relationship in Mental Health Service

An important function of the counselor is to provide the teacher with the kind of assistance and services which will result in the most favorable environment possible for a youngster. The emotional and educational welfare of each student is the major concern. The exact nature of the service may vary somewhat among schools or within the same school, since conditions are different and the needs of teachers vary as do the competences of the counselors providing the assistance. However, these differences are not important so long as the working relationship is favorable and the needed aid and encouragement are provided. The teacher-counselor relationship can be strengthened and made more meaningful as certain procedures are followed and as attention is given to specific services which will aid the students. The counselor assumes the major role in making certain that essential services are provided and that conditions are conducive to the emotional well-being of students. These services are outlined here, after which attention is given to the important functions of the teacher.

Providing effective counseling. Effective student counseling is the greatest service rendered by the counselor. Its benefits are felt by students in terms of better adjustment in the classroom. As student adjustment improves, and children become more intellectually receptive, emotionally stable, and better prepared to gain from the educational endeavor, classroom achievement and behavior also show improvement. With good mental health there are fewer distractions and classroom incidents, better time utilization, more efficient study habits, and a greater receptivity to learning experiences; thus the results of the teacher's efforts, too, are more rewarding. Occasional counseling contacts with the majority of the students will generally suffice. However, there are typically about two students in each classroom of thirty who require more than basic counseling. Their problems are more intense and their resources for handling problems less adequate than those of the well-adjusted child. The counseling provided should prove beneficial to these students, and the counselor can also be of help to the teacher by suggesting ways in which these students may best be aided.

Maintaining consultation activities. Periodic consultations between counselor and teacher are mutually beneficial as information, ideas, and suggestions about student behavior are exchanged, either following counseling or after the counselor has observed a student in his classwork.

Acquainting students with the counselor. The teacher as well as the counselor himself can help in acquainting students with the counselor and the nature of his services. The teacher may make referrals to the counselor and thus encourage students to take advantage of the assistance he can provide. The appointments may be arranged by the teacher and time allowed for the student to see the counselor.

Providing counseling for teachers and counselors. The counselor-teacher relationship can be improved and the professional competences of the teacher and counselor strengthened if these people are given the advantage of counseling. Since personal and professional growth is an aim of both the teacher and the counselor, they too may profit from counseling or therapy. The counselor may thus provide counseling time for members of the teaching staff as well as their students. He may do likewise as he becomes the client for another counselor or therapist. This concept is not readily acceptable to all professional people. However, the anxieties and frustrations of the teacher and counselor are debilitating and often result in reduced professional effectiveness. A competent counselor can supply other professional persons with the therapy needed, or he can suggest other sources of help within the community.

The Teacher-Counselor Role in Mental Health

In addition to the working relationship between counselor and teacher, there is also a cooperative role through which specific activities are carried out. The representative activities reviewed here not only characterize this cooperative role but also emphasize the role of the teacher and constitute suggestions as to what he can do in the cooperative effort with the counselor.

The teacher's key role in mental health. Most of the benefits gained by students in their relationship with their teachers occur rather naturally by virtue of that relationship. The influence of the teacher on a child is often subtle and imperceptible. The teacher's ability to create an atmosphere conducive to high productivity and emotional well-being is of great consequence in the life of each student. The positive aspects of this power extend far beyond the classroom and for many years following formal schooling. The actions of a teacher may stimulate youngsters and encourage them toward unusual achievements and life accomplishments, or teacher's actions may dishearten and discourage them.

Making the classroom appealing. The foremost responsibility of the teacher is to make the classroom an attractive, delightful place with an atmosphere that encourages and stimulates learning. Reasonable comfort with a minimum of anxiety is essential to the promotion of self-confidence, which in turn is essential to academic progress and satisfactory adjustment. Appropriate controls and guidelines help students maintain appropriate behavior and maximize accomplishments. Students find stimulation in this type of environment and profit from their associations with a highly competent, dedicated teacher.

Teaching with enthusiasm based on competence. The teacher should be enthusiastic and have a profound knowledge of students and of the learning process. He should be familiar with at least the basic intricacies and complexities of the learning process. He should be able to structure learning experiences in such a way as to make them highly meaningful, practical, and challenging for students. The procedures sometimes used by teachers are reflections of their habit patterns and staid reflexes, and have only a remote relationship to true learning. The development of good mental health will be curbed and impeded under this kind of teacher, just as it will be aided and enhanced under a competent teacher.

Providing children with necessary assistance. The teacher must provide youngsters with the necessary guidance to ensure their success in accomplishing tasks within their range of competence. Floundering, trial and error, and meaningless probing are frustrating and inefficient. Appropriate reinforcement for correct responses is essential to learning, as are immediate feedback and correction of incorrect responses. The teacher, then, is a highly trained, professionally competent person who knows how to utilize his knowledge and skill in promoting the academic learning of his students. He provides guidance, direction, and encouragement, and also stimulates youngsters to experiment and probe new depths on their own with confidence and the assurance that they have their teacher's support and trust.

Demonstrating interest in children. A genuine interest in each child characterizes the teacher, and it should be made evident in his relationships with the children. Good mental health depends upon feelings of adequacy and self-confidence, which in turn depends upon a sense of being liked and appreciated by other people—particularly by the teacher. The teacher has many opportunities for demonstrating this interest, and he will find that these expressions will bring him delight and satisfaction as a youngster responds. Burdensome problems become less formidable to a child as the teacher expresses an interest and concern.

Providing appropriate counseling. As coworkers the counselor and teacher both do some counseling. It may be more casual and informal with the teacher, but it is of no less importance than the work of the counselor. An attitude of interest and concern by the teacher eliminates barriers and makes it easier for a student to seek counsel from him. The teacher thus has the opportunity to provide information, to be a sympathetic listener, and to give structure to a student's plans. As a result counseling received from the school counselor also has more meaning, and the possibilities for student growth are enhanced as the teacher-student relationship suggests the counselor-student relationship.

Maintaining contact with students. The teacher may also take the initiative in maintaining close, personal contact with each student and particularly with those whose behavior is symptomatic of developing problems. The teacher is alert and observant as he notes unusual pupil behavior, and he lends his strength to the guidance service as he initiates the necessary action to aid these youngsters. The casual, indifferent, apathetic teacher lacks the necessary alertness to identify and assist these pupils, and he may also lack professional competence to deal with them.

Participating in making case studies. The participation of the teacher in case studies and case conferences is essential. The initiation of and the leadership in, case studies may come from the counselor, but the teacher is essential to the activity. The teacher's position is unique, and the attainment of certain information about a child depends upon a teacher's alertness and willing participation. His insights and understanding of youth and his familiarity with the usual problems of youngsters make him a valuable member of the team. His orientation and experiences demand a practical approach in a consideration of problems. Logical explanations for behavior may be reached and judicious decisions for action attained by the study group as the teacher makes his contributions.

Becoming involved in research. Research is an area of activity to which relatively few teachers are attracted. However, they are often closer to the sources of difficulties and are in a position to profit better from research findings than anyone else. Explanations for this slight commitment to research activities are at once apparent, and if there is an indictment to be assessed, it may be against the educational system rather than the teacher.

Research requires time, energy, interest, and skill. Teaching also has its demands upon the energies and skills of the teacher. And if a choice must be made, it had better be one which favors the boys and girls in the classroom. However, activity in research endeavors can and should be a function of the teacher, without sacrificing his influence in the classroom. This can be done by having research projects directed by a competent person on the staff who makes use of the contributions of teachers. The major burden is thus assumed by a person employed for that purpose, but the teacher also takes an active part. Floundering due to lack of knowledge on how to proceed is kept to a minimum, and teachers are also protected against encroachments upon their time and energies. Research is vital to progress, and greater provision should be made for this activity in the school program.

The teacher may also be the ego ideal for many students, and he can serve as a model for them if he is aware of his influence potential and makes an effort to improve his image in the minds of students. This involves a more subtle influence; it is a guidance function which lacks the specificity of some of the others but carries no less capacity for good. As Farnsworth so aptly states,[16] "The

[16] Dana L. Farnsworth, "Mental Health Education: Implications for Teachers," *Teachers College Records*, vol. 62, p. 267, January, 1961.

potential worth of the teacher as a model, as an admirable human being with whom his students can profitably identify, is hard to overestimate." Serving as a model for youngsters places considerable responsibility upon the person so honored; however, such a role is both inevitable and desirable. Emulation of others is a dynamic force in the development of youngsters. They gain strength from the confidence they have in their teachers, and their activities and behavior become more appropriate and profitable when they have someone to observe and follow.

SUMMARY/

Good mental health and the emotional stability and well-being of all citizens is a concern of every responsible adult. No one agency can rightfully be assigned this responsibility or be expected to provide the necessary preventive or therapeutic measures. All community agencies and all individuals share in these responsibilities. The school, however, by virtue of its contributions to, and demands from, individuals is in a favorable position to prevent maladjustments. Some treatment is also possible through the guidance service and referral resources.

Areas of major concern to students can be identified by the school and measures taken to alleviate problems. An alert school staff, bolstered by a well-organized school program of special services, will be able to determine the general quality of a student's schoolwork and assess his status in all aspects of his school and social life.

The guidance service is unique in its ability to provide for the needs of students through activities not carried on in the classroom. Its aims include supplementing other educational services and diligence in providing preventive measures and treatment. It can promote conditions which are favorable to good mental health and encourage teachers to improve the general climate of the classroom in the interest of the emotional well-being of the students.

The roles of the counselor and the teacher in the interest of mental health are reciprocal and supportive, but also distinctive and unique. The counselor's role includes aiding the teacher by providing special services for him and his students. The good teacher considers and provides for the emotional welfare of his students in his teaching.

PROBLEMS/

1   The school should show considerable concern for the emotional well-being of each student. Why? What is the real purpose of the school? How does this purpose relate to mental health?

2   Justify the position that good mental health should be a concern of everyone and of all agencies. What can each individual do in the interest of his own mental health?

3   Describe the responsibility of the school in terms of the mental health of students. What factors favor the school as an agency for promoting good mental health?

4   Briefly describe the position of the guidance service in its relationship to the rest of the educational program where mental health is concerned.

5   Perhaps there is more talk than action in providing for the mental health needs of students. Account for the fact that school people are relatively ill informed on this subject. What can be done about it?

6   Is the function of the school primarily prevention or cure? Defend your answer. How might it be both?

7   The prevention of school failure, including leaving school, and the promotion of worthy academic achievement are aims of the guidance service. What does this service do in an attempt to fulfill these aims? In what ways are these activities different from the regular classroom activities?

8   There is far more to the promotion of good mental health than just providing certain services. What else is involved?

9   What are the merits and weaknesses of the approach which refers to the work being done in the interest of mental health as a "counselor-teacher relationship"?

10   In what ways is the work of the teacher like that of the counselor? How does their work differ?

Selected References

Textbooks

ARBUCKLE, DUGALD S.: *Pupil Personnel Services in American Schools*, Allyn and Bacon, Inc., Boston, 1962, chap. 2.

BARR, JOHN A.: *The Elementary Teacher and Guidance*, Holt, Rinehart and Winston, Inc., New York, 1957, chap. 2.

BERNARD, HAROLD W., JAMES C. EVAN, and FRANKLIN R. ZERAN: *Guidance Services in Elementary Schools*, Chartwell House, New York, 1954, chap. 2.

CARROLL, HERBERT A.: *Mental Hygiene,* 4th Edition, Prentice-Hall, Inc., Englewood Cliffs, N.J., 1964.

D'EVELYN, KATHERINE E.: *Meeting Children's Emotional Needs,* Prentice-Hall, Inc., Englewood Cliffs, N.J., 1957.

HUMPHREYS, J. ANTHONY, ARTHUR E. TRAXLER, and ROBERT D. NORTH: *Guidance Services,* Science Research Associates, Inc., Chicago, 1961, chap. 4.

KOWITZ, GERALD T., and NORMA G. KOWITZ: *Guidance in the Elementary Classroom,* McGraw-Hill Book Company, New York, 1959, chap. 5.

REDL, FRITZ, and WILLIAM W. WATTENBERG: *Mental Hygiene in Teaching,* Harcourt, Brace & World, Inc., New York, 1959, chaps. 8 and 11.

ROGERS, DOROTHY: *Mental Hygiene in Elementary Education,* Houghton Mifflin Company, Boston, 1957, chaps. 3 and 9–12.

WILLEY, ROY DE VERL, and DEAN C. ANDREW: *Modern Methods and Techniques in Guidance,* Harper & Row, Publishers, Incorporated, New York, 1955, chap. 18.

———— and MELVIN DUNN: *The Role of the Teacher in the Guidance Program,* McKnight & McKnight Publishing Company, Bloomington, Ill., 1964, chaps. 4, 7, and 9.

Journals

ACKERLY, S. SPAFFORD, and others: "Fostering Mental Health in the Classroom," *Journal of Teacher Education,* vol. 11, pp. 365–369, September, 1960.

BINDMAN, ARTHUR J.: "The School Psychologist and Mental Health," *Journal of Education,* vol. 146, pp. 5–9, February, 1964.

BOWER, E. M.: "Mental Health in Education," *Review of Educational Research,* vol. 32, pp. 441–454, December, 1962.

GAFFNEY, PHILLIP: "Youth Fitness as Related to Discipline," *Arizona Teacher,* vol. 50, pp. 14–15, November, 1961.

HOLLISTER, WILLIAM B.: "Child Guidance in Your School," *National Parent Teacher,* vol. 55, pp. 29–31, October, 1960.

HOPKINS, M. L.: "Mental Hygiene in the Classroom," *School and Community,* vol. 51, p. 19, May, 1965.

ISAKSEN, HENRY L.: "The Role of the School Counselor in School Mental Health," *Journal of Education,* vol. 146, pp. 11–15, February, 1964.

JOHNSON, RICHARD W.: "Proposed Psychological Service Plan for Public Schools," *Bulletin of the National Association of Secondary-school Principals,* vol. 46, pp. 33–39. November, 1962.

KLEIN, DONALD C.: "Some Concepts concerning the Mental Health of the Individual," *Journal of Consulting Psychology,* vol. 24, pp. 288–293, August, 1960.

MORSE, W. C.: "Mental Hygiene Viewpoints on School Discipline," *High School Journal,* vol. 48, pp. 396–401, March, 1965.

REAVES, G. C., and L. E. REAVES: "Counselor and Preventive Psychiatry," *Personnel and Guidance Journal,* vol. 43, pp. 661–664, March, 1965.

RYAN, W. CARSON: "People Are Not Things," *Educational Leadership,* vol. 16, pp. 72–74, November, 1958.

SHOBEN, EDWARD J.: "Personal Responsibility, Determinism, and the Burden of Understanding," *Personnel and Guidance Journal,* vol. 39, pp. 342–348, January, 1961.

SIRES, ELY: "Mental Health in the Classroom," *Wisconsin Journal of Education,* vol. 92, pp. 13–14, March, 1960.

FOURTEEN

/THE GUIDANCE SERVICE AND THE EXCEPTIONAL CHILD

The concept that every child should be given an appropriate amount of attention and that he should be assisted in accordance with his particular needs is basic to the guidance service. Every child should be helped to attain his goals and develop his potentialities no matter what his capabilities or limitations may be. The youngster with physical, emotional, or mental handicaps should be given the attention through which his handicaps are minimized and his best capabilities exploited. The typical classroom is expected to provide the essential experiences for heterogeneous groups. However, the guidance service is needed to supplement the efforts of the teacher to aid all youngsters, including those with special needs not normally met within the classroom.

Nearly every child suffers from some neglect. Even the best efforts by teachers and counselors are not adequate for meeting the needs of the child who is in some manner exceptional. The guidance service attempts to reduce the inadequacies of the educational system in this area among others.

This chapter attempts to identify the responsibilities of the guidance service for the exceptional child and to show how its services will supplement the activities of the classroom in providing for each child's needs. We begin with a review of classifications of the types of exceptionality, including giftedness.

What Is an Exceptional Child?

Some confusion still persists as to what constitutes exceptionality. A mild handicap or some deviation from the norm does not justify regarding a child as exceptional. He can be different from the typical child in some characteristic and still be within the range of the normal. However, if this deviation is sufficiently pronounced to make him stand out from his peers, then he may be appropriately considered exceptional and treated accordingly. Hunt [1] states that "Exceptional children are those who deviate from the average child in physical, mental, emotional, or social characteristics to such an extent that they require special educational services in order to develop to their maximum capacity." An understanding of what constitutes exceptionality is necessary for the protection and welfare of the children and to ensure appropriate educational experiences.

Information as to the approximate number of children within a population who may be exceptional is helpful. Although figures will vary among different areas, an average figure is about 15 percent, or one child in each seven or eight.[2] The guidance service should be cognizant of these children, aware of the nature of their problems, and prepared to assist them.

Classification of the Exceptional Child

For purposes of this discussion exceptionality may be classified as (1) physical, (2) mental, (3) emotional and social, and (4) characterized by giftedness. This arrangement closely parallels Cruickshank's classification: (1) intellectual differences, (2) physical differences, and (3) emotional differences.[3] The exceptional child is

[1] J. T. Hunt, "Guidance and the Exceptional Children," *Education,* vol. 80, p. 344, February, 1960. Reprinted by permission of the publisher, The Bobbs-Merrill Company, Inc., Indianapolis.

[2] *Ibid.*

[3] William M. Cruickshank and G. Orville Johnson, (eds.), *Education of Exceptional Children and Youth,* 1958. Reprinted by permission of Prentice-Hall, Inc., Englewood Cliffs, N.J.

defined as follows: [4] "Essentially, an exceptional child is one who deviates intellectually, physically, socially, or emotionally so markedly from what is considered to be normal growth and development that he cannot receive maximum benefit from a regular school program and requires a special class or supplementary instruction and services." This definition also suggests that there are degrees of deviation among children and that the seriousness of this deviation should be known.

The physically handicapped child. The child with a physical handicap sufficiently serious to set him apart from other children should be given the attention and aid necessary to minimize the impairment imposed by the handicap. Impediments of sight, hearing, and speech are generally less observable than a physical handicap; hence the need for alertness by school personnel in order to detect these problems. Diagnosis and appropriate treatment may then follow, and efforts may be made to help the child make the best adjustments possible.

The child with an intellectual handicap. The child with limited scholastic aptitude who is unable to achieve at the same level as his classmates has an intellectual handicap. There are degrees of mental retardation and of intellectual competence, resulting in a great range of ability in the typical classroom. A reliable assessment of a child's intellectual capacity is therefore necessary in order to determine the most appropriate educational experiences for him. Pronounced retardation should be dealt with through special classes and individual attention. Institutionalization may be called for where a child is below the educable level and therefore unable to profit from the school.

The emotionally maladjusted child. Most children experience some emotional stress at various times. These stressful situations are usually temporary, and the adjustments are generally satisfactory. Emotional upsets and frustrations are a part of a child's development. However, there is the child whose emotional problems are not transitory and therefore constitute a serious threat to his emotional well-being. If he is unable to make satisfactory adjustments, if his problems become increasingly more formidable, and if his behavior

[4] *Ibid.*

becomes a confirmation of his distress, the teacher and counselor must have some awareness of the nature and possible causes of his trouble in order to help him.

The gifted child. The child with unusual ability and the promise of superior achievement is one who also should receive special attention. The exceptional child is generally regarded as one with a handicap and as one who is thus less fortunate than other children. The gifted child, however, deviates in the direction of superiority and thus requires a more challenging educational program than the typical child. He can be neglected just as readily as the child whose deviation is below the average, and with equally costly results. More attention will be given to this topic in another section of this chapter.

Responsibilities of the Guidance Service for the Exceptional Child

Major educational and guidance service objectives are essentially the same for all children, as are the principles underlying the educational offerings. The technique, materials, and procedures are a little different with the exceptional child, but these differences are readily manageable once the objectives have been established.

Aims of the Guidance Service

A major aim of the guidance service is to aid each child toward full self-realization. The attainment of full and maximum development of each child is a matter of degree. The exceptional child requires special attention in order to realize significant progress toward this aim.

The exceptional child must be identified and accommodated early in the primary grades. This will permit the appropriate structuring of educational experiences at a time when they will be most beneficial to him.

More specifically the guidance service aims to assist each child toward:

1 Better self-understanding and the ability to recognize his strengths and weaknesses and exploit each to his advantage.
2 A strong, positive, realistic self-concept, with adequate self-confidence to make aspirations become achievements.
3 The knowledge, skills, and techniques by means of which he can continually progress and gain satisfaction.

4 Satisfying, stimulating experiences and warm relationships with other people.
5 The establishment of a realistic vocational goal and appropriate preparation for his lifework.
6 Knowledge about the human personality and the intricacies of behavior, and mature judgments by which he can control his behavior.
7 Abilities and insights through which he can make satisfactory adjustments to life situations and through which his life can be made more enriching and meaningful.
8 Emotional strength and the ability to deal with unpleasant incidents and to resolve problems as they occur.

As fulfillment of these and related aims is approached through the intelligent application of school resources, the life of each child is enriched and the possibilities for his making greater contributions to himself and to others are increased. A sound educational program, made possible by dedicated, resourceful teachers and counselors, can make the aspirations of young people become realities. The child to himself is too naïve to do the careful planning for action that adults and the educational system can provide for him.

Guiding Principles for an Effective Guidance Service

Progress toward the attainment of worthy goals is enhanced through the directions provided and the resources made available through the guidance service. Basic to this progress and to the effectiveness of the guidance service are established principles which provide the structure, the guidelines, and the stimulation from which effective action comes.

The principles outlined here are appropriate for all children rather than limited to the exceptional child. However, they have particular significance for the exceptional child and are given as aids to his guidance.

1 Start guidance early in the life of each child. Existing or potential problems should be identified early and appropriate steps taken to treat existing problems and to avoid future difficulties. The organized guidance service combined with an effective instructional program will make appropriate aid available to the child when it will be of the greatest benefit to him.
2 Provide a variety of rich, meaningful experiences for each child throughout his school day. A narrow, restricted offering limits the opportunities for growth and fails to provide the exceptional

child with the stimulation needed for his continuous growth and improvement.

3 Make certain that each child achieves a degree of success in some endeavor. Feelings of success and achievement in one endeavor bolster the student's self-esteem and compensate for the areas where his performance may be mediocre. Success serves as a stimulus to more intensive effort, while failure tends to foster discouragement, reduced effort, and low production.

4 Encourage superior teaching and high-level professional competence with all teachers. This involves self-encouragement and personal efforts on the part of all staff members to strive toward constant improvement. The administration too should recognize and encourage superior teaching. The exceptional child depends upon the wisdom and competence of the teacher for his progress and welfare, and the teacher's effectiveness is determined in part by the leadership given by the administration and in part by the aid of the guidance service.

5 Promote activities which provide for pupil interaction. A child's handicaps may be minimized as he profits from his experiences with other children. A child's strengths may also be exploited for his benefit through interaction with others. A child stimulates and is in turn stimulated by another child; he gains from both roles.

6 Aid and encourage each child in self-appraisal. Test data, teacher observations, and school achievement all assist a child toward better self-understanding. Logical decisions and appropriate plans for the future depend upon the student's having some facts about himself and seeing their implications.

7 Integrate learning about the human personality with academic learning, not to minimize academic learning in order to accommodate other kinds of learning, but rather to broaden the understandings and learnings of each student. Some understanding of the personality is necessary for the student to capitalize upon his capabilities and profit from his interaction with others. The goal is really the integration of all kinds of learning.

8 Help each child develop his intellectual and social skills. As educational objectives are extended and given greater depth, the offerings of the school must be modified to accommodate these objectives better. Horizons are broadened for the student whose development is keeping pace with increasing opportunities.

9 Avoid conditions which may cause frustrations and anxieties. The exceptional child generally encounters more frustrations by virtue of his differences. Anxieties inevitably result unless steps are taken to avoid situations which are thwarting and frustrating, particularly since the child with a handicap may lack the needed resources for continuous adjustments.

The Gifted Student

Belief in the need to identify the gifted child early in life and to provide him with opportunities to maximize his development is well accepted in modern education. The practices lag considerably behind the belief, but prospects for the future are encouraging. Providing special attention and experiences for the gifted child is no longer regarded by the modern educator as a violation of democratic principles. The needs of each child should be ascertained and supplied in accordance with his productive capabilities.

Evidence of this mounting concern for the gifted is found in much of the Federal legislation enacted during recent years. The National Defense Education Act of 1958 signaled the concern felt for the need to capitalize upon the capabilities of the more talented individuals. This act provides, among other things, for the training of counselors through whom the more capable students can be identified and more appropriately educated. Youth with the potential for making significant contributions to the strength and welfare of the country are the focus of this legislation. Counseling programs have been initiated and strengthened in the schools as a result of the incentives provided through Federal legislation. Considerable improvement is being made in overcoming an unfortunate condition of neglect in providing challenging educational experiences for gifted children.

This section outlines the purposes and concerns of the guidance service with the gifted. Suggestions are given on how to identify the gifted child, and his characteristics are reviewed. Some attention is also given to the matter of providing special activities for the gifted youngster.

The Guidance Service and the Gifted Child

The guidance service has an obligation to the school and to the gifted child. This includes identifying the nature of his giftedness and making the information available to the school for purposes of improving his learning environment. The unique qualities of the guidance service make it possible to locate and appraise the gifted student. Giftedness, as we have seen, is a matter of degree. It should also be remembered that every normal child has potentialities which would make him an unusual person if these potentialities were developed into superior abilities. Obviously, efforts should be made to help each child develop his abilities to the highest degree possible.

This discussion, however, concerns the child who already shows unusual ability and the characteristics by which he is identified.

A second major function of the guidance service is to aid in providing the stimulation and direction essential to the child's making proper use of his abilities and to his planning intelligently for the future. This function, of course, depends upon the classroom and the challenges and stimulation it provides. Guidance and instruction are engaged in a team effort. Curricular offerings and educational experiences should be in keeping with the capabilities of the student and in harmony with his interests and aspirations. To coerce a student into an area of study incongruent with his aptitudes and interests would not be in keeping with the best interests of the school or of society. The superior scientist and the gifted mathematician are indeed essential to the welfare of the nation, but it also needs the thinking and influence of the person with unusual abilities as a social scientist, artist, or humanitarian. Beals notes that there is a need for people who contribute to the solutions of all kinds of problems. The ability of many people to make greater contributions of a social nature would have been much higher if they had been given better guidance.[5]

Many young people with promising talents will continue to be overlooked in the schools. These youngsters will follow the usual educational program with greater success than the typical child, but often with accomplishments no more startling. This may continue to be the case even with a strong guidance program. However, the number of students being overlooked can be reduced considerably, and certainly the opportunities for these youngsters to develop their talents will be increased and improved through the guidance service. No one activity will locate and aid these gifted children; a variety of services and the dedication of many people are necessary.

The concern of guidance for the gifted. Locating the gifted child, ascertaining the nature of his giftedness, and then providing the educational experiences which will produce maximum development are all concerns of the guidance service. Adequate tools and procedures are essential. There must be concentrated effort to accommodate these youngsters; otherwise they may accomplish very little more than the typical students. An awareness by school personnel that the gifted child has talents which should be developed is a sound starting point.

[5] Lester Beals and Patricia Simmons, "Counseling Needs of Gifted High School Students," *Personnel and Guidance Journal,* vol. 40, p. 712, April, 1962.

Some agreement should also be reached by the school staff as to what constitutes giftedness. It should be known how the gifted child differs from the typical child and how he can be best accommodated. High achievement in one or more subjects generally characterizes the gifted child; however, he may be gifted in areas outside the typical school program. The identification of qualities made manifest apart from the atmosphere of the school is difficult but no less important. A child's unusual ability in mathematics or English will soon become apparent to the teacher. Another youngster may possess great spiritual, altruistic, or aesthetic qualities that are never recognized by the teacher. The guidance service has an interest in the development of all kinds of talents and abilities, and realizes that the academic talents of a child are perhaps no more important than those talents not identified with school subjects. Talents in art, music, speech, and writing are often overlooked, since the conventional school subjects do not always provide for the use and development of these abilities. A more alert staff, a broader offering of school subjects, and better opportunities for participation in a variety of activities should result in less neglect of students with these talents.

Current research provides some needed information as to the nature and origin of special abilities, but not with such conclusiveness that any broad generalizations can yet be made.[6] Guidance people can be satisfied with the knowledge that giftedness is attributed to both hereditary influences and rich environmental stimulation. More knowledge is needed on this problem. However, the important consideration is one of identifying giftedness, providing for its development, and stimulating all youngsters to their maximum performance in all creditable endeavors.

Identifying the gifted child. The gifted child is often neglected in school because he is able to do superior or satisfactory work with very little teacher time or direction. This permits the teacher to devote his time and energies to the less able student, but not without cost. Many talents remain undeveloped for want of needed direction and stimulation that only the teacher can provide. An organized system by which the students with unusual potentialities are identified early in life seems most essential. The development of capabilities beyond the typical level of performance is also possible with a num-

[6] See Jack Birch and Maynard Reynolds, "The Gifted," *Review of Educational Research*, vol. 33, pp. 83–98, February, 1963.

ber of children in a highly stimulating environment where development and productivity are emphasized.

Mead discusses six kinds of giftedness but adds that these are only illustrations of the variety of gifts possessed by people. These areas of giftedness include (1) intellectual gifts, (2) giftedness of aesthetic character, (3) superb physical gifts, (4) high moral and spiritual values, (5) high-level social understanding and living, and (6) great economic ability.[7] More recent literature provides some information with excellent possibilities for increasing the educator's understanding of the gifted, including characteristics by which he can be identified.[8] It should also be remembered that one child may exemplify talent in a number of areas while another is limited to perhaps just one area. The latter may attract less attention and be less spectacular in his performances, but he should receive the same attention and encouragement as the multitalented pupil. Shannon states,[9] "It seems, empirically, that a larger proportion of five-talent than of one-talent men bury their talents—or worse, dissipate or squander them. This waste of our most precious of natural resources is America's greatest educational tragedy." The guidance service has a genuine interest in locating all talents among students and in not neglecting any student irrespective of the number of talents possessed.

Characteristics of the gifted child. There there is a large chance that a gifted child will be overlooked in the typical school is quite evident. In order for this child to be noticed, he has to be well above other capable children in his performance, and he must perform somewhere near his level of competence. In many cases he does neither, simply because he is unaware of his talents, because he fails to realize their significance, or because he is insufficiently motivated to perform well. The school must take the initiative in helping each child discover his most promising abilities and in stimulating him toward superior performance.

Some general guides for the teacher and counselor by which superior abilities may be identified are stated here as descriptions

[7] A. R. Mead, "Who Are the Gifted?" *Education*, vol. 79, pp. 3–7, September, 1958. Reprinted by permission of the publisher, The Bobbs-Merrill Company, Inc., Indianapolis.

[8] Birch and Reynolds, *op. cit.*, pp. 84–89.

[9] Dan C. Shannon, "Our Greatest Educational Tragedy," *Education*, vol. 79, p. 8, September, 1958. Reprinted by permission of the publisher, The Bobbs-Merrill Company, Inc., Indianapolis.

of the child's behavior and characteristics which are readily observable by the teacher. The teacher and the counselor should be alert in noticing these characteristics and cognizant of their implications.

1 He may demonstrate unusual ability in several areas. These may be in academic subjects or in other areas.

2 He often demonstrates unusual ability as a leader. This may be attributed to his superior knowledge rather than unusual social skills. Indeed, the gifted child may also be a lonely child.[10]

3 He grasps quite readily the meaning and significance of difficult concepts and can deal with abstractions without the benefit of concrete examples and detailed explanations.

4 He can see the application possibilities of a concept and is able to describe the practical aspects of the concept. He does not limit himself to just the basic point.

5 He is able to see relationships between old and new concepts and usually can transfer and make generalizations quite readily.

6 He is inclined toward creativeness in one or more fields such as writing, music, art, mechanics, or design.

7 He goes beyond enumeration and description and is able to make adequate interpretations of information.

8 His attention span on challenging material is relatively long. He learns more quickly and retains information longer than the average student.

9 His verbal expressions, vocabulary, reading ability, and spelling skill are usually superior.

10 He usually responds quickly to a problem, is able to reach a solution quickly, and can see related problems without receiving help.

11 He shows unusual interest in world problems and in adult affairs, and is curious about a number of things.

12 He generally gets along well with others and has several friends. He might, however, show some impatience with a slower child.

13 His general maturity level is above average, and he may give the impression of being older than he is.

There will of course be exceptions to these guides and various degrees of competence. As a better understanding of a child's ability is acquired, curricular adjustments and enrichment experiences may be made.[11]

[10] George Kaluger and Ruthe Martin, "The Loneliness of the Gifted Child," *The Elementary School Journal,* vol. 61, no. 3, pp. 127–132, December, 1960.

[11] John A. Barr, *The Elementary Teacher and Guidance,* Holt, Rinehart and Winston, Inc., New York, 1958, pp. 302–303, has an excellent discussion on the characteristics of the gifted.

Specific functions of the guidance service with the gifted. Many of the functions of the guidance service have already been inferred. A more specific identification of these functions should result in a better understanding of the role of the guidance service with the gifted child. Following is a list of functions and suggestions on how they might be carried out.

1 The proper identification of the gifted child and an appropriate assessment of his abilities. Teacher and counselor observations of children under many circumstances should be combined with test results and other data collected on each child.

2 The initiation and promotion of activities which will stimulate a child to exert his best efforts and aid in developing his interests and talents. These can be accomplished through a variety of enrichment experiences including field trips, intensive study, discussion groups, and personal interviews. The school must take the initiative in providing such experiences and in noting their influences upon the student.

3 Assistance given the student that will promote a strong desire to excel. This can be done by showing the student personal attention, praising his work, encouraging him in his efforts, and showing a personal interest in him.

4 Encouraging the student to go beyond the normal classroom requirements in his study, reading, and experimentation. This requires special or additional materials or equipment by which challenging experiences can be made possible. A cooperative effort within the school should meet these needs.

5 Aiding the student in ways that will promote desirable study habits, leadership competence, diligence, and dependability. These are desirable habits for anyone but may have special significance for the youngster with unusual potential for making outstanding contributions to his society. To accomplish these ends he must be given challenging experiences which will stimulate him toward greater achievement and which will require diligent, concentrated effort.

6 Helping the student acquire information from which realistic self-appraisal might be made. Self-understanding is essential to the progress of the gifted student. The guidance service provides tests, inventories, and other materials for self-appraisal and an increased self-understanding. All elements of the guidance service are designed to promote self-understanding.

7 The development of strong articulation between instruction and the guidance service to help the gifted student as it strengthens the total educational offering and provides him with a number of appropriate experiences. Classroom visits by the counselor and teacher-counselor conferences should help to accomplish this.

8 The provision of high-quality service through well-qualified personnel. This suggests the need for care in employing teachers and counselors and in making appointments to positions upon which the quality of the program depends. It is a function of the guidance service to see that quality service is provided for the gifted child and that he is given many opportunities for full development.

Special Activities for the Gifted Child

The gifted child is capable of doing more work and work of a higher quality than the average child. The work requirements within the typical classroom are not adequate for the gifted child; therefore the necessity arises for enrichment activities which permit learning experiences beyond the average. He may perform the usual tasks of the class, but he also engages in other, related activities. The alert teacher will soon note the quality of achievement of the gifted child and encourage him to extend his activities to related but more challenging tasks. The pressure of time and inadequate facilities are discouragements to be dealt with by the teacher. However, genuine teacher interest goes a long way in overcoming these deterrents. The resourceful teacher provides the necessary direction to keep the child progressing in accordance with his capabilities. The counselor is of assistance as he capitalizes on the resources of his office and as he brings to bear his judgment and imagination.

Since many gifted youngsters are not identified or given enrichment experiences, society fails to profit from the unusual capabilities of these individuals. Often their latent talents and potentialities for great contributions go undiscovered and undeveloped. Many of these youngsters fail to receive an adequate educational experience in the elementary and secondary schools, and are not stimulated to go on to college. Any failure to develop the abilities of a gifted child through additional schooling following high school graduation constitutes a serious loss in human resources. It is also an indictment of the educational system and of the society in which that system exists.

Providing for adequate motivation of the gifted youngster is a problem. True, he already has some motivation and is striving toward self-fulfillment. However, external encouragement and appropriate guidance are necessary for him to continue to be motivated and for that motivation to be associated with his own development. Motivation of an appropriate kind cannot be left to chance or to the whims of the individual. A strong educational offering of a variety of worthwhile experiences must be provided by highly competent, enthusiastic teachers and counselors. The guidance service and the instructional program have the responsibility for initiating procedures designed to motivate each child toward a realization of his greatest potential.

Some Guiding Principles for Helping the Gifted Child

Following certain guides results in less neglect of the gifted child and provides him with a broader, more stimulating educational experience. Even the superior guidance service will fail to do everything that should be done for this pupil. Some omissions of vital services are inevitable, and the child may fail to take advantage of all his opportunities. However, the school with a well-organized service and competent personnel will be more aware of the child's needs and more proficient in meeting these needs than the school that lacks a guidance program. Encouragement, proper direction, and a demonstrated personal interest in each child are vital to a child's progress. These necessities can be provided if the school is aware of its responsibilities and opportunities, and if the leadership and skills are present. The principles to be observed by the school for better accommodation of the child with unusual talents are:

1. Demonstrating a sincere personal interest in each child, thus indicating the confidence the school has in him and in his ability to achieve great heights
2. Providing opportunities for enrichment experiences which will take him beyond the rather arbitrary limits of the typical classroom
3. Capitalizing on his interests by structuring appropriate experiences which will develop these interests and by encouraging flexibility in his academic program
4. Making no distinction between the gifted student and other students in social activities but being certain he makes the contacts and has experiences which will be stimulating and fruitful
5. Helping him realize the magnitude of his opportunities for superior development through tactful encouragement in the classroom and in personal interviews
6. Structuring the classroom situation in such a way as to protect him against chiding or cynical remarks by students who may resent his superior ability
7. Praising him for superior effort and encouraging better performance when his achievement is not commensurate with his ability

8   Aiding him in recognizing his limitations as well as his strengths and in adjusting to his weaknesses as well as developing his capabilities.

Certainly the talents of the gifted child should be appropriately developed by the school during his growing years and intelligently utilized by society after he reaches maturity. A sense of fulfillment is essential to the person with unusual ability. His adjustment to society and the quality of his productivity depend upon a feeling of accomplishment. Mediocrity of performance or of product does not satisfy this person. He is capable of rich output, and anything less can be frustrating and discouraging. He depends upon the school for the stimulation, encouragement, and resources needed for full development. If the school does its job well, it is helping to produce a citizen whose contributions will more than compensate for the costs.

SUMMARY/

The guidance service has an interest in, and commitment to, every child in the school. Adjustments are made in the educational offering to accommodate every child best in accordance with his particular needs. The exceptional child is different in some respects from the normal child and will therefore require some special attention. The guidance service helps to determine just what his greatest needs might be and uses its influence in making the necessary arrangements by which his needs can be met.

Although the exceptional child may in some ways be very much the same as his classmates, he is also sufficiently different in some characteristic to justify his receiving special attention. Once the nature of his handicap or exceptionality is established, he may be aided through the cooperative efforts of the school personnel.

The gifted child is characterized by his ability to perform and produce at a high level of proficiency. He too is a concern and responsibility of the guidance service, because of the possibilities present for him to develop into an unusually capable person and, therefore, a very productive person. He needs to experience the feelings of satisfaction that come from fulfillment, and society needs his contributions. Identifying the gifted, ascertaining and assessing the nature and quality of his giftedness, and aiding in providing experiences and resources essential to his maximum development are major functions of the guidance service.

Each child should constitute the center of attention no matter what his limitations or capabilities may be. He needs the educational offering that the school can provide, and society in turn needs him and his productive capabilities.

PROBLEMS/

1 Defend the position that the guidance service has responsibilities for the exceptional child no matter what the nature of his exceptionality might be. What principle underlies this concept?

2 What are the advantages to come from classifying a child according to a handicap or characteristic? What is undesirable about this?

3 The guidance service can do some things for the exceptional child, but not everything. What are some of the essential activities designed for the exceptional child which depend upon the cooperative efforts of other phases of the school program?

4 Can you find weaknesses in the principles of an effective guidance program given in the chapter? What are they? How can these principles be improved?

5 Note some sound reasons for including the gifted child as a topic in this chapter.

6 Outline the school's major responsibilities for the gifted child.

7 Enumerate the major functions of the guidance service in providing for the gifted youngster. Suppose a school has no organized guidance service; what happens in this case to the gifted student?

8 How does the gifted child differ from the typical child? What qualities characterize his behavior?

Selected References

Textbooks
BARR, JOHN A.: *The Elementary Teacher and Guidance*, Holt, Rinehart and Winston, Inc., New York, 1957, chaps. 16 and 17.
CRUICKSHANK, WILLIAM M., and ORVILLE G. JOHNSON: *Exceptional Children and Youth*, Prentice-Hall, Inc., Englewood Cliffs, N.J., 1958.
JOHNSON, MAURITZ, WILLIAM E. BUSACKER, and FRED Q. BOWMAN: *Junior*

High School Guidance, Harper & Row, Publishers, Incorporated, New York, 1961, chap. 11.

JOHNSON, WALTER F., BUFORD STEFFLRE, and ROY A. EDELFELT: *Pupil Personnel and Guidance Services,* McGraw-Hill Book Company, New York, 1961, chap. 3.

MARTINSON, RUTH A., and HARRY SMALLENBURG: *Guidance in Elementary Schools,* Prentice-Hall, Inc., Englewood Cliffs, N.J., 1958, chap. 11.

Journals

BARBE, W. B.: "Meeting the Needs of Exceptional Children," *Education,* vol. 84, pp. 476–479, April, 1964.

BEALS, LESTER, and PATRICIA SIMMONS: "Counseling Needs of Gifted High School Students," *Personnel and Guidance Journal,* vol. 40, pp. 712–716, April, 1962.

BIRCH, JACK, and REYNOLDS MAYNARD: "The Gifted," *Review of Educational Research,* vol. 33, pp. 83–98, February, 1963.

BORST, S. W.: "Dangers in a Crash Program for the Gifted," *Ohio School,* vol. 38, pp. 10–11, December, 1960.

BOWER, E. M.: "Education as Primary Prevention," *California Journal of Elementary Education,* vol. 31, pp. 54–61, August, 1962.

COMBS, CHARLES F.: "Perception of Self and Scholastic Underachievement in the Academically Capable," *Personal and Guidance Journal,* vol. 43, pp. 47–51, September, 1964.

DREWS, ELIZABETH M., and SUSAN MONTGOMERY: "Creative and Academic Performance in Gifted Adolescents," *High School Journal,* vol. 48, pp. 94–101, November, 1960.

FURMAN, S. S.: "Suggestions for Refocusing Child Guidance Clinics," *Children,* vol. 12, pp. 140–144, July, 1965.

GIVENS, PAUL: "Creativity and the Gifted Child," *Educational Theory,* vol. 13, pp. 128–131, April, 1963.

GORDON, JULIA M., and others: "Child Who Demands Excessive Attention," *Instructor,* vol. 71, p. 52, September, 1961.

————: "The Child Who Is Listless and Indifferent," *Instructor,* vol. 71, pp. 30–31, January, 1962.

GOWAN, J. C.: "What Makes a Gifted Child Creative?" *Education Digest,* vol. 31, pp. 12–14, September, 1965.

HIVELY, WELLS: "Implications for the Classroom of B. F. Skinner's Analysis of Behavior," *Harvard Educational Review,* vol. 29, pp. 37–42, Winter, 1959.

HOEDT, KENNETH C., and JOHN W. M. ROTHNEY: "Guidance For Superior Students: Some Problems," *Vocational Guidance Quarterly,* vol. 11, pp. 199–201, Spring, 1963.

HUNT, J. T.: "Guidance and Exceptional Children," *Education,* vol. 80, pp. 344–348, February, 1960.

JOHNSON, NORMAN C., and OCTAVIA B. KNIGHT: "Can Enrichment Help the Academically Retarded?" *Elementary School Journal,* vol. 66, pp. 83–86, November, 1965.

KLAUSMEIER, HERBERT J.: "Research and Educational Improvement," *Teachers College Journal,* vol. 34, pp. 139–141, March, 1963.

KVARACEUS, WILLIAM C., and BURTON BLATT: "Selected References from the

Literature on Exceptional Children," *Elementary School Journal*, vol. 64, pp. 341–347, March, 1964.

LAMBERT, SAM M.: "What a National Survey of Teachers Reveals about Pupil Behavior," *Journal of the National Education Association*, vol. 45, pp. 339–342, September, 1956.

LESSINGER, L. M.: "Enrichment for Gifted Pupils: Its Nature and Nurture," *Exceptional Child*, vol. 30, pp. 119–122, November, 1963.

MAMMARELLA, RAYMOND, and JOSEPH CRESCIMBENI: "Need for Perspective in Problem Identification," *Education*, vol. 85, pp. 162–165, November, 1964.

NEWLAND, T. ERNEST: "The Gifted in the High School," *High School Journal*, vol. 48, pp. 76–81, November, 1964.

ROTHNEY, JOHN W. M., and NORBERT E. KOOPMAN: "Guidance Of The Gifted," Fifty-seventh Yearbook of the National Society for the Study of Education part II, pp. 347–361, 1958.

———: "State-wide Approach to the Discovery and Guidance of Superior Student," *School and Society*, vol. 89, pp. 271–274, Summer, 1961.

SCHLEIN, JOHN M.: "The Self Concept in Relation to Behavior," *Religious Education*, vol. 57, pp. 111–127, July, 1962.

STRANG, RUTH: "Self Concepts of Gifted Adolescents," *High School Journal*, vol. 48, pp. 102–106, November, 1964.

TORRANCE, E. PAUL: "Priming Creative Thinking in the Primary Grades," *Elementary School Journal*, vol. 62, pp. 34–41, October, 1961.

———: "What Kinds of Persons Do We Want Gifted Children to Become?" *High School Journal*, vol. 48, pp. 88–93, November, 1964.

TRIPPE, M. J.: "Stigma and Schooling," *High School Journal*, vol. 49, pp. 241–247, March, 1966.

WITTY, P. A.: "Recent Publications Concerning the Gifted and the Creative Student," *Phi Delta Kappa*, vol. 46, pp. 221–224, January, 1965.

YOUNG, F.: "Program for Preventing School Maladjustment," *School and Community*, vol. 50, pp. 16–17, May, 1964.

FIFTEEN

/BEHAVIOR PROBLEMS OF CHILDREN AND YOUTH

The frequent use of the term "behavior" in current literature suggests a healthy, growing interest in the child and a greater concern for his welfare. An increasing understanding of child development has also contributed to the significance being placed upon child behavior. A genuine interest prevails in behavior beyond the observable conduct itself. The observant, competent educator is now aware of symptoms of possible maladjustment. Possible causes are determined and isolated, and efforts are made to remove or modify these causes. Prevention and treatment procedures are also being given more attention.

Child behavior has become a matter of concern because of the great implication it has for welfare of the total society. A more intelligent use of the human resources of the country has been recognized as a priority factor by leaders in government and education for some time. Inefficiency in time utilization and the dissipation of energies are often the result of personality instability and inappropriate behavior. Such losses should be reduced or eliminated. The better understanding of human behavior by teachers and counselors, by the pupils themselves, and by society in general must be converted into action through the application of this knowledge.

Everyone is in the act of behaving in some fashion at all times. An intensive study of behavior yields information on how children, and adults too, may become more productive and better adjusted individuals. Although the term "behavior" has a rather broad connotation and includes virtually all aspects of human endeavor, including learning, some limits are placed on its meaning in this chapter. Here our concern is with identifying the kinds of child behavior which are in disharmony with the established pattern and expectations of the school and which constitute a deterrent to the child's progress, development, achievement, and adjustment. When a youngster's conduct is disturbing to others, interferes with the normal procedure of the school, or results in his being a nuisance, he may be regarded as having behavior problems. The frequency and persistence of the behavior must be considered, however, before a hasty or arbitrary classification is made.

The nature of misbehavior and the functions of the guidance service in dealing with it are discussed in the chapter, as well as a more detailed coverage of some representative kinds of misbehavior with suggestions as to possible causes and methods of treatment. Although no one chapter or textbook is likely to do more than provide a superficial coverage of a very broad topic, procedures for carrying out the functions of the guidance service in relation to behavior problems are suggested.

The Nature of Behavior

Behavior of any kind is the result of a variety of influences upon a person during his years of development. His conduct is his way of reacting to these influences and experiences, and it denotes an attempt to make satisfactory adjustments. A person's behavior is to a degree a reflection of his attitudes and values, and it provides the mechanisms for self-fulfillment and the realization of ambitions. Some kinds of behavior actually thwart one's progress rather than aid it; however, the same behavior might serve as an adjustment mechanism for the individual. An aim of the guidance service is helping to prevent frustrations and the thwarting of plans, and helping each child make the maximum use of his energies and potentialities. The removal of the causes of frustrations and anxieties should receive first attention. The dissipation of energies upon minor stumbling blocks and the failure to make efficient use of time and energies constitute serious deterrents to the progress and productivity of children and youth.

All behavior should be purposeful and hold the promise of beneficial results. The fact that all behavior is purposeful to the behaver may be accepted as an explanation for the behavior, but it is unacceptable as an excuse or rationalization for inappropriate conduct. It might well be purposeful to the behaver, but there may be inadequacies or deprivations in the life of the person which have precipitated the behavior. These inadequacies should be avoided where possible and deprivations minimized in order for the behavior of each person to be positive and constructive. No one can afford the luxury or the inconvenience of debilitating, time-consuming conduct which retards rather than facilitates development and learning.

The school has a great influence on the life of a child and can either contribute to his emotional well-being through appropriate experiences and helpful guidance or add to his frustrations and maladjustment. What happens in each case is determined by the quality of the school environment provided for each child, and the willingness and ability of the school to aid, direct, and stimulate each pupil. The school can, through its preoccupation with a variety of problems, easily overlook the plaintive plea of the child who needs help but lacks the maturity either to demand it or to know how to use it when it is provided. The school typically expects everyone to conform, but this expectation often has little meaning for the child who neither has learned conformity nor understands its significance. And conforming behavior may be incongruous to his particular needs. Misconduct may be the logical procedure for him. A related idea is expressed in this statement: [1] "The frustration of an existence in which individuality is sacrificed on the altar of mass conformity is communicated to children, who may act out their uneasiness in the classroom."

Some conformity is indeed essential to the proper management of the classroom, and children welcome limits which aid them in keeping their feelings and conduct under control. Some flexibility is also desirable, to permit individual expression and the release of emotional tension. The causes underlying misbehavior may include either an absence of logical limits or a rigid, highly restrictive environment which invites rebellion.

[1] I. W. Fellner, "When Children Are Disturbed," *Elementary School Journal*, vol. 61, p. 254, February, 1961.

Causes of Misbehavior

If it were possible to pinpoint and to identify accurately the exact causes of undesirable conduct on the part of youngsters, the whole problem would be relatively simple. But since human behavior is a rather baffling phenomenon and the ramifications and implications are so varied, the problem is indeed complex, challenging, and fascinating. It might be said that if all of a child's experiences are most appropriate for him and all of life's influences are of the best, then his conduct may be generally acceptable and conforming. This too is an oversimplification and can be only theoretically true. In practice two obstacles must be considered:

1   Each youngster is unique and therefore requires treatment a little different from every other child's. The environment has inevitably some undesirable elements and omissions. Even with the best of intentions by adults the experiences and the environment will not be completely satisfactory. The quality of the environment helps to determine the degree of adjustment attained by the person, and the adjustment realized is reflected in his behavior.

2   The human personality is very complex and dynamic, thus presenting a formidable problem to the counselor who attempts to probe the depths and to understand another person. The attempt both to understand and to provide satisfactorily for each child in school requires an omniscience not possessed by even the best of teachers and counselors.

Underlying each act of misbehavior is a combination of factors or conditions which contribute to the behavior and even make the behavior appear logical to the behaver. Although individuals are different and vary in their needs and resources for adjustment and in their reactions to circumstances and events, there are nevertheless some common causes for misbehavior which are quite basic to most people.

General insecurity of the times.   The current conditions within the society tend to breed feelings of insecurity which create tensions and anxieties. Threats of nuclear war, rumors of impending chaos, and dishonest practices by irresponsible individuals at all levels of government constitute threats to the security of all citizens including children. This problem is magnified by television and other news media which keep the public informed of these events. Parents are inclined to discuss these matters rather freely before children, and certainly the news is a topic of discussion within the classroom.

Home conditions.   By the time a child starts school, his basic per-sonality structure is quite well established. How well his needs have been met within the home during these tender years of dependence is a major factor in the determination of his emotional strength in school. If inadequacies, deprivations, and inconsistencies character-ize the home, the child will enter school with anxieties and per-sonality problems which may well indicate impending behavior difficulties. A home characterized by warmth, acceptance, love, and consideration will, on the other hand, produce a child with much more promising prospects for good adjustment and a happy, profit-able school experience.

The school.   The school situation often contributes to the anxieties of a child and, as a result, to some maladjustment which may lead to misbehavior. Since the school is the very agency for the allevia-tion of problems and tensions, the fact that it sometimes contributes to the problem is an indictment of the school. If the home has failed to prepare the child for school properly and the school also fails to accommodate him appropriately, the prospects for desirable behav-ior are rather dim. The requirement to attend school is sometimes frightening to a child, and unless the teacher is prepared to reduce this fear, a healthy adjustment is unlikely. The potential for mal-adjustment finds fulfillment in the soul of a frightened, unhappy child.

Harper points out that the disturbed child builds the strongest possible defenses against a violent world and that self-protective efforts sap his emotional and intellectual energies.[2] The demands of the typical school program in respect to learning and emotional control are quite rigorous for the most typical child. Every child must be at his best and have all his resources under control and at his command if his progress and adjustment are to be satisfactory. School officials must be constantly alert to the appearance of any situation which may cause a child to feel threatened or anxious. The immediate alleviation of such a situation is of maximum im-portance.

Economic status.   Some economic deprivation in the life of a child may be tolerated satisfactorily so long as basic psychological needs are being met. And if the discrepancy between what one child is

---

[2] Louis E. Harper and Benjamin Wright, "Dealing with Emotional Prob-lems in the Classroom," *Elementary School Journal*, vol. 58, p. 316, March, 1958.

receiving and what another is receiving is not too great, the former may adjust without mishap. However, the feelings of inferiority often spawned by the inability of parents to provide for a child pose threats to his development, and these feelings may cause him to behave inappropriately. If a child is hungry, shabbily dressed, or unable to maintain status with his peers because of financial deprivation, he might harbor resentments or develop hostile feelings which could erupt into misconduct. The reasons for the behavior are not likely to be either intellectually or emotionally evident to the child, and his conduct may be the same even if an awareness of causes is present. The teacher and the counselor must be sufficiently alert to note the causes, and they should know how to deal with each child who has such problems.

Economic affluence or deprivation are relative terms, thus maximizing the importance of knowing how a child feels about his particular situation. If one child feels neglected and deprived because of his relatively low status, problem behavior may develop. Another child may have no such feelings, although equally deprived, and is therefore likely to give no trouble. It is therefore more important to know how a child feels about his status than it is to know just what his financial status is.

Racial status.   A child's racial status may also be a source of problem behavior if he feels, or is made to feel, that he is inferior. Children rarely pay any heed to racial differences, but adults often do, either innocently or deliberately. Once the matter of differences is brought to the attention of a child, he may react to it either to his favor or disfavor. If his position is a favorable one, he may react with arrogance and self-satisfaction. This attitude could contribute to his misbehaving or provoking another child to misconduct. Feelings of inferiority are devastating to the personality of a child and underlie much of the unhappiness, frustration, and anxiety he experiences. Problem behavior can often be traced to feelings of inadequacy and inferiority. The logical attack upon such problems is one which permits and encourages the bolstering of the self-esteem and the strengthening of the self-confidence of the child who has been made to feel inferior.

The Avoidance of Problems

Certainly considerable effort is directed by the school toward the alleviation of behavior problems. This effort is prompted primarily by the desire to minimize or eliminate the trouble and inconvenience caused by a nonconforming child. If each child is busily engaged in appropriate activities, the classroom is a pleasant place for everyone, and the learning experience is enjoyable. Unacceptable behavior on the part of even one child may, on the other hand, create tensions and disturbances which impede learning and detract from an otherwise pleasant atmosphere. Remedial or disciplinary action may then be necessary.

The anticipation and avoidance of problem behavior are generally simpler and more economical in regard to both financial and human resources than dealing with misbehavior after it has occurred. To anticipate possible difficulty the teacher must have an understanding with some depth of each child and a willingness to plan the classroom activities carefully and, by structuring, avoid disrupting incidents. If Billy has a history of problems, this should be known by the teacher, and steps should be taken to minimize his difficulties in class. If Mary is experiencing unusual stress at home or difficulties with her schoolwork, this too should be understood by the teacher, who may then make an effort to reduce these stresses and avoid adding any additional problems. Problem behavior may often be avoided if there is awareness by the staff of the existence of conditions which may provoke a child to misbehave.

A multiplicity of causes.   Misbehavior generally has a multiplicity of causes; no one cause is likely to be identified as the one behind the problem. The child's behavior is a reaction to the many influences in his life, some of which bring frustration and disappointment while others bring satisfaction and enjoyment. Since his behavior is the product of many influences, combining a variety of preventive and treatment procedures must be considered as a possible way to help him.

Avoidance techniques.   Even to imply that by using certain techniques the school may avoid behavior problems of pupils is an oversimplification of a complex problem. However, the use of certain techniques should reduce the intensity of many problems. The seriousness of problem behavior is partially determined by the depth of feeling experienced by the youngster and by the persistence of the behavior. As problem behavior is anticipated by the school and as preventive measures are employed, there may be a reduction in the number of expressions of maladjustment by youngsters and in the seriousness of the behavior. In addition, certain procedures may stimulate the school staff to try additional practices by which behavior problems may be reduced and controlled. The school should provide for:

1 The identification of potential problems early in the school life of a child through observations and appropriate screening devices.
2 A team approach by staff members in which everyone plays an important part in noting developing problems and in planning appropriate methods for handling them.
3 A wholesome, accepting school environment which minimizes frustrations and aids each youngster in his self-promotion toward greater self-actualization.
4 A sound structure of controls as well as freedoms which will set limits on behavior and will provide students with the needed support to keep their impulses under control.
5 A system of instruction which enlivens the imagination and curiosity of students and which encourages the expression of deep feelings.
6 Remedial and therapeutic services by which students may be aided in controlling and managing their emotions.

An attitude of serious intent by the staff to be of assistance to students is perhaps more valuable than any particular techniques. Dedication to a cause piques the imagination of the participants and prompts them to act on the behalf of youngsters in desperate need of help.

The Perceptual View of Behavior

There is no one theory of learning, of counseling, or of behavior that is likely to satisfy the typical educator. However, theories can provide the foundation for additional exploration, experimentation, and speculation. They also provide the elements from which an integrated guide is devised that serves professional persons in their work. Typically the behavior of another person is judged by the standards of the observer. This approach is inevitably fraught with the biases, prejudices, values, and opinions of the one doing the observing. No person can possibly see a situation as another person sees it. The behavior of a child may be perfectly logical to him but quite illogical to the teacher. To gain even a superficial understanding of the causes behind the behavior of any one person the observer must be able to view the behavior from the position of the behaver. Neither a complete understanding of the perceptual view of behavior nor an adherence to its proposals is entirely necessary in order to understand or treat a child with behavior problems, but a knowledge of the concepts included in this view should prove helpful in both preventing and treating behavior problems.

Combs states [3] that the primary principle of perceptual psychology is that "All behavior, without exception, is a function of the behaver's perceptual field at the instant of behaving." Although the implications for perceptual psychology extend beyond the topic of behavior problems, certain aspects of it help in identifying causes of misbehavior.

The same writers further emphasize the importance of looking at behavior from the point of view of the behaver. This approach [4] seeks to understand behavior by making its observations from the point of view of the behaver himself. It attempts to understand the behavior of the individual in terms of how things seem to him.

An effective teacher is certainly cognizant of the fact that a child may view the environment, with its attractions and threats, somewhat differently from the teacher. He also knows that a child may either be unaware of his behavior and thus be innocently oblivious of his actions or that he may regard his behavior as quite appropriate. The complexity of factors underlying all behavior and the multiplicity of causes are beyond the comprehension of even the most astute counselor and teacher. Since a complete understanding of behavior is beyond the realm of possibility, efforts should be directed toward improving the school situation for the child and all staff members encouraged to be sympathetic, helpful, and resourceful in their relationships with each child.

If people behave in a fashion consistent with their personal perceptions, any attempt to dictate behavior through coercion and in accordance with external criteria is likely to meet with little success. "People do not behave according to the facts as *others* see them. They behave according to the facts as *they* see them. What governs behavior from the point of view of the individual himself are his unique perceptions of himself and the world in which he lives, the meanings things have for him." [5] It is not the intent to imply that misbehavior is an inevitable evil to be tolerated but not understood. There are ways to deal with behavior, the success of which depends

[3] Arthur W. Combs, "Some Basic Concepts in Perceptual Psychology," paper given at the American Personnel and Guidance Convention, Apr. 14, 1965, Minneapolis, Minn.

[4] Arthur W. Combs and Donald Snygg, *Individual Behavior*, Harper & Row, Publishers, Incorporated, New York, 1959, p. 16.

[5] *Ibid.*, p. 17.

more upon the attitudes, patience, and skill of the staff than it does upon the procedure used. To assist effectively a child with behavior problems four essential elements are needed: (1) a basic understanding of the human personality, (2) a sensitivity to people, (3) patience and a willingness to explore for possible causes, and (4) the ability to separate behavior from the child, making it possible to like and accept him while disapproving of his behavior.

The Functions of Guidance with Behavior Problems

Basic to the guidance program is the principle that all youngsters be accorded the assistance they need to ensure their progress no matter what the level of adjustment might be and irrespective of the nature or seriousness of their problems. The child whose behavior may suggest some underlying emotional disturbances should receive immediate attention by both the teacher and the counselor. Such attention should include using the resources of the guidance service and the patience, skill, and stimulation of the classroom. The child who experiences frustrations and problems of adjustment constitutes a serious challenge to the school. The imagination, ingenuity, and energies of the teacher and the counselor may be taxed to the limit. However, the results in improved behavior by the child and greater progress toward self-actualization should serve as rewards to the staff for efforts expended.

Coleman has stated: [6] "All behavior—successful, unsuccessful, wise, foolish, flexible, rigid—is an attempt by the organism to meet the demands facing it or perceived as facing it. Behavior, in other words, is an attempt to adjust." If a child's behavior is a manifestation of his attempts to make a better adjustment, then any undesirable behavior should signal the need for assistance in finding more appropriate ways of fulfilling needs. The teacher and the counselor must recognize that the behavior is symptomatic of the child's failure to adjust, and they must provide the needed assistance.

Whether problem behavior is essentially a responsibility of the classroom or of the guidance service should not be an issue. In fact, any such arbitrary division of responsibilities could result in very little being done by either side. The teacher and the counselor both have responsibilities and prerogatives. The activities of both should be in harmony with the aims of the school and designed to assist

[6] James C. Coleman, *Personality Dynamics and Effective Behavior*, copyright 1960 by Scott, Foresman and Company, Chicago.

the student. The teacher should foster those services closely allied with his main function—teaching. The counselor will provide for counseling sessions and for any needed diagnosis. The teacher and counselor, in a cooperative endeavor with a mutual concern for the child's well-being, exchange ideas and augment one another's efforts to help the child. The present discussion, however, emphasizes the place of the guidance service in aiding the youngster with behavior problems. Some of the specific functions of the guidance service are enumerated, and the procedures by which these functions may be carried out are also considered in the following paragraphs.

Specific Functions of the Guidance Service

The underlying philosophy of the guidance service is a determining factor in the quality and nature of the services provided for youngsters. If there is a prevailing belief that the accommodation of each child according to his particular needs is a major function of the school, appropriate steps will be taken to meet this need. The absence of this belief will be reflected in the attitudes of the staff and in the number and quality of activities provided. A strong philosophy which embraces a commitment to serving youngsters and which includes a belief in the efficacy of man and a confidence in his potentialities is essential to any guidance service. This philosophy constitutes one important aspect of the guidance program. The activities and services provided constitute another aspect. Both aspects are needed if the child with developing problems is to be helped. The guidance service meets some of his needs, while other needs are met through the classroom. The following paragraphs suggest functions of the guidance service in the matter of behavior problems.

Appraisal of aptitudes and personality. The tools of the guidance service and skills of the counselor are utilized in determining a child's strengths and weaknesses and unique personality characteristics. A knowledge of his aptitudes, interests, and personality should prove helpful in determining the most logical procedures to use in aiding him toward the necessary insights for behavior improvement. The counselor's judgment is somewhat dependent upon this knowledge, and the child should also be apprised of the meaning of data obtained on him in order to use them profitably for self-improvement.

Evaluation of behavior. Some determination as to the meaning, seriousness, and implications of behavior needs to be made. The guidance service takes the initiative and provides the tools and skills needed to assess behavior objectively. Symptoms of maladjustment have meaning if objectivity and sound judgment are used in identifying them. A cautious approach is required in which the best judgments of a number of people are considered. Sufficient time must be available, and the careful appraisal of all evidence should precede these judgments. Just as the behavior of children varies, so, too, may the significance of particular conduct be quite different for any two children. Some aggressive behavior may be quite appropriate for Mark and should be regarded as such. The same conduct by Kendall may, however, be symptomatic of impending difficulties. Merely casual observations by either the teacher or the counselor are not satisfactory. Wisdom, born of academic training and experience, and a genuine interest in each child are essential.

Establishment of a framework for specialized services. The guidance service must provide the structure and the organization for appropriate preventive, remedial, and therapeutic services. Provisions must be made for competent personnel, appropriate tools, adequate facilities, coordination of efforts, and sufficient time. Developing problems are noted and necessary assistance is provided by design and through planning, not by chance. The efficiency with which services are performed and coordinated, and their value to the student depend to a high degree upon the stability and quality of the organization providing the service. If the administrative structure for a program is defensible, practicable, and understood by the staff, specialized services for students become possible.

Conduct of research activities. Judgments, opinions, and actions of the staff are often of limited worth because of the absence of research data. Conclusions as to the possible causes of behavior and opinions about how a child should be handled depend upon empirical data. The guidance department should be aware of and provide research data. The subjects for such research should contribute something to the school's program. The findings and conclusions might also have implications for other schools, and if so these should be made available elsewhere. An attitude of healthy inquiry and curiosity should characterize a guidance department, and the subsequent accomplishments should improve the existing program.

The Tools and Procedures for Accomplishing
Guidance Functions with Behavior Problems

The functions described above are broad and of necessity include a number of related activities. Not all guidance procedures for handling behavior problems are necessarily included under one of these four headings. However, these specifically stated functions do identify and partially explain the role of the guidance service with behavior problems. The tools, knowledge, and skills of the guidance service are needed to carry out these functions.

A well-organized guidance program provides a variety of activities and services for each youngster. However, students vary in their adjustments and needs; hence, the requirement for flexibility and breadth in the school's services in order to meet these needs. So a child with developing behavior problems receives some benefits from the guidance service by virtue of its existence and the nature of its activities. However, the needs of some youngsters are more urgent than those of others, making it necessary to take special cognizance of them. Timely, appropriate help may reduce the possibilities of more serious problems later. The resources of the guidance service should be utilized at these times to a higher degree than for the typical student. The responsibilities of the guidance service in both preventing and assisting with behavior problems must be met through the use of its tools and techniques.

Providing for appropriate measuring devices and experiences. A good basic testing program which covers all students will yield helpful information. Testing beyond this minimum should be available, however, where additional information is needed on a particular child. Working through an inventory, questionnaire, or checklist may have a special appeal for a student or contain information from which he can profit. An increased awareness by the student as to the nature of his own personality development and the significance of his behavior may come from just the experience of responding to the items on the instrument. In other words, there are benefits to be gained from a testing experience beyond the accumulation of scores.

Utilizing all objective data properly. Proper interpretation of test results by the counselor is of paramount importance. The data serve no purpose unless their use benefits the child. Misleading statements and vague references may result in erroneous conclusions formed by the student or may add to his anxieties. The improvement of each child's behavior as a result of better adjustment is the aim of the testing service.

Capitalizing on opportunities to observe children. The child with behavior problems makes them known in many ways. The observant teacher or counselor notes behavior which is symptomatic of developing problems and makes an effort to determine its significance. Observing youngsters in the various activities of the school should result in identification of those whose behavior suggests possible difficulties or maladjustments. A casual, superficial perusal of children at work or play is not adequate. The observer must know the possible significance of certain conduct; he must observe with a purpose. His observations should contribute to his knowing how to proceed in order that his help will have a lasting effect.

Providing for teacher-counselor conferences. The counselor is a consultant to the teacher. His knowledge is utilized to improve the effectiveness of the school in working with a child whose behavior is inappropriate. He is also the teacher's coworker as they pool their resources, exchange ideas, and together arrive at procedural decisions. The guidance service permits and encourages this close relationship between counselor and teacher. The teacher might review a case with the counselor, describing the child's behavior. Together the teacher and counselor may then consider possible causes of the behavior, and methods and procedures for future action.

Maintaining contact with the home. Some appraisal of the home is essential to the guidance service as background information which may have far-reaching effects upon a plan of action. Family attitudes should be ascertained and knowledge gained on the willingness and ability of the parents to assist in any program designed to reduce frustrations and improve the behavior of a child. Parents should be apprised of any problems experienced with a child, and their assistance and understanding should be solicited. Misunderstandings may be avoided between the home and the school and decisions for action facilitated if a spirit of cooperation and mutual concern prevails.

Conducting case studies. The case-study approach is an excellent way to collect specific information about a child. A concerted effort

is made to accumulate data and review them before making decisions. This method makes possible an intensive study of a child by
several competent people. Possible causes for the child's behavior
may be determined and decisions reached on how to better the situation for the child. What is learned in making a study of one child
also promotes better understanding of other children. Thus, many
children may benefit directly from a case study made on just one
child.

Providing for group guidance activities.   The child is benefited in
several ways by his experiences in groups. Some comfort is gained
by a group member from the knowledge that others too have problems, that he is not alone or unique. A group session also provides
the opportunity for a free expression of feelings. The student gains
some satisfaction from the mere fact that he had the necessary
courage to put his feelings into words and actions. Ideas on how to
handle one's problems may also be gained through an honest exchange with other group members. Suggestions for behavior
improvement made by one student may be utilized with equal effectiveness by another person. Group guidance sessions also provide a
setting in which the counselor may do some structuring and thereby
give the participants the benefit of his thinking and his experiences
for their self-improvement. A critical look at oneself is possible in
group sessions with a minimum of threat and anxiety. Defensiveness is reduced as the student reaches a point where he feels no
need to defend his behavior and as he begins to see the advantages
associated with appropriate behavior. Behavior improvement becomes an attainable goal when the student begins to see that his
situation can be bettered through such change.

Stressing personal contacts with students.   Informal contacts between counselor and student may help the student realize that other
people are interested in him, and this may encourage him toward
more appropriate behavior. As a student's faith and confidence in a
trusted adult increase, his own self-confidence is bolstered, and he
is better able to fulfill needs in a legitimate manner. Appropriate,
acceptable behavior gradually replaces misbehavior as a child's ability to adjust becomes stronger and more flexible. These informal
contacts may occur by accident, but they generally require a deliberate attempt by the counselor to bring them about. He makes it a
point to see and visit with each student who may be experiencing
adjustment problems.

Counseling sessions represent a formal, planned approach to problem resolution. Time is designated in the day for counseling and therapy when both student and counselor can give full attention to this activity. These sessions provide the opportunity for a student to explore and express his feelings about matters that are bothering him. Insights are gained from which improvements and better adjustments are made. More serious problems may also be avoided as the causes of undesirable behavior are identified and preventive measures taken.

Providing for remedial assistance. Misbehavior often has a close relationship with low academic ability and low achievement. Behavior problems might be avoided by locating the low-achieving student early and providing the special assistance necessary to bring about better academic achievements. Remedial assistance is primarily a responsibility of instruction, but the guidance service has a role in identifying these students, in gaining data needed for proper appraisal, and in prescribing remedial action. An understanding, sympathetic counselor and teacher find many ways of encouraging, aiding, and stimulating a youngster toward higher motivation and better achievement. He can be helped to make more effective use of his time and energies, and he can be aided in the development of his potentialities.

Making research findings available. Program improvement is an aim of the school. As times and conditions change, appropriate modifications in the offerings of the school must also be made. Research activities should be an integral part of the total school program, designed to find solutions to immediate problems and structured to make an early application of findings possible. Research conducted in the school should have practical significance for that school, and the conclusions reached should lead to program improvements. The major objective is of course to gain information which can be utilized in aiding students toward better adjustment.

No school is likely to explore or utilize more than a fraction of its resources in dealing with behavior problems. The traditional view that a child's behavior makes him subject to punishment still prevails in many places. A more enlightened approach includes plans and means for identifying the child with developing problems early and for providing special activities and services through the guidance program and the classroom for aiding this child.

Inappropriate Kinds of Behavior

The child whose behavior is inappropriate for the school setting is a source of disturbance to other children, and he often constitutes a problem for the teacher. Aggressive behavior, for example, attracts attention and generally tends to interfere with normal classroom processes. An undue amount of the teacher's energies are often dissipated in combating the distracting influence of the misbehaving child. The timid child who tends to withdraw from most activities is less disturbing than the boisterous child, but he still requires special attention from the teacher. So, no matter what the nature of a child's problems or behavior are, he is still a source of irritation to the teacher and to the other children. Learning is less effective, and the achievements and accomplishments within a classroom are obstructed as long as any child is experiencing difficulties in making proper adjustments. The kinds of behavior that give trouble should be identified and described. What constitutes inappropriate behavior? What are the labels given to this behavior? In this section the kinds of behavior problems encountered in the typical school are discussed, and suggestions are given on how the school might help with these problems.

The child whose behavior deviates markedly from the normal expectations of the school is the subject of this discussion. He is the student who requires special attention, the one who is most likely to be the source of difficulties in the classroom. He cannot always be ignored, nor should he be merely tolerated. He should receive the necessary aid and attention to bring about his better adjustment. An understanding teacher can help as modifications are made in the school program. An imaginative, resourceful approach by the teacher with the student's problems in mind will often result in better self-control by the student and greater academic progress. The usual routine of the classroom with its typical demands and expectations often fails to provide the needed opportunities for self-expression and release of feelings. This often causes or contributes to frustrations and anxieties, which in turn result in misbehavior by the child.

It is also important that the teacher and counselor be sufficiently well informed on child behavior that they can determine the seriousness of the behavior of any particular child. It would be wrong to conclude that a pupil is a behavior problem because of a single incident or to arrive at such a conclusion through impressions gained from superficial and infrequent contacts. Any behavior which appears to be in opposition to the established standards of the school may well evoke the displeasure of the teacher. Any behavior which poses a threat to the orderly process of the classroom may be looked upon with disdain. The sincere teacher makes an effort to determine the possible causes of the problem and strives to assist the child toward better adjustment. However, the energies of teachers are so strained and the resources in time and facilities are so limited that too often nothing is done to help the child or to improve the classroom climate.

Typically, then, the child whose behavior is a source of irritation is soon regarded as a problem and as a child in need of disciplinary action. The seriousness of the problem should be determined early and corrective measures taken. However, only the child who is indeed a behavior problem should be regarded as such. The ordinary, typical kinds of misconduct should be accorded the attention they require and no more. The seriousness of the behavior can be ascertained by reference to certain criteria for determining if a child needs special help or if the behavior is in keeping with his particular moods and needs at the time.

Criteria for the Assessment of Problem Behavior

Snap judgments and premature conclusions about a child should be avoided. One or two displeasing incidents do not warrant the immediate placement of a label upon a child. Fred's fighting on the playground might have just as much meaning for good adjustment as for poor adjustment. The same behavior might, however, have quite a different meaning for Tim or Joe. Each situation and each student must be considered individually and in accordance with the circumstances of each case. Although the behavior may displease the adults, it might in reality be desirable conduct for that child at that time in terms of his needs and personal development. Considerable trial-and-error behavior occurs as a child attempts to compete successfully with others and feels his way without benefit of absolute knowledge on how to conduct himself. He often recognizes his mistakes and profits from them; as his judgment improves, he finds more acceptable ways to express himself. Each student can be helped by his teacher and counselor to realize self-fulfillment through expressions of feelings and aspirations, if they will be guided by the following criteria in their appraisal of his behavior.

Normality of the behavior for this person. Since the background and experiences of one child may be quite different from those of another child and since children vary markedly in their responses to experiences, closely similar behavior by two children may have entirely different meanings. If the conduct is compatible with the established habit patterns of the child, then it is normal behavior for him and should be regarded as such. If, however, the conduct is incongruous with his normal habit pattern, it may suggest impending difficulties. No radical change in temperament or behavior is likely to occur without some good reasons. The determination of these reasons should be one goal of the school as it attempts to assist the child toward better adjustment. In order to reach a sound decision as to the seriousness of the behavior for a particular child, it is necessary to know him quite well and be aware of his background. A careful, intensive study of the child is imperative.

The enduring nature of the problem. If a child persists in his undesirable behavior despite concerted efforts to dissuade him, the problem may be serious, and additional attention is necessary. Conduct of an unusual nature may occur with any child, but there is little need for concern if the behavior is soon abandoned. It is the permanence of the behavior and its persistence in the face of remedial measures that suggest the presence of a serious problem. Most children respond favorably to the guidance of the teacher on matters of conduct. It is the disturbed child who fails to respond to the teacher, who gives cause for concern. His behavior does not change appreciably under normal classroom procedures, and he persists in a pattern of conduct which is in disharmony with the school's expectations. His failure to respond to directions and his apparent inability to alter his behavior serve as warnings that his case calls for special help and consideration.

A failure to respond to treatment. A child may demonstrate no improvement in his conduct despite the attention and best efforts of the school. This indicates that the problem is deep-seated and that the usual procedures are too superficial to be effective and a more intense approach involving the specialized services of the guidance program is needed. The desired changes may also be slow in coming even if the student receives expert counseling or therapy. Special consideration should also be given to him in the classroom. An understanding, sympathetic teacher may to some extent reduce the anxieties and bolster the self-esteem of the student by planning and structuring classroom activities with his needs in mind. The inability or disinclination of the student to respond to intelligently applied treatment should be taken as a warning that the problem has serious implications, that it needs careful study, and that appropriate remedial measures should be initiated.

The degree of self-control manifested. A normal, well-adjusted child is able to exercise a degree of self-control and impose limits upon himself. He may need an occasional reminder from his teacher, but the potential for behavior change and improvement is present. Compulsive, unrestrained, illogical behavior, on the other hand, suggests an inability to cope with feelings and denotes the presence of personality weaknesses and related problems. Such a child does not respond to normal procedures, nor is he able to deal with the problem by himself. Circumstances have contributed to a weakening of his control structure and a diminution of his adjustment resources, making it imperative that he be given special aid and attention.

Kinds of Behavior Problems

As we have seen, if behavior is inappropriate for a particular person, if it endures despite treatment procedures, and if there is an obvious inability of the child to control his behavior, he is in need of special help. If his behavior does not meet these particular criteria, he may just be giving expression to current feelings due to present frustrations, and these expressions need not be regarded as serious problems. The guidance service is helpful in assessing the relative seriousness of problems and in providing the necessary treatment. Although the criteria discussed here do not include all that might be used, they do emphasize the point that some such guides should be used.[7]

There are many kinds of behavior which may be regarded as problem behavior. The more pronounced the behavior is, the more attention it attracts, and the greater its nuisance is to the school. This is to be expected, since the school tries to maintain order and efficiency. Timidity may be just as serious from the standpoint of the child's welfare, but it will normally receive less attention in the typical school setting. It is of major importance to identify all types of behavior and to provide every child with appropriate aid and

[7] See Fritz Redl and William W. Wattenberg, *Mental Hygiene in Teaching*, Harcourt, Brace & World, Inc., New York, 1959, pp. 412–416.

direction in accordance with his particular needs. Any classification of problem behavior must be arbitrary, since there are several labels that might be attached to any particular kind of conduct.[8]

The material in the remaining pages of this chapter is intended to serve as a guide in identifying and dealing with behavior problems. The areas of problems selected and the suggestions concerning symptoms and treatments should, however, be regarded as representative and not as a comprehensive coverage. The same basic outline might be used in considering other kinds of problems.

The arbitrary classification of causes, symptoms, and treatment has definite limitations. It suggests simplicity, when in reality the matter of behavior is very complex. It also tends to place certain symptoms and treatment procedures with one particular kind of labeled behavior and not with another, whereas actually, there are no hard-and-fast lines of distinction. Perhaps the essential points here can be summarized in four statements:

1 A child with problems of behavior is likely to manifest symptoms which may be placed in any one of several classifications. For example, a child might be regarded as overly aggressive because of his inclination to fight, bully, and dominate others. In classifying him arbitrarily as an aggressive child one may tend to ignore other problems of equal importance.

2 The symptoms associated with one problem area may be equally appropriate for describing behavior which has been classified in another area. A reluctance to recite in class may place a child in the timid category, whereas this same behavior may be symptomatic of a low self-concept and the need for improved status.

3 The conditions which may cause one child to steal, cheat, and lie may contribute to another child's becoming fearful or jealous. There is no predictable cause-and-effect relationship between particular conditions and the behavior that results from those conditions.

4 Treatment recommended for one kind of behavior problem may also be suitable for a different kind of behavior.

Careful thought, study, imagination, and resourcefulness are all essential in aiding the child with behavior problems. There are no exact formulas for action. The quality of the relationship developed between the youngsters and the school is more important than the exact techniques employed to assist him. How he feels toward

[8] For a general discussion on behavior problems see Ervin Winfred Detjen and Mary Ford Detjen, *Elementary School Guidance*, 2d ed., McGraw-Hill Book Company, New York, 1963.

his teacher and the counselor is a determining factor in his progress toward improved behavior.

In the remainder of this chapter under each behavior-problem category there is a brief summary of (1) symptoms, (2) possible causes, and (3) suggested treatment. These summaries are for illustrative purposes and are not an attempt to discuss the various problem areas in detail.

The overly aggressive child. Some children are by nature more aggressive than others. Therefore, unless the conduct is extreme and incongruent for a particular child, it may only be indicative of the child's personality. The overly aggressive child's conduct [9] is extreme; it is in disharmony with the child's personality and a source of concern to the school. Aggression may also be a desirable quality under certain circumstances, since it may indicate leadership ability, and it may also suggest taking the initiative in solving a problem or getting a job done.

Some symptoms of the overly aggressive child are listed below. He may manifest his disturbance by:

1 Breaking, tearing, or destroying property.
2 Causing unnecessary and excessive disturbances.
3 Attacking other children.
4 Interrupting others in a loud, boisterous voice.
5 Resisting authority.
6 Expressing a quarrelsome attitude.

Any number of causes can contribute to this kind of behavior. Some such possible causes are:

1 General feelings of insecurity stemming from an inadequate home, school failure, or lack of acceptance by other pupils.
2 Fear of failure or of displeasing parents or teachers.
3 Lack of attention, love, and consideration by parents and other adults.
4 Rigid, demanding disciplinary controls or inconsistencies in disciplinary measures.
5 An absence of controls with too much responsibility placed on the child for the management of his conduct.

What approaches might be used in assisting the child? What are the treatment possibilities? The aggressive child might be helped by:

[9] The Detjens include such behavior as temper tantrums, vandalism, fighting, bullying, teasing, and angry feelings under this classification. *Op. cit.,* pp. 86–105.

1. Bolstering his self-esteem through showing him special attention and by complimenting him on his work.
2. Providing experiences through which he can achieve and gain recognition.
3. Increasing his opportunities for physical activity where hostile feelings may be dissipated.
4. Showing him personal attention and interest and encouraging him as he shows progress.
5. Being friendly, relaxed, and patient and displaying a sense of humor as well as a sincere interest in his welfare.
6. Providing for group counseling or discussion sessions in which problems and feelings may be aired.
7. Promoting positive feelings and an attitude of good fellowship.
8. Minimizing the need for a youngster to find it necessary to defend himself.

The child who bullies.   The bully may be regarded as overly aggressive. However, aggression manifests itself in a number of ways, not all of which are necessarily of the bullying type. A child may be unduly aggressive and still not bully other children. The youngster who expresses his hostility by picking on others in all probability feels very inadequate and insecure himself. He is attempting to compensate for his inadequacies by asserting himself and thus proving to himself and to others that he is an adequate, competent person. There is something amiss in his life. His needs are not being met satisfactorily, and his efforts to fulfill needs are being blocked. Frustration, anxiety, humiliation, and unhappiness are the results of these efforts. He needs and wants friends, and he is often dismayed by his lack of status. He is not easily discouraged, and he keeps trying despite repeated rebuffs. However, his efforts are often misguided and misdirected, and instead of winning friends he alienates himself from others.

The behavior of the bully may take many forms, but it generally involves picking on other people and making a general nuisance of himself. The youngster who bullies others may be observed:

1. Attacking other children, generally smaller than himself, by pushing, tripping, or hitting and annoying others in a variety of ways.
2. Engaging in verbal attacks by calling names, poking fun, criticizing, and arguing.
3. Expressing belligerence and defensiveness in a loud, boisterous, agitated voice.

As with all problem behavior, the bullying student's behavior has been prompted by inadequacies or unfavorable circumstances in his life. His problems may stem from:

1 Deprivations of the psychological needs of love and attention or inadequacies in fulfilling his physical needs.
2 A strong need for identification with another person, resulting in his identifying with someone whose behavior is inappropriate as a model.
3 An aggressive, domineering, demanding teacher whose unrealistic expectations bring frustration and anxiety to the student.
4 Undesirable home conditions which may include financial problems, low educational and social status, and lack of parental supervision.
5 Lack of friends, inadequate social skills, and lack of ability to interact favorably with peers.
6 A bullying family member, teacher, or peer who creates a situation in which the child feels the need to get even.
7 Academic failures which bring frustration, anger, and an attitude of futility.

The child who bullies may be given some assistance by:

1 Correcting or improving the undesirable conditions in his life which are precipitating the problem.
2 Assisting him in finding suitable friends and people with whom he might associate or identify.
3 Providing for conferences through the guidance service with teachers and other adults who may be contributing to the problem through unreasonable demands.
4 Encouraging the parents to show an interest in the child and aiding them in improving conditions which may be precipitating the problem.
5 Giving him instructions in social skills and creating opportunities for him to work with, and assume responsibilities in, group projects.
6 Correcting any situation in which he is being bullied by another person.
7 Providing classroom enrichment experiences by which he can gain a feeling of success.
8 Modifying the school program to enable him to fulfill his needs more satisfactorily and always keeping demands and expectations realistic in terms of his capabilities.

The timid, backward, withdrawing child. The timid child is the one who stays in the background, and he generally has a good reason for keeping himself isolated. He sometimes gives the impression of being backward; however, his problem is not so much a lack of ability as it is low self-esteem and low self-confidence. Occasional evidence of timidity is sometimes welcome to the teacher and may be refreshing in contrast to the boisterous, uninhibited behavior of some children. Withdrawal may thus be innocently encouraged by the teacher in his efforts to maintain quiet and order. Measures taken to reduce the spontaneity and enthusiasm of the more extroverted youngsters may constitute a threat to the timid child, resulting in his withdrawing even more. His feelings of inadequacy and guilt may be intensified, thus adding fuel to the fire and creating a never-ending vicious cycle for him.

Excessive daydreaming often serves as an escape for the timid child. Life fails to provide adequately for his needs, so he finds thrills and satisfaction in escaping from reality through daydreams. Such behavior only adds to his problems, since the time and energy being expended on flights into fantasy could be better spent in facing and dealing with problems. Daydreaming as an escape from reality is more than an adjustment mechanism and can be a forerunner to more serious maladjustments. Maturity, strength, and the ability to make adjustments come with effort and the desire to improve. Escape mechanisms provide nothing but temporary relief, and they fail to provide any direction for better adjustment.

Although the timid child is easily spotted in a group because of his atypical behavior, he is often overlooked in deference to the more vociferous demands of other children. The behavior of the shy, withdrawing child is characterized by his:

1 Reluctance to take part in class recitations and failure to complete assignments although he is intellectually capable of doing the work.
2 Preference for working alone and his quiet, bashful, well-behaved manner in the presence of others.
3 Avoidance of physical activity which includes contact or competition with others and a reluctance to defend himself against abuse or attacks.
4 Tendency toward nervous habits such as twisting his clothing, squirming, or biting his fingernails.
5 Discomfiture when teased or engaged in an argument, which he tries to avoid.
6 Preoccupation with his thoughts and personal activities with an apparent lack of awareness of activity and people around him.

Causes underlying the problems of the withdrawing child may have their inception in inevitable conditions such as hereditary factors of body build, disabilities, and limited mental capacity. However, environmental conditions over which some control can be exerted also play a significant part. Factors or conditions which precipitate or contribute to his problems are:

1 Physical immaturity, handicaps, or deficiencies, and limited athletic skill.
2 Low academic ability or limitations in study habits or facilities for effective study.
3 Inadequate special skills and low interest in school.
4 Parental overprotection or domination or insufficient love and attention.
5 Unrealistic standards on the part of the school or his family.
6 An unfavorable position in comparison to siblings whose successes may magnify his inadequacies.
7 Previous experiences which have proved unpleasant and embarrassing.

Every effort should be made to assist the shy child, since he is unhappy with himself and the world, and he is seriously handicapped in his development. Any treatment or assistance provided should be directed toward building up his self-esteem and self-confidence. Increasing self-regard should result in a reduction in his withdrawing tendencies. The school may thus assist the shy child by:

1 Arranging for activities where strength or skill are unessential for success.
2 Modifying the level of expectations established by the school and making it possible for him to succeed.
3 Encouraging him to participate in activities in which he can perform adequately and aiding him in the development of social skills.
4 Conferring with his parents and deciding upon procedures which will provide reassurance and bolster his self-confidence.
5 Investigating and modifying disciplinary procedures in order to make certain that they are appropriate and consistently applied.
6 Winning his confidence through a friendly, personal, approach.

The dishonest child. Cheating, stealing, and lying are all regarded as forms of dishonesty. There are other forms, but these three are of the greatest concern to the school because of their seriousness in respect to the child's development and their frequency of occurrence. There are degrees of honesty, and there are opportunities for rationalizing one's behavior. The student himself may logically regard his behavior as appropriate for the circumstances. He must earn a passing grade in mathematics to avoid the stigma of failure, to be eligible for extracurricular activities, or to satisfy his parents. Copying another student's work may be the logical solution to his dilemma, in which case the behavior is not really dishonest.

Stealing is also dishonest behavior, and it requires the attention of the school when the behavior persists. The personal wishes of a very small child are paramount with him. Unselfishness and a willingness to share are learned by the child through his experiences with other people. The child with strong, positive feelings of security and adequacy profits from these experiences and has no real need for dishonest behavior. The insecure, neglected, abused, or rejected child has a greater justification for such behavior as he strives to fulfill his needs for status. Dishonest behavior has underlying causes, and the behavior has some meaning for the child; it is purposeful for him. The temptation experienced by school people to moralize, to pass judgments, and to impose immediate punishment should be avoided. The conduct should not be ignored, but neither should a child's problems be intensified by hasty judgments and illogical punishment. Dishonesty is merely a symptom of some deep, underlying problems or frustrations. The child can be helped by a patient attempt to correct the causative conditions. A child may cheat, steal, or lie, or he may do all three. In any case there are reasons for the dishonesty, and in most cases he can be helped.

The symptoms of dishonesty may be present in the conduct of a child who:

1 Loiters around cloakrooms, lockers, or desks, or who casually looks at another student's work during tests or personal assignments.
2 Has an excessive amount of candy or other items in his possession and is generous in his sharing with others.
3 Resorts to untruths in explaining his behavior or possessions.
4 Gives the appearance of being apprehensive, nervous, and on guard.
5 Is oversolicitous and unduly anxious to please and may either verbalize in excess or withdraw.
6 Resorts to various devices for ascertaining the location of money or other items in the classroom.
7 Uses notes, marks on his desk, or other devices as aids in schoolwork and may attempt to add points to the score given his work.

Again, there are many causes underlying dishonest behavior. These causes cannot be specifically identified. However, some general possible causes can be noted. Factors which may result in dishonest behavior by a student may include the following:

1 An actual need for certain items in order to maintain himself properly within a class or to meet physical needs
2 Unfavorable home conditions where a youngster's physical or psychological needs are not met
3 Inadequate social skills, low academic ability, lack of interest in school, and inability to compete successfully
4 Undue stress upon grades by the school or family, or a rigid, demanding grading system
5 Loneliness, feelings of inadequacy and inferiority, and lack of status with peers

Treatment should be provided for the youngster who evidences some deprivation in his life. There is no prescribed procedure for helping this student any more than there is one particular cause for his behavior. The student with the behavior problem of dishonesty may be helped by:

1 Making certain his basic needs for survival and comfort are met.
2 Visiting the home and in various ways encouraging the parents to express their affection and appreciation for the child, and demonstrating a genuine interest in him at school.
3 Providing special attention in the classroom and through counseling, and helping him develop his talents, abilities, and social skills.
4 Providing opportunities for him to assume responsibility, make decisions, and become less dependent upon others.
5 Initiating demonstrations, role-playing, and dramatizations which emphasize the importance of honesty and encouraging activities which will raise the child's self-esteem and build self-confidence.
6 Encouraging the more popular students to include the troubled youngster in school activities and providing opportunities for him to excel.
7 Planning schoolwork to make successful performance possible and modifying academic standards to permit a realistic appraisal of his performance.
8 Encouraging maximum effort without undue stress upon grades and incorporating some flexibility in the grading system to permit the granting of satisfactory marks for sincere, maximum effort.
9 Encouraging participation in extraclass activities in which he may gain some ego-strengthening experiences and in which he can realize some success.

10 Providing group-work experiences in school and the opportunities for students to cooperate, share, and assist rather than to compete.

11 Permitting and encouraging the free expression of the imagination in which a child can be creative and uninhibited, with no need always to separate the mythological from the facts.

The highly emotional child.   The highly emotional child [10] reacts in an extreme fashion to conditions in the environment. He lacks the emotional balance generally manifested in the well-adjusted youngster. He may fret, cry, talk in loud tones, chew his finger nails, or become physically ill over relatively minor incidents. Usually the child is unaware of the reasons for his feelings and behavior, and he might even be unaware of the behavior itself or show no concern for how it might appear to others. Such behavior can become habitual and extremely difficult to change. Some degree of emotional maladjustment exists with any youngster whose behavior deviates markedly from the normal expectations of the society. Therefore, all behavior problems are in a way indicative of emotional disturbances, no matter what the symptoms may be. However, the topic is given separate consideration here because the emotional well-being of a student has so many implications for his behavior under all circumstances.

The behavior of the highly emotional child is often characterized by such symptoms as the following:

1 Excessive squirming, purposeless movements, nervous hand movements, twisting clothing, thumb-sucking, and biting objects

2 Short attention span with a tendency to abandon a task before its completion

3 Excessive movement about the room to sharpen a pencil or dispose of waste paper, and frequent requests to leave the room

4 Easily aroused anger, becoming upset over minor incidents, often being on the defensive, and sometimes being cruel, destructive, and unmanageable

5 Uncontrollable muscle movement, facial tics, muscle rigidity, and abnormal bodily movements

6 Unpredictable and sporadic performance with achievement generally below the level of capability

7 Occasional temper tantrums with extremes in moods, becoming highly elated or depressed with no apparent cause

[10] See Dorothy Rogers, *Mental Hygiene in Elementary Education*, Houghton Mifflin Company, Boston, 1957, pp. 315–345, for an excellent discussion on the emotional difficulties of children.

The causes underlying the behavior and the problems of the emotional youngster may be very much the same as for other kinds of disturbances. The degree of adjustment potential that he possesses also determines how well a youngster adjusts to unfavorable circumstances at home and at school. Although a broad generalization as to causes of emotional disturbances may be inaccurate, the general conclusion is valid that high anxiety usually accompanies and contributes to emotional disequilibrium. The problem obviously becomes one of discovering and removing the causes of the anxiety. With a reduction in anxiety comes an improvement in behavior. Reacting to or treating the symptoms serves no purpose.

In working with the highly emotional child the school should consider the following items as possible causes of the problem:

1   Unfavorable family relationships, including neglect, rejection, arguments, and friction
2   An absence of controls at home or school, or inconsistencies in discipline
3   Severe, unreasonable, or harsh treatment and unrealistic demands and pressures
4   Frequent failures in school, limited social skills, and anxieties associated with a low level of success
5   Frustration due to failure of the school to challenge the bright child adequately or to provide appropriate experiences for him
6   Confusion and uncertainty due to conflicting standards of conduct and morality within the child's environment

The best possible treatment for the highly emotional child is prevention. Responsible adults should be able to anticipate how certain conditions may contribute to emotional instability and thus take corrective measures before maladjustments occur. This is an ideal, however, and emotional difficulties will continue to occur, so that an effort must be made to aid the child when such problems do arise. This aid depends upon a knowledge of the child and a realization that he has certain basic needs which must be met. Harper and Wright note that certain experiences are crucial in enabling the disturbed child to learn and that these experiences vary in priority. They state that these needs are in the following sequence: safety, basic comfort, pleasures of his own, self-respect, success, and challenge.[11] Certainly the child must feel comfortable in his school environment and gain a degree of personal satisfaction from his achievements. Incentives in the form of praise, grades,

[11] *Op. cit.*, p. 319.

and rewards all help the child to gain in self-confidence. However, there is no substitute for the thrill he feels from having satisfied himself that he can do a thing well. As self-satisfaction and self-confidence improve, anxieties lessen, the emotions become more stable, and behavior improves.

Any treatment suggested for the highly emotional child must take into consideration his basic needs, and it must include a genuine interest in the child as a separate person worthy of love and deserving of the respect of his peers. In attempting to provide for the highly emotional child the school might:

1 Take the initiative in alleviating undesirable home conditions through parent conferences, study groups, and home visits.
2 Keep disciplinary and control measures reasonably consistent and appropriate, and avoid extremes of harsh treatment.
3 Provide adequate controls and assist the child to control his emotions and manage his behavior.
4 Modify the expectations of the school to make it possible for the child to succeed with a minimum of anxiety, and provide counseling through which he may gain confidence.
5 Provide for enrichment experiences in which the child is adequately challenged and given the opportunity to experience the thrill of success.
6 Make known to each child acceptable moral standards and codes of conduct to serve as guides in his own thinking and behavior.

Other Behavior Problems

There are behavior problems other than those included in this chapter. This discussion identifies some of the more common problems and suggests procedures for dealing with them. The psychological explanations underlying behavior are essentially the same no matter what the particular nature of the conduct might be. An understanding of the human personality and an awareness as to the needs of a child by the school constitute the first steps in devising a program which will help him make a better adjustment to school and to life. The individual child should be the focus of attention, and he should experience the warmth of a favorable school environment. The particular nature or causes of his problems are significant only as such knowledge will be used to improve the environment and stimulate the child toward maximum personal fulfillment and self-actualization.

SUMMARY/

Most children and youth make satisfactory adjustments to life and conduct themselves in an acceptable fashion appropriate for their school and community. However, there are some youngsters who do not conform and whose behavior constitutes a source of concern for the teacher. These children require special attention from school personnel and must receive remedial or therapeutic assistance if they are to resolve their difficulties and progress toward better adjustment.

All problems of behavior have a background of causes, with various experiences and conditions having some influence upon a child's development and conduct. Determining the causes of maladjustment is a principal function of guidance, to be followed by recommendations and services for remedial action.

A procedure that might be followed in dealing with behavior problems consists of these main steps: (1) noting symptoms, (2) determining possible causes, and (3) taking remedial action or providing treatment. It is most essential that the teacher and counselor make a cooperative effort to do everything possible to assist each youngster in making a satisfactory adjustment.

Behavior of any kind has a multiplicity of causes. It is also true that there is a relationship among behavior traits. A child who misbehaves in a particular fashion is more likely to misbehave in some other area of conduct than a child with acceptable behavior in the first instance. As self-understanding improves, as insights are gained, and as the child's needs are met, the likelihood of his resorting to inappropriate behavior is reduced considerably.

PROBLEMS/

1   What is meant by the term "behavior"? Define it in your own words, and then show how your definition differs from the usual understanding of the term.

2   What determines how a child will conduct himself? What are the factors and conditions which have the greatest influence on a child for desirable or undesirable conduct?

3   Although two children may show the same symptoms, that is, behave in a similar fashion, treatment procedures may

be entirely different. Why is this true? What are the dangers involved in treating children alike on the basis of symptom similarities?

4   Enlarge upon the concept that a person will behave in a fashion which is in harmony with his self-concepts and with his phenomenal self. Suppose a teacher does not understand or accept this concept but believes instead that a child can control his conduct if he wishes. Explain how he will probably deal with a child with behavior problems.

5   Why do you suppose it is particularly difficult for the teacher to view behavior from the viewpoint of the behaver rather than from the viewpoint of the observer? Which is better? Why?

6   Why is the counselor more likely than the teacher to look at conduct from the viewpoint of the behaver? Why is the teacher more likely to be inclined to regard and judge conduct from the position of an observer?

7   Why is it often difficult or even impossible for a child to change his behavior after having been asked to do so by the teacher or principal? What procedures would be used if the requests of the teacher or principal are ineffective?

8   What are some important implications for the statement that behavior has a multiplicity of causes?

9   Review the principal functions of guidance in dealing with behavior problems.

10   Why is it so difficult for behavior problems to be handled entirely within the classroom by the teacher with no additional help? What can the guidance program provide in services and materials that are not normally provided in the classroom?

11   What are some of the criteria to be used for making a distinction between appropriate, acceptable behavior and problem behavior?

12   How might the approach which includes noting symptoms, possible causes, and treatment be improved or in some way modified for greater effectiveness?

13   List other kinds of behavior problems worthy of consideration which are not included in this chapter.

Selected References

Textbooks

BARR, JOHN A.: *The Elementary Teacher And Guidance,* Holt, Rinehart and Winston, Inc., New York, 1957, chaps. 4 and 5.

COLEMAN, JAMES C.: *Personality Dynamics and Effective Behavior,* Scott, Foresman and Company, Chicago, 1960, chaps. 5–7.

COMBS, ARTHUR W., and DONALD SNYGG: *Individual Behavior,* Harper & Row, Publishers, Incorporated, New York, 1959.

COTTINGHAM, HAROLD F.: *Guidance in Elementary Schools,* McKnight & McKnight Publishing Company, Bloomington, Ill., 1956, chap. 8.

DETJEN, ERVIN WINFRED, and MARY FORD DETJEN: *Elementary School Guidance,* 2d ed., McGraw-Hill Book Company, New York, 1963.

KOWITZ, GERALD T., and NORMA G. KOWITZ: *Guidance in the Elementary Classroom,* McGraw-Hill Book Company, New York, 1959, chaps. 12 and 13.

PETERS, HERMAN J., and GAIL F. FARWELL: *Guidance: A Developmental Approach,* Rand McNally & Company, Chicago, 1959, chap. 13.

REDL, FRITZ, and WILLIAM W. WATTENBERG: *Mental Hygiene in Teaching,* Harcourt, Brace & Company, Inc., New York, 1959, chaps. 3–6.

ROGERS, DOROTHY: *Mental Hygiene in Elementary Education,* Houghton Mifflin Company, Boston, 1957, chaps. 9–13.

WRENN, C. GILBERT: *The Counselor in a Changing World,* American Personnel and Guidance Association, Washington, D.C., 1962, chap. 3.

Journals

AMIDON, EDMUND, and ANITA SIMON: "Teacher-Pupil Interaction," *Review of Educational Research,* vol. 35, pp. 130–139, April, 1965.

BRADFIELD, R. H.: "Guidance: Too Little, Too Late?" *California Journal of Educational Research,* vol. 16, pp. 42–45, January, 1965.

DREIKURS, R., and V. SOLTZ: "Your Child and Discipline," *NEA Journal,* vol. 54, pp. 33–47, January, 1965.

EATON, M. T.: "Problem Behavior in School," *Journal of Educational Psychology,* vol. 47, pp. 350–357, October, 1956.

FELLNER, I. W.: "When Children Are Disturbed," *Elementary School Journal,* vol. 61, pp. 254–259, February, 1961.

GALLAGHER, J. J.: "Expressive Thought by Gifted Children in the Classroom," *Elementary English,* vol. 42, pp. 559–568, May, 1965.

GLIDWELL, JOHN C., HERBERT R. DOMKE, and MILDRED B. KANTOR: "Screening in Schools for Behavior Disorders: Use of Mother's Report of Symptoms," *Journal of Educational Research,* vol. 56, no. 10, pp. 508–515, July-August, 1963.

GOLDMAN, R.: "Behavior and Personality Problems of Adolescence," *High Points,* vol. 41, pp. 40–43, April, 1959.

HAMPTON, P. J.: "Helping the Child Who Steals," *Childhood Education,* vol. 41, pp. 242–243, January, 1965.

HANVIK, LEE J.: "Child Who Is Afraid of School," *Elementary School Journal,* vol. 62, pp. 27–33, October, 1961.

HARPER, L. E., and B. WRIGHT: "Dealing with Emotional Problems in the Classroom," *Elementary School Journal,* vol. 58, pp. 316–325, March, 1961.

HARRISON, A.: "Discipline Problems," *School and Community,* vol. 52, pp. 12–13, December, 1965.

HARTUP, W. W.: "Social Behavior of Children," *Review of Educational Research,* vol. 35, pp. 122–129, April, 1965.

HAVIGHURST, ROBERT J.: "Problem Youth in the Junior High School," *Bulletin of the National Association of Secondary-school Principals,* vol. 42, pp. 367–372, April, 1958.

KAPLAN, SYLVAN J., and S. M. ANDERSON: "Help Ahead for Troubled Children," *Texas Outlook,* vol. 44, pp. 28–29, December, 1960.

KELLEY, R.: "Limits to Deviant Behavior in the Gifted," *Education Digest,* vol. 30, pp. 37–39, February, 1965.

KLAUSMEIER, HERBERT J.: "Using Research: Improving Problem Solving," *Wisconsin Journal of Education,* vol. 96, pp. 15–16, March, 1964.

KOWITZ, G. T.: "On Understanding Human Behavior," *Educational Forum,* vol. 29, pp. 59–63, November, 1964.

KVARACEUS, WILLIAM C.: "School as a Catalyst in Precipitating Delinquency," *Elementary School Journal,* vol. 59, pp. 211–214, January, 1959.

LOUGHLIN, RICHARD L.: "Short Answer Test on Discipline," *Bulletin of the National Association of Secondary-school Principals,* vol. 45, pp. 117–120, November, 1961.

MC CLEARY, ROLAN D.: "Group Psychotherapy Aids Problem Children: In-school Therapy Relieves Pressures," *Chicago School Journal,* vol. 46, pp. 343–351, May, 1965.

MANGAN, THOMAS, and D. SHAFFER: "Behavior Problems of Children as Viewed by Children in the Fifth through Eighth Grades," *Journal of Educational Research,* vol. 56, pp. 104–106, October, 1962.

MARSHALL, H. H.: "Behavior Problems of Normal Children: A Comparison between the Lay Literature and Developmental Research," *Child Development,* vol. 35, pp. 469–478, June, 1964.

MARSICO, A.: "Control without Punishment," *High Points,* vol. 47, pp. 9–19, April, 1965.

MICHAEL, J., and L. MEYERSON: "Behavioral Approach to Counseling and Guidance," *Harvard Education Review,* vol. 33, pp. 239–241, Spring-Summer, 1963.

MURRAY, WALTER I., and IRVING BLOOM: "Characteristics of Slow Learners and Pupils of Normal Intelligence Referred to a Child Guidance Clinic," *Journal of Educational Research,* vol. 54, pp. 43–48, October, 1960.

OHLSEN, M. M.: "Increasing Youth's Self-understanding," *Educational Leadership,* vol. 22, pp. 239–241, January, 1965.

OJEMANN, R. H.: "Causes and Consequences of Behavior," *Education,* vol. 85, pp. 78–83, October, 1964.

QUAY, H. C.: "Behavior Problems in Early Adolescence," *Child Development,* vol. 36, pp. 215–220, March, 1965.

RADIN, S. S.: "Teacher and the Rehabilitation of the Emotionally Disturbed Child," *School Health,* vol. 35, pp. 97–100, March, 1965.

RYAN, W. C.: "Mental Health Problems of School Leaving," *Understanding the Child,* vol. 25, pp. 98–102, October, 1956.

SCHACTER, NORMAN: "It Figures in Social Adjustment," *Bulletin of the National Association of Secondary-school Principals,* vol. 48, pp. 43–47, September, 1964.

SCHUL, B. D.: "Counselor Listens to Johnny," *Catholic School Journal*, vol. 65, p. 75, September, 1965.

SKINNER, C. E.: "Some Thoughts about Children Who Have Problems," *Education*, vol. 78, pp. 349–350, February, 1958.

WARNKEN, R. G., and T. F. SIESS: "Use of the Cumulative Record in the Prediction of Behavior," *Personnel and Guidance Journal*, vol. 44, pp. 321–327, November, 1965.

WATTENBERG, WILLIAM W.: "Causes of Child Behavior," *Understanding the Child*, vol. 25, pp. 81–83, June, 1956.

WILLIAMSON, E. G.: "New Look at Discipline," *Journal of Secondary Education*, vol. 38, pp. 10–14, January, 1963.

PART 4/

*A look at evaluation
and issues*

SIXTEEN

/EVALUATION AND RESEARCH

The need for a continuous evaluation of the guidance service is generally known and accented by guidance personnel. The degree to which this need is being met, however, is a moot question. There is widespread recognition that evaluation is most essential to the progress of the service. Guidance people cannot honestly or ethically think otherwise. There is also some reluctance to face the problem, and embarrassment best characterizes the reaction of some counselors when the issue is presented. It takes some rationalizing to justify the limited activity given to evaluation. Perhaps it is a case of first things first with some disagreement as to the position of evaluation in the hierarchy of tasks to be accomplished. The statement [1] that "Guidance services, like many others in education, are still offered largely on the bases of hope and faith" appears to have strong support. Although the quantity and quality of research on evaluation precedures have increased and improved

[1] John W. Rothney and Gail F. Farwell, "The Evaluation of Guidance and Personnel Services," *Review of Educational Research,* vol. 30, p. 168, April, 1960.

considerably since Cottle's statement in 1957, it still bears repeating today: [2] "This review for the three year period indicates the paucity and limited nature of published research on the evaluation of guidance services. There is great need for cooperative research among institutions and for research designs of better quality."

It should also be noted that some commendable work is being done in many schools in the interest of evaluation at the local level. The fact that most of these accomplishments are not published should be taken into consideration in any current criticism of the schools. Evaluation and some informal research are being done, but not with the intensity or care necessary for publication. There are also many school people who lack the motivation to prepare research findings properly for publication. Counselor interests, orientation, and research competence are all factors with some influence in the research productivity of a staff. Current counselor preparation programs are giving research activities more emphasis, resulting in greater competence, stronger orientation, and more intense interest on the part of graduate students in pursuing research activities. Historically and traditionally, too little stress has been given to evaluation in the guidance services, and too little time has been given to training graduate students for research and related productive endeavors. Conditions in the graduate schools are, however, much more favorable than they were a generation ago and permit a greater commitment of time and resources to research.

More recent reviews of the literature provide some ground for optimism. There is evidence that some interesting and worthwhile research is being accomplished. Only a small segment of the research deals with program evaluation, but even this is encouraging, since it indicates an interest in a vital problem. The building up of an impetus in this type of research may require some time, even with competent researchers. Patterson notes that there is a continuing scarcity of studies evaluating counseling and guidance services, but with some improvements in quality.[3] A similar report [4] was made three years later: "The literature in this field pertinent to total program evaluation is limited. A perusal of the last three issues of *The Review of Educational Research* on the current topic reveals quite clearly the paucity of total program research."

[2] William C. Cottle, "The Evaluation of Guidance Services," *Review of Educational Research*, vol. 27, p. 234, April, 1957.

[3] C. H. Patterson, "Program Evaluation," *Review of Educational Research*, vol. 33, no. 2, p. 214, April, 1963.

[4] R. Wray Strowig and Gail F. Farwell, "Programmatic Research," *Review of Educational Research*, vol. 36, no. 2, p. 327, April, 1966.

These reports suggest the need for some intensive research in the area of program development and improvement. Perhaps as other areas of research improve in quantity and quality, evaluation studies will likewise improve. Greater effort should also be given to the evaluation of currently functioning guidance programs. A school district might profit from a periodic evaluation of its guidance service conducted by a competent person or team of individuals. Such evaluations would result in an identification of weaknesses in the program together with recommendations for improvements.

The excellent work of the ACES and the ASCA, both divisions of the American Personnel and Guidance Association, in the establishment of standards for the training of school counselors should lend considerable strength to the evaluation of the guidance programs in the schools. Strengthening of the standards for counselor education can be expected to produce more competent counselors, which should inevitably bring improvements in the programs being established and conducted in the schools. Attitudes toward evaluation and research should also improve as guidance people become better informed, more adequately prepared, and less defensive.

This chapter presents a discussion of the place of evaluation in the guidance service, the purposes of evaluation, and some appropriate methods and instruments for conducting evaluation studies. The place of research in the guidance service is also reviewed.

Evaluation and the Guidance Service

Evaluation procedures should be under way continuously with some phase of the program constantly under scrutiny. Assignments may be made to staff members and designated times set aside for them to concentrate on a particular area of guidance periodically, thus making possible a more intensive study of the service. The proof of a program's effectiveness is in the degree of success realized in accomplishing its objectives. Periodic evaluation is suggested by the need for constant improvement in a program. It denotes a recognition by the staff that weaknesses and omissions exist and that something should be done to strengthen the service.

The aims of the guidance service are often rather vaguely stated, if indeed they are stated at all. A general agreement may exist among the staff as to expected accomplishments, but this agreement is likely to be obscure and subject to personal interpretations. The objectivity of evaluation studies and other research projects permits an organized attack upon the solution of a problem and minimizes guesses and subjective judgments. Evaluation fulfills another important need as it helps in the identification of weak or unrealistic objectives. The services may be inappropriate or weak, in which case corrections should be made. However, inappropriate objectives are equally serious. These too may be discovered through evaluation. Congruity between established objectives and the services designed to meet them is essential. The aims of the total guidance program and of each service should be subjected to the same intensive scrutiny as that directed toward the way the services themselves are performed. Needed corrections in both areas may then be made.

The Purposes of Evaluation

The major purpose of evaluation is to determine the quality and effectiveness of a particular program. This can be accomplished only if the strengths and weaknesses of the program are identified in terms of established standards and if appropriate efforts are made to correct the weaknesses and maintain the strengths. Riccio clarifies this point when he says: [5] "Briefly then, the major purpose of evaluation is to ascertain the current status of a service or activity within a frame of reference, and on the basis of this knowledge, to improve the activity in terms of quality and efficiency." The "frame of reference" in this case presumably includes the use of standards against which a service is checked. Acceptable criteria with which current services may be compared are essential to evaluation. Otherwise a judgment about a service will be the result of subjective, personal observations rather than of studying objective data.

Once the strengths of the program are located through evaluation procedures, they may be reinforced, continued, and improved beyond their present level. These stronger areas may also be utilized in strengthening the weaker services, since there is a reciprocal give-and-take relationship among all aspects of the program. For example, the testing service in a school may be of high quality, while the counseling is weak. Data gained from testing might be utilized to improve the counseling.

[5] Anthony C. Riccio, "The Evaluation of Guidance Services," *Bulletin of the National Association of Secondary-school Principals*, vol. 46, p. 100, November, 1962. Reprinted by permission of the National Association of Secondary-school Principals, Washington, D.C., copyright 1962.

Just as predictions may be made as to the expected progress and quality of a guidance program in terms of the seriousness with which a school regards evaluation, so may predictions be made in terms of the efforts given to evaluation. An attitude of acceptance and concern on the part of the staff and a willingness to look objectively at itself and its activities must prevail. An overly sensitive, evasive, or insecure staff will resist criticisms and suggestions and will probably rationalize its inactivity to conduct and submit to evaluation. As Riccio notes, evaluation is not intended to be a threatening process but is intended to aid everyone to do his job better.[6] Certainly it should be a threat to no one. Indeed, it should be an active, meaningful, integral part of the guidance service. As such, evaluative activities are appreciated and enjoyed by the staff, and the results are beneficial to everyone. The students are ultimately benefited most as the quality of the guidance service continues to improve.

To ignore evaluation is to invite at least four undesirable conditions: (1) a weak or mediocre service at a level of quality far below the possibilities, (2) an apathetic, indifferent staff and a student body with little motivation for improvement, (3) a general failure to provide and utilize the proper activities, tools, and procedures essential to the educational progress of youth, and (4) inefficiency in the use of staff members and the school's resources.

Specific Problems to Consider in Evaluating a Program

Program improvement, then, is the fundamental purpose of evaluation. A prerequisite to this improvement is a serious look at each of the basic elements of the guidance service. It is necessary to know just what the status of each service is. How good is each of the basic services of the guidance program as measured against the standards being used? Where are the major weaknesses? Ultimately these questions too call for an answer: how can the weaknesses be overcome, now that they are identified, and what are the procedures for strengthening the total guidance service? The points to be considered under each of the major elements, or services, of the guidance program are outlined below. A careful consideration of each of the points listed is a major step in evaluating the guidance service, and the attention given should result in a more thorough knowledge of the existing program. This knowledge may then be

[6] *Ibid.*

used in modifying and strengthening the service and in achieving better results. Although group guidance activities and the organization of the guidance service are not regarded as basic services in the guidance program, they should be subjected to a critical appraisal in any evaluation study.

The pupil inventory service

1 Adequacy of the present system of guidance records, and quality and appropriateness of the forms used
2 Accessibility of data to the staff and the utilization of data
3 System of filing and recording information and adequacy of clerical help for maintaining records
4 Policies and system for promoting the use of information by the staff and pupils
5 Utilization of accumulated data in curriculum planning and improvements, and the use made of data in teaching and in counseling
6 System for receiving and transferring records for pupils who change schools and the use made of information in aiding the adjustment of such pupils

The testing program

1 Current philosophy of the school toward the use of tests and inventories for guidance purposes and the quality of the leadership directing the program
2 Support given to testing in the form of finances and time allotment in the school schedule
3 Competence of the staff in selecting, administering, and interpreting tests, and the provisions made for reviewing test results with students
4 Adequacy of the basic or minimum testing program and the availability of special tests and inventories beyond the minimum program
5 Utilization of test data for adjustments in teaching and in providing enrichment experiences, and in the counseling service
6 Adequacy and appropriateness of the system for scoring tests and in reporting the results

The counseling service

1 Nature of prevailing counseling philosophies and competence of the counselors

2   Nature of the services provided for all students, the adequacy of these services, and the counselor-student ratio

3   Program of orientation for acquainting the staff and students with the counseling service and the quality of communication between teachers and counselors

4   Quality of the service to the more serious problem cases and the effectiveness of this service

5   Suitability of facilities and conditions for counseling including office, privacy, and accessibility of the counselor to students

6   Existence and quality of in-service training opportunities for staff members

The information services

1   Adequacy and suitability of current information files and their location for immediate access and use

2   Funds available for this service, adequacy of subscriptions and other sources of information, and a system for intelligent use of data

3   Utilization of information by teachers for instructional purposes and utilization by counselors

4   Program for informing students about the school's offerings and opportunities and availability of literature on post-high school educational and vocational training opportunities

5   Availability of bulletin-board space and the quality of displays, and the uses made of existing facilities

6   Provisions made for field trips, career days, conferences, and group guidance activities for informing and stimulating students toward wise vocational and career choices

The placement service

1   The philosophy and commitment of the school on placement and the nature of the activities provided for placement in the various curricular areas

2   Structure of the service for aiding students in part-time and full-time job placement for in-school youth, dropouts, and graduates

3   Adequacy of the placement service in aiding students in college or training school placement and in helping students plan for the future

4   Appropriateness and effectiveness of the system for maintaining contact with prospective employers, colleges, and training schools

The follow-up service

1 Provisions made for ascertaining periodically the status of each student following educational or vocational placement and the utilization of the staff and students in conducting follow-up studies

2 Adequacy of staff time given to follow-up activities, competence of the staff, and use made of findings

3 Amount, quality, and appropriateness of forms, data sheets, questionnaires, and other materials used for studies and research

4 Adequacy of research programs, disposition and use of data gained, and number of staff members involved

5 Appropriateness of procedures used for the coordination of efforts and the implementation of findings

Group guidance activities

1 Degree to which group guidance is used in augmenting and facilitating other guidance services and the accomplishments realized by these procedures

2 Competence of the staff in conducting group guidance activities

3 Quality of the structure of group procedures and the effectiveness of the plan through which students are given additional help

4 Harmony between group guidance and the instructional program, and the quality of the program as it provides for more effective learning and better adjustment by students

5 Ability of the program to accommodate all students and the quality of the service as determined by results

The organization and administration of the guidance service

1 The philosophy of the administration toward guidance and the amount of leadership and support given to the guidance service

2 The amount of effort given to public relations, and the extent of parents' and public interest and participation in the guidance service

3 The competence of the guidance director and the amount of participation by staff members in formulating and implementing policies

4 Effectiveness of the service in bringing about better student adjustment and in reducing problem behavior

5 Adequacy of funds for personnel and material, and the suitability of facilities

Devices, Methods, and Procedures for Evaluating the
Guidance Service

We turn now to the means by which evaluation may be carried out —the tools, aids, devices, and suggested procedures to be utilized in both simplifying and making more effective all efforts given to evaluation. The availability and proper utilization of established criteria are of basic importance to any evaluation study.

Evaluation studies may be conducted by using some rather standard procedures, thus reducing the amount of effort given to preliminaries. However, some thought should be given to the fact that each school has its differences and unique characteristics, thus requiring the application of procedures which take these differences into consideration. Since schools also have many characteristics common to all, the problem is relatively minor and can be handled quite readily. A realization, too, that each tool and each procedure has its limitations will protect the staff against the mistakes of hasty preparation or acceptance of an instrument and a naïve acceptance of the results. Considerable care must be given to the selection and preparation of the instrument to be used. The tools and procedures are merely means to the accomplishment of ends. The objectives to be attained through evaluation should be established early and prior to the selection of tools and procedures. Problems to consider before deciding which methods to use may include (1) the purpose of the study, (2) the best tools and techniques available for use, (3) the amount of time to be given to the project, (4) the number and competence of the personnel to do the work, and (5) the scope and intensity of the study.

Essential precaution in evaluation.   The observance of certain precautions in conducting evaluative studies should produce more valid and useful results and a greater likelihood of being able to improve the guidance service as a whole. Some people resist planning, since it requires time and energy. However, appropriate planning accomplished early will generally be more economical ultimately. Evaluation is facilitated if the people making the study will:

1   Take sufficient time to plan the entire program carefully, including the preliminary planning and the establishment of the groundwork for the program.
2   Utilize the suggestions and assistance of other staff members, thus broadening the participation and giving greater strength to the study.

3   Strive for simplicity in the survey instruments used to obtain information from other people in order to achieve a high return and for purposes of simplifying and objectifying the tabulation of results.
4   Make certain the wording in the instrument is clear and understandable and the directions are explicit.
5   Plan specifically in advance the system to be used in tabulating and reporting the results, thus minimizing subjectivity and confusion.
6   Test the instrument on selected subjects prior to its use and encourage criticisms by these people as to how the instrument might be improved.
7   Do an actual tabulation on the preliminary administration and follow through with a reporting of the data in order to discover and correct the weaknesses.
8   Keep the welfare of the respondent in mind by protecting him against unwise or unethical use of the information he gives you and against unreasonable infringements upon his time.
9   Make certain that all requests in the instrument are purposeful and that the information requested is relevant to the study.
10   Provide for the return of the instrument by including a return container properly addressed and with sufficient postage for its return by first class mail.

The above suggestions are primarily for studies which require soliciting information from people by mail. Evaluation studies may, of course, be done locally by other means. The same care should be exercised in the preparation or selection of the materials and instruments to be used, and the same consideration should be accorded the people who are asked to participate in the study.

Using the questionnaire.   The questionnaire calls for the reporting of certain information as directed by the researcher. The nature of the information sought is indicated by a short phrase or statement preceding a blank which is to be completed by the respondent. Considerable care should be given to preparation and use of the questionnaire in order to avoid or minimize the weaknesses inherent with this type of instrument. Simplicity and objectivity should characterize the questionnaire in order to obtain a good response and useful information.

The usual duplicating processes are satisfactory for the preparation of the questionnaire. Multilith, mimeograph, or Ditto duplicating processes are suitable. If the information being sought is limited to a very few items, a double-postcard arrangement may be used instead of a standard-sized sheet of paper. One card contains the address of the person, while the other card has the return address on one side and the items to be completed on the opposite side. This is a simple, inexpensive procedure for gaining information, but it does have a space limitation. A follow-up study of graduates or of some other group may be conducted with this arrangement where the information sought may be limited to five or ten items.

SAMPLE QUESTIONNAIRE

To the Graduates of Ellis High School, 1963

Your high school is conducting a survey of a selected group of former students for purposes of learning (1) the nature of the vocation now being pursued by these individuals and (2) how the school might improve its educational offering in order to do a better job of preparing its students for successful adult life. We know you can be of help to us in this important project, and we are looking forward to receiving your completed questionnaire.

NAME: _____ SEX: _____
      (Last)   *(First)*   *(Middle)*

PRESENT ADDRESS: _____

MARITAL STATUS: _____ IF MARRIED, NAME OF SPOUSE:

_____

EMPLOYED: _____ EMPLOYER: _____
     (Yes or no)

NATURE OF YOUR WORK: _____

HOW LONG WITH PRESENT EMPLOYERS: _____

DO YOU REGARD THIS AS PERMANENT EMPLOYMENT? _____

WOULD YOU PREFER SOME OTHER TYPE OF JOB? _____

    IF SO, WHAT? _____

LIST IN ORDER OF IMPORTANCE SCHOOL SUBJECTS WHICH

    HAVE BEEN MOST HELPFUL TO YOU: (1) _____

(2) _____ (3) _____

WHICH SUBJECTS HAVE BEEN OF THE LEAST VALUE? (1) __

    _____ (2) _____ (3) _____

YOUR RECOMMENDATIONS FOR THE IMPROVEMENT OF THE

    SCHOOL PROGRAM: _____

The sample questionnaire given here illustrates how certain information might be obtained. The purpose of this questionnaire is to learn the whereabouts and type of work engaged in by former students who did not attend college and to get their suggestions as to the relative merits of the various school subjects for graduates who move directly into employment. This questionnaire is too long for a postcard, but one sheet of paper is adequate for the information requested. Some space should also be given to a brief explanation of the purpose of the study and to the necessary directions to the respondent.

The Use of Checklists

Although the nature and purposes of information sought should determine the type of instrument to be used, the checklist has some advantages over the questionnaire and in most instances is preferable, or one might use a combination of the two within one instrument.

The questionnaire has the advantages of permitting free response and expression and obtaining information peculiar to each respondent. The checklist provides such advantages as (1) some control over exactly what information will be given, (2) more responses, because of the ease and speed of responding as compared to answering a questionnaire, (3) ease and simplification of tabulating results, and (4) possibilities for assigning numerical ratings to the various responses.

In the usual kinds of checklists, responses are made by circling or checking the most appropriate word or number given after the item. It may call for a yes-or-no answer, or the degree of feeling may be denoted by selecting the most appropriate number given among the alternatives. The yes-or-no type of question is usually inadequate, since in most instances the answer is not that clear-cut. It may be partly yes and partly no to the respondent, but he is, nevertheless, forced to choose one or the other.

When there are degrees of feeling about a matter, provisions should be made for answers which are accurate and in close harmony with one's feelings. A five-point rating scale is usually desirable, since it provides for a variety of responses, one of which should be satisfactory to the respondent. However, whereas a five-point scale may be adequate for some matters, it has the disadvantage of not providing for the "middle," or average. A choice of three answers is in many instances better than the yes-or-no response, but this too has the disadvantage of providing an insufficient number of responses.

At the beginning of the checklist a clear explanation should be given of each possible response. Each respondent should know exactly what his particular response on an item means. If standards of meaning have been established for each possible response, the data will have considerably more validity than if the matter is left to chance or the individual judgment of each person responding.

A few representative items are given in the following sample checklist. This illustration is given for purpose of showing the form that a checklist may take. It is not intended to represent a complete checklist, which obviously would take up considerably more space.

The questionnaire-checklist. As already noted, a combination of the questionnaire and the checklist is sometimes desirable. In this way more information is obtained than with the checklist alone. Names, birth dates, addresses, schools attended, employment record, and other personal data may be obtained in this manner. It is generally advisable to group the questionnaire items together and do likewise with the checklist items rather than to mix the two. This arrangement avoids the possibility of confusing the respondent by his having to make the frequent transitions from one type of item to the other.

The interview method. The personal interview method for obtaining information for use in evaluation has both advantages and disadvantages when compared with other methods. The interview has the advantages of (1) providing for personal contact in which the respondent may express himself freely, (2) making it possible to explain and clarify questions posed, (3) realizing a higher return than where the contact is limited to the mails, (4) lending dignity and importance to the study, and (5) yielding more information than can be obtained within the limits of a printed form.

The interview has the disadvantages of (1) being very time-consuming and presenting many administrative problems related to setting up satisfactory interview schedules, (2) being subject to respondent resistance and resentment because of its personal nature and the time it takes, (3) demanding skills and tact on the part of the interviewer, (4) being subject to whims, opinions, and sub-

CHECKLIST

A Follow-up Study of Graduates of Brown High School, 1963

Your high school is concerned about the improvement of its guidance program, and feels that as a former student you can be of some help. Your responses will be kept confidential; you need not sign your name.

> Directions: Please circle the number which most nearly represents your feelings about this phase of the program, particularly in respect to the benefits you gained from it which have proved helpful since your graduation.

3   EXCELLENT—This service or activity has been of great help to me.

2   GOOD—This service has been quite helpful.

1   FAIR—There have been some benefits from this service, but they have been rather weak.

0   POOR—No help was received in this area. I would have managed just as well without it.

1   The record system, which included the use of cumulative records and information   3   2   1   0

2   The counseling, where each student had the opportunity to discuss his problems and plans with a counselor   3   2   1   0

3   The information service's files and literature dealing with vocations, colleges, and training schools   3   2   1   0

4   The testing program, where tests of various kinds were administered and the results interpreted for students   3   2   1   0

5   The placement service, from which students received assistance in finding part-time jobs and with job or college location following high school   3   2   1   0

6   Follow-up activities, through which students were contacted periodically to learn how they were getting along while in school, on a job, or in college after high school   3   2   1   0

Comments on any of the above:

_____

_____

_____

_____

_____

jective judgments of the respondent which may have little value for the study, and (5) difficulty in tabulating data in meaningful numerical terms.

If the interview method is used, its strengths may be capitalized upon and its weaknesses minimized. Many of its limitations can be at least partly overcome through an objective awareness of these limitations and careful planning.

The interview-instrument method. Some kind of recording and reporting form should be used in the interview method. The interview-instrument method combines the interview and the instrument into a meaningful procedure which makes use of both the oral responses of the person and the information recorded during the interview. The subjectivity of the personal interview is avoided as specific information is recorded. The instrument should favor the obtaining of data which may be reported in meaningful numerical terms. Personal opinions of the respondents may be solicited, but they should be reported apart from the objective data.

It must be borne in mind that questionnaires, checklists, interviews, or combinations of these instruments or procedures are merely means to ends and nothing more. It is not a matter of whether evaluations should be done but rather one of considering the quality of the evaluation and the strength of the organization responsible for its conduct. Hatch has a point when he says: [7] "We cannot escape evaluation; we can only improve it."

Using Established Criteria in Evaluation

An excellent procedure for ascertaining the weaknesses of the guidance service is to use established criteria. Several instruments have been developed for this purpose that are currently available for use. They may be obtained by purchasing copies directly from the publishers or, if they have not been published separately, by obtaining permission to use them from the publishers of the textbooks or other publications in which they appear.

Some major sources of these criteria are the following:

1   Arthur L. Benson, *Criteria for Evaluation Guidance Programs in Secondary Schools,* Misc. 3317, 1949, and *How to Use the Criteria for Evaluating Guidance Programs in the Secondary Schools,* Misc. 3317A, both published by the U.S. Department of

[7] Raymond N. Hatch and Buford Stefflre, *Administration of Guidance Services,* Prentice-Hall, Inc., Englewood Cliffs, N.J., 1958, p. 299.

Health, Education, and Welfare, Office of Education, Division of Vocational Education. These instruments have had considerable use for a number of years; they are an excellent guide for schools as to how to go about their evaluation studies and what to include. Modifications may, of course, be made in these or any other instruments according to local needs.

2   North Central Association Sub-committee on Guidance, "Report of the Self-study Survey of Guidance Practices in North Central Association High Schools for the School Year 1947–48," *North Central Association Quarterly*, vol. 23, January, 1949. This instrument has had wide usage in the improvement of many guidance programs. It is more inclusive than the typical evaluation guide; it covers certain elements of instruction and the community as well as the usual basic elements of the guidance service. It is particularly helpful for promoting wide involvement and participation in the guidance program. Its approach may be a little too ambitious, however, for the typical school.

3   Frank E. Wellman and Don D. Twiford, "Guidance, Counseling, and Testing Program Evaluation," U.S. Department of Health, Education, and Welfare, Office of Education, 1961. This publication suggests procedures for evaluating the guidance service either within a school or for the whole state. The basic elements of the guidance service are included, and suggestions are given on how to gather data needed for properly evaluating a program.

Other sources of evaluative criteria are also available in textbooks.[8] These criteria may be more readily accessible than those found in government publications. Each school should ascertain its particular needs and select materials which will be of the greatest aid in fulfilling these needs and realizing its objectives. As noted previously, appropriate modifications may be made of published criteria according to the needs of a particular school.

For an instrument prepared by the author to be used in evaluating the guidance service see Appendix B of this text. These criteria might be used during the initial stages of program development as guides for the school in deciding what kinds of services to include. It also has an advantage over the instrument that requires a simple yes-or-no answer after each item, in that it provides for a numerical rating of the relative quality of the service, with five possible responses.

[8] *Ibid.*, appendixes C and D; and George E. Hill, *Management and Improvement of Guidance.* Appleton-Century-Crofts, Inc., New York, 1965, appendixes B and C.

Research Activities in the Guidance Service

Although evaluation is not synonymous with research, a form of research is required in doing an evaluation study. Research is, furthermore, in itself a vital part of the guidance service.

Guidance departments at all levels of education have been subjected to criticism for their apparent low productivity in research efforts. The need for the guidance service has become quite evident to most school people and to the public. This attitude has resulted in rather consistent growth by the guidance service in many areas, and with this has come an awareness as to the critical part research plays in such a program. However, the research effort has not kept pace with the growth of the guidance service and has certainly been inadequate to meet the needs of the guidance movement as a whole.[9] The research accomplishments at the public school level have generally been considerably below those of college and university counseling services. This is to be expected in terms of the research potential typically found in a university counseling center compared to the typical elementary school or high school. Greater research effort, however, should be encouraged at all educational levels.

It is to be hoped that the critics of the guidance services will give direct attention to providing the leadership by which guidance personnel may become more productive. Unless tactfully and judiciously applied, criticisms may serve as added deterrents to progress rather than as sources of stimulation. More than talk, either positive or negative, is needed in stimulating people to dedicate a part of themselves to an objective exploration of problems. The guidance people best qualified to assume the leadership in conducting research should be identified and given the necessary time, resources, and incentives to move ahead with this task.

The particular source of this help is not too important just so long as it is forthcoming. Resource people at the national and state levels can be of assistance through published directives, conferences, and personal contacts. Individual school districts might also provide for research through appropriate budgeting and by providing competent people to direct the research effort. Intentions in many cases are exceptionally good, and involvement in research is an objective of a substantial number of school people; however, the formidable demands upon time and energy and the inade-

[9] For a more detailed discussion and for references dealing with this problem, see *ibid.*, p. 230.

quacies of personnel and resources have all been deterrents to actual accomplishment.

The valid comment is occasionally made that more research should be done by people actively engaged in teaching and counseling. However, this also has some obvious limitations, and unless adequate provisions are made for these people to become involved, they are not likely to do so. Generally the people who are closest to the problems are also the busiest in providing personal assistance for their students and clients and are thus faced with the inevitable dilemma of insufficient time and depleted energies. Personnel at the district level in the schools and at the university level are less restricted by the urgent demands of students and are therefore freer to do research, and they also generally have a stronger orientation toward and inclination to do research. A reasonable approach is to recognize the existing problems and deterrents to research and for all school people at the various educational levels to give their best efforts to encouraging and promoting research activities among all staff members who can contribute to the effort. The realization should obviously prevail that research activities are means to worthy ends and not ends in themselves. There are purposes and reasons, then, underlying all research efforts.

Purposes of Research

It is highly unlikely that even the devoted researchers will agree as to the major purposes underlying their efforts. Perhaps the positive attitude of the worker toward research is no closer to a clear-cut, logical, defensible explanation than is the enthusiasm of the mountain climber, the daring of the big-game hunter, the strivings of the artist, the passions of the composer, or the discontent of the writer. The "divine discontent" which so poignantly characterizes the behavior of many men may press a bit harder for expression in the soul of the man who finds at least some satisfaction in his search for answers to problems. The realization of the striving researcher that he has not succumbed to mediocrity or to maintaining the *status quo* and that he is giving at least minimal expression to his desires to move on and up might be all that it takes to keep him moving in his task. The results he hopes for may continue to elude him, and rewards and recognition may be vague unrealities in an uncertain future, but his spirits may still be high and his efforts unfaltering.

Some rather tangible purposes also underlie research that constitute good reasons for being involved in it and justification for the necessary expenditure of time and money. A few representative purposes, of the many that research serves, are discussed in the paragraphs that follow.

To gain important information.   Sound improvements in any service or program depend upon having and utilizing essential information. Studies properly initiated and carried to a conclusion will yield this information. Subjective judgments, guesses, impressions, and intuition should not be entirely ignored, but neither should they be used as the base, or framework, upon which to build a program. Objective data are a prerequisite to planning, which in turn leads to the establishment and maintenance of services which hold promise for advancement, strength, and permanence.

To meet professional responsibilities.   One's enthusiasm for, and interest in, doing research may be quite low if it is motivated only by a sense of professional obligation. Usually this is only one of many reasons for doing research. However, it is an important one. Any professional or vocational pursuit should have the commitment and dedication of its workers. The professional guidance worker has an obligation to lend his efforts to the task of extending the horizons of knowledge. Society has a rather substantial investment in every professionally trained person. His obligation to society is quite obvious. The contributions of each person throughout his career should result in improvements and innovations upon which others can build for continuous progress. Research is only one area of service, but it is a critical one for the guidance worker.

To promote one's professional development.   The completion of the requirements for a graduate degree at a university presumably suggests a level of competence for engaging in specified professional work and therefore opens the doors of opportunity for service. However, as most commencement speakers manage to say in one way or another, this is only the beginning. A formal education provides the stimulation and the direction, and it helps to set the course for a lifetime of activity and service. If the spark for personal and professional progress was well kindled in the mind of the learner while he was in school, then it should blaze into a conflagration of intensity and permanence during his years of service to other people. A worker's professional development takes place as a result of engaging in activities which are academically, personally, and professionally rewarding. Research activities hold this promise for many guidance workers.

To gain personal satisfaction. Personal satisfaction from one's efforts is one of the ultimate criteria by which the value of the activity may be assessed. Not all people, even within the counseling profession, find satisfaction in research or feel that it holds much promise for self-actualization. However, the orientation of the guidance worker should include an interest in problem solution, a curiosity about better ways of doing things, and an enthusiasm for helping people. Some research activity, therefore, is inevitable. Weak or doubtful interests may be strengthened through activity, and thus greater enthusiasm and higher competence may follow involvement with research. The reluctance of some people to do research is often due to a lack of familiarity with research procedures. The assistance of a competent researcher from whom they can learn research techniques is of great value to these people. Confidence follows understanding, and a reduction of inhibitions will result in greater productivity.

To meet the challenges of the times. The best efforts by all guidance personnel would not be adequate to keep pace with our rapidly changing society. Industrial and technological advancements have been almost beyond comprehension. Current evidence suggests even greater advancements in the future. The social sciences are not experiencing changes at the same rapid pace, but advancements in those areas too are pronounced and provide some warning for what may lie ahead. The challenges to the guidance worker are strikingly evident, as is the inevitability of his facing up to these challenges. A dedication to his work and a responsibility to his society are basic requirements and assumptions. Research, exploration, and the creative effort are all essential aspects of the counselor's commitment to his profession and his obligation to his society to meet the challenges of his time.

To provide for exploration. The term "research" suggests to many people a systematic attack upon a problem with its solution as the ultimate goal. There is another side to research. This is the opportunity it provides the worker to explore, to try, to test out, to guess, and to anticipate. Many brilliant ideas and excellent improvements have resulted from the uninhibited explorations of a curious mind. The good researcher is often more interested in the activity and in the involvement than he is in a specific problem or its solution. The exhilaration of the search and the stimulation of the adventure are nearly all that are needed for productivity to occur. The more formal aspects of the research will take place at the appropriate time, but in the meantime the person is thinking, discovering, speculating, and laying the groundwork for productivity.

Informal exploration, then, also has a place in the research activities of the guidance service. The results of such research may not warrant space in the journals, but they still contribute something to the researcher and to his school. Furthermore, much research starts with a naïve curiosity. Who is to say what the outcome may be? There must be a start some place, and with an unheralded beginning may come some creditable discoveries, even without benefit of formality.

Problems Associated with Research

The problems associated with initiating a solid research program and keeping it going are numerous. These problems may be disposed of with excuses and rationalizations, or they may be recognized as real and dealt with accordingly.

Research activities are extremely demanding of time, personnel, resources, and money. This being the case, it is understandable why the status of research is relatively low among guidance workers. Also, problems of negative attitudes and indifference are often encountered. The existence of resources is no guarantee that the effort in research will be anything but feeble. The sense of dedication and responsibility felt by the guidance staff are prime determiners of research achievements. The key to research activities, then, rests with the staff. Solutions to the other deterrents may be found if the attitude of the staff is positive toward research. The problems to be considered prior to and during research are represented in the following:

1 The centralization of responsibility for research
2 The role of the guidance personnel in research
3 The role of the teachers in doing research
4 The sources of data to be tapped and explored
5 The kinds of problems to be considered
6 The approximate costs to be expected
7 The sources of financial assistance for research purposes
8 The purposes to be served through the research effort
9 The amount of time to be given to research activities

10 The utilization of findings and the implementation of results
11 The disposition to be made of accumulated data and study findings
12 The degree of involvement by students in research

The nature and seriousness of the problems will vary with each school or district. It is therefore necessary to determine locally just what the more serious problems are, and each school must consider each problem and each suggested solution in terms of its own needs and resources.

Some one person should be the designated head of the research effort, and he should be given the authority, support, and resources required to meet this responsibility. Leaving the work to chance with no centralization of responsibility is an invitation to inaction. The person chosen may be a member of the guidance staff and should be the one most competent for doing and directing research. The roles of the various staff members will vary depending upon the number and competence of the staff. However, everyone on the guidance staff should have some involvement with, and participation in, research.

Teacher involvement will vary considerably, depending again, upon local circumstances. A teacher with an interest in and the competence to do research should be encouraged through load reduction or being provided secretarial or other needed help. The typical teacher might contribute most effectively by supplying information to, and working with, the guidance person who has research responsibilities, rather than assuming the task himself. The teacher might also conduct limited studies associated with the classroom which could be handled with less effort than would be required for a major study. The teacher is a member of the research team primarily as a contributor and coworker, not as one having major responsibilities for research.

Sources of data are generally known locally, and efforts should be made by the researchers to locate and use these sources, among which are cumulative records, test information, school achievement records, and teacher observations.

The kinds, nature, and severity of problems existing within a school should be general knowledge. However, there is the danger of disagreement as to what constitutes a problem. The judgment of the staff will need to be brought to bear in deciding which problems have priority and how much attention each problem should be given. The head researcher should also have the prerogative of helping to identify problems and should have the final word on how to go about doing the research.

Costs will of course vary with the intensity of the research. Salaries will generally constitute by far the greatest expenditure. Load adjustments can often be made, and providing a staff member with relatively inexpensive secretarial help will often make it possible for him to give some time to research activities. The employment of additional staff to do research is not necessary in the typical school. Ambitious requests for new personnel are often a frightening prospect for the school board. Progress can be realized and research will be done if the current staff of a school will assume its rightful role as contributors to the research effort. Additional staff may be desirable, but the lack of it should not be an excuse for avoiding research.

Local districts are generally hard put to meet their financial demands and are not likely to budget much for research without some outside help. State funds are available for such purposes, and Federal funds are also being made available through the states and local district. This money might augment local funds, thus increasing the possibilities for greater research activity. Information about these sources is generally available in the state departments of education.

The purposes underlying local studies should be determined at least tentatively prior to initiating the studies. An attitude of doing research as an end in itself is not likely to be very productive. Immediate and long-term objectives should provide direction and structure for the activities. Improved programs, more satisfactory educational experiences, better personal adjustment by students, higher achievement, and greater maturity are some of the purposes of research. Other purposes were reviewed earlier in the chapter.

The time to be given to research is closely related to other problems discussed. The total guidance service should provide for an appropriate allotment of time to the various activities, of which research is just one. Since research activities are often interrelated with other ongoing activities, there may be no way or necessity to determine the exact amount of time being given to research. However, since research should not be neglected, it may be reasonable to devote about 15 percent of the total time allotted to the guidance effort. This may vary somewhat with local conditions, but a substantial amount of staff time should be given to research.

How to utilize findings and implement the results should not be difficult problems if these aspects of the guidance service are given due consideration prior to and during the actual research. The nature of the research undertaken and the problem to be explored should be determined somewhat specifically before initiating the research, so that possible procedures for the utilization and implementation of the results can receive attention while the study is in progress, with no time gap between the completion of the study and the application of the results. The specific techniques chosen for data application will depend upon the judgment and resourcefulness of the school staff. The stated objectives of the study will serve as guides in the implementation of program changes in keeping with research findings.

In the disposition of research findings it is important that they be properly recorded, with appropriate conclusions, since they provide the framework upon which action is taken. Also, studies undertaken and completed should be made available to other people through journals or other media. Some studies may be limited to local interest, in which case publishing facilities of the district may be used in reporting results. Some studies may also be relevant to state programs and should be reported accordingly. Certainly, research of value for a wide audience should be reported in a national journal. However, the motivation of much of the research within a district should be one of program improvement for local schools. Some researchers show more enthusiasm for the activities of the study than they do for reporting the findings. The latter should not be neglected if the investment of time and resources is to be justified.

Rather extensive involvement by a number of staff members in research activities has been suggested. The benefits to be gained from an application of the findings should also be widely shared. Presumably all research has as its ultimate goal a better educational offering for the student. It is quite possible, however, to lose sight of this objective and all but exclude the student from the picture. The student should benefit from study findings and should also have an active part in conducting the studies. His role should extend beyond serving as the subject or guinea pig. A mature student can make himself useful in many ways to the researcher. There are many students capable of doing library work, clerical tasks, interviewing, and simple statistics. This will permit the researcher to give more time and effort to the more technical aspects of the research and at the same time provide the student with valuable, practical experience. A drastic change is called for in the present attitudes and inhibitions of school personnel concerning the involvement of students in the research effort. The talents and abilities of students can indeed be utilized in many phases of research work, and this should be done with due regard for the welfare of the student and in a manner in keeping with his best interests.

The Guidance Worker as a Researcher

The guidance worker is a researcher by virtue of his training and commitment and by the very nature of his position. The general quality of the service and its effectiveness is determined to a degree by the nature and quality of the research effort. Most counselor preparation programs in university graduate schools provide at least the fundamentals of research for their students. The more demanding programs generally require a fairly high level of sophistication in research techniques, particularly at the doctorate level. The properly certified guidance worker is capable of conducting research, and in some cases he may be able to provide the necessary leadership for others.

Walker notes three reasons for the counselor's being able to do research: (1) the nature of his training, (2) the nature of his staff assignments, and (3) the demands of his position. He should be competent to do research. He is in an unusually excellent position to collect and organize useful information. His less rigidly defined time schedule allows the opportunity to do research.[10] Research, then, is one of the major responsibilities of the guidance worker. If he has a master's degree or its equivalent, he should have received at least a basic foundation for doing research. His own interests and resourcefulness should see him through from there.

The guidance service requires constant appraisal if it is to fulfill its function. The guidance personnel should make certain that the various services are subjected to careful scrutiny and that weaknesses are being identified and corrected. The guidance service also has an obligation to the total educational program. The unique contributions of the guidance service can be brought to bear on all other aspects of the education program.[11] It should be the intent of the researcher in the guidance program to give first consideration to

[10] Robert N. Walker, "Guidance Contributes to the School's Research Efforts," *High School Journal*, vol. 44, pp. 210-214, March, 1961.
[11] *Ibid.*, p. 212.

problems directly related to that program. However, there should be no fast lines of distinction between areas of educational activity. The research will have implications for one or more of these areas other than guidance. The guidance worker might also provide some leadership in the research effort in instruction or administration, or some other designated area. Improvement in the total educational program is the objective of research. A rigid observation of discrete lines between areas of service is unwise. Flexibility should enhance the research effort as the researcher seeks solutions to all important educational problems.

Sources of Information on Research

Excellent sources of research data are available in current publications. However, the fact that these publications are to be found in libraries and not immediately accessible to the worker is often a source of discouragement. At least a partial answer to this rests with the school, department, or college which might maintain subscriptions to a few of these periodicals and thus make at least a minimum of these sources known and available to the staff. Counselors, teachers, and professors might also receive some of these publications by virtue of their membership in professional organizations. A general sharing of these materials among various staff members is recommended. Since each publication has its unique characteristics, some care should be taken in making selections in order to realize the most help from their use. Some representative and highly recommended sources are given here.

The Review of Educational Research. This periodical is published by the American Educational Research Association of the National Education Association, Washington, D.C. It includes significant studies on guidance, counseling, and personnel services in its April issues every third year: 1966, 1963, 1960, and so forth. A school might make it a point to get copies of these particular issues if it does not have a regular subscription. However, it would be to a school's advantage to subscribe regularly to all the publications suggested here, since they provide equally valuable information for other areas of the educational program.

Professional journals of the American Personnel and Guidance Association (APGA). Every guidance worker should affiliate himself with this association. As a member he will receive a copy of the

Personnel and Guidance Journal each month.[12] Many of the articles in this journal are reports of research conducted by fellow workers. They provide possible answers to problems and serve as guides to other workers in conducting studies. There are also eight divisions of APGA, each of which publishes a journal for the benefit of its members.

The Journal of Counseling Psychology. Although relatively new, this journal has become very popular with counselors and clinicians. Its scholarly articles dealing with topics of current interest in counseling and its reports on research are written to appeal to both the practicing counseling psychologist and the beginning counselor. This journal should be accessible to counselors at all educational levels.[13] Many other journals are available, some of which should be made available to guidance personnel through regular subscriptions.

Government agencies under the U.S. Department of Health, Education, and Welfare, in Washington, D.C., also constitute sources of helpful information on research procedures. State departments of education likewise provide publications designed to aid the schools in their research efforts. State universities too have facilities for aiding schools in making studies of local interest. Consultants are generally available in these universities, and their services may be obtained for very little cost to the district. Expert assistance is usually accessible to a school if it will take some initiative in locating and requesting aid. Frequently the school can continue its research program with little or no additional aid once it has been given the necessary assistance to get under way

SUMMARY/

Evaluation is a vital part of the guidance program. It is through evaluation that weaknesses in the program are identified and needed improvements thus made possible. Objectives can be realized only as the services being offered are congruent with those objectives. Realistic aims are thus established and appropriate service provided as the needs of the school become evident to the staff. As an integral

[12] Application forms for membership may be obtained by writing to the American Personnel and Guidance Association, 1605 New Hampshire Ave., NW, Washington, D.C. 20009.

[13] Subscriptions may be obtained by writing to *Journal of Counseling Psychology,* 1945 North High Street, Columbus, Ohio 43210.

part of the guidance service, evaluation is an ongoing, long-term activity with neither a beginning nor an end. It works hand in hand with all elements of the guidance service, involving a careful consideration of problems and questions associated with each phase of the service. As solutions to the prevailing problems are found, the services are improved. This is accomplished with the proper use of available tools and procedures. Questionnaires, checklists, and interviews are all methods for obtaining needed information. Established evaluative criteria are available for an objective study of the guidance service.

The guidance service also has a concern for research, and staff members are encouraged to give a part of their time to conducting organized studies or research projects. Considerably more effort is currently being given to research than formerly, but the effort is still inadequate in terms of the growth of the guidance movement and the great number of unsolved problems.

Research has many purposes which must be fulfilled if the guidance service is to meet its responsibilities and fulfill its destiny. There is no shortcut to the accumulation of needed data or the solution of problems. Objectivity in an organized pursuit of problem resolution is essential. Both general and specific problems associated with research confront the school. Each problem should be handled in accordance with the needs and available resources of the particular district or school.

The guidance worker is a researcher by virtue of his training, experience, and commitment to his profession. His capabilities are appropriately utilized in research. He must be aware of the major sources of research data in periodicals and other publications. These sources should be made available through subscriptions and used by everyone interested and involved in the research effort.

PROBLEMS/

1 Explain why continuous evaluation is essential for maintaining a strong guidance service.

2 Account for the fact that evaluation is a neglected activity in many schools. Give some suggestions on how to overcome these deterrents to more effective evaluation.

3 The literature suggests that while there is still a scarcity of studies dealing with program development, there are also some encouraging signs. What are these?

4 Some schools initiate evaluation studies but with no stated reasons for doing so. Purposes or objectives should be essential elements in evaluation. What are the major purposes of evaluation?

5 Some specific points to consider in evaluating a program are given in the chapter. Of what advantage are these to a school as it evaluates its guidance program?

6 Discuss the advantages and disadvantages of the questionnaire as a research instrument.

7 Enumerate some principles, or guides, to follow in preparing and using a questionnaire.

8 What advantages does the checklist have over the questionnaire? Explain the circumstances which should help you decide whether to use a questionnaire or a checklist.

9 Point out the advantages of using established criteria for evaluating the guidance service rather than attempting evaluation without criteria.

10 Account for the fact that a counseling service at the university level is likely to be more involved in research than a counseling service in the elementary or secondary schools.

11 In the chapter some "purposes of research" are reviewed. What are some other such purposes?

12 Some formidable deterrents to research are lack of sufficient time, money, or resources, negative attitudes, and incompetent staff. Make some suggestions on how to overcome these deterrents.

13 The guidance person should perhaps be more involved in research than teachers. Why?

14 What journals should be accessible to the school as aids in the research effort?

Selected References

Textbooks
BERNARD, HAROLD W., C. EVAN JAMES, and FRANKLIN R. ZERAN: *Guidance Services in Elementary Schools*, Chartwell House, New York, 1954, chap. 14.
COTTINGHAM, HAROLD F.: *Guidance in Elementary Schools*, McKnight & McKnight Publishing Company, Bloomington, Ill., 1956, chap. 15.
FARWELL, GAIL F., and HERMAN J. PETERS: *Guidance Readings for Counselors*, Rand McNally & Company, Chicago, 1960, chap. 10.

FROEHLICH, CLIFFORD P.: *Guidance Services in Schools,* McGraw-Hill Book Company, New York, 1958, chap. 15.

HILL, GEORGE: *Management and Improvement of Guidance,* Appleton-Century-Crofts, Inc., New York, 1965, chap. 9.

HUMPHREYS, J. ANTHONY, ARTHUR E. TRAXLER, and ROBERT D. NORTH: *Guidance Services,* Science Research Associates, Inc., Chicago, 1960, chap. 11.

HUTSON, PERCIVAL W.: *The Guidance Function in Education,* Appleton-Century-Crofts, Inc., New York, 1958, chap. 19.

JONES, ARTHUR J.: *Principles of Guidance and Pupil Personnel Work,* 5th ed., McGraw-Hill Book Company, New York, 1963, chap. 15.

MARTINSON, RUTH A., and HARRY SMALLENBURG: *Guidance in Elementary Schools,* Prentice-Hall, Inc., Englewood Cliffs, N.J., 1958, chap. 15.

MC DANIEL, HENRY B.: *Guidance in the Modern School,* The Dryden Press, Inc., New York, 1956, chap. 16.

——— and others: *Readings in Guidance,* Holt, Rinehart and Winston, Inc., New York, 1959, chap. 14.

MILLER, FRANK W.: *Guidance Principles and Services,* Charles E. Merrill Books, Inc., Englewood Cliffs, N.J., 1961, chap. 8.

MORTENSEN, DONALD G., and ALLEN M. SCHMULLER: *Guidance in Today's Schools,* John Wiley & Sons, Inc., New York, 1959, chap. 15.

OHLSEN, MERLE M.: *Guidance Services in the Modern School,* Harcourt, Brace & World, Inc., New York, 1964, chap. 17.

ROTHNEY, JOHN W. M.: *Guidance Practices and Results,* Harper & Row, Publishers, Incorporated, New York, 1958, chap. 5.

SHERTZER, BRUCE, and HERMAN J. PETERS: *Guidance: Techniques for Individual Appraisal and Development,* The Macmillan Company, New York, 1965, chap. 19.

SMITH, GLENN D.: *Principles and Practices of the Guidance Program,* The Macmillan Company, New York, 1951, chap. 11.

STOOPS, EMERY, and GUNNAR L. WAHLQUIST: *Principles and Practices in Guidance,* McGraw-Hill Book Company, New York, 1958, chap. 14.

WILLEY, ROY DE VERL: *Guidance in Elementary Education,* Harper & Row, Publishers, Incorporated, New York, 1960, chap. 10.

——— and DEAN C. ANDREW: *Modern Methods and Techniques in Guidance,* Harper & Row, Publishers, Incorporated, New York, 1955, chap. 22.

Journals

AMEREDES, WILLIAM N.: "Students Evaluate the Guidance Program," *Ohio School,* vol. 41, pp. 16–17, January, 1963.

ANDERSON, ROBERT P., and GORDON V. ANDERSON: "Development of an Instrument for Measuring Rapport," *Personnel and Guidance Journal,* vol. 41, pp. 18–24, September, 1962.

ARBUCKLE, DUGALD S.: "Client-centered Therapy in Counseling Students with Behavior Problems," *Journal of Counseling Psychology,* vol. 8, no. 2, pp. 136–139, Summer, 1961.

CALLIS, ROBERT: "Counseling," *Review of Educational Research,* vol. 33, pp. 179–187, April, 1963.

CARLIN, LESLIE O.: "Negative Responses to Counseling," *Vocational Guidance Quarterly,* vol. 13, pp. 287–289, Summer, 1965.

CARNES, EARL F., and EUGENE B. DOUGHTIE: "The Appraisal Function," *Review of Educational Research*, vol. 36, no. 2, pp. 288-295, April, 1966.

CHENAULT, JOANN: "Research and the Monolithic Tradition," *Personnel and Guidance Journal*, vol. 44, pp. 6-10, September, 1965.

COTTLE, WILLIAM C.: "Evaluation of Guidance Services," *Review of Educational Research*, vol. 27, pp. 229-235, April, 1957.

DAUBNER, E. V.: "Classification of Problems in Counseling," *Catholic Education Review*, vol. 63, pp. 376-392, September, 1965.

DE LONG, A. R.: "Data Collection for Research in the Public Schools," *Educational Administration and Supervision*, vol. 46, pp. 1-4, January, 1960.

DEMOS, GEORGE D.: "Every Guidance Worker a Researcher," *Education*, vol. 85, pp. 242-244, December, 1964.

————: "Guidance and Research," *Education*, vol. 84, pp. 41-43, November, 1963.

FITZGERALD, PAUL W.: "Evaluation of a County Guidance Program," *Personnel and Guidance Journal*, vol. 39, pp. 507-509, February, 1961.

GOLDMAN, LEO: "Appraisal Function," *Review of Educational Research*, vol. 33, pp. 188-196, April, 1963.

————: "Guidance, Counseling, and Personnel Services," *Review of Educational Research*, vol. 33, pp. 139-226, April, 1963.

HAMILTON, CURTIS L.: "Self-evaluation Can Help Your Guidance Program," *Illinois Education*, vol. 51, p. 378, May, 1963.

HILL, GEORGE E.: "Elementary School Guidance: Criteria for Approval by State Departments of Education," *Counselor Education and Supervision*, vol. 2, pp. 137-143, Spring, 1963.

————: "Evaluation of Guidance Services," *Clearing House*, vol. 37, pp. 275-280, January, 1963.

HOYT, KENNETH B., and G. D. MOORE: "Group Procedures in Guidance and Personnel Work," *Review of Educational Research*, vol. 30, pp. 158-167, April, 1960.

ISAACSON, LEE: "Role of Research in Counselor Education," *Teachers College Journal*, vol. 35, p. 228, May, 1964.

KASPER, E. C.: "Student Perceptions of the Environment in Guidance and Non-guidance Schools," *Personnel and Guidance Journal*, vol. 43, pp. 674-677, March, 1965.

KRUEGER, ALBERT H.: "Counselor Holding Power: Clinical vs. Client-centered," *Personnel and Guidance Journal*, vol. 43, pp. 981-984, June, 1965.

METZLER, J. H.: "Evaluating Counseling and Guidance Programs: A Review of Literature 1946-62," *Vocational Guidance Quarterly*, vol. 12, pp. 285-289, Summer, 1964.

MILLER, C. H.: "Foundations: Concepts and Purposes," *Review of Educational Research*, vol. 33, pp. 146-148, April, 1963.

PETERS, HERMAN J., and W. J. MUELLER: "Counseling Function," *Review of Educational Research*, vol. 30, pp. 131-140, April, 1960.

PETERS, MILDRED: "Need for Careful Appraisal Evaluating the Guidance Program," *National Elementary Principal*, vol. 43, pp. 26-27, April, 1964.

RICCIO, ANTHONY C.: "Evaluation of Guidance Services," *Bulletin of the National Association of Secondary-school Principals*, vol. 46, pp. 99-108, November, 1962.

————: "New Dimensions," *Theory into Practice,* vol. 4, pp. 129–130, October, 1965.

RIPPEE, BILLY D., WILLIAM E. HANVEY, and CLYDE A. PARKER: "Influence of Counseling on the Perception of Counselor Role," *Personnel and Guidance Journal,* vol. 43, pp. 696–701, March, 1965.

ROTHNEY, JOHN W. M., and GAIL F. FARWELL: "Evaluation of Guidance and Personnel Services," *Review of Educational Research,* vol. 30, pp. 168–175, April, 1960.

SARAH, SISTER MARY: "Evaluation: Focus on Guidance," *Catholic School Journal,* vol. 66, p. 35, January, 1966.

SCHUTZ, R. E., and G. E. MAXER: "Factor Analysis of the Occupational Choice Motives of Counselors," *Journal of Counseling Psychology,* vol. 11, pp. 267–271, Fall, 1964.

SHAW, MERVILLE C.: "Research: Stepchild of School Guidance," *Journal of Counseling Psychology,* vol. 9, pp. 364–366, Winter, 1962.

SHOUKSMITH, GEORGE, and W. TAYLOR: "Effect of Counseling on the Achievement of High-ability Pupils," *British Journal of Educational Psychology,* vol. 34, pp. 51–57, February, 1964.

SLINGER, GEORGE E.: "Evaluating Professional Growth," *Vocational Guidance Quarterly,* vol. 11, pp. 247–253, Summer, 1963.

STABLEIN, JOHN E.: "Critique of Counseling Evaluation," *Personnel and Guidance Journal,* vol. 41, pp. 66–68, September, 1962.

STEFFLRE, BUFORD: "Research in Guidance: Horizons for the Future," *Theory into Practice,* vol. 2, pp. 44–50, February, 1963.

STILLER, ALFRED: "School Guidance Needs Research," *Personnel and Guidance Journal,* vol. 41, pp. 798–802, May, 1963.

STOUGHTON, ROBERT W.: "The Preparation of Counselors and Personnel Workers," *Review of Educational Research,* vol. 37, pp. 174–182, April, 1957.

STROWIG, R. WRAY, and GAIL F. FARWELL: "Programmatic Research," *Review of Educational Research,* vol. 36, no. 2, pp. 327–333, April, 1966.

WALKER, ROBERT N.: "Guidance Contributes to the School's Research Efforts," *High School Journal,* vol. 44, pp. 210–214, March, 1961.

WAETJEN, WALTER B.: "Pupil Personnel Work: A Prospectus for Research," *Personnel and Guidance Journal,* vol. 42, pp. 97–98, September, 1963.

———— and J. K. FISHER: "Needed Research in Pupil Personnel Services," *Educational Leadership,* vol. 21, pp. 21–29, October, 1963.

WHETSTONE, BOBBY D.: "Personality Differences between Selected Counselors and Effective Teachers," *Personnel and Guidance Journal,* vol. 43, pp. 886–890, May, 1965.

SEVENTEEN

/PROBLEMS, ISSUES, AND DEVELOPMENTS

The total program of education has had and is continuing to have problems as it endeavors to meet the needs of the young people within its charge. This is inevitable in view of the rapidity with which changes are occurring and scientific advancements are being made. The guidance program of the school is no exception; it is constantly beset with problems. In some cases these problems are peculiar to guidance while other phases of the educational program appear to be immune. Generally, however, the total educational program is involved, and existing problems evoke some degree of concern from everyone.

Three statements can be made at the outset concerning the topics to be discussed in this chapter:

1 Although the problems are found in many schools, they still have to be dealt with locally according to their severity and the nature of the local conditions. What constitutes a serious problem in one commun-

ity may cause little or no concern in a neighboring school.

2   There is a concomitant change in problems with the advancements occurring in the society and even within the immediate community. Rather noticeable and challenging problems of today may no longer exist five years from now—having been resolved or simply having vanished as improvements were made.

3   Problems, issues, and developments are so closely related that an attempt at separating them may be unwise—perhaps even impossible, since a problem may become a development or a trend as it is resolved and as new insights are gained.

In this discussion it is assumed that there are no permanent hard-and-fast lines of distinction between problems and issues and between trends and developments. Certain areas have been identified in this chapter because of their relevance to the guidance movement. Some existing problems are noted, and trends and developments are in some cases identified and in other cases implied. The omission of other issues that are equally vital is both inevitable and desirable within the space limitations of one chapter.

Administrative Phases of the Guidance Service

Administrative leadership, support, and initiative are vital to the success of the guidance service. The attitude that the guidance service fulfills vital needs in the lives of students must prevail. Sound administrative policies and procedures are also essential to the service.

Representative Problems for Local Consideration

Since certain problems and issues are common, each school and district must initially consider the most urgent local problems in terms of national trends and developments. Brief reference is made in the following paragraphs to some representative issues, most of which are matters of concern to many schools.

Effective communication must be maintained. This involves a free flow of ideas between the administration and the staff, keeping everyone informed on developments. Communication procedures must be kept clear, precise, and understandable, and efficient, economical methods must be employed.

Adequate budgets constitute problems of concern to many schools. This being the case, careful planning must precede the formulation of budget requests, and an attitude of economy must prevail in making effective use of all resources. Sources of funds should be known and intelligently utilized, and proper allocations made to the various services within the program.

The scope of the guidance service—how extensive and inclusive it should be—must be determined. The relationship of the guidance service to other areas of the educational program must be defined and some agreement reached as to how these various services can aid each other. This problem becomes less formidable as school people become better informed.

The effect of school-district reorganization has been felt but not always understood or properly utilized. Adjustments in the program should be made and new and better opportunities for a strengthening of the guidance service capitalized upon as larger administrative units, more personnel, and better facilities become available.

A cooperative, dedicated staff may be the aim of many schools, but it is often difficult to achieve. How to establish a high level of cooperative spirit and effort has many related questions but few precise answers. Strong leadership is at least a partial answer. This combined with a plan for the employment and retention of only highly competent and professionally dedicated staff should reduce the problem to a minimum.

Setting aside adequate time in the school schedule for guidance activities is not easily done. Decisions must be made as to the amount of time needed, how these activities can be accommodated without neglecting other activities, and how the efficiency of time utilization can be improved throughout the program.

The separation of counseling and discipline is only one of several problems which depend upon the philosophy of the school and the competence of the staff for their answers. An understanding of the concept that the counselor works with all kinds of youngsters with a variety of problems in an attempt to aid them in their development should serve as one answer to this and to related problems. Misunderstandings can be avoided and program effectiveness improved through professional competence and understanding gained from appropriate study and adequate preparation for one's duties.

To what extent secretarial and clerical assistance is needed constitutes another problem area. A separation must be made between tasks to be performed by the professionally trained person and those to be handled by other types of workers. Efficiency and effectiveness in operation of the program are, of course, the major considerations.

Representative Problems at the National Level

The number and breadth of the problems and issues receiving national attention and their implications are staggering. Wrenn, in a chapter called "New Directions in American Society,"[1] identifies seven major problems and trends that affect the guidance service:

1 The pressure of population
2 Jobs in the future
3 The changing family
4 Living together in metropolis
5 The growth in wealth
6 The impact of Federal government
7 The world next door

Obviously, it is not the guidance service alone that is affected by these trends, but they have some significant implications for this service.

Stefflre[2] adds other issues briefly summarized here:

1 The kinds of people needed to do the counseling—their professional and personal competences
2 The number of counselors needed—total number of counselors and counselor-student ratio
3 The work of the counselor—the nature of his work with students and staff

Problems of the organization and administration of the guidance service include such questions as what to call the special services; for example, the term "pupil personnel services" is becoming more common. Naming the services becomes more of a problem, as school districts increase in size and as service teams are added to the staff.[3] The autonomy of the principal in respect to guidance

[1] C. Gilbert Wrenn, *The Counselor in a Changing World*, American Personnel and Guidance Association, Washington, D.C., 1962, chap. 2.

[2] Buford Stefflre, "Issues in School Guidance: Varying Perceptions of Administrators, Counselors, and Counselor Educators," *Teachers College Journal*, vol. 36, no. 5, pp. 195–200, March, 1965.

[3] Richard P. Koeppe and John F. Bancroft, "Elementary and Secondary School Programs," *Review of Educational Research*, vol. 36, no. 2, p. 219, April, 1966.

services is another issue, with some question as to the division of responsibility between the principal and the guidance personnel, some support being given to the concept that the responsibilities of the guidance service rest with the chief guidance officer.[4]

The issue of the establishment and maintenance of sound public relations is also a matter for concern. Public interest and support are essential to the program's success and are achieved through planning and effort, not by chance.

An allied problem is one of the ethics to be observed by all professional people. This problem is met by having well-trained, highly competent members on the staff who understand their work, recognize their obligations, and observe high standards of practice.

Further consideration is given to related issues in the topics that follow. Many of these issues are also covered under other major topics.

Federal Aid and Guidance

Programs of Federal aid to education that have been in operation for many years have to some degree indirectly influenced the guidance movement at all educational levels. Problems arise and issues demand attention as legislative enactments that help to solve problems at the same time create new ones. Many school districts welcome sources of new revenue but resist controls or coercion associated with Federal aid programs. Irrespective of personal or political beliefs as to the role of the Federal government in education, the fact remains that its involvement in education has increased tremendously, and current indications are that this will continue.[5]

The National Defense Education Act of 1958

This act was at least partly prompted by the concern of the Congress of the United States for the security and welfare of the nation. It was felt that there was a need to provide better educational opportunities for the youth of the country in terms of requirements and expectations of the society. Students were not realizing their full potential, and young people were not being adequately prepared for

---

[4] *Ibid.*

[5] For some revealing facts and figures see Galen Saylor, "The Federal Colossus in Education: Threat or Promise?" *Educational Leadership*, vol. 23, no. 1, pp. 7–14, October, 1965.

positions of leadership in a nation that requires a highly skilled and technologically well-informed citizenry for its survival and advancement. It was the intent of this act to identify and more adequately provide for the talented youth of the country.

Title V of the National Defense Education Act provides, among other things, for the training of counselors to serve in the schools. The number of NDEA institutes organized and conducted for this purpose by universities has been on the increase since the original enactment, and the act has been extended and broadened. A notable change, for example, was one which included elementary schools, public junior colleges, and public technical institutes for eligibility under the act. This makes possible the training of counselors to serve in these schools as well as in the secondary schools. Summer and year-long institutes sponsored under this act and conducted in a number of universities have contributed markedly to the supply of counselors. Guidance programs have been benefited by these institutes, and the general quality of many programs has been improved.

Some Problems and Issues

With increasing involvement by the Federal government in education have come additional problems and indications of concern on the part of school people and the public. For example, the ultimate purpose of the National Defense Education Act is not always well understood. The nature and extent of Federal participation in the promotion of guidance programs is still a matter of interest and concern.

Federal funds are available to school districts for the development of their guidance services, but with certain conditions and stipulations. These conditions may be interpreted as controls and may therefore evoke resistance from some schools. Just how well the objectives of the act are being realized is not known to the satisfaction of the schools or the government agencies. The amounts of money to be dispensed to school districts and the soundness of the criteria used for these allocations are still sources of concern. What are the prerogatives of the schools and of the government agencies under aid programs such as NDEA? For the sake of efficiency, harmony on major issues must prevail.

The identification and education of the talent of the nation were objectives of the original act; as one statement [6] suggests, "We

[6] National Defense Education Act of 1958, Public Law 85–864.

must increase our efforts to identify and educate more of the talent of our Nation." The possibilities for misunderstandings and differences in interpretations are obvious. The need for sound criteria by which the gifted can be identified becomes evident. The nature of the educational experiences to be provided for these students may also be a controversial issue. Any suggestion that one child is to receive preferential treatment over another by virtue of his superior academic endowment is open to immediate attack. The principle to be kept in mind in attempting to resolve these problems is that each student is a responsibility of the guidance service and that each should be assisted in terms of his needs.

These and many other problems challenge the educational leaders of the schools and are likewise concerns of government officials with responsibilities for the improvement of education. The list of problems and issues is growing and will continue to do so as new legislation is enacted and as efforts are made to meet the challenges of innovation and change.

Changing Educational Emphases

There is support for the belief that the whole structure of the democratic society is undergoing gradual change. Therefore, appropriate adjustments by the populace to these changes are called for, and significant modifications must be made in the educational program in keeping with the demands and expectations of the times. Modern education must, for example, prepare a substantial number of people for service in a highly technical and complex society. It must also provide appropriate educational experiences for all its young citizens in anticipation of considerable involvement in civic and government affairs as well as dedication to a vocation or career. The traditional "three R's" are no longer adequate. Much more than basic academic competence is necessary. Time is precious and must be utilized intelligently to develop the potentialities of young people and to make certain that each young person is adequately equipped to live successfully and dynamically in his world.

These changes are not limited to areas of technology; they also encompass attitudes, morals, and value systems. How well prepared is the typical high school or college graduate to meet and successfully resolve the problems and issues confronting him personally, his community, and his nation? This question no doubt nags the conscience of every sincere educator. The lag between technological and social advancements and the ability of the people to apply new knowledge intelligently is often formidable. Educational procedures generally fail to reflect to any high degree recently acquired knowledge and truths. This takes time, but it should and must take considerably less time than has been typically the case. The waiting can be too costly in terms of lost human resources.

Education for dynamic leadership thus becomes the goal, and the full development of the creative capabilities of all students becomes a realistic objective through which that goal might be achieved. The lockstep procedures of the past have no place in the modern educational scheme, and mediocrity is to be avoided even with the less gifted.

Creativity in the Modern School

Among the responsibilities of the school is that of recognizing students with special talents and capabilities and assessing the aptitudes of all students for purposes of proper training and appropriate placement. For school counselors this is a challenge, and they are meeting it with enthusiasm and dedication.

Research in creativity helps to focus attention upon this critical area of education and can provide possible answers to hitherto unanswered problems.[7] The guidance service, by utilizing appraisal instruments and techniques, assesses the capabilities and potentialities of students. Through these and other activities the guidance service encourages youngsters to explore new ideas, to experiment, and to extend themselves beyond the minimum expectations of a teacher or a class. If creativity can indeed be taught,[8] the possibilities for the development of the creative powers of each child within an educational setting characterized by cooperative effort between teacher and counselor are virtually without limit.

The research and contributions of several leaders in this field are gaining widespread attention, and there is an increasing awareness as to the tremendous significance the concept of creativity has for the future of education and for the welfare of the nation.[9] The pioneering efforts of the people currently engaged in seeking truths about creativity are yielding results in the form of a rapidly expanding interest in it.

[7] Earl F. Carnes and Eugene B. Doughtie, "The Appraisal Function," *Review of Educational Research,* vol. 36, no. 2, pp. 289–290, April, 1966.

[8] H. J. Hallman, "Can Creativity Be Taught?" *Education Theory,* vol. 14, pp. 15–23, January, 1964.

[9] Some leading contributors are Joy P. Guilford, Calvin W. Taylor, and E. Paul Torrance. There are many others.

Educational Excellence as a Goal

A more economical and intelligent utilization of the resources of the community and nation to promote greater educational excellence for each student is an immediate goal of education. The ultimate goal is a well-informed, highly trained, skillful, competent citizen and worker. Resources, then, are provided by the school, capitalized upon and exploited by students and the school staff, and made serviceable in the lives of the students who are seeking an education and appropriate preparation for a profession or vocation.

Such excellence is to be realized only as each student is carefully studied and as he is properly stimulated and guided in the use of his capabilities and in the development of his potentialities. Only a well-organized, carefully structured school program can achieve this end. The challenges to the guidance service, to instruction, and to the administration are well established. How well they are met depends upon the quality of the leadership and the staff of a school and upon the community that supports it.

Education for a Vocation

Education has charge of providing experiences which will help to prepare young people for adulthood in a highly competitive society with an ever-increasing emphasis upon automation and technology. Just what this program should include and the nature of the experiences to be provided are questions of considerable concern and controversy. This is particularly true in terms of rapid advancements, technological and scientific innovations in the world of work, and man's changing concepts about how much of himself he should commit to earning a living. The percentage of the female population currently employed and the percentage anticipated for the future are also important factors.

Since many students are not academically suited for the typical college program, the responsibility for preparing these people for vocations rests with the high schools and the trade and technical schools, and to a degree with the community or junior college. Some universities are also realistically assuming this responsibility by including divisions of trade and technical training in their offerings.

The fact that many of the jobs of the future are not currently in existence complicates the attempt to prepare young people for a vocation. It suggests the importance of stressing basic knowledge which can be extended to include information and skills needed on a job. Adaptability is an essential requirement in this respect, as workers will need to make rapid adjustments to new conditions, different tools and products, and even personality changes within themselves and in coworkers.

Research provides not only important information about the world of work but also some revealing information about personal and psychological factors associated with vocation selection and success within a chosen field.[10] The personal and psychological factors are of major importance in vocational choice. This has tremendous implications for the school and particularly the guidance service. There are, indeed, as Hoyt suggests, some challenges for guidance in vocational education.[11] The counselor is just as concerned about the student who plans, or should be planning, to enter some type of vocational training as he is about the student with aspirations toward one of the professions.

The Counselor—His Work and Preparation

The quality of the guidance service is determined to a considerable degree by the competence of the guidance people providing the leadership and conducting the activities of that service. This suggests the need for some sound criteria by which competence can be assessed, and it also implies the establishment and use of standards in admitting people to counselor training programs. Appropriate standards are also needed in the issuance of counseling certificates to candidates.

Although a final statement of what constitutes high-level competence for the counselor has not yet been developed, three areas are generally emphasized in considering competence and apparent readiness to function as a professionally qualified counselor: personal qualities and characteristics, experience, and educational preparation. Understanding and agreement as to what constitutes counselor proficiency can be achieved only if there is consensus as to the nature of the tasks to be performed by the counselor. This agreement then makes it possible to develop appropriate educational programs for counselors.

[10] Philip A. Perone, "Vocational Development," *Review of Educational Research,* vol. 36, no. 2, pp. 298–305, April, 1966.

[11] Kenneth B. Hoyt, "New Challenges for Guidance in Vocational Education," *Bulletin of the National Association of Secondary-school Principals,* vol. 49, pp. 131–141, May, 1965.

Counselor Functions

Progress is being made toward greater specialization for the counselor. With better training programs the counselor is emerging with skills, competences, and understandings not possessed by the counselor of the past. He is no less active than his predecessor, but his functions are more specialized and more in keeping with the dignity of the profession. Although to some extent problems in these matters persist, the counselor in today's school is less likely to find himself involved in the performance of routine clerical and administrative functions and therefore is able to give more time and energy to his work as a counselor.

The functions of the counselor are becoming quite well established and accepted. As his responsibilities have become more clearly defined, he has been able to provide the school with better services, and his relationship with students has improved.

In addition to his leadership functions, Wrenn suggests that the counselor has four direct responsibilities: [12] "(*a*) Counseling with students . . . (*b*) consulting with staff and parents . . . (*c*) studying changes in the character of the student population and making a continuing interpretation of this information . . . (*d*) performing a liaison function between other school and community counseling resources and facilitating their use by teachers and students." The counselor in the modern school, then, is not only a counselor to students but also a consultant, a researcher and observer, and a coordinator of guidance functions. Any activity outside these categories belongs more appropriately with other staff members.

A review of at least some of the recent research suggests that progress is being made in refining the role of the counselor.[13] Although confusion has existed as to the functions of the counselor, studies dealing with this and related problems are continuing, and divisions of the American Personnel and Guidance Association have taken on the herculean task of determining the counselor's role and of establishing standards for his preparation.[14]

[12] Wrenn, *op. cit.*, p. 141.

[13] William L. Cash, Jr., and Paul F. Munger, "Counselors and Their Preparation," *Review of Educational Research*, vol. 36, no. 2, p. 256, April, 1966.

[14] One of several excellent reports on the work of the counselor is John W. Loughary, Robert O. Stripling, and Paul W. Fitzgerald (eds.), *Counseling: A Growing Profession*, joint publication of the Associations for Counselor Education and Supervision and the American School Counselors Association,

Counselor Competences

A problem closely related to counselor functions and counselor preparation is one of competences. What traits, characteristics, and qualities should the counselor possess? How can these be assessed in the person aspiring to be a counselor? Can these traits, once they are identified, be taught? These and other problems have received and will continue to receive attention through research and in university counselor preparation programs. An example of a related problem is whether or not the counselor should be certified as a teacher and have teaching experience. Controversy and disagreement on these issues exist among school people, but progress is being made toward their resolution, and satisfactory solutions are emerging.

Since considerable emphasis is being given to the concept that the counselor's abilities, characteristics, and qualities are of major importance, it may [15] be well to consider how best to select people for counselor training and counseling positions who possess these characteristics or who have the potential for their development. If it is true that "the counselor as a person is the most important factor in counseling," [16] then appropriate action might be taken to promote greater self-understanding by people selected for counselor training.

Counselor Preparation

Through the work of the American Personnel and Guidance Association with its divisions of ACES and ASCA considerable progress is being realized in the development of standards for the preparation of counselors. Courses are designated and blocks of time recommended to training institutions.[17] Considerable research, particularly on subjects enrolled in NDEA counselor training institutes, also provides possible answers to many persistent, critical problems.[18]

Divisions of the American Personnel and Guidance Association, Washington, D.C., 1965. Also see Calvin J. Daane and C. Patrick McGreevy, "The Counseling Process and Function," *Review of Educational Research*, vol. 36, no. 2, pp. 264–271, April, 1966.

[15] Cash and Munger, *op. cit.*, p. 257.

[16] Wrenn, *op. cit.*, p. 168.

[17] *Ibid.*, pp. 167–168; and George E. Hill, *Management and Improvement of Guidance*, Appleton-Century-Crofts, Inc., New York, 1965, pp. 386–405. Copies of these standards are also available from ACES and ASCA.

[18] Cash and Munger, *op. cit.*, pp. 259–261.

Although complete agreement has not been reached on what the nature of counselor preparation programs should be, considerably more is known about the problems, and action is being taken in terms of this increasing knowledge.

Other Issues and Developments concerning the Counselor

The issues and developments concerning the training and the work of the school counselor are too far-reaching to permit more than a brief, cursory reference in this presentation to a few of the pressing issues. Most of these issues are centered upon the kinds of people to be admitted to counselor education, the nature of the work to be performed by the counselor, the kinds of professional experience the counselor should have, the nature and extent of experiences to be provided by universities in the preparation of counselors, the length and quality of counselor preparation programs, and appropriate placement procedures in terms of school needs and counselor competence. Many of the other problems, issues, and developments are closely related to these.[19]

Counselors in Elementary Schools

Since the concept of a counselor for the elementary school is rather generally accepted by school people, in this section attention is given to some trends and developments in, and to specific problems associated with, organized guidance services in the elementary school. The idea has had its advocates for a long time, but conditions apparently have not been sufficiently favorable to result in its receiving adequate support. The initiation of organized services within the elementary school is definitely a current development, and the prospects for the future in terms of financial support from the district, the state, and the Federal government are encouraging.

The Work of the Elementary School Counselor

With an acceptance of the idea that there is a need for counselors in the elementary school has come the problem of determining just what his function is to be. Since the problem has not been researched sufficiently to justify any strong conclusion, dependence

[19] Hill, *op. cit.*, pp. 406–418, identifies and discusses in some detail and depth eight problems.

upon the judgments of the best-qualified people has been inevitable. Although much of his work is similar to that of the secondary school counselor, there are some differences. One of the problems is to determine just what these differences are and then to proceed accordingly to identify what appear to be the major functions of the counselor in the elementary school.

A review of some of the stronger studies dealing with this problem [20] suggests the following conclusions: (1) there is some general agreement as to the nature of the work this person is to perform; (2) some school people see the counselor as one who spends most of his time working directly with the teacher, while others regard him as a highly trained specialist providing considerable help for individual students; (3) progress is being made toward a common understanding of just how the counselor's functions should be carried on. From the research and other information currently available the following statements may serve as guides in furthering the development of guidance services for the elementary schools.

The concept of developmental guidance is emphasized in the elementary school. This concept suggests that these services should be available to all pupils and that the total development of each child is a major concern of this service. The counselor is to work closely with the teacher in an effort to improve the learning and living environment of each child. Parents are important figures in the scheme, and the counselor consults with them and advises them on appropriate procedures for assisting a child.

The counselor is a very busy person and therefore finds it advantageous to work with small groups of children in planning sessions and in the resolution of problems. The teacher too may direct some group activities. Some individual counseling, therapy, or remedial work are to be performed by the counselor. However, he may spend less time in these activities than his counterpart at the secondary level and proportionately more time with the teacher. Another of his functions may be summarized as providing a variety of experiences for youngsters from which growth is realized. Most of these are conducted in cooperation with the teacher in the classroom and are designed to promote the learning and the adjustment of each child. He is also the coordinator of the various services and activities of the guidance program.

[20] Richard P. Koeppe and John Bancroft, "Elementary and Secondary School Programs," *Review of Educational Research*, vol. 36, no. 2, pp. 225–226, April, 1966.

The Preparation of the Elementary School Counselor

Training programs for the elementary school counselor can be developed and strengthened as knowledge is gained about his functions and responsibilities. Each state has its particular requirements for the certification of counselors, but these have generally been designed to certify the counselor for the secondary school. Currently, however, there has been an attempt to provide for the certification of counselors for elementary schools. In one arrangement certification is given to those who hold or are eligible for the elementary school teaching certificate and who have taken essentially the same counselor-certification courses as the secondary school counselor.

A representative study suggests that although there has been support for the idea that the training programs for the elementary school counselor should be somewhat different from those for secondary school counselors, this has not been true in practice.[21] This is understandable, since there is generally a lag between what the leaders of a movement regard as desirable and what is taking place. Time is needed to put these ideas and beliefs into practice. A more recent and intensive study provides some encouraging data in terms of progress in the development of training programs for elementary school counselors and in making distinctions between the nature of the training provided for secondary school counselors and for elementary school counselors.[22] Additional studies anticipated for the immediate future should provide more data which may serve as guides in developing training programs and in informing the elementary schools on what they can expect in services from the elementary school counselor. Among the many decisions reached should be one concerning the title to be given to this person. "Child guidance specialist," "child development specialist," or "child guidance consultant" may be more appropriate terms than "counselor."

In the meantime aid is being provided through research, and intensive consideration is being given to these problems by guidance leaders. The matter of preparation has received careful attention, including the place of internship and practicum experiences.[23] As

[21] George E. Hill and Dale F. Nitzschke, "Preparation Programs in Elementary School Guidance," *Personnel and Guidance Journal,* vol. 40, pp. 155–159, October, 1961.

[22] Dale F. Nitzschke and George E. Hill, *The Elementary School Counselor: Preparation and Functions,* Ohio University Center for Educational Research and Service, Athens, Ohio, 1964.

[23] Dale F. Nitzschke, "Preparation Programs in Elementary School Guidance," *Personnel and Guidance Journal,* vol. 43, no. 8, pp. 751–756, April 1965; Bill Raines, "An Approach to Practicum for the Elementary School Counselor," *Personnel and Guidance Journal,* vol. 43, no. 1, pp. 57–59, September, 1964.

ideas are consolidated and integrated, rapid progress in the development of elementary school guidance programs throughout the country may be expected.

Aids and Innovations—Technological Developments

No one book on guidance and counseling services as a whole can do justice to this topic. The few pages devoted to these important subjects in this chapter can do little more than note that significant gains are being realized in the development of tools, machines, and programs designed to facilitate the learning process and to alert the reader to the tremendous implications these developments have for the future. Automation, mechanization, and programming all have implications for the counselor. Considerable experimentation characterizes the educational program of the modern school, as new and better ways are devised for facilitating pupil learning and pupil adjustment.

The programming of materials, the use of IBM equipment for storing and providing important data, and the many types of audio-visual aids are all receiving considerable attention. The counselor is concerned and involved because of his commitment to the learning process and because he is interested in any proved tool or procedure that will enhance his relationship and improve his effectiveness with students.

Wrenn suggests four "changing procedures within the school." Two of these deal with the use of television, radio, and films and with programmed instruction.[24] Considerable evidence is available to show the rapid increase in the use of these new aids. The challenge to the guidance service is a formidable one if these innovations are to be properly evaluated and intelligently utilized.

Programming as a Guidance Tool

Although the programming of materials has concentrated primarily upon instruction, there is no reason for its being limited to instruction. It lends itself very well to the guidance function for some good reasons: (1) programming is designed to accommodate the individual student; (2) some guidance functions are largely clerical and can thus be handled with mechanical devices; (3) the demands on the counselor's time are such as to necessitate the use of various

[24] Wrenn, *op. cit.*, pp. 88–90.

tools to facilitate his work; (4) as articulation between the guidance service and the classroom is strengthened, the possibilities for co-operating and sharing in the uses of appropriate educational devices are also increased.

Filep suggests three areas of use for individualized learning devices: (1) as support or adjunct to the work of the classroom teacher, (2) as a means of conveying occupational and college-admissions information, and (3) as a help to the student in developing search or problem-solving techniques applicable to self-discovery or other complex problem-solving tasks.[25] Many other uses are possible, and the counselor in the schools today may well anticipate their extension in the near future.

Data Processing as an Aid to the Counselor

At least two conditions augur well for counseling: (1) better-qualified people entering the counseling field and (2) the development of laborsaving devices which will free the counselor to engage in professional activities for which he was trained. The use of data processing has increased tremendously in many areas of education, including student personnel services. Reports on the research being done in an effort to develop and refine methods for the use of data processing to facilitate guidance services further are very encouraging.[26] Relieving the counselor of routine clerical tasks is one of the objectives of data processing.[27] Conceivably, a number of other uses will be found for data-processing procedures as the counseling function gains in the importance given to it and as its various specialties are extended and given greater depth.

A Variety of Audio-visual Aids

As with many other teaching media, the use of a number of audio-visual aids is increasing markedly, their benefits are being demonstrated, and their use in the guidance service is being extended. Tape recorders and film projectors have a most important part to play in the training of counselors and in the work of the practicing counselor, as well. Charts, graphs, and other related media are also useful to the counselor.

[25] Robert T. Filep, "Programming: A Three-pronged Counseling Tool," *Audio-visual Instruction,* vol. 8, no. 1, pp. 36–39, January, 1963.
[26] Koeppe and Bancroft, *op. cit.,* pp. 221–222.
[27] Alvin Grossman and Robert Howe, "Human Economy and Data Processing," *Personnel and Guidance Journal,* vol. 43, pp. 343–347, December, 1964.

A more resourceful counselor better prepared to utilize the tools available to him intelligently and a more creative counselor with the imagination to develop some additional tools are anticipated in the future. Counselors are better prepared than ever for their work, and this preparation is likely to continue to improve in the years ahead.

The future for guidance is indeed bright. Significant progress is being made in overcoming hampering elements and outright resistance. Awareness of the need for, and importance of, the guidance service as an integral part of the educational program of every school is gradually becoming a reality. The dedication of many fine counselors and teachers who have not lost hope and the interest and support of a concerned public are all contributing to the growth and strength of the guidance movement.

SUMMARY/

The guidance movement has had its share of problems as efforts have been made to make the guidance service an integral part of the educational process. Issues develop as an inevitable concomitant to problems and to progress. As issues are met, debated, and resolved, progress is realized. It is from these differing views that stronger programs of services are evolving. Dissent and discussion are contributing to progress.

The total guidance service depends upon the administrative leadership of the school for its ultimate strength and worth. A number of the problems and issues of the guidance service are of an administrative nature, and they depend upon local conditions for their solution. Broader problems with implications at the national as well as the local level also persist.

An issue with tremendous ramifications is that of Federal aid. Many programs of Federal participation in education exist, and they are on the increase. The National Defense Education Act of 1958 has had tremendous impact upon the guidance movement. Financial assistance to schools and universities has resulted in stronger guidance programs in the schools and improved counselor preparation programs in universities.

The emphases in education are changing as new information and research findings become available. The promotion of the creative capabilities of youngsters and the stimulation of each student toward educational excellence are receiving attention. Appropriate educational experiences for each student as preludes to later vocational or professional choices are also matters of concern.

The work of the counselor, his competences, his preparation, and related problems are matters of considerable concern to the counselors themselves and to all dedicated school personnel. There is considerable support for having counselors in the elementary schools, and significant progress is being made toward this end.

The innovations of programming, data processing, and the utilization of a variety of audio-visual aids are having an impact upon guidance. Procedures are being developed for the intelligent utilization of these aids in making the counselor's work more professional and more effective.

PROBLEMS/

1   Make some recommendations that might prove useful to a school staff in dealing with the issues and problems associated with the initiation and development of the guidance service.

2   The chapter identifies some representative problems of an administrative nature at both the local and national levels. Name some additional problems of perhaps equal importance.

3   Why is the matter of Federal aid such an important issue at this time?

4   In what ways has the National Defense Education Act aided the guidance movement? What recommendations can you make for changes in this act?

5   Explain why the counselor has an interest in the creativity of students. What are some of the implications of creativity for the guidance service?

6   Describe the responsibility of the school in aiding students toward the selection of a vocation.

7   Explain the relationship between the work of the counselor and the university program of counselor education. How well are the two generally integrated?

8   Identify some of the major sources of information and guidelines on the preparation of counselors.

9   Why is it necessary that special attention be given to the problem of what constitutes an appropriate training program for elementary school counselors?

10 Identify the major developments and innovations in educational tools and practices which will have the greatest impact upon the counselor and his work.

Selected References

Textbooks

BARRY, RUTH, and BEVERLY BARRY: *Modern Issues in Guidance: Personnel Work*, Bureau of Publications, Teachers College, Columbia University, New York, 1957, chap. 15.

JOHNSON, WALTER F., BUFORD STEFFLRE, and ROY EDELFELT: *Pupil Personnel and Guidance Services*, McGraw-Hill Book Company, New York, 1961, chap. 18.

TRAXLER, ARTHUR E., and ROBERT D. NORTH: *Techniques of Guidance*, Harper & Row, Publishers, Incorporated, New York, 1966, chap. 22.

Journals

ARBUCKLE, DUGALD S.: "The Education of the School Counselor," *Journal of Counseling Psychology*, vol. 5, Spring, 1958.

BARCLAY, J. R.: "Attack on Testing and Counseling: An Examination and Reappraisal," *Personnel and Guidance Journal*, vol. 43, pp. 715–716, 1046–1048, March, June, 1965.

BELANGER, LAURENCE L.: "Guidance Trends in High School," *California Education*, vol. 1, November, 1963.

———: "NEDA Adds 300 Guidance Personnel to California High Schools," *California Education*, vol. 1, no. 2, p. 23, October, 1963.

———: "Surge toward Excellence: The Impact of Title V in California," *Journal of Secondary Education*, vol. 36, pp. 500–506, December, 1961.

BLOCHER, DONALD H.: "Issues in Counseling: Elusive and Illusional," *Personnel and Guidance Journal*, vol. 43, pp. 796–800, April, 1965.

BOY, ANGELO V., and A. H. KRUEGER: "Counselor Holding Power: Clinician vs. Client-centered with Comment," *Personnel and Guidance Journal*, vol. 43, pp. 981–985, June, 1965.

CAMPBELL, DAVID P.: "Achievement of Counseled and Non-counseled Students Twenty-five Years after Counseling," *Journal of Counseling Psychology*, vol. 12, pp. 287–293, Fall, 1965.

CASH, WILLIAM L., JR., and PAUL F. MUNGER: "Counselors and Their Preparation," *Review of Educational Research*, vol. 36, no. 2, pp. 256–261, April, 1966.

CATTELL, RAYMOND B.: "Some Deeper Significances of the Computer for the Practicing Psychologist," *Personnel and Guidance Journal*, vol. 44, pp. 160–166, October, 1965.

COOLEY, WILLIAM W.: "A Computer-measurement System for Guidance," *Harvard Educational Review*, vol. 34, pp. 559–572, Fall, 1964.

COTTINGHAM, HAROLD F.: "National Level Projection for Elementary School Guidance," *Personnel and Guidance Journal*, vol. 44, pp. 499–502, January, 1966.

CRITES, JOHN O.: "Research Frontier: The Vocational Development Project at the University of Iowa," *Journal of Counseling Psychology*, vol. 12, pp. 81–86, Spring, 1965.

DE MILLE, RICHARD: "The Creativity Boom," *Teachers College Record*, vol. 65, pp. 199–208, December, 1963.

DEMOS, GEORGE D.: "Suggested Uses of Tape Recordings in Counselor Supervision," *Personnel and Guidance Journal*, vol. 42, pp. 704–705, March, 1964.

ERICKSON, KENNETH A.: "Principal and the Counselor in a Changing World," *Bulletin of the National Association of Secondary-school Principals*, vol. 46, pp. 186–192, April, 1962.

FEDER, DANIEL D.: "Perspectives and Challenges," *Personnel and Guidance Journal*, vol. 40, pp. 6–10, September, 1961.

FILEP, ROBERT T.: "Programming: A Three-pronged Counseling Tool," *AV Instruction*, vol. 8, pp. 36–39, January, 1963.

GLASSER, EDWARD M.: "Research Frontier: Utilization of Applicable Research and Demonstration Results," *Journal of Counseling Psychology*, vol. 12, pp. 201–205, Summer, 1965.

GROSSMAN, ALVIN, and ROBERT HOWE: "Human Economy and Data Processing," *Personnel and Guidance Journal*, vol. 43, pp. 343–347, December, 1964.

GUILFORD, J. P.: "Factors That Aid and Hinder Creativity," *Teachers College Record*, vol. 63, pp. 380–392, 1962.

HALLMAN, H. J.: "Can Creativity Be Taught," *Education Theory*, vol. 14, pp. 15–23, January, 1964.

HOYT, KENNETH B.: "New Challenges for Guidance in Vocational Education," *Bulletin of the National Association of Secondary-school Principals*, vol. 49, pp. 133–141, May, 1965.

JOHNSON, RAY W.: "Number of Interviews, Diagnosis and Success of Counseling," *Journal of Counseling Psychology*, vol. 12, pp. 248–251, Fall, 1965.

JOSEPH, E. A.: "Guidance May Become Residual," *Clearing House*, vol. 38, pp. 81–84, October, 1964.

LORETAN, JOSEPH O.: "How Are Federal Programs Working in the Large City?" *Educational Leadership*, vol. 23, pp. 20–24, October, 1965.

MC CULLY, C. HAROLD: "School Counselor: Strategy for Professionalization," *Personnel and Guidance Journal*, vol. 40, pp. 681–689, April, 1962.

MC DANIEL, CARL: "Financial Aid for Guidance and Personnel Graduate Study 1965–66," *Personnel and Guidance Journal*, vol. 43, pp. 492–507, January, 1965.

———:"Recent Federal Legislation Affecting Guidance," *High School Journal*, vol. 49, pp. 223–230, February, 1966.

MILLMAN, JASON, and MARVIN D. GLOCK: "Trends in the Measurement of General Mental Ability," *Review of Educational Research*, vol. 35, pp. 17–24, February, 1965.

MORMAN, ROBERT R.: "Automation Dropouts and Guidance," *Bulletin of the National Association of Secondary-school Principals*, vol. 48, pp. 83–98, November, 1964.

NEIHAUS, STANLEY W.: "Title V-A Influence in Illinois," *Personnel and Guidance Journal*, vol. 42, pp. 791–793, April, 1964.

OLSEN, LEROY C., and LYNTON M. PIATT: "Certification Trends in Guidance," *Bulletin of the National Association of Secondary-school Principals*, vol. 45, pp. 55–59, May, 1961.

ORTON, JOHN W.: "Areas of Focus in Supervising Counseling Practicum Students in Groups," *Personnel and Guidance Journal,* vol. 44, pp. 167–170, October, 1965.

PATTERSON, C. H.: "Supervising Students in the Counseling Practicum," *Journal of Counseling Psychology,* vol. 11, pp. 47–53, Spring, 1964.

PATTERSON, DALE C., and WALTER M. LIFTON: "Of Things to Come: Automation and Counseling," *Personnel and Guidance Journal,* vol. 37, pp. 282–287, December, 1958.

PETERS, HERMAN J., and JAMES C. JANSEN: "Counseling Practicum: Bases for Supervision," *Counselor Education and Supervision,* vol. 11, pp. 82–85, Winter, 1963.

PRITCHARD, D. H.: "Impact of Government Programs on the Development and Employment of Counselors," *Vocational Guidance Quarterly,* vol. 14, pp. 36–40, Autumn, 1965.

RAINES, BILL: "Approach to Practicum for the Elementary School Counselor," *Personnel and Guidance Journal,* vol. 43, pp. 57–59, September, 1964.

SANBORN, MARSHALL P.: "A Comparison of Four High School Guidance Programs in Terms of Four Criteria," *Personnel and Guidance Journal,* vol. 43, pp. 293–298, November, 1964.

SAYLOR, GALEN: "The Federal Colossus in Education—Threat or Promise?" *Educational Leadership,* vol. 23, pp. 7–14, October, 1965.

SHEDD, MARK R.: "The Federal Colossus in Education—Curriculum Planning," *Educational Leadership,* vol. 23, pp. 15–19, October, 1965.

SHOBEN, E. J.: "Dilemmas of Guidance," *Teachers College Record,* vol. 64, pp. 719–722, May, 1963.

STEFFLRE, BUFORD: "Issues in School Guidance: Varying Perceptions of Administrators, Counselors, and Counselor Educators," *Teachers College Journal,* vol. 36, pp. 195–200, March, 1965.

———: "What Price Professionalization," *Personnel and Guidance Journal,* vol. 42, pp. 654–659, March, 1964.

STOCKMAN, VERNE, DONALD MOLER, and JAMES LISTER: "AVA Materials in Guidance," *Education Screen,* vol. 39, pp. 220–223, May, 1960.

STRAIGHT, DANA G.: "Relating Guidance to the Philosophy of the School," *Clearing House,* vol. 37, pp. 271–275, January, 1963.

UTHOFF, HARRY: "One Full Year NDEA Institute; An Over View," *Personnel and Guidance Journal,* vol. 40, pp. 735–736, April, 1962.

VANATTA, RALPH E., and HERMAN J. PETERS: "Professional Staffing of Guidance Positions," *Personnel and Guidance Journal,* vol. 41, pp. 509–512, February, 1963.

VAN HOOSE, W. H.: "Elementary Guidance Is Moving Forward," *Ohio School,* vol. 40, pp. 8–9, December, 1962.

WARREN, D. M.: "High School Guidance in 1970: A New Frame of Reference," *Journal of Secondary Education,* vol. 38, pp. 142–147, March, 1963.

WEITA, HENRY: "Shifting Image of the Counseling Psychologist," *Personnel and Guidance Journal,* vol. 40, pp. 184–185, October, 1961.

WIEBE, ARTHUR J.: "High School Guidance in 1970," *Journal of Secondary Education,* vol. 37, pp. 12–16, January, 1962.

ZACCARIA, JOSEPH S.: "Developmental Tasks: Implications for the Goals of Guidance," *Personnel and Guidance Journal,* vol. 44, pp. 372–375, December, 1965.

PUBLISHERS OF TEXTS AND GUIDANCE MATERIALS

Allyn and Bacon, Inc.
150 Tremont St.
Boston, Mass. 02111

American College Testing Program
Box 168
Iowa City, Iowa 52240

American Council on Education
1785 Massachusetts Ave., NW
Washington, D.C. 20006

American Guidance Services, Inc.
720 Washington Ave., SE
Minneapolis, Minn. 55400

American Personnel and Guidance
  Association
1605 New Hampshire Ave., NW
Washington, D.C. 20009

American Psychological Association,
  Inc.
1333 16th St., NW
Washington, D.C. 20006

Appleton-Century-Crofts, Inc.
440 Park Ave. So.
New York, N.Y. 10016

B'nai B'rith Vocational Service
1640 Rhode Island Ave., NW
Washington, D.C. 20036

William C. Brown Co.
Dubuque, Iowa 52001

Bureau of Occupational Information
  and Guidance
California State Department of
  Education
721 Capitol Ave.
Sacramento, Calif. 95801

Bureau of Publications
(Teachers College Press)
Teachers College
Columbia University
501 W. 120th St.
New York, N.Y. 10027

California Test Bureau
Del Monte Research Park
Monterey, Calif. 93940

College Entrance Examination Board
475 Riverside Drive
New York, N.Y. 10027

Columbia University Press
2960 Broadway
New York, N.Y. 10027

Consulting Psychologists Press
270 Town and Country Village
Palo Alto, California 94300

Coronet Films
Coronet Building
Chicago, Ill. 60601

The Department of Publications
State University of Iowa
Iowa City, Iowa 52240

Doubleday & Company, Inc.
Garden City, N.Y.

Educational Records Bureau
21 Audubon Ave.
New York, N.Y. 10032

Educational Test Bureau
720 Washington Ave., SE
Minneapolis, Minn. 55400

Educational Testing Service
Princeton, N.J. 08540

Ginn and Company
Statler Building
Back Bay
P.O. 191
Boston, Mass. 02117

Guidance Information Center
Academy Ave.
Saxtons River, Vt. 05154

Harcourt, Brace & World, Inc.
757 Third Ave.
New York, N.Y. 10017

Harper & Row, Publishers,
  Incorporated
49 E. 33rd St.
New York, N.Y. 10016

Harvard University Press
44 Francis Ave.
Cambridge 38, Mass.

D. C. Heath and Company
285 Columbus Ave.
Boston 16, Mass.

Holt, Rinehart and Winston, Inc.
383 Madison Ave.
New York, N.Y. 10017

Houghton Mifflin Company
2 Park St.
Boston, Mass. 02100

J. B. Lippincott Company
East Washington Square
Philadelphia, Pa. 19100

McGraw-Hill Book Company
330 W. 42d St.
New York, N.Y. 10036

McKnight & McKnight Publishing
  Company
Towanda Ave.
Bloomington, Ill. 61701

The Macmillan Company
60 Fifth Ave.
New York, N.Y. 10011

Charles E. Merrill Books, Inc.
Route 9W
Englewood Cliffs, N.J. 07631

National Education Association
1201 16th St., NW
Washington, D.C. 20036

W. W. Norton & Company, Inc.
55 Fifth Ave.
New York, N.Y. 10003

The Odyssey Press, Inc.
55 Fifth Ave.
New York, N.Y. 10003

Ohio State University
Columbus, Ohio 43200

The Personnel Press, Inc.
20 Nassau St.
Princeton, N.J. 08540

Prentice-Hall, Inc.
Englewood Cliffs, N.J. 07631

The Psychological Corporation
304 E. 45th St.
New York, N.Y. 10017

G. P. Putnam's Sons
200 Madison Ave.
New York, N.Y. 10016

Rand McNally & Company
P.O. 7600
Chicago, Ill. 60680

Science Research Associates, Inc.
259 E. Erie St.
Chicago, Ill. 60611

Sheridan Supply Company
P.O. Box 837
Beverly Hills, Calif. 90210

Stanford University Press
Stanford, Calif.

State University of Iowa
(See under The Department of
  Publications)

Superintendent of Documents
Government Printing Office
Washington, D.C. 20402

Teachers College
(See under Bureau of Publications)

The University of Chicago Press
5750 Ellis Ave.
Chicago, Ill. 60637

D. Van Nostrand Company, Inc.
120 Alexander St.
Princeton, N.J. 08540

Vocational Guidance Center
371 Bloor St., W.
Toronto 5, Canada

Wadsworth Publishing Co.
Belmont, California 94002

Western Psychological Services
10655 Santa Monica Boulevard
Los Angeles 25, Calif. 90000

John Wiley & Sons, Inc.
605 Third Ave.
New York, N.Y. 10016

The H. W. Wilson Company
950 University Ave.
New York, N.Y. 10052

World Book Company
Tarrytown-on-Hudson, N.Y. 10591

CRITERIA FOR EVALUATING A SCHOOL'S GUIDANCE PROGRAM

Rating Scale

In evaluating the guidance services of any designated school, please use the rating scale given below. Circle the number (or letter) which corresponds with the most accurate description of the service as it exists at the time of the evaluation.

4   Excellent—this service is of very high quality.

3   Very good—this service is of high quality.

2   Good—the service is adequate but needs to be improved.

1   Fair—there is some evidence of activity, but this service is unsatisfactory as a whole.

0   Poor—this service is virtually nonexistent or seriously neglected.

A   Does not apply—this service is not appropriate for this school.

Pupil Inventory Service

		Circle one					
1	The present record system is adequate for this school.	4	3	2	1	0	A
2	The forms used are in sufficient number, appropriate, and usable.	4	3	2	1	0	A
3	The system for transferring and receiving records is satisfactory and properly utilized.	4	3	2	1	0	A
4	Competent secretarial help is provided, keeping to a minimum the amount of secretarial work performed by professional staff.	4	3	2	1	0	A
5	The staff makes use of the records.	4	3	2	1	0	A
6	The records are used in curriculum planning and revisions.	4	3	2	1	0	A
7	The records are immediately accessible to the staff and easily obtained.	4	3	2	1	0	A
8	There is a plan for using accumulated data.	4	3	2	1	0	A
9	Data are interpreted for students, and use is made of them.	4	3	2	1	0	A
	Total, or general, rating.	4	3	2	1	0	A

Tests and Inventories

1	The philosophy of the school is favorable toward the use of tests for guidance purposes.	4	3	2	1	0	A
2	The leadership is strong and well-informed on test usage.	4	3	2	1	0	A
3	The funds for purchase of materials are adequate.	4	3	2	1	0	A
4	Staff members are competent in the administration and interpretation of tests.	4	3	2	1	0	A
5	Sufficient time is given to preliminary experience and to the administration and interpretation of tests.	4	3	2	1	0	A
6	There is a minimum or standard testing program which is appropriate for this school.	4	3	2	1	0	A
7	Special tests of various types beyond the minimum are available.	4	3	2	1	0	A
8	There is a plan for interpreting test results to students.	4	3	2	1	0	A
9	Test data are used in considering curricular improvements.	4	3	2	1	0	A
10	The system used for scoring tests is adequate and satisfactory.	4	3	2	1	0	A
11	Total, or general, rating.	4	3	2	1	0	A

Counseling

1	The philosophies of the counselors are in harmony with current points of view of specialists.	4	3	2	1	0	A
2	The counselors are competent, with a good background of training and experience.	4	3	2	1	0	A
3	The counselor-student ratio is satisfactory.	4	3	2	1	0	A
4	The services are adequate for reaching and serving all the students.	4	3	2	1	0	A
5	There is sufficient counselor time to deal satisfactorily with the more serious problem cases.	4	3	2	1	0	A
6	Counseling facilities, including space, privacy, and accessibility of offices to students, are satisfactory.	4	3	2	1	0	A
7	There is a program for familiarizing students with the counseling services, and with the nature of counseling.	4	3	2	1	0	A

8	Communication procedures between teachers and counselors are satisfactory.	4	3	2	1	0	A
9	An in-service training program is under way.	4	3	2	1	0	A
10	Arrangements are made for interviewing students during the school day.	4	3	2	1	0	A
	Total, or general, rating.	4	3	2	1	0	A

Information Services

1	The adequacy, appropriateness, and suitability of current information files are all satisfactory.	4	3	2	1	0	A
2	Vocational files are suitably located for easy access and use.	4	3	2	1	0	A
3	There is a system for making use of accumulated information.	4	3	2	1	0	A
4	The teachers make use of data in the information files in teaching.	4	3	2	1	0	A
5	There is a program of subscriptions for receiving vocational literature each month.	4	3	2	1	0	A
6	College catalogs, vocational training school literature, and other literature dealing with post-high school training are available.	4	3	2	1	0	A
7	Adequate funds are appropriated for these services.	4	3	2	1	0	A
8	There is a program for informing students about the curricular and extracurricular offerings of their school.	4	3	2	1	0	A
9	There is adequate bulletin-board space, and it is utilized in displaying posters and other types of guidance information.	4	3	2	1	0	A
10	Provisions are made for conducting field trips and career days for informing students about vocations.	4	3	2	1	0	A
	Total, or general, rating.	4	3	2	1	0	A

Placement Services

1	The philosophy of the school encompasses the belief that the school has some responsibilities for the educational and vocational placement of students.	4	3	2	1	0	A
2	A program of placement procedures is followed.	4	3	2	1	0	A
3	There is an organization set up to help students find part-time and full-time jobs.	4	3	2	1	0	A
4	Provisions are made for the placement of school dropouts.	4	3	2	1	0	A
5	Graduates are assisted in locating jobs.	4	3	2	1	0	A
6	Students planning to attend a college or training school of some type are assisted with their plans.	4	3	2	1	0	A
7	There is a system for maintaining contact with prospective employers, and with colleges and training schools.	4	3	2	1	0	A
	Total, or general, rating.	4	3	2	1	0	A

Follow-up Services

1	Provisions are made for contacting students for purposes of determining how well they are doing following placement in an educational curriculum or job.	4	3	2	1	0	A
2	Follow-up responsibilities are assumed by designated staff members.	4	3	2	1	0	A
3	Adequate forms and materials are provided for these activities.	4	3	2	1	0	A
4	Sufficient time is given to research and follow-up activities.	4	3	2	1	0	A
5	Staff members and students are included in these activities.	4	3	2	1	0	A
6	The findings gained from the studies are used in improving the school program.	4	3	2	1	0	A
7	There is a program for the coordination of efforts and for implementing the findings.	4	3	2	1	0	A
	Total, or general, rating.	4	3	2	1	0	A

Group Guidance Activities

1	Distinctions are made between group guidance and the instructional program.	4	3	2	1	0	A
2	There is a harmonious working relationship between group guidance and instruction.	4	3	2	1	0	A
3	These activities accommodate all students.	4	3	2	1	0	A
4	Staff members conducting group activities are competent.	4	3	2	1	0	A
5	Sufficient time is devoted to group guidance activities including multiple counseling and group therapy.	4	3	2	1	0	A
6	The organizational procedures are of high quality, and established criteria are used in the selection of individuals for special group activities.	4	3	2	1	0	A
7	There is a plan for making referrals and for providing additional assistance as needed.	4	3	2	1	0	A
	Total, or general, rating.	4	3	2	1	0	A

Organization and Administration of Guidance

1	The administration has a guidance point of view and supports the aims of guidance.	4	3	2	1	0	A
2	There is an organized program of public relations which functions effectively in keeping the public informed.	4	3	2	1	0	A
3	The director of guidance is well-qualified and competent and meets the certification requirements for the state.	4	3	2	1	0	A
4	Staff members are included in the formulation of policies and in conducting the various services.	4	3	2	1	0	A
5	The program is highly effective in contributing to the adjustment of pupils and in the reduction of pupil problems.	4	3	2	1	0	A
6	Funds are provided for in the budget; these are adequate.	4	3	2	1	0	A
7	The facilities are suitable, adequate, and of good quality.	4	3	2	1	0	A
	Total, or general, rating.	4	3	2	1	0	A

PERSONAL-DATA PROFILE FOR TEST INTERPRETATION

Subject: _____ Sex _____ Age _____ Grade_____

Examiner: _____ Date _____

Aptitudes   Quintile graph
Differential Aptitude Tests:

Norms _____

	Raw score	Per- centile	0	20	40	50	60	80	100
Verbal	_____	_____							
Numerical	_____	_____							
Abstract	_____	_____							
Space	_____	_____							
Mechanical	_____	_____							
Clerical	_____	_____							
Spelling	_____	_____							
Sentences	_____	_____							
Scholastic aptitude	_____	_____							

Achievement
California Achievement Tests:

Norms _____

	Raw score	Per- centile	0	20	40	50	60	80	100
Reading: Vocabulary	_____	_____							
Comprehension	_____	_____							
Arithmetic: Reasoning	_____	_____							
Fundamentals	_____	_____							
Language: Mechanics	_____	_____							
Spelling	_____	_____							
Totals:									
Reading	_____	_____							
Arithmetic	_____	_____							
Language	_____	_____							
Battery	_____	_____							

Interests
Kuder Preference Record:

Norms _____

	Raw score	Per-centile	0	20	40	50	60	80	100
Outdoor									
Mechanical									
Computational									
Scientific									
Persuasive									
Artistic									
Literary									
Musical									
Social service									
Clerical									

Kuder—Personal:

			0	20	40	50	60	80	100
Group activity									
Stable situations									
Dealing with ideas									
Avoiding conflicts									
Directing others									

Quintile scale		Quartile scale
100		100
99		99
80		
60		75
50	Midpoint	50
40		
20		25
1		1
0		0

SUGGESTED ACTIVITIES TO BE UTILIZED IN THE CLASSROOM

Chapter 1

1 Have each student write his own definition of guidance, and then exchange papers and evaluate each definition with the following criteria: (a) clarity: clearly stated, understandable, and free of vague terms; (b) comprehensiveness: important areas covered with no serious omissions; (c) brevity: brief and to the point; (d) practicability: practical, logical and applicable.

LEGEND: 1 Excellent, all criteria met to a high degree.
            2 Very good, most of the criteria met to a high degree.
            3 Good, some criteria met and some not met.
            4 Fair, some criteria met to a low degree.
            5 Poor, no criteria met satisfactorily.

2 Divide the class into two major groups: (a) those who are to describe the work of the teacher, and (b) those who are to describe the work of the counselor. Summarize on the blackboard: (a) the functions of the teacher that are distinct from those of the counselor, (b) the work of the counselor which is quite distinct from that of the teacher, and (c) the shared or overlapping functions.

3 Divide the class into sections according to individual preferences for doing guidance work at the elementary or secondary school level. Have each group make a list of the most essential competences to be acquired by each of these groups.

4 Divide the class into four sections for some role-playing. Section a represents teachers who are skeptical of guidance and must be convinced. Section b represents parents who regard guidance as a costly frill. Section c represents teachers and counselors who regard guidance as essential. Section d members serve as scribes and write the major summary points on the blackboard.

Chapter 2

1 Organize the class into groups of four or six. Half of the group are to pretend they are classroom teachers and the other half are to pretend they are counselors. The teachers are to outline their major functions, after which the counselors will show how their efforts can supplement the work of the teacher.

2 Have each student select one of the following groups for participation: (a) preschool, (b) early elementary, (c) late elementary, (d) junior high,

and (*e*) high school. Organize the class into these groups by student choice, and then encourage each group to assume the problems and behavior of its particular age group. Make a summarization of the most critical problems of each age group, and then have the class as a whole show how the guidance service can be of assistance in helping youngsters deal with these problems.

Chapter 3

1 A number of teacher activities are discussed in this chapter. Have each student select one of these and write a list of suggestions showing how the activity can be carried out. These lists may then be reviewed and discussed.

2 Do some role-playing. Divide the class into three groups: number ones are to represent counselors, twos parents and threes are to serve as observers and critics. Role play a counselor's visit to the home wherein the counselor is soliciting the aid of the parent in assisting his child in the resolution of his problems and in making a better adjustment to school. Have the class reassemble and then give the observers a few minutes in which to react to the procedures used by the counselor, taking into consideration the counselor's use of tact and patience. Modifications in the above may be made to suit the particular class.

3 Gain permission to use a class in a nearby elementary or secondary school for a sociometric problem. After the students in the selected class have responded to the structured problem, such as "Name the person with whom you would like to work on a team project in class," return the data to the university class and have the students draw a sociogram. Numbers should be substituted for names in order to avoid revealing the identity of the student.

Chapter 4

1 Divide the class into groups of four with the following assignment for each group: (*a*) group one are students who assume the role of counselors for the lower elementary grades; (*b*) group two are counselors for the upper elementary grades; (*c*) group three are counselors in junior high schools; and (*d*) group four are counselors in the senior high school. Have each group make a list of the principal functions of the counselor at the level of its assignment. Have each group make a brief report to the whole class and permit questions and discussion on each report.

Chapter 5

1 Divide the class into five groups and have each group represent one of the basic elements of the guidance service (testing, counseling, information services, placement, and follow-up). Have each group show how an adequate record system is essential to the success of the basic element it represents. Also, have each group show how its service contributes to the record system.

2 Have each student draw a rough sketch of a cumulative folder and indicate the nature of the information to be included in a folder.

3 Have the students design a system by which cumulative folders may be checked out of a central office.

4 In this activity the instructor is to select a cumulative folder and use it as a guide in doing the following. Select the major sections of the folder and divide the class into the same number of groups, in order to have one group for each section. Have each group select a hypothetical case and record on a sheet of paper just how certain information should be recorded in the cumulative record. After the groups have completed this task, have them shift their papers to the next group and permit each group to criticize or comment on the work of the neighboring group. Allow time for each group to observe the work of all other groups.

5 Borrow enough cumulative records from a nearby elementary or secondary school to equal about half the class total. Have class members pair off. One is to serve as the counselor and interpret the record entries to the partner, who assumes the role of the student. NOTE: Precautions should be taken to protect the identity of the student whose record is being used.

Chapter 6

1 Have class members arrange themselves in teams of two for a role-playing experience. One person is to act as the student and present his problems to the other person, who is to act as the counselor. After about ten minutes have the counselor make a list of the kinds of information he feels he needs in order to be of help to the student. The person acting as the student may at the same time list the areas where the counselor was of no help to him. The purpose of this activity is to impress upon the counselor the need for having certain information about a student available.

2 Divide the class into groups of three to five members and have each group represent a committee of teachers and counselors with the responsibility for carrying out one of the five major functions of the testing service, as outlined in the chapter. One group member may then report to the whole class on its principal functions in carrying out this particular activity.

3 Prepare a profile sheet similar to the one found in Appendix C. Have each student transfer test results to this profile and prepare to interpret this information to another class member. This activity will necessitate borrowing some cumulative folders from a nearby school, or a hypothetical case could be developed. The idea here is to give every student some experience in preparing and interpreting test data.

Chapter 7

1 Appoint a panel of about five members and have each person represent some area of business or industry as a "counselor." For example, there could be a financial counselor, a real estate counselor, an investment counselor, a purchasing counselor, and a banking counselor. Have each member of the panel report briefly on the nature of his work. Have the class members point out the major differences between this kind of "counseling" and the counseling done by a professional counselor.

2 Divide the class into two major groups. One group is to represent teachers and the other group counselors. Have the teachers enumerate the ways that their work supplements that of the counselors, and then have the counselors indicate how their work aids the teacher.

3 Organize the class into groups of four. One person in each group is to act as the student and present his problem to the other three members of the group, each of whom will assume one of the following roles: a client-centered counselor, a directive or counselor-centered counselor, and an eclectic counselor. Have each of the three counselors respond to each client statement according to the particular approach he represents.

Chapter 8

1 Appoint a panel of eight class members and have each lead the discussion on one of the eight "Essential Elements in Counseling," as discussed in the text. Each discussion leader should show what the counselor is to do in carrying out this particular element or function.

2 Organize the class into groups of about three to five members and have each group complete this assignment: (*a*) make a list of the major functions to be performed by the counselor; (*b*) prepare a second list and indicate the courses and experiences the counselor should receive in his preparation in order to be prepared to carry out each of the functions in the first list.

Chapter 9

1 Arrange to take the class to the university counseling center and see the materials and facilities provided for vocational advisement of students.

2 Visit a nearby high school that has a system for the filing and use of vocational and educational materials. Determine the strengths and weaknesses of the system upon the return of the class to the classroom.

Chapter 10

1 A simple and effective system for assisting students with job placement is the maintenance of a card file of students seeking jobs and also of employers looking for help. Have each student prepare a model card for each of the above. Discuss these in class and permit some of the students to diagram their cards on the blackboard.

2 Have each student prepare a simple instrument designed to gain information in a follow-up study. This might be a questionnaire or a checklist.

Chapter 11

1 Have each class member write on a sheet of paper a statement as to what he considers his most serious problem to be. Assign a number to each student and have him write this number in the upper left-hand corner. Collect the papers and arrange them in groups according to the nature of the problem. Arrange the groups according to these problems and encourage a free discussion of these problems within the groups.

2 Arrange for other kinds of group experiences in which the memberships of the groups are changed periodically. Take a few minutes after each group experience to evaluate its effectiveness in terms of its acceptability, suitability, and effectiveness.

Chapter 12

1 Have each class member draw an organizational chart to show the relationship of the various school personnel with each other. Since the size of the district is an important factor in this organization, the student might have his choice of: (a) a large district with a director of pupil personnel services, (b) an average-sized district with one director of guidance and part-time counselors in each building, (c) a small district or school with one head counselor and two part-time counselors.

2 Organize the class into groups of three and have each group design a form to be used in surveying a school for purposes of gaining information that might be used to aid the school in organizing a guidance program.

3 Appoint a panel of four students, to represent a teacher, a counselor, an administrator, and a parent; have each one point out his major responsibilities to the guidance program.

Chapter 13

1 Organize the class into groups of five and have the members of each group assume the roles of the counselor, teacher, administrator, parent, and observer. Each person is to outline to the group his major responsibilities in the promotion of good mental health with students—the observer is to report last and indicate how the services of these four people can be coordinated and implemented.

2 Have a panel of about five class members lead a discussion on the function of the guidance service in providing for the mental health needs of students.

Chapter 14

1 Divide the class into four groups, and let each represent one of the four classifications of the exceptional. Devote about fifteen minutes to a discussion and interchange of ideas centered upon each member role playing or

describing the nature of his deviation. This should result in a better understanding of the term "exceptional" and provide some insights into the problems encountered by some of these youngsters. Have a member of each group report briefly to the entire class on the highlights of the discussion in his group. As time permits, entertain questions from individuals, and have other class members propose answers.

2 Have each student imagine that he is the guidance director of a school. He has been asked by the administration to establish a set of criteria to be used in identifying the gifted children in the school. Do this as a written assignment and then have the students exchange papers several times in class in order that each person may learn from the ideas presented by other class members.

3 Have each student do one of the following: (*a*) You are the teacher of a class in which two students have been identified as "gifted." Make a list of the things you would do to assist them toward the maximal use of their abilities. (*b*) You are the head counselor in a high school in which ten youngsters have been classified as gifted. Show how you would use the facilities and services of the guidance program to assist these students.

Chapter 15

1 Organize the class into small groups and have each group prepare a brief case study that includes home background information, progress in school, interests and activities, medical record, and a description of behavior. Have each group make a brief report to the class and then arrive at decisions on the following problems: (*a*) is the behavior normal and to be expected under the circumstances, or does the child have problems; (*b*) what factors in his life or background are contributing to his problems; (*c*) how can he be helped?

2 Have each student make a list of those elements in a child's life which have the greatest influence on his behavior. Attempt to list these in order of importance, and be prepared to defend choices in the class discussion.

3 Arrange for a situation in the classroom which will constitute a threat to the self-esteem or comfort of one or more class members. Have a class member who was included in the planning of the incident explain how the threatened person acted and then explain why he behaved in a particular fashion.

4 Divide the class into three groups. Have group one represent teachers, and group two counselors, with the responsibility of listing their most important functions in dealing with behavior problems. Group three is to serve as critics of the first two groups and to make corrections or suggestions where applicable. This group is also to point out how the teachers and counselors may coordinate their functions.

5 Arrange for some role playing interviews by having the students pair off, one acting as the counselor and the other as a child with particular behavior problems.

6 Invite a counselor, psychologist, or child specialist in to talk with the class about the behavior problems of children, and to answer the questions of the students about these problems.

Chapter 16

1 Have each class member make a list of the major weaknesses in the guidance program of the high school he attended. Assign a committee to the task of making a consolidated list of the most frequently mentioned items; duplicate this list and make copies available to the class. In the class discussion show how an evaluation study would help to get at these weaknesses.

2 Organize the class into small groups for purposes of planning and carrying out a simple evaluation study. This could be done within the class or by mailing brief questionnaires to selected schools for the purpose of having these schools evaluate their programs according to criteria prepared by the students. (A number of modifications may be made in the procedures.)

3 Have each student list and write a brief annotation on the major sources of information on guidance research. Have a committee edit and consolidate this information and duplicate it for class members.

Chapter 17

1 Give a select group of students the assignment of determining the nature of federal participation in guidance services. Have these people report their findings to the class and be prepared to answer questions about these programs.

2 Appoint a group of students to prepare a list of the major issues confronting guidance and counseling programs. Organize the class into groups and assign a number of these issues to each group; instruct them to prepare some logical solutions to these issues.

Name Index

Subject Index